Orson Ferguson Whitney

History of Utah

Orson Ferguson Whitney

History of Utah

ISBN/EAN: 9783337297541

Printed in Europe, USA, Canada, Australia, Japan

Cover: Foto ©ninafisch / pixelio.de

More available books at **www.hansebooks.com**

HISTORY OF UTAH

COMPRISING

PRELIMINARY CHAPTERS ON THE PREVIOUS HISTORY OF HER FOUNDERS, ACCOUNTS OF EARLY SPANISH AND AMERICAN EXPLORATIONS IN THE ROCKY MOUNTAIN REGION, THE ADVENT OF THE MORMON PIONEERS, THE ESTABLISHMENT AND DISSOLUTION OF THE PROVISIONAL GOVERNMENT OF THE STATE OF DESERET, AND THE SUBSEQUENT CREATION AND DEVELOPMENT OF THE TERRITORY.

IN FOUR VOLUMES.

By ORSON F. WHITNEY.

. . . Illustrated. . . .

"This I hold to be the chief office of history, to rescue virtuous actions from the oblivion to which a want of records would consign them; and that men should feel a dread of being considered infamous in the opinions of posterity, from their depraved expressions and base actions." — TACITUS

SALT LAKE CITY, UTAH:
GEORGE Q. CANNON & SONS CO., PUBLISHERS.
MARCH, 1892.

COPYRIGHT APPLIED FOR.

PREFACE.

HE author here presents the first volume of his history of Utah, a work which has engaged his attention, though not uninterruptedly, since May, 1890. As will be seen, it is a continuous historical narrative of the early settlement and formation of the Territory and its growth and development up to the year 1861, a point of time just prior to the advent of the electric telegraph, and not long before the arrival of the great Pacific Railway. This period, which marks in local annals the close of one era and the beginning of another, seemed a fitting place for the author's pen to pause, while the press gave the first fruits of his present labor to the public.

Necessarily this volume has most to say of the Mormon people. Being the pioneers and earliest builders of our inter-mountain commonwealth, it was as proper as it was unavoidable to give them first and foremost mention in a work of this character. It was also deemed essential, for reasons stated elsewhere, that the opening chapters should deal more or less comprehensively with the history of Utah's pioneers and founders prior to their advent into the Great Basin. Something of their religious and political views, their early experiences in the east and the motives which impelled them westward, are therefore herein contained. Of the non-Mormon portion of the community, and the important part played by them in the stirring drama of our social, political and material development, as much will be said hereafter.

As the author has endeavored, in volume one, to present a fair and truthful statement of facts antedating and leading up to the new era that was ushered in by the telegraph and the locomotive,—which came as it were on the wings of the lightning, or on the back of the enchanted iron horse,—he will as diligently strive, in the succeeding volumes, to deal faithfully and impartially with events that have since taken place. It is the design, after completing the general narrative here begun, to give the histories of the various counties of the Territory, and the professions and pursuits of the people. Special chapters on agriculture, manufacture, mining, commerce, etc., may be looked for; as well as others on churches, newspapers, theaters, railways and other agencies of civilization. Literature, music and the drama, poets, painters and sculptors will each be placed in an appropriate niche, while bench and bar, civil and military affairs in general and in detail will all be duly represented. Biographies of prominent citizens, men and women, will also form a feature of the work.

In conclusion, the author expresses his grateful appreciation to all who have in any way assisted or encouraged him in his literary labors: to Dr. John O. Williams, to whom belongs the credit of originating the history project—of which he was once the main proprietor—and of pushing forward the business pertaining to it with characteristic energy and ability; to Mr. J. H. E. Webster, his partner, who, in conjunction with Dr. Williams, has ably conducted and continues to conduct the canvass for the work. With these gentlemen and their associates my relations have been of the most pleasant character. To President Wilford Woodruff and council, and other leading citizens, for their warm approval and endorsement of the project: to Governor Arthur L. Thomas, for various courtesies extended: to the Church historian, Apostle Franklin D. Richards, his assistant, John Jaques, General Robert T. Burton and A. M. Musser, Esq., for advice and assistance such as an author can best appreciate, I feel deeply indebted. Nor should the name of Hon. F. S. Richards be omitted, he being one of the first to recognize the importance of the history enterprise, as a public benefit, and to give it his hearty encouragement and support. To the press of Salt Lake City and the Territory in general, to the Union Pacific, Rio Grande Western and

Utah Central railways, and the Salt Lake City Railroad Company, I return hearty thanks for favors bestowed. The share of credit due the publishers and now main proprietors of the history—Messrs. George Q. Cannon and Sons—is manifest from the appearance of the work itself.

I shall begin immediately upon the second volume, and while taking time and pains to do the work in a manner worthy the subject, it is my intention to push it to completion with all possible dispatch.

Orson F. Whitney.

Salt Lake City,
    February, 1892.

CONTENTS.

CHAPTER I.
1805–1827.

PAGE.

Antecedents of Utah's Early Settlers—Joseph Smith and Mormonism—The Prophet's Birth and Boyhood—Social and Religious Phases of Seventy Years Ago—Seeking for the True Church—Joseph's First Vision—The Father and the Son—Forbidden to Join any of the Churches—The Youth tells his Story—Prejudice and Persecution—The Angel Moroni—Discovery of the Golden Plates—The Prophet on Probation—The Record of Mormon, the Nephite, in the Hands of Joseph, the Translator. . 17

CHAPTER II.
1827–1830.

Translation of the Book of Mormon—Poverty and Persecution—The "Money-Digging and Wife-Stealing" Stories—Martin Harris—The Prophet Removes to Pennsylvania—Description of the Plates and the Urim and Thummim—Martin Harris and Professor Anthon—The Reputed Method of Translation—The Stolen Manuscript—Oliver Cowdery—John the Baptist and the Aaronic Priesthood—Baptism of Joseph and Oliver—Joseph Knight's Beneficence—David Whitmer—Joseph and Oliver Remove from Harmony to Fayette—The Melchisedek Priesthood—The Three Witnesses—The Eight—The Translation Complete and the Book of Mormon Given to the World. . 28

CHAPTER III.

What the Book of Mormon Claims to be—The Narrative of the Nephite Record—How the World Received it—The Spaulding Story—"Mormonism Unveiled"—The Sidney Rigdon Anachronism—Discovery of the Original "Manuscript Story"—Its Condensed Narrative—Mormon's Record and Spaulding's Romance Compared—Reynolds' "Myth of the Manuscript Found"—President Fairchild's Opinion—Numerous Editions of the Translated Work. 37

CHAPTER IV.
1830.

Organization of the Church of Jesus Christ of Latter-day Saints—The Doctrine of Common Consent—Oliver Cowdery the First Public Preacher of Mormonism—Newel Knight—The First Conference of the Church—The Elders at Colesville—Joseph Smith Arrested for "Preaching the Book of Mormon"—His Trial and Acquittal at South Bainbridge—Re-arrested and Tried at Colesville—Another Failure to Convict—Return to Pennsylvania—A Schism Threatening the Church—Revival of Opposition at Harmony—The Prophet Removes with his Family to Fayette—The Schism Averted—A Mission to the Lamanites Announced. 57

CONTENTS.

CHAPTER V.
1830-1831.

Mormonism's Mission to the Lamanites—Its Significance—Oliver Cowdery, Parley P. Pratt, Peter Whitmer, Junior, and Ziba Peterson the Chosen Evangelists to the Red Men—Their Departure for the West—The Catterangus Indians—Kirtland and the Campbellites—Sidney Rigdon—His Conversion to Mormonism—Edward Partridge—Newel K. Whitney—Success of the Elders in Ohio—Their Pilgrimage Resumed—Elder Pratt's Arrest and Escape—Simeon Carter Among the Wyandots—Storms and Privations—Arrival at Independence, Missouri—Preaching to the Delawares—Government Agents and Christian Missionaries—The Elders Ordered out of the Indian Country. 66

CHAPTER VI.
1830-1833.

The Church Removes to Ohio—The United Order—Organization of the Bishopric—Joseph Smith's First Visit to Missouri—Jackson County the Chosen Site of the City of Zion—The Land Dedicated for the Gathering of Israel and the Building of the New Jerusalem—The Return to Kirtland—The Prophet and Elder Rigdon at Hiram—A Vision of Human Destiny—The Mobbing of Joseph and Sidney—A Second Visit to Missouri—The War of the Rebellion Predicted—The First Presidency organized—The Kirtland Temple Projected. 79

CHAPTER VII.
1833.

The Jackson County Expulsion and its Causes—Mobocratic Mass Meetings at Independence—Destruction of the Office of the "Evening and Morning Star"—Bishop Partridge Tarred and Feathered—The Mormons Required to Leave the County Forthwith—A Truce Agreed upon—The Mob Break their Pledge—Renewal of Depredations—The Mormons Appeal to Governor Dunklin—He Advises them to seek Redress in the Courts—Legal Proceedings Instituted—The Mob Enraged—The October and November Riots—A Battle on the Big Blue—Lieutenant-Governor Boggs calls out the Militia—The Mormons Disarmed and Driven—Clay County receives the Refugees—Jackson County, Missouri, still "The Land of Zion." 100

CHAPTER VIII.
1833-1837.

Brigham Young, the Founder of Utah, Embraces Mormonism—Heber C. Kimball Enters the Fold—Wilford Woodruff—George A. Smith—Jedediah M. Grant—Erastus Snow—The First High Council Organized—Zion's Camp—The Twelve Apostles Chosen—The Seventies Selected—A Revelation on Priesthood—Mormonism and Education—The Kirtland Temple Dedicated—Lorenzo Snow—The Missouri Mormons—Their Removal from Clay County to Caldwell—The Founding of Far West. 111

CONTENTS.

CHAPTER IX.
1836-1838.

The Kirtland Apostasy—The Temporal at War with the Spiritual—Financial Disasters—"Something New must be done to Save the Church"—Opening of the British Mission—Heber C. Kimball and his Confreres in Lancashire—Marvelous Success of Mormonism Abroad—Affairs at Kirtland Continued—A Dark Hour—Brigham Young's Fidelity—John Taylor—Setting in Order the Church—Flight of the Prophet and his Friends from Kirtland—The Church Removes to Missouri—Excommunications—New Calls to the Apostleship—The Law of Tithing Instituted. 131

CHAPTER X.
1838-1839.

The Mormons in Missouri—Far West, Diahman and Dewitt—A Slumbering Volcano—Celebrating the Nation's Birthday—The State Election—Attempt to Prevent Mormons from Voting—The Gallatin Riot—The Volcano Awakes—Daviess County in Arms—Joseph Smith and Lyman Wight Arrested—The Mob Army Threatens Diahman—The Mormons arm in Self-defense—Generals Atchison, Parks and Doniphan—The Saints Exonerated—Siege and Bombardment of Dewitt—Governor Boggs Appealed to—He Declines to Interfere—Dewitt Evacuated and Diahman again Threatened—Gilliam's Guerillas—The Mormon Militia Make War upon the Mob—The Danites—Battle of Crooked River—Death of David W. Patten—Governor Boggs Espouses the Cause of the Mobocrats—The Mormons to be "Exterminated or Driven from the State"—The Haun's Mill Massacre—Fall of Far West—The Mormon Leaders in Chains—Liberty Jail—The Exodus to Illinois. . . 142

CHAPTER XI.
1839-1842.

Nauvoo—The Saints in Illinois and Iowa—Daniel H. Wells—The Apostles Depart for Europe—The Prophet lays the Grievances of His People Before the General Government—President Van Buren's Reply—"Your Cause is Just, but I can do Nothing for You"—Illinois Politics—Whigs and Democrats—The Mormons Hold the Balance of Power—A Cloud on the Horizon—Missouri Demands of Illinois the Mormon Leaders as Fugitives from Justice—The Requisition Returned Unserved—The Nauvoo Charter—The Apostles in Great Britain—The Beginning of Mormon Emigration from Abroad—The Saints Concentrate at Nauvoo—The Politicians Alarmed—Rise of the Anti-Mormon Party—The Missouri Writ Re-issued and the Prophet Arrested—Habeas Corpus—Judge Douglas—Liberation—John C. Bennett—The Shadow of a Coming Event—The Prophet Predicts the Flight of His People to the Rocky Mountains. 167

CHAPTER XII.
1842-1843.

Again in the Toils—Joseph Smith and Porter Rockwell Arrested, Charged with Attempted Murder—Ex-Governor Boggs of Missouri the Alleged Victim—How the Deed was Done—The Prisoners Released by Habeas Corpus—They Evade Re-arrest—Rockwell Kidnapped and Carried to Missouri—Governor Ford Succeeds Governor Carlin—The Prophet Submits to a Judicial Investigation—Judge Pope—The Mormon Leader Again Liberated—Another Requisition—Joseph Smith Kidnapped—His Rescue and Release—Anti-Mormon Depredations Around Nauvoo. 197

CHAPTER XIII.
1843–1844.

Celestial Marriage—Why the Mormons Practiced Polygamy—The Prophet and the Politicians—Joseph Smith a Candidate for President of the United States—His Platform of Principles—Planning the Western Exodus—The Laws, Fosters, and Higbees Excommunicated—The "Expositor" Abatement—Arrest of the Mayor and City Council of Nauvoo—A Gathering Storm—Nauvoo under Martial Law—Governor Ford Demands the Surrender of the Mormon Leaders—The Prophet and his Friends Start for the Rocky Mountains—The Return—The Surrender—Carthage Jail—Murder of the Prophet and Patriarch. 210

CHAPTER XIV.
1844–1845.

Brigham Young Succeeds Joseph Smith—The Man for the Hour—Sidney Rigdon Rejected and Excommunicated—Factions and Followings—The Prophet's Murder Proves an Impetus to Mormonism—The Crusade Renewed—The Apostles Driven into Retirement—The "Bogus Brigham" Arrest—Repeal of the Nauvoo Charter—Josiah Lamborn's Opinion of the Repeal—Governor Ford Advises a Mormon Exodus—The Prophet's Murderers Acquitted—The Anti-Mormons Change Their Tactics—The Torch of the Incendiary in Lieu of the Writ of Arrest—Sheriff Backenstos—The Mobocrats Worsted and put to Flight—Governor Ford Interposes to Restore Order—General Hardin and the Commissioners—The Mormons Agree to Leave Illinois. . 233

CHAPTER XV.
1845–1847.

The Exodus—Brigham Young Leads his People Westward—Sugar Creek—Samuel Brannan and the Ship "Brooklyn"—Garden Grove and Mount Pisgah—The Saints Reach the Missouri River—The Mexican War and the Mormon Battalion—Elder Little and President Polk—Colonel Kane—More Anti-Mormon Demonstrations—The Battle of Nauvoo—Expulsion of the Mormon Remnant from the City—Colonel Kane's Description of Nauvoo—The Church in the Wilderness—Winter Quarters. 248

CHAPTER XVI.
1540–1847.

The Beginning of Utah History—Why the Mormons did not Colonize the Pacific Coast—The Great Basin—Utah's Physical Features—Daniel Webster on the "Worthless West"—Early Spanish Explorations—Escalante in Utah Valley—La Hontan's Hearsays—American Trappers on the Shores of the Great Salt

CONTENTS.

Lake—Colonel Bridger—Captain Bonneville—Colonel Fremont—Early Emigrations from the Missouri to the Pacific—The Donner Disaster.   281

CHAPTER XVII.
1847.

The Mormon Pioneers—Their Journey Across the Great Plains—Pawnees and Sioux—The Pioneer Buffalo Hunt—Fort Laramie—The Mississippi Mormons—South Pass—Major Harris—Colonel Bridger—"A Thousand Dollars for the First Ear of Corn Raised in Salt Lake Valley"—A Discouraging Prospect—Elder Brannan Again—Some of the Battalion Boys—Fort Bridger—Miles Goodyear—Echo Canyon—The Valley of the Great Salt Lake.   298

CHAPTER XVIII.
1847.

Pen Picture of Salt Lake Valley—How it Looked to the Pioneers—Contrasted Impressions—Orson Pratt and Erastus Snow the First Explorers—The Camp on City Creek—Plowing and Planting—Arrival of the President—The First Sabbath Service in the Valley—Orson Pratt's Sermon to the Pioneers—Brigham Young Lays Down the Law—Apostle Lyman and Elder Brannan Arrive—Exploring and Colonizing—Ensign Peak Named—The Great Salt Lake Visited—Black Rock Christened—Tooele Valley—Utah Lake Seen—Salt Lake City Planned and Located.   325

CHAPTER XIX.
1847.

The Pioneer Settlers Reinforced—Captain James Brown and his Company—The Mississippi Mormons—An Indian Affray—Utes and Shoshones—The "Old Fort" Projected—The First City Survey—Utah Valley Explored—"Renewing Covenants" and "Selecting Inheritances"—Cache Valley Visited—Ascent of Twin Peaks—The First House Finished in Salt Lake City—The First White Child Born in Utah—First Death in the Pioneer Colony—The Ox-team Companies Return to Winter Quarters—Great Salt Lake City Named—The Pioneer Leaders Recross the Plains—Immigration of 1847—Captains of Hundreds and Fifties—The First Stake of Zion in the Rocky Mountains—Arrivals from the West—Winter at the Fort—Harriet Young's Adventure—Indian Captives and Captors—Cedar and Rush Valleys Explored—Close of the Year 1847.   342

CHAPTER XX.
1847-1849.

Founding New Settlements—Brigham Young as a Colonizer—Davis County Occupied—The Goodyear Purchase—The Cricket Plague—Saved by the Gulls—Days of Famine—The First Harvest Feast—How Gold was Discovered in California—Immigration of 1848—Matters Spiritual and Temporal—Lands Distributed to the Settlers—The First Utah Currency—More Apostles Ordained—The Stake Reorganized—Salt Lake City Divided into Bishops' Wards.   370

CONTENTS.

CHAPTER XXI.
1849.

Beginning of Utah's Political History—The Provisional Government of Deseret—Utah Valley Settled—The Ute Indians—Sowiette and Walkara—The Gold-Hunters—"Winter Mormons"—Deseret Applies for Statehood—First Celebration of Pioneer Day—The Stansbury Expedition—The Perpetual Emigrating Fund—The First Missionaries Sent from the Rocky Mountains—Why Brigham Young Discouraged Mining—The Great Salt Lake Valley Carrying Company—Sanpete and Tooele Valleys Settled. . . 389

CHAPTER XXII.
1849–1851.

Salt Lake, Weber, Utah, Sanpete, Juab and Tooele Counties Created—Parley P. Pratt Explores Southern Utah—The First Indian War—A Skirmish at Battle Creek—The Two Days' Fight at Provo—Table Mountain—A Treaty of Peace—The Pioneer Newspaper of the Rocky Mountains—Death of Presiding Bishop Whitney—The First P. E. Fund Emigration—George A. Smith Pioneers Iron County—Educational Beginnings—The University of Deseret—The Cities of Salt Lake, Ogden, Provo, Manti and Parowan Receive their Charters—The First Municipal Government in the Great Basin. 420

CHAPTER XXIII.
1850–1852.

Utah Territory Created—Brigham Young Governor—How the News Reached Deseret—Dissolution of the Provisional Government—Its Acts Recapitulated—The First Utah Census—The First Territorial Election—John M. Bernhisel Delegate to Congress—Arrival of the Federal Officials—Brandebury, Brocchus and Harris—A Discontented Trio—Judge Brocchus Insults the Mormon People at Their Conference—Brigham Young's Reply—The Three Officials Leave the Territory—Governor Young's Letter to President Fillmore—Report of the "Runaway" Judges and Secretary—A Case of Moral and Official Hari-Kari—The Grant Letters—Utah's First Legislative Assembly—Its Initial Acts—The First Murder Trial in Utah—Fillmore, Millard County, the Chosen Capital of the Territory—Box Elder and Juab Counties Settled—The San Bernardino Colony—A Territorial Library—Probate Judges and Their Jurisdiction. 442

CHAPTER XXIV.
1852–1853.

A Great Pacific Railway Wanted—The Governor and Legislature of Utah Petition Congress for its Construction—Celestial Marriage Proclaimed to the World as a Mormon Doctrine—Orson Pratt Preaches the First Sermon on Polygamy—His Mission to Washington—The "Seer"—Utah's offering to the Washington Monument—Governor Young on Manual Training and Home Industries—His Views of Slavery—Feramorz Little and the Mail Service—The Pioneer Merchants of Utah—Dramatic Beginnings—The Salt Lake Temple Begun—Arrival of the New Federal Officials. 486

CONTENTS.   xiii

CHAPTER XXV.
1853-1854.   PAGE.

Another Indian War—Causes of the Outbreak—Pedro Leon and his Associates—Governor Young Proclaims Against the Mexican Slave-traders—Purchase of Fort Bridger—Walker on the War Path—Indian Raids in Utah and Sanpete Valleys—The War Becomes General—Colonel George A. Smith Given Command of the Southern Utah Military Districts—Governor Young's Letter to Chief Walker—The Gunnison Massacre—End of the Walker War—Other Events of 1853-4—Summit, Green River and Carson Counties Created—Utah Settlements at the Close of 1853—John C. Fremont at Parowan—Death of President Willard Richards—A Grasshopper Visitation.   .   .   508

CHAPTER XXVI.
1854-1856.

Brigham Young's Record as Governor—An Administration Acceptable to Both Mormons and Gentiles—They Unitedly Petition for his Reappointment—Colonel Steptoe—The Gunnison Massacre Investigated and the Murderers brought to Justice—Death of the Ute Chief Walker—The Triumph of Brigham Young's Indian Policy—Why the Savages Drew a Distinction Between "Americans" and "Mormons"—Death of Chief Justice Reed—Judge Kinney Succeeds Him—Morgan County Settled—The Elk Mountain and Salmon River Missions—The Carson Colony—George Q. Cannon and the "Western Standard"—Death of Associate-Justice Shaver—The Mormon People Honor the Memory of Their Departed Friend—Judge Drummond Succeeds Judge Shaver—The Utah Legislature Convenes at Fillmore—Another Movement for Statehood—Cache, Box Elder and Other Counties Settled.   .   .   .   532

CHAPTER XXVII.
1856.

A Year of Calamities—Another Famine in Utah—More Indian Outbreaks—Death of Colonel Babbitt—Massacre of the Margetts Party—The Hand-cart Disaster—Narratives of Messrs. Chislett and Jaques—The Reformation—Death of Jedediah M. Grant.   547

CHAPTER XXVIII.
1856-1857.

The Utah Expedition—Buchanan's Blunder—Some of the Causes which Led to It—An Historic Review—The Magraw Letter—Judge Drummond's Charges—Clerk Bolton's Reply—Indian Agent Twiss and his Complaint—The B. Y. Express Carrying Company—The Real Reason why the Troops were Sent to Utah—Secretary Floyd and his Record—Mormondom Sacrificed to Favor Secession—Blaine on Buchanan's Cabinet—General Scott's Instructions to the Army—Feramorz Little and the New York Herald—The Expedition Starts Westward—Mayor Smoot Brings the News to Utah.   567

CHAPTER XXIX.
1857.

Pioneer Day in the Tops of the Wasatch Mountains—The Celebration at Silver Lake

CONTENTS.

—Tidings of the Coming of the Troops—How the News was Received—Brigham Young Determines to Resist the Entry of the Army into Salt Lake Valley—General Johnston and his Command Leave Fort Leavenworth—Captain Van Vliet Precedes the Expedition to Utah—His Interviews with Governor Young—The Mormon Leader's Ultimatum—"When those Troops Arrive They shall find Utah a Desert"—A Second Moscow Threatened—Van Vliet's Official Report. . 600

CHAPTER XXX.
1857–1858.

The Echo Canyon Campaign—Utah Under Martial Law—Colonel Burton Takes the Field—The United States Troops Enter the Territory—General Wells Goes to the Front—Echo Canyon Fortified—Lot Smith Burns the Government Trains—Major Taylor's Capture—Mormon Cossacks—Colonel Alexander's Dilemma—He Starts for Soda Springs—Colonel Burton Intercepts Him—The Project Abandoned—Correspondence Between Colonel Alexander and Governor Young—Apostle Taylor's Letter to Captain Marcy—Arrival of General Johnston—A March of Misery—Forts Bridger and Supply Burnt—Colonel Cooke's Experience—Camp Scott—The Federal Army goes into Winter Quarters—Return of the Militia—Preparing for the Spring Campaign. . 619

CHAPTER XXXI.
1858.

President Buchanan Begins to see His Blunder—Colonel Kane the Mediator—His Mission to Utah—The Mormons Agree to Receive Governor Cumming, but not With an Army at his Heels—Colonel Kane Visits Camp Scott—He Escorts the New Executive to Salt Lake City—Cordial Meeting of the Two Governors—Judge Drummond's Falsehood Exploded—The Court Records Found Intact—The "Move" South—The Peace Commissioners—President Buchanan's Pardon—Johnston's Army Enters the Valley—Camp Floyd—The Citizens Return to Their Homes. 664

CHAPTER XXXII.
1858–1861.

After "The War"—The Federal Courts in Operation—Judge Sinclair Seeks to Renew the Strife—He Sentences a Murderer to be Hung on Sunday—Judge Cradlebaugh's Administration—The Story of the Mountain Meadows Massacre—Cradlebaugh's Vain Attempt to Fasten the Awful Crime upon the Mormon Leaders—He Summons the Military to his Aid—The Court House at Provo Surrounded by Federal Bayonets—The Citizens Protest and the Governor Proclaims Against the Military Occupation—A Conspiracy to Arrest President Young Thwarted by Governor Cumming—Attorney-General Black Rebukes the Utah Judges—The Anti-Mormons Seek the Removal of Governor Cumming—Colonel Kane to the Rescue—How Utah was Affected by Johnston's Army—Horace Greeley at Salt Lake City—More Newspapers—The "Valley Tan" and the "Mountaineer"—William H. Hooper Delegate to Congress—The Pony Express—The Civil War—Camp Floyd Abandoned. 689

ILLUSTRATIONS.

	PAGE.		PAGE.
BRIGHAM YOUNG	[*Frontispiece*]	MARY J. DILWORTH HAMMOND	433
JOSEPH SMITH	57	JULIAN MOSES	434
HYRUM SMITH	62	NATHANIEL H. FELT	436
PARLEY P. PRATT	70	SETH M. BLAIR	452
HEBER C. KIMBALL	111	JOHN M. BERNHISEL	458
WILLARD RICHARDS	231	WILLIAM C. STAINES	483
WILLIAM MILLER	236	WILLIAM JENNINGS	500
GEORGE A. SMITH	250	ALONZO H. RALEIGH	502
LEVI RICHARDS	260	JESSE W. FOX	504
WILFORD WOODRUFF	298	TRUMAN O. ANGELL	506
AMASA M. LYMAN	300	ANSON CALL	522
CLARA D. YOUNG	302	DIMICK B. HUNTINGTON	526
ELLEN S. KIMBALL	306	JOHN NEBEKER	529
WILLIAM CLAYTON	310	SALT LAKE CITY IN 1853	530
THE PIONEER ROUTE, 1847	318	LEONARD W. HARDY	542
FIRST GLIMPSE OF "THE VALLEY"	322	JOHN NEFF	548
GREAT SALT LAKE VALLEY, 1847	325	JEDEDIAH M. GRANT	564
ERASTUS SNOW	330	ABRAHAM O. SMOOT	567
JOHN PACK	334	JOHN R. MURDOCK	586
LORENZO D. YOUNG	338	FERAMORZ LITTLE	596
CAPTAIN JAMES BROWN	344	NICHOLAS GROESBECK	598
CHARLES C. RICH	348	SILVER LAKE	600
JOHN YOUNG	358	LAKE MARTHA	604
DANIEL SPENCER	360	LAKE BLANCHE	608
JOSEPH HORNE	362	DANIEL H. WELLS	619
JOSEPH B. NOBLE	364	JAMES FERGUSON	622
JACOB HOUTZ	366	ROBERT T. BURTON	626
HARRIET PAGE WHEELER YOUNG	368	ANDREW CUNNINGHAM	630
PEREGRINE G. SESSIONS	372	J. D. T. McALLISTER	640
JOHN STOKER	374	EDWIN D. WOOLLEY	648
LORIN FARR	376	JOHN R. WINDER	661
HORACE S. ELDREDGE	384	SAMUEL W. RICHARDS	666
CHARLES CRISMON	386	COLONEL THOMAS L. KANE	674
EDWARD HUNTER	416	REUBEN MILLER	710

HISTORY OF UTAH.

CHAPTER I.
1805-1827.

ANTECEDENTS OF UTAH'S EARLY SETTLERS—JOSEPH SMITH AND MORMONISM—THE PROPHET'S BIRTH AND BOYHOOD—SOCIAL AND RELIGIOUS PHASES OF SEVENTY YEARS AGO—SEEKING FOR THE TRUE CHURCH—JOSEPH'S FIRST VISION—THE FATHER AND THE SON—FORBIDDEN TO JOIN ANY OF THE CHURCHES—THE YOUTH TELLS HIS STORY—PREJUDICE AND PERSECUTION—THE ANGEL MORONI—DISCOVERY OF THE GOLDEN PLATES—THE PROPHET ON PROBATION—THE RECORD OF MORMON, THE NEPHITE, IN THE HANDS OF JOSEPH, THE TRANSLATOR.

AS IT would be natural, in describing a lake or large body of water, to give some account of the origin, course and character of the streams flowing into and forming it, so is it expected of the historian, who describes a city or country and its inhabitants, to dwell to some extent upon their antecedents, to speak of the sources whence they sprang. The history of Utah, therefore, must include the history of her founders, and with their general narrative, as a religious community, it now suits our purpose to begin.

In the early part of the present century, in the little town of Sharon, Windsor County, Vermont, there lived an humble family of the name of Smith. Joseph and Lucy were the parents' names, and their children, seven sons and three daughters—some born prior, some subsequent to the time of which we write—were Alvin, Hyrum, Sophronia, Joseph, Samuel H., Ephraim, William, Catharine, Don Carlos and Lucy. The father was a farmer, though not a flourishing one, having lately lost his property through the dishonesty of a trusted friend, and was now renting a farm in Sharon, and toiling early and late for a bare livelihood. They were a God-fearing folk, honest, straightforward in their dealings, and of good repute among their neighbors.

It was on the 23rd of December, 1805, that the son was born to whom was given the paternal name. This son, Joseph Smith, junior, was the famous Mormon Prophet, the founder of the Church of Jesus Christ of Latter-day Saints.

The boy was about ten years old when his parents migrated from Vermont and made their home at Palmyra, Ontario—now Wayne—County, New York; whence they removed, four years later, to Manchester in the same county.

A brief glance at some of the social conditions of those early times and primitive places may here be necessary. Western New York, the arena of our story's immediate action, was then an almost new country. Farm and forest, society and solitude, civilization and semi-savagery divided it. The red man, though no longer roaming wildly, had not disappeared from its borders, and the whites, who of course predominated and held sway, if, like all Yankees, shrewd and intelligent, were mostly illiterate and untaught. The masses were poor, but there were farmers and artisans who were prosperous, and the people, as a rule, were industrious and provident. Their style of living was exceedingly plain. Houses were usually small, unplastered, unpainted and rudely furnished. A huge fire on the hearth, fed with pine knots from the neighboring forest, gave light and warmth to those within the house, or the flickering flame of the tallow-dip shed its uncertain lustre over the scene. The floors were often without carpets, the tables without cloths, and the frugal meal, cooked amid the glowing embers on the hearth, or in the iron pot suspended by a chain from the chimney hook, was eaten from pewter or wooden plates, with horn-handled knives and iron spoons. Clocks were a rarity, the "time o' day" being commonly "guessed" by the sun; pictures and musical instruments were few and of inferior kind, and the family library consisted, in most instances, of the Bible, an almanac and what books were in vogue at the village school. In short, it was just such a social condition as life in our own Utah once presented, and in rare cases yet presents, in sparsely settled localities, where primitive taste or poverty still reigns.

The people of those times, or at any rate of that region, were generally religious, and were great Bible readers; though many spiritually inclined and well versed in scripture, were neither communicants nor church-goers. The leading sects of today were nearly all represented in the ecclesiastical category of the period, each having its doughty champions, its Davids in the field, armed *cap-a-pie* and confronting with valorous zeal the gigantic Philistines of sin and unbelief. The infidel, however, did not abound, as at a later day. Nearly every one professed some sort of religion. Religion, indeed, and not agnosticism, was the fashion and flavor of the times. Yet the tide of spiritual thought and emotion, like any other tide, was subject to the extremes of ebb and flow.

Soon after the removal of the Smith family to Manchester, a wave of religious excitement, of a character common to the period, began rolling over the land, and camp-meetings and revivals, like bubbles on the crest of the mighty billow, were held far and near under the auspices of the various Christian sects. The whole region rang and resounded with the echoing notes of the evangelic trumpet. The village of Manchester shared in the general excitement and enthusiasm,—Methodists, Baptists, Presbyterians, etc., all vieing with each other in the work of "soul-saving," and crowds of converts flocking to the standards of the ministers of the rival faiths. Among the proselytes made by the Presbyterians were Lucy Smith, Joseph's mother, his brothers Hyrum and Samuel, and his sister Sophronia.

Fruitful as were the labors of the revivalists, however, one thing militated against their further success. It was lack of unity. They were not united; either in doctrine, sentiment or common Christian feeling. Divisions in doctrine among the Christian churches were neither shocking nor surprising; from the days of Wycliffe, Luther and Wesley the world had grown used to such things; and so long as modern Christians merely differed in opinion regarding the "one Lord, one faith, one baptism" of the ancients, and were careful to "love one another" and "avoid disputations," their course would occasion little comment and less complaint.

But strife and hatred among professed ministers of Christ, while provoking mirth and mockery from the infidel, are to all good Christians horrifying. And such things, sad to tell, were manifested by the ministers of whom we are speaking, and by many of their converts as well, and deprecated and deplored by divers thoughtful and pious minds, who consequently stood aloof and forbore to taste of the fountains that sent forth such bitter waters.

In matters of doctrine, as said, the sects were much divided,— though on certain points agreed. For instance, some held, as now, that the ordinance of baptism was non-essential to salvation. Others contended that it was essential. Some claimed sprinkling to be the proper mode of baptism; others, that pouring water upon the head was the true method, and others still that immersion of the whole body in the liquid element was necessary. And similar differences in other doctrines. The main points upon which most of the sects agreed were: that God was a being without body, parts or passions; that He no longer communicated His will to man; that the heavens were closed and the canon of scripture full; that the days of miracles and revelations were over; that faith without works was sufficient to save, and that all who died without hearing of or believing in Jesus Christ as the world's Redeemer, were doomed to never-ending torment. Even infants were not exempt, according to the Calvinistic creed, but were fated to eternally "roast in sulphur," if the Almighty had seen fit to cut short their lives ere they came to the knowledge of His only begotten Son. A chaos, a Babel of religious opinions and their professors, differing, yet all claiming to be right, and to have the Bible as their basis of belief and source of inspiration; a ceaseless clash and war of words in support of those opinions. Such in brief was the spiritual condition of the Christian world at the period of which we are writing.

Among those who stood aloof, surveying the scene of strife,

wondering which of all these wrangling sects was the true Church of Christ, was Joseph Smith, the farmer's boy, then a little over fourteen years of age. Anxious for his soul's salvation,—for he was a thoughtful and conscientious lad,—he much desired to know the true way, in order that he might walk therein. Unable to solve the problem, though feeling assured that the contending churches were not all divine, he forbore to join with any, but attended their meetings as often as convenient, particularly those of the Methodists, to whom he was somewhat partial.

One day, he relates, while reading the scriptures, his eye chanced to rest upon the fifth verse of the first chapter of the Epistle of James, running as follows: "If any of you lack wisdom, let him ask of God, that giveth to all men liberally, and upbraideth not, and it shall be given him." The sacred words sank deeply into the boy's simple soul. He did "lack wisdom," wisdom to know the truth; and he would "ask of God," who had thus promised, by His ancient apostle, to hear and answer prayer. Such was his simple faith. Such was his earnest resolve.

Joseph's record then relates how on a bright spring morning in the year 1820, he retired to the woods,—a sylvan solitude not far from his father's home,—and finding himself alone, bowed down in prayer. It was his first attempt to orally address Deity. He had scarcely begun, he declares, when suddenly he was seized by some mysterious power which paralyzed his tongue so that he could no longer speak. Simultaneously a cloud of darkness encompassed him, filling his soul with horror and presaging instant destruction. So literal were his sensations that he felt himself in the fell grasp of some actual, though unseen, personage or influence of another world. Exerting all his powers, he called upon God for deliverance—his thoughts now praying in the absence of speech—and just as reason seemed tottering, and hope was hovering on the brink of despair, he saw a light descending from heaven, directly over his head, of such surpassing brilliance as to exceed that of the noon-day sun. The pillar of splendor gradually fell until it rested upon the prostrate youth, who, the moment it appeared, found himself delivered from the deadly influence that had held him bound. In the midst of the pillar were two personages of ineffable glory, in the form of men, one of whom, addressing Joseph by name, and pointing to the other, said, "This is my beloved Son, hear him!"

The amazed and enraptured youth, so soon as he could collect his thoughts and command utterance, recalling the object of his quest, asked of the glorious oracles which of all the religious sects was right, and which one should he join? To his astonishment he was told that none of them were right, and that he must not unite with any; that their creeds were an abomination and their professors corrupt; that they taught for doctrine the commandments of men, drawing near to the Lord with their lips while their hearts were far from Him, and having a form of godliness but denying the power thereof. Again forbidding him to join any of the churches, the two personages withdrew, the pillar of light ascended and vanished, and the rapt youth, recovering from his vision's ecstacy, found himself lying upon his back gazing up into heaven.

Naturally enough, the boy's story, being told, and its truth persisted in—and that, too, with every evidence of solemn sincerity—created no small sensation. Some were amazed, some simply amused at its audacity; others horror-stricken at its blasphemy,—for such it seemed to them. In the midst of a generation which doubted and even denied the Creator's personality, applying to Him, in thought if not in word, Pope's eloquent definition of the all-pervading Spirit, which

> Warms in the sun, refreshes in the breeze,
> Glows in the stars and blossoms in the trees,
> Lives through all life, extends through all extent,
> Spreads undivided, operates unspent,

he, an untutored lad, had had the temerity to assert, in full face of the teachings and traditions of the sects and schools, that God the universal Father was a man, a living, breathing, glorified man, and that God the Son was a man also, made, like other men, in the image of that Father's person.* Moreover, that he had both seen and heard them. The idea was preposterous—blasphemous! It was a matter-of-fact, even skeptical age,—skeptical as to modern miracles and spiritual manifestations,—that Joseph Smith confronted, and such a tale, however sincerely told, was altogether too marvelous for belief. Such an event was very much too literal to suit the temper of the times. To speak of Christ's coming to earth at some future period was one thing; to claim that He had already come, and had appeared to so insignificant a person as young "Joe Smith" was quite another thing. The fellow must be mad, or else a wicked and designing imposter. So thought that generation—so thinks this—with comparatively few exceptions.

Joseph had a friend, a Methodist minister, prominent in the religious movement then agitating the neighborhood. To him, among the first, he confided his story, thinking that his clerical friend would rejoice at the recital. In this, however, he was disappointed. The minister treated the matter with utter contempt, flatly telling him that it was "all of the devil;" that there were no such things now as visions and revelations, that they had all ceased with the Apostles, and that the world would never have any more of them.

But the matter did not end there. With the usual zeal of the heretic-hunter, the minister, forgetting his former friendship for the boy, went about prejudicing the minds of his fellow preachers and the people against him. The result was that the lad, who had formerly been a favorite with the preachers, suddenly found himself an object of their distrust and derision,—the target of their bitterest scorn. Continuing to affirm the truth of his tale, prejudice increased, and the arrows of persecution began falling around him. The preachers and professors, so disunited before, all united now upon one point,—to deride and denounce "Joe Smith the imposter." Nay, more; his very life was attempted by the bullet of the ambushed assassin. Still, said he, "I had seen a vision. I knew it, and I knew

---

* "God Himself was once as we are now, and is an exalted man, and sits enthroned in yonder heavens."—JOSEPH SMITH.

that God knew it, and I could not deny it; at least I knew that by so doing I would offend God, and come under condemnation."

Three years elapsed, and still this strange boy,—for strange he must have seemed,—scorned and buffeted and belied, steadfastly maintained his testimony. Driven from the ranks of the religious and respectable because of his convictions, he was often forced for companionship, which his genial and kindly nature craved, into society not the most select, and was led in the way of temptations which he did not always resist. During those days he did things, as he candidly confesses, that were "offensive in the sight of God." Self-condemned for his youthful follies, accusing conscience finally drove him to seek forgiveness of his Maker, and implore a fresh proof of his "state and standing before Him."

For what followed in his experience we again refer to his own record, which necessarily forms the principal basis of this portion of our narrative. It was the night of September 21st, 1823.' Joseph, retiring to rest, began pleading with the heavens and pouring out his soul in penitent supplication. While so engaged he saw a light appearing in his room, increasing in brilliance until brighter than the blaze of noon-day. Immediately a glorious being, clad in a loose robe of radiant whiteness, his countenance lustrous as lightning, stood at his bedside, his feet seemingly resting on air. The head, neck, hands and feet were bare, and the body, wherever exposed, of all but transparent purity. He called the youth by name, and giving his own name as Moroni, proclaimed himself a messenger from the presence of God. He told Joseph that the Lord had a work for him to do, and that his name should be spoken both well and evil of among all nations; showed him in vision where there was a record deposited, written upon plates of gold, giving an account of the ancient inhabitants of America and their origin, and containing the fullness of the Everlasting Gospel as delivered by the Savior to those inhabitants; also that an instrument called the *Urim and Thummim*, consisting of two stones set in a silver bow and fastened to a breast-plate, was deposited with the plates, having been prepared by the

Almighty for the purpose of the book's translation. The angel then quoted from the scriptures various prophecies relating to the restoration of the Gospel and the Priesthood, the setting up of Messiah's latter-day kingdom and the ushering in of the Millennium. These prophecies,—including part of the third and all of the fourth chapters of Malachi, the eleventh chapter of Isaiah, the twenty-second and twenty-third verses of the third chapter of Acts, and the last five verses of the second chapter of Joel,—he said were about to be fulfilled. He also declared that "the fullness of the Gentiles" would soon come in. He warned the youth that when he obtained possession of the plates, he must not show them to any save those to whom he should be commanded to show them,—otherwise he should be destroyed. Having delivered his message the angel departed, ascending by what seemed "a conduit opening right up into heaven," and the room made radiant by his presence again grew dark. But while musing and marveling over this visitation, with its new and strange revealings, Joseph saw the light returning. In an instant the same messenger stood at his bedside. Rehearsing without the least variation the things before related, the oracle added that great and grievous judgments, desolations by famine, sword and pestilence were coming upon the earth in this generation. Again he departed, but still again returned, and after repeating his former message, cautioned the youth against giving way to a mercenary spirit that would tempt him, owing to the poverty of his father's family, to obtain the plates for purposes of worldly gain. This he must not attempt to do, but seek only to glorify God and build up his kingdom. A third time the messenger vanished, when almost immediately the village cock crew, and the first faint streaks of dawn shot athwart the eastern horizon.

From loss of sleep and the severe strain upon his physical powers, incident to his extraordinary experience, Joseph, going into the field to labor that day, found himself exhausted and utterly unable to toil. Noticing his condition, his father, who was near, bade him return to the house and rest. He attempted to obey, but in crossing the fence from out the field his strength completely failed, and he fell helpless and unconscious to the ground. A voice calling him by name aroused him. He looked, and lo! the angel messenger of the past night standing above him in a halo of glory. For the fourth time Moroni delivers his message, which now burns as in letters of fire upon the young man's mind, then bids him return to his father and tell him all. Joseph obeys, his sire declares it to be divine, and directs him to go and do all that the angel has commanded.

Accordingly, as the record continues, he set out for the spot where he had been shown the plates were deposited. It was a hill, two or three miles from the village of Manchester. "On the west side of this hill," says he, "not far from the top, under a stone of considerable size, lay the plates deposited in a stone box; this stone was thick and rounding in the middle on the upper side, and thinner towards the edges, so that the middle part of it was visible above the ground, but the edges all round were covered with earth. Having removed the earth and obtained a lever, which I got fixed under the edge of the stone, with a little exertion I raised it up; I looked in and there indeed did I behold the plates, the *Urim and Thummim* and the breast-plate, as stated by the messenger. The box in which they lay was formed by placing stones together in some kind of cement. In the bottom of the box were laid two stones cross-ways of the box, and on these stones lay the plates and the other things with them."

Attempting to possess himself of the box's contents, Joseph finds himself restrained, and at that moment the angel who has directed him thither appears and forbids him to touch them. Four years, he is informed, must elapse before the season will be ripe and the records delivered into his hands. Meantime he must lead a godly life, and visit the hill once a year, until the four years' term has expired; then and there to be further taught in relation to his prophetic mission. Much more does the angel unfold,—among other thing that he, Moroni, while living in the flesh, was the last of a line of prophets who ministered to an ancient people called Nephites, who inhabited this land; that he was the son of Mormon, a Nephite prophet, general and historian, whose record it is that there lies deposited, where

Moroni, divinely directed, hid it fourteen centuries before; that this hill was called by the Nephites Cumorah, but to the Jaredites, their historic predecessors, it had been known as the hill Ramah. Having finished his course of counsel and admonition, the messenger departs, and the youth, after carefully covering the box containing the records and replacing the surrounding soil, seeks his home to tell to the astonished household the marvelous things revealed by the heavenly messenger. Unlike the minister in whom he formerly confided, they believe his words and rejoice in his strange and wondrous story.

Agreeable to his instructions, Joseph, at the end of each year, or on the 22nd of each of the four succeeding Septembers, repairs to the hill Cumorah, meets and receives further teachings from Moroni. Finally, at the end of the fourth year—September 22nd, 1827—the angel custodian of the golden plates and the *Urim and Thummim* delivers the ancient relics into his keeping.

CHAPTER II.
1827-1830.

TRANSLATION OF THE BOOK OF MORMON—POVERTY AND PERSECUTION—THE "MONEY-DIGGING" AND "WIFE-STEALING" STORIES—MARTIN HARRIS—THE PROPHET REMOVES TO PENNSYLVANIA—DESCRIPTION OF THE PLATES AND THE URIM AND THUMMIM—MARTIN HARRIS AND PROFESSOR ANTHON—THE REPUTED METHOD OF TRANSLATION—THE STOLEN MANUSCRIPT—OLIVER COWDERY—JOHN THE BAPTIST AND THE AARONIC PRIESTHOOD—BAPTISM OF JOSEPH AND OLIVER—JOSEPH KNIGHT'S BENEFICENCE—DAVID WHITMER—JOSEPH AND OLIVER REMOVE FROM HARMONY TO FAYETTE—THE MELCHISEDEK PRIESTHOOD—THE THREE WITNESSES—THE EIGHT—THE TRANSLATION COMPLETE AND THE BOOK OF MORMON GIVEN TO THE WORLD.

NOT for some months, according to Joseph, after receiving the golden plates, was he enabled to begin the task of their translation. In the first place he was very poor, and having married, was obliged to labor more diligently than ever for his daily bread. In the next place he was constantly harassed by enemies.

He tells that while on his way home with the plates, he was repeatedly set upon by unknown men, who strove to wrest them from him. Once they dealt him a severe blow with a bludgeon. Thanks to his superior strength, for he was now a stalwart youth of nearly twenty-two, and aided as he believed by the Almighty, he successfully withstood his assailants, and finally reached home in safety. But his enemies did not rest. Falsehood like a flood pursued him, and the waves of prejudice rose higher and higher. The house in which he lived was beset by mobs; armed assassins lay in wait for him and shot at him as he passed; robbers broke into his rooms to carry off the records, and every means imaginable, both of force and strategy, was vainly employed to get them from him.

In the interim of his fourth and fifth visits to Cumorah, Joseph had married Miss Emma Hale, daughter of Isaac Hale, of Harmony,

Susquehanna County, Pennsylvania. He had formed her acquaintance in the fall of 1825, while working for a Mr. Josiah Stoal, a resident of Chenango County, New York, who had hired him to go with him to Pennsylvania and dig for a silver mine. While thus employed, Joseph boarded in the family of Mr. Hale, and became enamored of his daughter, who returned his affection. The silver mine proving an *ignis fatuus*, after a month's fruitless labor Joseph persuaded his employer to abandon the useless enterprise. Subsequently he made overtures for the hand of Miss Hale, but her parents withheld their consent to the union. Emma, however, was of age, and a girl of high mettle, and her lover no less spirited and determined. They acted without consent, and went elsewhere to be married; the nuptial knot being tied by one Esquire Tarbill, at his home in South Bainbridge, Chenango County, New York, on the 18th of January, 1827.

From these two incidents in his career,—his being employed to dig for a silver mine, and his marriage with Miss Hale away from her father's home,—arose the prevalent stories of "money-digging" and "wife-stealing," used against him by his enemies.

The anger of Emma's parents over the independent action of the young couple, now happily wed, evidently soon abated; for at the expiration of a few months after their marriage, we find them contemplating a removal to the home of the Hales in Pennsylvania. And this, owing to the annoyance and persecution to which they were subjected at Manchester. Too poor to pay the expenses of the trip,—a distance of about a hundred miles,—Joseph at this juncture received timely aid from a Mr. Martin Harris, a well-to-do farmer residing in Palmyra Township, a few miles from Manchester. Mr. Harris, who had previously become interested in Joseph, gave him fifty dollars to assist him on his journey. This enabled the young couple to reach their destination. They arrived at Harmony in December, 1827. On their way thither, the wagon in which they traveled was twice stopped by officers, or men claiming to be such, armed with search warrants, who ransacked the vehicle in quest of the golden plates. They were secreted, it is said, in a barrel of beans, and thus escaped discovery.

These plates are thus described. They were of uniform size, about eight inches in width, each one a little thinner than ordinary tin. They were bound together by three rings running through one of the edges, forming a book about six inches in thickness, one-third of which was sealed. This part was not to be opened; the time not having come for its contents to be known. The unsealed two-thirds of the volume,—the plates of which could be turned like the leaves of a book, and were covered, both sides, with strange characters, "small and beautifully engraved,"—were left free to be translated by means of the *Urim and Thummim*.

This instrument consisted of two precious stones, set in the rims of a silver bow, and fastened to a breast-plate. The breast-plate, like the record plates, was of gold, the inside concave, the outside convex, and four golden bands attached served to fasten it to the person of the wearer.

In February, 1828, Martin Harris, the Palmyra farmer, visited his young friend at Harmony. Being shown certain mystical characters, which Joseph informed him he had copied from the golden plates and translated, Martin, by permission, took these characters to the city of New York, to exhibit them to the savants and linguists of the metropolis.

According to his account, he first submitted them to Professor Charles Anthon, of Columbia College, who stated that the translation was correct, and as to the characters, translated and untranslated, that they were Egyptian, Chaldaic, Syriac and Arabic—true and genuine. Being asked for a certificate to that effect, he willingly gave one, addressing it to the people of Palmyra.

"How did the young man learn that there were gold plates there?" asked the Professor, as Harris, having folded the certificate and put it in his pocket, turned to go.

"An angel of God revealed it to him," answered the farmer.

A look of dismay, as if doubting the speaker's sanity, stole over the face of the Professor, who, as soon as he could regain himself, exclaimed "Let me see that certificate."

Martin returned the paper, whereupon Professor Anthon tore it in pieces, remarking that there were no such things now as ministering of angels, but that if the plates were brought to him he would translate them.

Martin informed him that a portion of the golden book was sealed, and that he would not be permitted to bring it.

"I cannot read a sealed book,"* replied the Professor, and the interview abruptly ended.

Harris next consulted Dr. Mitchell, another scholar, who seconded all that Professor Anthon had said concerning the characters and the translation.

Such was the report of his errand with which Martin Harris returned to Joseph Smith. So far was he now converted to the latter's views, that he then and there offered to act as his scribe in the work of translation. As Joseph was a poor penman, this offer was gratefully accepted.

The following is the reputed method of translation. The Prophet, scanning through the *Urim and Thummim* the golden pages, would see appear, in lieu of the strange characters engraved thereon, their equivalent in English words. These he would repeat, and the scribe, separated from him by a veil or curtain, would write them down. A peculiarity of the process was that until the writing was correct in every particular, the words last given would remain before the eyes of the translator, and not disappear. But on the necessary correction being made, they would immediately pass away and be succeeded by others. In this manner the Book of Mormon is said to have been translated. Hence the claim of the Latter-day Saints,—called "Mormons" for their belief in the book,—to its plenary inspiration.

From the 12th of April to the 14th of June, 1828, Joseph and Martin continued, with some intermissions, their joint labor of translating. In that interim the latter copied by dictation one hundred

---

* The Latter-day Saints regard this as a literal fulfillment of Isaiah xxix–11.

and sixteen pages of foolscap manuscript. These pages he much desired to show to his wife and other curious or skeptical persons, with a view to their conversion. After many entreaties and refusals, he obtained Joseph's permission to do so, on condition that they should be shown only to certain persons who were named. Martin, however, broke his pledge and permitted others to see them. The result was that the manuscript was stolen. Neither he nor Joseph ever again beheld it. A temporary estrangement ensued between them, and the Prophet, it is said, having angered the Almighty, lost his gift for a season. Martin, though eventually forgiven, never again acted as Joseph's scribe.

Oliver Cowdery next comes upon the scene. He is a schoolteacher by profession; by trade a blacksmith; young in years, but a man of intelligence and education. Pursuing his vocation of pedagogue at Manchester, New York, during the winter of 1828-9, while boarding in the family of Joseph Smith, senior, he hears of young Joseph, his visions and the golden plates, and is impressed with a belief in their genuineness. He is also imbued with the idea that his future destiny and that of the Prophet are in some manner interwoven. At Sabbath sunset, April 5th, 1829, he presents himself at Joseph's door in Harmony, and volunteers his services as a scribe and secretary. The proffered aid is eagerly accepted. Two days later the youthful twain,—who are yet to be known as the first and second Elders of the Church of Jesus Christ of Latter-day Saints,—continue the work of translating the Nephite record. The rendering into English progresses rapidly under their united and almost incessant labors, and by the middle of May the greater part of the translation is complete.

Joseph and Oliver testify that on a certain day they suspended their task and went out into the woods to pray and inquire of the Lord concerning the doctrine—then well nigh obsolete in Christendom—of baptism for the remission of sins, which they had found mentioned in the translation of the plates. While calling upon the Lord, they declare, a heavenly messenger descended in a cloud of light, and laying his hands upon their heads, spake these words: "Upon you, my fellow servants, in the name of Messiah, I confer the Priesthood of Aaron, which holds the keys of the ministering of angels, and of the gospel of repentance, and of baptism by immersion for the remission of sins; and this shall never again be taken from the earth, until the sons of Levi do offer again an offering unto the Lord in righteousness."

The angel who thus ordained them said that his name was John, the same who was anciently surnamed "the Baptist," and that he acted under the direction of Peter, James and John, who held the keys of the Melchisedek Priesthood; this, the higher authority, should in due time be conferred upon them, and Joseph should then be the first Elder and Oliver the second Elder in the Church of Christ. The Melchisedek Priesthood would authorize them to bestow the Holy Ghost by the laying on of hands, a power not conferred by the Priesthood of Aaron. They were then directed to baptize each other by immersion; Joseph first to baptize Oliver, Oliver then to baptize Joseph; after which, in the same order, they were to re-ordain each other to the Aaronic Priesthood. These instructions were carefully obeyed. The date given for these events is May 15th, 1829. According to the record, it was soon after this that the Melchisedek Priesthood was conferred upon Joseph and Oliver by the Apostles Peter, James and John.

In the latter part of May the mobocratic spirit, which till then had lain dormant in that locality, manifested itself at this place of peaceful name, Harmony, where a violent assault upon the two young men was only prevented by the personal influence of Mr. Hale, Joseph's father-in-law. Joseph was now living in his own home, but the gaunt wolf of poverty still hovered round his door. Hearing of his straitened circumstances and having faith in his professions, an elderly man named Joseph Knight, residing at Colesville, Broome County, New York—thirty miles distant—came bringing supplies of food and other necessaries, to enable him and his scribe to continue their work without interruption. This act of beneficence was several times repeated.

A family named Whitmer, friends of Oliver Cowdery, at Fayette, Seneca County, New York, had also been apprised of the situation. Early in June David Whitmer arrived at Harmony with a message from his father. Peter Whitmer, senior, inviting Joseph and Oliver to come to Fayette and make their home in his household. This offer was thankfully accepted.

At the home of Father Whitmer, to which they at once repaired, they zealously prosecuted their labors. At intervals Joseph and Oliver would converse with the Whitmers and other people of the neighborhood upon the subject of religion, baptizing such as believed and desired to embrace their principles. During the month of June, Hyrum Smith, David Whitmer and Peter Whitmer, junior, were baptized in Seneca Lake; the first two by Joseph Smith, the last-named by Oliver Cowdery. Samuel H. Smith had been baptized by Oliver at Harmony some time before.

Among the predictions of the Book of Mormon is one to the effect that three special witnesses should be chosen to behold the plates from which it was translated. These plates were to be shown them by an angel. Oliver Cowdery, David Whitmer and Martin Harris were selected as these witnesses. The event is thus recorded in their own words, forming a portion of the preface to the Book of Mormon:

THE TESTIMONY OF THE THREE WITNESSES.

Be it known unto all nations, kindreds, tongues, and people unto whom this work shall come, that we, through the grace of God the Father, and our Lord Jesus Christ, have seen the plates which contain this record, which is a record of the people of Nephi, and also of the Lamanites, their brethren, and also of the people of Jared, who came from the tower of which hath been spoken; and we also know that they have been translated by the gift and power of God, for his voice hath declared it unto us; wherefore we know of a surety that the work is true. And we also testify that we have seen the engravings which are upon the plates; and they have been shown unto us by the power of God, and not of man. And we declare with words of soberness, that an angel of God came down from heaven, and he brought and laid before our eyes, that we beheld and saw the plates, and the engravings thereon; and we know that it is by the grace of God the Father, and our Lord Jesus Christ, that we beheld and bear record that these things are true; and it is marvelous in our eyes, nevertheless the voice of the Lord commanded us that we should bear record of it; wherefore to be obedient unto the commandments of God, we bear testimony of these things. And we know that if we are faithful in Christ, we shall rid our garments of the blood of all men, and be found spotless before the judgment-seat of Christ, and shall dwell with him eternally in the heavens. And the honor be to the Father, and to the Son, and to the Holy Ghost, which is one God. Amen.

OLIVER COWDERY,
DAVID WHITMER,
MARTIN HARRIS.

Eight others also testify, as follows:

THE TESTIMONY OF THE EIGHT WITNESSES.

Be it known unto all nations, kindreds, tongues, and people unto whom this work shall come, that Joseph Smith, Jun., the translator of this work, has shewn unto us the plates of which hath been spoken, which have the appearance of gold; and as many of the leaves as the said Smith has translated, we did handle with our hands; and we also saw the engravings thereon, all of which has the appearance of ancient work, and of curious workmanship. And this we bear record with words of soberness, that the said Smith has shewn unto us, for we have seen and hefted, and know of a surety that the said Smith has got the plates of which we have spoken. And we give our names unto the world, to witness unto the world that which we have seen; and we lie not, God bearing witness of it.

CHRISTIAN WHITMER,	HIRAM PAGE,
JACOB WHITMER,	JOSEPH SMITH, SEN.,
PETER WHITMER, JUN.,	HYRUM SMITH,
JOHN WHITMER,	SAMUEL H. SMITH.

Among the revelations recorded as "given through Joseph the Seer" during the month of June, 1829, is one making known the calling of the Twelve Apostles of the coming Church. The mission to "search out the Twelve" was given to Oliver Cowdery and David Whitmer. In other revelations, addressed to various individuals, it is reiterated that "a great and marvelous work is about to come forth among the children of men."

As the translation drew to a close, the Prophet and his friends visited Palmyra, the home of Martin Harris, to arrange for the publication of the Book of Mormon. They secured the copy-right and contracted with Mr. Egbert B. Grandin to print five thousand copies for the sum of three thousand dollars. Martin Harris was to furnish the money. The copy-right was secured June 11th, 1829.

Respecting the final disposition of the plates and the *Urim and Thummim*, Joseph states that the same heavenly messenger who committed them to his care, reclaimed them when the work of translation was over.

The manuscript of the Book of Mormon was carefully copied, the original retained by the translator, and the copy,—said to be in the writing of Oliver Cowdery,*—placed in the hands of the printer. Joseph then paid a visit to his home in Pennsylvania, leaving his more scholarly friend Cowdery to superintend the proof-reading and other details of publication. Early in the year 1830 the first edition of the Book of Mormon was given to the world.

* This manuscript is now in the possession of the family of the late David Whitmer, at Richmond, Ray County, Mo.

CHAPTER III.

WHAT THE BOOK OF MORMON CLAIMS TO BE—THE NARRATIVE OF THE NEPHITE RECORD—HOW THE WORLD RECEIVED IT—THE SPAULDING STORY—"MORMONISM UNVEILED"—THE SIDNEY RIGDON ANACHRONISM—DISCOVERY OF THE ORIGINAL "MANUSCRIPT STORY"—ITS CONDENSED NARRATIVE—MORMON'S RECORD AND SPAULDING'S ROMANCE COMPARED—REYNOLDS' "MYTH OF THE MANUSCRIPT FOUND"—PRESIDENT FAIRCHILD'S OPINION—NUMEROUS EDITIONS OF THE TRANSLATED WORK.

THE Book of Mormon claims to be a record of two great races that flourished successively upon the American continent ages prior to its discovery by Columbus. Their combined histories, written by a succession of authors—prophets and kings—cover a period extending from the time of the Tower of Babel down to about the beginning of the fifth century of the Christian era. The records of these authors comprise fifteen books, named in their order as follows: I. Nephi, II. Nephi, Book of Jacob, Book of Enos, Book of Jarom, Book of Omni, The Words of Mormon, Book of Mosiah, including the Record of Zeniff, Book of Alma, Book of Helaman, III. Nephi, IV. Nephi, Book of Mormon, Book of Ether, and the Book of Moroni.

The first of the ancient races referred to, whose histories are briefly given in these records, were the Jaredites, who, in the dispersion following the confusion of tongues, came across the great deep and peopled what is now North America. Their leaders were Jared and his brother, Mahonri Moriancumr, from the former of whom the nation derived its name. Their greatest national character, however, was this "brother of Jared,"—otherwise nameless in the record,*—under whose inspired leadership the colony left the land of Shinar, and crossing one of the great oceans in ships or "barges" of their own building, landed on these northern shores, made glorious during

---

* Joseph Smith supplied the proper name, Mahonri Moriancumr.

the lapse of centuries by their power, wisdom, wealth and civilization.

The Jaredite leaders were democratic in their instincts, abhorring the idea of kings and monarchies, which they had been taught to believe could not long flourish upon this goodly land,—a land destined to be "free from bondage." But their people, like the Israelites of a later period in the far-off land of Canaan, desired a king, and besought them ere they died to anoint one of their sons to rule over them. The thought was repugnant to the great and good founders of the nation, who foresaw the inevitable result,—the captivity, perchance the destruction of their people. However, they yielded reluctant assent, and one of the sons of Jared—Orihah—his three brothers and all the sons of the brother of Jared having declined the proffered purple, was anointed king.

A short period of prosperity followed, for the people served God and were righteous. Then came wealth, class divisions, pride, tyranny, with their usual concomitants,—luxury, licentiousness and crime. The worship of God was neglected, then abandoned. Self-interest dethroned patriotism, and passion usurped the place of principle. Civil wars broke out, dismembering and dividing the nation. From civilization and refinement the race sank into brutality and savagery, until finally, over the precipice of destruction, of utter annihilation, swept the awful torrent of a mighty people's ruin.

The last of many prophets who taught and warned the Jaredites, seeking in vain to avert their coming doom, was Ether their historian, who, having witnessed the destruction of his people, hid up their records for discovery in after ages, and disappeared from view.

A few passages from the Book of Ether*, as abridged by Moroni the Nephite, are here presented:

And now I, Moroni, proceed to finish my record concerning the destruction of the people of whom I have been writing.

For behold, they rejected the words of Ether; for he truly told them of all things, from the beginning of man; and that after the waters had receded from off the face of this

---

* Chapter xiii. 1–14.

HISTORY OF UTAH. 39

land, it became a choice land above all other lands, a chosen land of the Lord; wherefore the Lord would have that all men should serve him who dwell upon the face thereof;

And that it was the place of the New Jerusalem, which should come down out of heaven, and the Holy Sanctuary of the Lord.

Behold, Ether saw the days of Christ, and he spake concerning a New Jerusalem upon this land;

And he spake also concerning the house of Israel, and the Jerusalem from whence Lehi should come; after it should be destroyed, it should be built up again a holy city unto the Lord, wherefore it could not be a New Jerusalem, for it had been in a time of old, but it should be built up again, and become a holy city of the Lord; and it should be built unto the house of Israel;

And that a New Jerusalem should be built up upon this land, unto the remnant of the seed of Joseph, for which things there has been a type:

For as Joseph brought his father down into the land of Egypt, even so he died there; wherefore the Lord brought a remnant of the seed of Joseph out of the land of Jerusalem, that he might be merciful unto the seed of Joseph, that they should perish not, even as he was merciful unto the father of Joseph, that he should perish not;

Wherefore the remnant of the house of Joseph shall be built upon this land; and it shall be a land of their inheritance; and they shall build up a holy city unto the Lord, like unto the Jerusalem of old; and they shall no more be confounded, until the end comes when the earth shall pass away.

And there shall be a new heaven and a new earth; and they shall be like unto the old, save the old have passed away, and all things have become new.

And then cometh the New Jerusalem; and blessed are they who dwell therein, for it is they whose garments are white through the blood of the Lamb; and they are they who are numbered among the remnant of the seed of Joseph, who were of the house of Israel.

And then also cometh the Jerusalem of old; and the inhabitants thereof, blessed are they, for they have been washed in the blood of the Lamb; and they are they who were scattered and gathered in from the four quarters of the earth, and from the north countries, and are partakers of the fulfilling of the covenant which God made with their father Abraham.

And when these things come, bringeth to pass the scripture which saith, There are they who were first, who shall be last; and there are they who were last, who shall be first.

And I was about to write more, but am forbidden; but great and marvelous were the prophecies of Ether, but they esteemed him as nought, and cast him out, and he hid himself in the cavity of a rock by day, and by night he went forth viewing the things which should come upon the people.

And as he dwelt in the cavity of a rock, he made the remainder of this record, viewing the destructions which came upon the people by night.

The sole survivor of the final slaughter, which took place near the hill Ramah, between the two great contending factions of the fratricidal Jaredites, was Coriantumr, their king. Having slain Shiz, the leader of the opposing host, in a duel upon the bloody field, where all save this twain had fallen, Coriantumr lived long enough to tell the sad story of his people's ruin to their successors upon this northern land. These, the people of Mulek, were a colony led out from Jerusalem under Mulek, son of Zedekiah, king of Judah, about the time of the beginning of the Babylonian captivity. They did not remain a distinct nation, but coalesced with the Nephites, the second of the two great races mentioned.

The Nephites, with whose history the Book of Mormon begins, —the discovery of Mulek's colony and the finding and translating of the Jaredite Book of Ether being incidents in their career,—were likewise from Judea. They were mostly the descendants of Lehi, who, divinely guided, departed with his family from Jerusalem about the year 600 B. C.,—eleven years before Mulek's colony emigrated,— while the Prophet Jeremiah was pouring his solemn warnings in the ears of king, princes, priests and people of the sin-laden and doomed city. Lehi was descended from Joseph, through Manasseh. His wife's name was Sariah. Their children, when leaving Jerusalem, were four sons,—Laman, Lemuel, Sam and Nephi,—and several daughters whose names are not given. Subsequently were born to them two more sons,—Jacob and Joseph. The other members of Lehi's colony were Ishmael and his family, who were of Ephraim,* and a servant named Zoram. The sons and daughters of Lehi and Ishmael intermarried.

The course of the colony from Jerusalem led to the Red Sea and along its shores; thence eastward across the peninsula of Arabia. On the shores of the Persian Gulf, under the inspired direction of Nephi, who became the virtual leader of the colony, they built a ship, and in it crossed "the great waters"—the Indian and Pacific oceans —to South America. They are supposed to have landed on the coast of the country now called Chili. Thence, as their nation or nations

---

* Joseph Smith said that the manuscript lost by Martin Harris so stated.

grew, and the people multiplied, the descendants of Lehi spread over the whole face of South and North America.

After Lehi's death the colony divided; Laman and Lemuel, who had always been jealous of their younger and gifted brother Nephi, rebelling against his rule, and leading away others to form a separate people. Thenceforth there were two nations; the followers of Laman, who were known as Lamanites, and the adherents of Nephi, who took upon them his name in like manner. The Lamanites, for their iniquity, were cursed by the Almighty with dark skins. They became a loathsome and benighted race, savage and blood-thirsty, roaming the wilderness and subsisting upon wild beasts, killed for game, or by their frequent marauding incursions into the territory of the Nephites. The latter were highly civilized, dwelling in cities and cultivating the arts and sciences. Unlike their dark-skinned neighbors, they were "a white and a delightsome people," fair and beautiful to look upon. Gentle in peace, valorous in war, refined, intelligent, wealthy and powerful, they were at once the envy and the terror of their foes, the ferocious Lamanites, who hated them with an intensity indescribable. Many were the wars and conflicts between the two races; the Lamanites being generally the aggressors, while the Nephites fought in self-defense. Their warriors were highly disciplined, wore armor, and wielded the sword, spear and javelin, while the Lamanites, whose favorite weapons were the bow and sling, went half nude or clothed in skins, affording little protection against the sharp blades and keen points of their adversaries. Still they were fiercely brave, and frequently came off conquerors. When the Nephites served God they prospered, and in war were invincible and invulnerable. When they forgot Him, as they often did, their power waned and departed, and they fell an easy prey to their enemies. But as often as they repented, their strength and valor returned, and the God of battles fought with them and against their foes.

The religion of the Nephites, until the advent of the Savior,—who appeared to them shortly after His resurrection and established His church among them,—was the law of Moses; though they also understood and practiced the first principles of Christ's gospel, revealed to them prior to His coming. One of their first projects, after separating from Laman and his followers, who turned entirely from the Lord, was to build a temple to the Most High, constructed after the pattern, though not on the same scale of magnificence, as the temple of Solomon. Nephi, his brothers Jacob and Joseph and their descendants were the officiating Priesthood.

The Nephite government was originally a limited monarchy, with Nephi,—against his own will, for he, like the first Jaredite leaders, was an anti-monarchist,—as king or protector. His successors, for several centuries, were mostly wise and able rulers, during whose reigns the Nephites enjoyed many periods of prosperity, and the nation, though at times brought to the brink of ruin by the wickedness of its people, spread abroad and became powerful. The Lamanites likewise had kings, who were autocrats, but, as stated, they were a nomadic and savage race, and only at rare intervals,—and then by fusion or contact with the Nephites,—reached a standard of civilization.

In the year B. C. 91, the Nephite republic was proclaimed, and for a period of one hundred and twenty years the nation was ruled by judges elected by the people. Wars with the Lamanites and with bands of truculent outlaws known as Gadianton robbers; victories, defeats, internal dissensions, revolutions, disasters, works of glory and deeds of darkness mark this checkered period,—an era of violent vicissitudes. In the year A. D. 30 the republic was disrupted, and the people divided into tribes and factions.

Then came the greatest, most glorious, and withal most terrible event in the annals of the Nephite nation,—the advent of the risen Redeemer; His appearance to the more righteous portion of the people, preceded by the appalling, overwhelming destruction and desolation of the wicked. First, according to those annals, an awful tempest, unparalleled in force and fury, swept over the land, leaving death and devastation in its wake. Three hours it endured,—but what hours! During the prevalence of the storm, while the lightning's fiery falchion smote, and the batteries of heaven thundered and reverberated, the whole face of nature was changed, disfigured, like the rage-distorted visage of an angry man. Mountains disappeared, sunken or swept away. Valleys became towering peaks. Impelled by the whirlwind, great boulders hurtled through the air, as if thrown by Titan hands, or rolled grinding and crashing along the quivering earth. The mighty heart of nature throbbed tumultuously. Earthquakes with awful rumblings rent the ground. Great chasms opened, like monster jaws, engulfing cities with their living millions, while others were devoured by fire, or swallowed by the raging seas, heaving beyond their bounds. Three hours of fearful turmoil, with three days of thick darkness following, during which the affrighted inhabitants, survivors of the tempest and its terrors, lay shuddering half lifeless upon the quaking earth, listening to the horrible groanings and grindings of the storm; or when its fury lulled, loudly bewailing their own and their fellows' woes.

At length the tumult ceases; the earth no longer trembles, and the voice of Him who stilled with a word the stormy waves of Galilee is heard from heaven proclaiming in solemn tones the calamities that have befallen. A note of awful warning to the transgressor; a promise of peace and of pardon to the penitent. Subsequently the Savior appears. The more righteous of the Nephites behold Him. He shows to them His wounded side and the prints of the nails in His hands and feet; instructs them in the truths of His gospel; heals their sick, blesses their children, administers the sacrament and establishes His church in the midst of them. Therein are apostles, prophets, etc.,—the same orders of Priesthood, the same doctrines, ordinances, gifts and graces that characterize the church at Jerusalem. He informs the Nephites that they are the "other sheep," of whom He spake to His Jewish disciples—though they understood Him not—who were "not of that fold;" not of Judah but of Joseph; and that from them He goes to visit still "other sheep," not of this land, "neither of the land of Jerusalem." Having fully instructed them He departs; not, however, before giving to three of the Twelve whom He has chosen, power over death, insomuch that the destroyer cannot assail them, and to all the Apostles power to preach the gospel, administer its ordinances, work miracles, build up the Church and bring souls to Him.

Then ensue nearly two centuries of unexampled peace and prosperity, during which period the Church of Christ, a pure theocracy, reigns supreme. A community of interests, spiritual and temporal—more than realizing the theories of a Bellamy—is established; Nephites and Lamanites throughout the entire land are converted unto Christ, and bask in the light of an almost Millennial era. This happy state continues until the year A. D. 200, when the first signs of disintegration appear. Other churches are then founded, other creeds promulgated, and the order of unity, equality, fraternity, is abandoned. Thirty years later a great separation takes place, and the people are again known as Nephites and Lamanites.

It is the beginning of the end. The period of the nation's decline and downfall has arrived, and the descent is thenceforth ruinous and rapid. Contentions, crimes and disasters follow in succession. Nearly a century rolls by. The great international conflict has resumed. Again have wars between Nephites and Lamanites drenched and deluged the land with blood and tears. The Nephites now occupy " the land northward," whither they have been driven by their victorious foes, who hold possession of the southern continent. The "narrow neck of land" divides them. The struggle goes on. Each army invades alternately the territory of the other; only to be repulsed and driven back. Again and again sounds the tocsin of war. Again and again the two nations rush to battle. Peace after peace is patched up, only to be rent asunder. At length the Lamanites gain an advantage. They once more invade the northern continent. The degenerate Nephites no longer prevail against them. Bravely, desperately they contend, but vainly. The God whom they have offended is no longer with them, and victory perches permanently upon the banners of their adversaries. Backward, still backward they are driven, disputing with stubborn valor every inch of ground. The whole land reeks and smokes with blood and carnage. Rapine and slaughter hold sway. Each side, drunken with blood, besotted and brutalized, vies with the other in cruelties and atrocities. Finally the hill Ramah—Cumorah—is reached, and there, on the spot where ages before the Jaredite nation perished, the Nephites, similarly fated, make their final stand.

Their general, Mormon, foreseeing the destruction of his people, has committed to his son Moroni,—like himself one of a righteous few left of a degenerate nation,—the records of their race, including an abridgment of their history written with his own hand upon plates of gold. These are accompanied by certain instruments called "interpreters"—Urim and Thummim—used by the Nephite prophets in translating.

The carnage of Cumorah ensues; the Nephite nation is annihilated, and the Lamanites,—ancestors of the dusky aborigines whom Columbus, centuries later, found and named Indians,—are left in absolute, undisputed possession of the soil. Moroni, having survived the awful massacre, abridges the Jaredite record, adds it to the Nephite history written by his sire, and deposits the golden plates and interpreters in the hill Cumorah, A. D. 420.

Such, briefly, is the story of the Book of Mormon, which Joseph Smith and his confreres had now given to the world; the famous "Gold Bible," so styled in derision by opponents of Mormonism, but revered by the Latter-day Saints as an inspired record, of equal authority with the Jewish scriptures, containing, as they claim, the revelations of Jehovah to His Israel of the western world, as the Bible His revelations to Israel in the Orient. The Saints hold that the Book of Mormon is the veritable "stick of Joseph," that was to be one with the "stick of Judah"—the Bible—as foretold by Ezekiel.*

The book being published and circulated, speculation at once became rife as to its origin. Of course nobody believed, or compar-

---

* Chapter xxxvii. 16-19.

atively few, that it had come in the way its translator and the witnesses declared. The same skepticism that repudiated the idea of the Father and the Son appearing to Joseph Smith, now ridiculed the claim of the Book of Mormon to being a divine record. That it was purely of human origin, or worse, was very generally believed. Passing by the many minor theories put forth to account for it, we will merely take up one, the celebrated Spaulding story, which obtained greater credence and notoriety than any other, and still forms the back-bone argument of objectors to the divine authenticity of the Book of Mormon.

In the year 1816, at Amity, Washington County, Pennsylvania, died Solomon Spaulding, a native of Ashford, Connecticut, where he was born in 1761. A few years prior to his decease, he had resided at Conneaut, Ashtabula County, Ohio. At one time in his life he was a clergyman,—at least he wore to his name the prefix of "Reverend,"—and is said to have been a graduate of Dartmouth College. Though not a man of much ability, nor of much education, if we may judge from his work, he cultivated a taste for literature, and aspired to the distinction of authorship. His mind ran upon ancient and archaic themes, insomuch that about the year 1812, while living at Conneaut, he wrote a romance entitled "Manuscript Story," giving a fabulous account of the pre-historic races of North America. The romance was suggested by the discovery, near the author's home, of certain relics, such as bows and arrows, and the existence in that vicinity of the ruins of an ancient fort. Two years later, Spaulding removed from Ohio to Pennsylvania, stopping awhile in Pittsburg, and then settling at Amity, where, as stated, he died in 1816.

The romance, unpublished, remained in the possession of his widow until 1834,—four years after the Book of Mormon was published,—at which time she was living at Monson, Hampden County, Massachusetts, and having re-married was then Mrs. Matilda Davison.

During the year 1834, D. P. Hurlburt, an apostate Mormon, came to Mrs. Davison and procured the "Manuscript Story" written by her former husband. His avowed purpose was to use this work, of which he had heard in Pennsylvania, in an expose of Mormonism, which certain opponents of the Saints,—whose headquarters were then at Kirtland, Ohio,—were helping him to publish in that state. Hurlburt's reason for desiring the romance was that he had recognized, from the account he had obtained of it, a supposed resemblance between it and the Book of Mormon, which he was then zealously decrying. He agreed with Mrs. Davison to publish the story and give her half the profits realized from its sale. She reluctantly consented to part with the relic, giving him an order for it addressed to Mr. Jerome Clark, of Hartwick, Otsego County, New York, with whom she had temporarily left an old trunk containing the manuscript. Hurlburt, having secured it, returned to Ohio. A perusal of its pages, however, failed to afford him and his colleagues the satisfaction they had anticipated. The supposed resemblance between it and the Book of Mormon, they found to be indeed suppositional, or at all events so vague as to poorly subserve their purpose. They therefore suppressed it. Hurlburt wrote to Mrs. Davison that the manuscript "did not read as he expected," and that he should not publish it. He did not return it, however, though repeatedly urged by the owner so to do, but gave out that it had been accidentally destroyed by fire, claiming to have been so informed by Mr. E. D. Howe, a publisher at Painesville, with whom he had left the romance to be read and then returned to Mrs. Davison. From that time, until fully fifty years later, nothing further was known of the fate of the Spaulding manuscript.

"Mormonism Unveiled"—Hurlburt's expose—appeared in due time; not, however, in the name of D. P. Hurlburt, but of E. D. Howe, who had purchased the work and published it. It was a satirical assault upon Mormonism in general, and upon Joseph Smith in particular. It announced to the world that the Book of Mormon, in all probability, was Solomon Spaulding's romance revised and amplified. The assertion was supported, not by extracts from the two records, compared, but by depositions from various persons who claimed to be familiar with both, touching the points of alleged similarity between them. It denied, on the authority of these deponents, that the writing obtained of Mrs. Davison was the "Manuscript Story," and claimed that it bore no resemblance to it. Mrs. Davison, however, though no friend to Mormonism, stated that it was the "Manuscript Story," that Hurlburt obtained of her, and her statement is borne out by the fact that no other manuscript of like character, claiming Solomon Spaulding as its author, has ever yet appeared.

The theory put forth by the author of "Mormonism Unveiled" regarding the origin of the Book of Mormon was this: that Sidney Rigdon,—then Joseph Smith's "right-hand man,"—who had formerly resided at Pittsburg, where Mr. Spaulding once tarried for a time, had procured the dead clergyman's manuscript from the printing-office of Messrs. Patterson and Lambdin, in that city; that being a man of ability and education, Rigdon had altered and enlarged the original work, adding the religious portions, and then, through Joseph Smith, had palmed it upon the world as an ancient and inspired record. This hypothesis found many believers, and even to this day, among non-Mormons generally, is accepted as authentic and reliable.

On the other hand, Mormon pens and tongues have been busy for fifty years denying the truth and consistency of the Spaulding story. They have always affirmed that until after the Book of Mormon was published, Joseph Smith had not been seen, nor scarcely heard of, in those parts traversed by the Spaulding manuscript; that Sidney Rigdon did not visit Pittsburg until years after the removal of the Spauldings from that city; that he never was connected, as alleged, with a printing-office in that place; that up to the fall of 1830, several months after the Book of Mormon was published, he had not so much as seen the book, and that until December of the same year he and Joseph Smith had never met. In short, that Rigdon's alleged connection with the origin of the Book of Mormon was an anachronism pure and simple, and that any theory seeking to identify that record with the Spaulding romance was susceptible of the easiest disproof.

But all in vain. The world had made up its mind. The Mormon side of the story was too miraculous for belief; the Hurlburt-Howe theory too plausible for disbelief; and the Spaulding romance, with Sidney Rigdon or "some other designing knave" as its amplifier and embellisher, has continued to be regarded as the literary nucleus of the Book of Mormon.

In the year 1884, fifty years after its disappearance and alleged destruction, the missing Spaulding manuscript was brought to light. Its discoverer was Mr. L. L. Rice, of Honolulu, Sandwich Islands. Being visited that year by President James H. Fairchild, of Oberlin College, Ohio, Mr. Rice, at his suggestion, was looking through his papers in quest of certain anti-slavery documents, when he came upon a package marked in pencil on the outside "Manuscript Story—Conneaut Creek," which proved upon examination, to their great surprise, to be the long-lost romance of Dr. Spaulding. Its presence among the private papers of Mr. Rice was explained by the fact that about the year 1840 he and a partner had purchased from E. D. Howe, the publisher of "Mormonism Unveiled," the business and effects of the Painesville "Telegraph." At that time Mr. Rice,—who in Ohio was an anti-slavery editor,—had received from Howe a collection of miscellaneous papers, which, prior to Mr. Fairchild's visit, he had never taken time to thoroughly examine. The original of the "Manuscript Story" Mr. Rice presented to President Fairchild, but an exact copy, procured of the former by a representative of the Church of Jesus Christ of Latter-day Saints, was published *verbatim et literatim* at Salt Lake City in 1886.*

As stated by Howe—or Hurlburt—it is "a romance purporting to have been translated from the Latin, found on twenty-four rolls of parchment in a cave;" its author thus anticipating a method in vogue among popular novelists of the present period,—notably of the H. Rider Haggard school. It contains perhaps a tenth as much reading matter as the Book of Mormon, and unlike that record is

* Josephites—dissenting Mormons—have also published the "Manuscript Story." Their edition was the first to appear.

written in modern style. None of the proper names, and few if any of the incidents, are similar to those of the Nephite narrative. Its rhetoric is exceedingly faulty,—more so than the usually criticised passages of the Book of Mormon,—and the pamphlet throughout is largely mis-spelled and poorly punctuated. Rehabilitated and condensed, the story would run about as follows:

In the reign of the Emperor Constantine, a young patrician named Fabius, secretary to his imperial majesty, sails from Rome for Britain, with an important commission to the commander of his country's legions stationed there. After safely traversing the Mediterranean, the ship encounters near the British coast a terrific storm, which drives her oceanward until she is utterly lost in the midst of the watery wilderness. Five days the tempest rages, and the vessel flies westward before a furious gale. On the sixth day the storm abates. The black mists which have hung over the deep, obscuring the lights of heaven, are dispelled, and the sun dawns in glory upon a cloudless sky. But no land is in sight; only "water, water everywhere." Consternation reigns, and the ship is still driven westward. Finally a mariner comforts his fellow castaways by announcing that the Almighty has revealed to him that land is not far off, and that gentle breezes will soon waft them into a safe harbor and to hospitable shores. Five days later the prediction is fulfilled. Land heaves in sight, and the storm-beaten ship enters the mouth of a spacious river. Sailing up many leagues, it arrives at a town on the river's bank, the home of the king and chiefs of a savage nation, upon whose domain the outcasts have entered. They are the "Deliwares," one of several tribes or nations inhabiting the land. The Romans are kindly received, and conclude to remain. The seven damsels of the party select husbands from their male companions, leaving the residue to lead lives of celibacy, or choose mates from the ranks of the copper-colored maidens of the land. Two years later the white colonists leave the country of the "Deliwares," and migrating to the north-west, take up their abode among the "Ohons," another native tribe vastly more numerous, powerful and civilized.

The remainder of the story, which is disjointed and incomplete, includes a series of philosophic, geographic, and astronomical observations by Fabius; descriptions of the religious teachings and traditions of the natives, their social and political customs and an elaborate narration of their glorious antecedents. Their great oracle and law-giver, a sort of Moses and Hiawatha combined,—though there is no allusion to Israel in all the text,—was one Lobaska, an illustrious character, a portion of whose biography is given. After dwelling upon the manner in which Lobaska united all the tribes or kingdoms of the land under one government, gave them their "sacred roll" of religious tenets, and framed their political constitution, it describes their subsequent wars and dissensions, and closes abruptly on the eve of a great battle between the hosts of the militant empires of "Sciota" and "Kentuck."

The latter is by far the best written portion of the narrative, the quality of which differs so in places, and descends so often from the half sublime to the wholly ridiculous, as to tempt the reader to believe that more than one pen was employed in its composition.

To enable the reader to compare the respective styles in which the two books are written, brief selections from each are here presented:

BOOK OF MORMON. II. NEPHI, CHAP. I.	MANUSCRIPT STORY, CHAP. II.
And now it came to pass after I, Nephi, had made an end of teaching my brethren, our father, Lehi, also spake many things unto them, how great things the Lord had done for them, in bringing them out of the land of Jerusalem. And he spake unto them concerning their rebellions upon the waters, and the mercies of God in sparing their lives, that they were not swallowed up in the sea. And he also spake unto them concerning the land of promise, which they had obtained; how merciful the Lord had been in warning us that we should flee out of the land of Jerusalem. For, behold, said he, I have seen a vision,	As no alternative now remained, but either to make the desperate attempt to return across the wide boisterous ocean or to take up our residence in a country inhabited by savages and wild ferocious beasts we did not long hesitate. We held a solem treaty with the king & all the chiefs of his nation. They agreed to cede to us a tract of excellent Land on the north part of the town on which was six wigwams, & engaged perpetual amity & hospitality & the protection of our lives & property. * * * But now a most singular & delicate subject presented itself for consideration. Seven young women we had on board, as passengers, to visit certain friends they had in

BOOK OF MORMON.

in which I know that Jerusalem is destroyed; and had we remained in Jerusalem, we should also have perished.

But, said he, notwithstanding our afflictions, we have obtained a land of promise, a land which is choice above all other lands; a land which the Lord God hath covenanted with me should be a land for the inheritance of my seed. Yea, the Lord hath covenanted this land unto me, and to my children for ever; and also all those who should be led out of other countries by the hand of the Lord.

Wherefore, I, Lehi, prophesy according to the workings of the Spirit which is in me, that there shall none come into this land, save they shall be brought by the hand of the Lord.

Wherefore, this land is consecrated unto him whom he shall bring. And if it so be that they shall serve him according to the commandments which he hath given, it shall be a land of liberty unto them; wherefore, they shall never be brought down into captivity; if so, it shall be because of iniquity; for if iniquity shall abound, cursed shall be the land for their sakes; but unto the righteous it shall be blessed for ever.

MANUSCRIPT STORY.

Britain—Three of them were ladies of rank, and the rest were healthy bucksom Lasses.—Whilst deliberating upon this subject a mariner arose whom we called droll Tom—Hark ye shipmates says he, Whilst tossed on the foming billows what brave son of neptune had any more regard for a woman than a sturgeon, but now we are all safely anchored on Terra firma—our sails furled & ship keeled up, I have a huge longing for some of those rosy dames—But willing to take my chance with my shipmates—I propose that they should make their choice of husbands. The plan was instantly adopted. * * * The Capt. & myself, attended with our fair partners & two mariners repaired to a new habitation which consisted of two convenient apartments. After having partook of an elligant Dinner & drank a bottle of excellent wine our spirits were exhilerated & the deep gloom which beclouded our minds evaporated. The Capt. assuming his wonted cheerfulness made the following address. My sweet good soaled fellows we have now commenced a new voige—Not such as brot us over mountain billows to this butt end of the world. No, no, our voyge is on dry land & now we must take care that we have sufficient ballast for the riging—every hand on board this ship must clasp hands and condescend to each others humour, this will pro-good cheer and smooth the raging billows of life. Surrounded by innumerable hords of human beings, who resemble in manners the Ourang Outang—let us keep aloof from them & not embark in the same matrimonial ship (*with them*). At the same time we will treat them with good cheer & enlighten their dark souls with good instruction. By continuing a distinct people & preserving our customs, manners, religion & arts and sciences another Italy will grow up in this wilderness & we shall be celebrated as the fathers of a great & happy nation.

BOOK OF MORMON, ETHER, CHAP. XIV.

And it came to pass that Lib did pursue him until he came to the plains of Agosh. And Coriantumr had taken all the people with him, as he fled before Lib in that quarter of the land whither he fled.

And when he had come to the plains of Agosh, he gave battle unto Lib, and he smote upon him until he died; nevertheless, the brother of Lib did come against Coriantumr in the stead thereof, and the battle became exceeding sore, in the which Coriantumr fled again before the army of the brother of Lib.

Now the name of the brother of Lib was called Shiz. And it came to pass that Shiz pursued after Coriantumr, and he did overthrow many cities, and he did slay both women and children, and he did burn the cities thereof,

And there went a fear of Shiz throughout all the land; yea, a cry went forth throughout the land, who can stand before the army of Shiz? Behold he sweepeth the earth before him!

And it came to pass that the people began to flock together in armies, throughout all the face of the land.

And they were divided, and a part of them fled to the army of Shiz, and a part of them fled to the army of Coriantumr.

And so great and lasting had been the war, and so long had been the scene of bloodshed and carnage, that the whole face of the land was covered with the bodies of the dead;

And so swift and speedy was the war, that there was none left to bury the dead, but they did march forth from the shedding of blood to the shedding of blood, leaving the bodies of both men, women, and children, strewed upon the face of the land, to become a prey to the worms of the flesh;

And the scent thereof went forth upon the face of the land, even upon all the face of the land; wherefore the people became troubled by day and by night, because of the scent thereof;

MANUSCRIPT STORY, CHAPTER XV.

Determined to conquer or die, it was impossible to conjecture which Emperor would have gained the victory had the divisions or bands in the rear of each army remained inactive. But anxious to engage with the boldest warriors, the Kentuck-Bands, led on by their heroic princes, rushed between the division of the grand army & made a most furious charge upon the Sciotans—They broke thro' their Ranks—peircing with deadly wounds their indignant foes—heroes fell before them—& many of the Sciotans being struck with surprise & terror began to retire back—But the bands in the rear of their army instantly rushed forward & met their furious combitants—The battle was now spread in every direction. Many valiant chiefs who commanded under their respective Kings were overthrown—& many thousand robust & brave warriors, whose names were not distinguished by office, were compeled to receive deadly wounds & to bite the dust. —It was Elseon fortune to attack the division led by the valiant Ramoff—He broke his ranks & killed many warriors—while driving them furiously before him—he met Hamkol at the head of many thousand Sciotans—Hamkol beheld the young Prince & knew him & being fired with the greatest rage & thirst for revenge, he urged on the combat with the most daring violence. Now he thot, was a favorable chance to gain immortal renown —Elseon says he shall feel the effects of my conquering sword—The warriors on both side charged each other with incredible fury —& Elseon & Hamkol met in the center of their divisions—I have found you says Hamkol perfiduous monster—I will teach you to rob our empire of its most valuable treasure—He spoke & Elseon replied—Art thou Hamkol the Counsellor of Rambock. Your advice has produced this blood and slaughter—Hamkol raised his sword & had not Elseon defended himself from the blow, he never would have spoken again—But

BOOK OF MORMON.	MANUSCRIPT STORY.
Nevertheless, Shiz did not cease to pursue Coriantumr, for he had sworn to avenge himself upon Coriantumr of the blood of his brother, who had been slain, and the word of the Lord which came to Ether, that Coriantumr should not fall by the sword.	quick as the lightning Elseon darted his sword thro' his heart—[*Hamkol*] gnashed his teeth together & [*with a groan*] tumbling headlong with a groan expired.

A portion of Christ's prophecy to the Nephites, concerning the gathering of Israel and the destiny of the Lamanites in the last days, is also here given:

BOOK OF MORMON, III. NEPHI, CHAP. XXI.

And, verily, I say unto you, I give unto you a sign, that ye may know the time when these things shall be about to take place, that I shall gather in from their long dispersion, my people, O house of Israel, and shall establish again among them my Zion.

* * * * * * * * *

Therefore when these works, and the works which shall be wrought among you hereafter, shall come forth from the Gentiles, unto your seed, which shall dwindle in unbelief because of iniquity;

For thus it behoveth the Father that it should come forth from the Gentiles, that he may shew forth his power unto the Gentiles, for this cause, that the Gentiles, if they will not harden their hearts, that they may repent and come unto me, and be baptized in my name, and know of the true points of my doctrine, that they may be numbered among my people, O house of Israel:

And when these things come to pass, that thy seed shall begin to know these things, it shall be a sign unto them, that they may know that the work of the Father hath already commenced unto the fulfilling of the covenant which he hath made unto the people who are of the house of Israel.

And when that day shall come, it shall come to pass that kings shall shut their mouths; for that which had not been told them shall they see; and that which they had not heard shall they consider.

For in that day, for my sake shall the Father work a work, which shall be a great and marvellous work among them; and there shall be among them who will not believe it, although a man shall declare it unto them.

But behold, the life of my servant shall be in my hand; therefore they shall not hurt him, although he shall be marred because of them. Yet I will heal him, for I will shew unto them that my wisdom is greater than the cunning of the devil.

Therefore it shall come to pass, that whosoever will not believe in my words, who am Jesus Christ, whom the Father shall cause him to bring forth unto the Gentiles, and shall give unto him power that he shall bring them forth unto the Gentiles, (it shall be done even as Moses said,) they shall be cut off from among my people who are of the covenant.

And my people who are a remnant of Jacob, shall be among the Gentiles, yea, in the midst of them as a lion among the beasts of the forest, as a young lion among the flocks of sheep, who, if he go through both treadeth down and teareth in pieces, and none can deliver.

Their hand shall be lifted up upon their adversaries, and all their enemies shall be cut off.

Yea, wo be unto the Gentiles, except they repent, for it shall come to pass in that day, saith the Father, that I will cut off thy horses out of the midst of thee, and I will destroy thy chariots.

*   *   *   *

And I will execute vengeance and fury upon them, even as upon the heathen, such as they have not heard.

But if they will repent, and hearken unto my words, and harden not their hearts, I will establish my church among them, and they shall come in unto the covenant, and be numbered among this the remnant of Jacob, unto whom I have given this land for their inheritance.

And they shall assist my people, the remnant of Jacob, and also, as many of the house of Israel as shall come, that they may build a city, which shall be called the New Jerusalem:

And then shall they assist my people that they may be gathered in, who are scattered upon all the face of the land, in unto the New Jerusalem.

And then shall the power of heaven come down among them; and I also will be in the midst;

And then shall the work of the Father commence at that day, even when this gospel shall be preached among the remnant of this people. Verily I say unto you, at that day shall the work of the Father commence among all the dispersed of my people; yea, even the tribes which have been lost, which the Father hath led away out of Jerusalem.

Yea, the work shall commence among all the dispersed of my people, with the Father, to prepare the way whereby they may come unto me, that they may call on the Father in my name.

In a little work called "The Myth of the Manuscript Found,"* by Elder George Reynolds of Salt Lake City, the arguments pro and con upon the question of the alleged identity of the Book of Mormon and the Spaulding romance, are clearly and intelligently set forth. Mr. Reynolds, being a believer in the Book of Mormon, devotes himself to the task of puncturing and shattering the Hurlburt-Howe hypothesis, but this does not prevent him from doing justice to the other side in the controversy, by stating fully and fairly the position that he assails.

---

* "Manuscript Found" is the more generally known title of the Spaulding tale.

President James H. Fairchild, in the New York *Observer* of February 5th, 1885, speaking of the discovery by Mr. Rice of the Spaulding romance, says: "The theory of the origin of the Book of Mormon in the traditional manuscript of Solomon Spaulding will probably have to be relinquished. * * Mr. Rice, myself and others compared it (the Spaulding manuscript) with the Book of Mormon, and could detect no resemblance between the two, in general or detail. There seems to be no name nor incident common to the two. The solemn style of the Book of Mormon, in imitation of the English Scriptures, does not appear in the manuscript. * * * Some other explanation of the origin of the Book of Mormon must be found, if any explanation is required."

Here we take leave of the subject. Up to the present time— 1892—the Book of Mormon has passed through no less than thirty American and English editions, aggregating many tens of thousands of volumes, scattered broadcast upon both hemispheres. It has been translated and published in eleven foreign vernaculars, namely: English, Welsh, French, Spanish, Italian, German, Dutch, Danish, Swedish, Hawaiian and Maori,—including, as seen, all the leading languages of modern times. It has also been translated, but not published, in Hindoostanee and the Jewish. A Russian translation, unauthorized, is likewise reported to have passed through the press.

CHAPTER IV.
1830.

ORGANIZATION OF THE CHURCH OF JESUS CHRIST OF LATTER-DAY SAINTS—THE DOCTRINE OF COMMON CONSENT—OLIVER COWDERY THE FIRST PUBLIC PREACHER OF MORMONISM—NEWEL KNIGHT—THE FIRST CONFERENCE OF THE CHURCH—THE ELDERS AT COLESVILLE—JOSEPH SMITH ARRESTED FOR "PREACHING THE BOOK OF MORMON"—HIS TRIAL AND ACQUITTAL AT SOUTH BAINBRIDGE—RE-ARRESTED AND TRIED AT COLESVILLE—ANOTHER FAILURE TO CONVICT—RETURN TO PENNSYLVANIA—A SCHISM THREATENING THE CHURCH—REVIVAL OF OPPOSITION AT HARMONY—THE PROPHET REMOVES WITH HIS FAMILY TO FAYETTE—THE SCHISM AVERTED—A MISSION TO THE LAMANITES ANNOUNCED.

RESUMING from the spring of 1830 the thread of our historical narrative. On the 6th of April of that year, at the town of Fayette, Seneca County, New York, was organized the Church of Jesus Christ of Latter-day Saints. Mormonism at that time had two score or more disciples,—persons who had embraced its principles and been baptized. Only six of these, however,—no less than that number being required by law to form a religious society,—participated in the organization. They were Joseph Smith, junior, Oliver Cowdery, Hyrum Smith, Peter Whitmer, junior, Samuel H. Smith and David Whitmer. Other believers were present at this initial meeting, which was held at the house of Peter Whitmer.

From the first the doctrine of common consent was practically exemplified in all the meetings and deliberations of the Latter-day Saints; the right of the people to a voice in the selection of their leaders, and in the establishment of the laws which govern them, being a cardinal principle of their religious, no less than of their political faith. Accordingly, in this instance, Joseph Smith and Oliver Cowdery, who were to be the first and second Elders of the Church, prior to ordaining each other or proceeding at all with the organization, called upon the disciples present to manifest whether or not they would accept them as their spiritual teachers, and were willing to be organized as a religious body. Unanimous consent being given, the purpose of the meeting was effected. Joseph first laid hands upon Oliver and ordained him an Elder in the Church of Christ. Oliver then ordained Joseph in like manner. The sacrament of the Lord's supper was administered to those who had been baptized, and they were then confirmed members of the Church by the laying on of the Elders' hands. Others of the brethren—for the Saints were thenceforth to each other "brethren and sisters"—were likewise ordained to various offices in the Priesthood. While together on this occasion, the Prophet voiced to his flock the following revelation : *

Behold there shall be a record kept among you, and in it thou shalt be called a seer, a translator, a prophet, an apostle of Jesus Christ, an elder of the church through the will of God the Father, and the grace of your Lord Jesus Christ,

Being inspired of the Holy Ghost to lay the foundation thereof, and to build it up unto the most holy faith,

Which church was organized and established in the year of your Lord eighteen hundred and thirty, in the fourth month, and on the sixth day of the month, which is called April.

Wherefore, meaning the church, thou shalt give heed unto all his words and commandments which he shall give unto you as he receiveth them, walking in all holiness before me;

For his word ye shall receive, as if from mine own mouth, in all patience and faith;

For by doing these things the gates of hell shall not prevail against you; yea, and the Lord God will disperse the powers of darkness from before you, and cause the heavens to shake for your good, and his name's glory.

For thus saith the Lord God, him have I inspired to move the cause of Zion in mighty power for good, and his diligence I know, and his prayers I have heard.

Yea his weeping for Zion I have seen, and I will cause that he shall mourn for her no longer, for his days of rejoicing are come unto the remission of his sins, and the manifestations of my blessings upon his works.

For, behold, I will bless all those who labor in my vineyard with a mighty blessing, and they shall believe on his words, which are given him through me by the Comforter, which manifesteth that Jesus was crucified by sinful men for the sins of the world, yea, for the remission of sins unto the contrite heart.

---

* Doctrine and Covenants, Section xxi.

Wherefore it behoveth me that he should be ordained by you, Oliver Cowdery, mine apostle;

This being an ordinance unto you, that you are an elder under his hand, he being the first unto you, that you might be an elder unto this church of Christ, bearing my name,

And the first preacher of this church unto the church, and before the world, yea, before the Gentiles: yea, and thus saith the Lord God, lo, lo! to the Jews also. Amen.

Thus was founded the Church of Jesus Christ of Latter-day Saints. Thus arose, as a system, what the world terms Mormonism,—universally regarded as the most remarkable religious movement of modern times; detested and denounced throughout Christendom as a dangerous and soul-destroying imposture, but revered and defended by its disciples as the wonderful work of the Almighty, the veritable "marvelous work and wonder" foretold by Isaiah and other ancient seers, which was to prepare the world, by the preaching of a restored gospel and the founding of a latter-day Zion for Messiah's second coming and the advent of the Millennium.

Five days after the organization—Sunday, April 11th—at the house of Peter Whitmer, in Fayette, Oliver Cowdery preached the first public sermon delivered by a Mormon Elder. Many persons were present besides the Saints. The seed sown took instant root, and that day several more were added to the Church.

The following paragraphs of a revelation recorded about this time will give some idea of the Church government and discipline :*

The duty of the elders, priests, teachers, deacons, and members of the church of Christ. An apostle is an elder, and it is his calling to baptize,

And to ordain other elders, priests, teachers, and deacons.

And to administer bread and wine—the emblems of the flesh and blood of Christ—

And to confirm those who are baptized into the church, by the laying on of hands for the baptism of fire and the Holy Ghost, according to the scriptures;

And to teach, expound, exhort, baptize, and watch over the church;

And to confirm the church by the laying on of hands, and the giving of the Holy Ghost,

And to take the lead of all meetings.

---

* Doctrine and Covenants, Sec. xx., 38–59.

The elders are to conduct the meetings as they are led by the Holy Ghost, according to the commandments and revelations of God.

The priest's duty is to preach, teach, expound, exhort, and baptize, and administer the sacrament,

And visit the house of each member, and exhort them to pray vocally and in secret and attend to all family duties;

And he may also ordain other priests, teachers, and deacons.

And he is to take the lead of meetings when there is no elder present;

But when there is an elder present, he is only to preach, teach, expound, exhort, and baptize.

And visit the house of each member, exhorting them to pray vocally and in secret, and attend to all family duties.

In all these duties the priest is to assist the elder if occasion requires.

The teacher's duty is to watch over the church always, and be with and strengthen them,

And see that there is no iniquity in the church—neither hardness with each other—neither lying, backbiting, nor evil speaking;

And see that the church meet together often, and also see that all the members do their duty.

And he is to take the lead of meetings in the absence of the elder or priest—

And is to be assisted always, in all his duties in the church, by the deacons, if occasion requires;

But neither teachers nor deacons have authority to baptize, administer the sacrament, or lay on hands;

They are, however, to warn, expound, exhort, and teach and invite all to come unto Christ.

During the month of April the Prophet visited Colesville, the home of Joseph Knight, who had ministered to his necessities on a former occasion. Mr. Knight and several members of his family were Universalists. At his home the Prophet held several meetings, which subsequently bore fruit in the baptism of many. The first miracle recorded in the Church,—for it was a gospel of "signs" following the believer, as in days of old, that was being preached by the Elders,—is accredited to Joseph Smith during this visit. It was the casting out of Satan from the person of Newel, son of Joseph Knight. Newel was baptized at Fayette in the latter part of May. Martin Harris, Joseph Smith, senior, Lucy Smith, Orrin Porter Rockwell and other historic names, by this time had also been added to the Church roll of membership.

The first conference of the organized Church convened at

Fayette on the first day of June. Thirty members were present on the opening day, besides many others who were investigating the new faith. More baptisms followed, more Elders, Priests, Teachers and Deacons were ordained, and Mormonism began spreading rapidly. As a matter of course it encountered opposition, much excitement at times prevailing over the preaching of its strange doctrines and the exercise of its novel "gifts," and its disciples suffered more or less petty persecution. Still it spread. The smoking flax was everywhere bursting into flame, and all efforts to quench it proved powerless.

Again visiting his home in Pennsylvania, Joseph returned bringing his wife, and in company with her and three Elders repaired to Colesville. There they found many awaiting baptism. It was Saturday, and the Elders constructed a dam in a stream, which they designed using next day for baptizing. That night a party of men, instigated it was believed by ministers of other denominations, tore away the dam, thus preventing the Elders from executing their purpose on the Sabbath. Early Monday morning, however, before their opponents could assemble in sufficient force to prevent, they reconstructed their dam, and Oliver Cowdery, entering the water, immersed thirteen converts to the faith ; Emma Smith, the Prophet's wife, being one of the number.

Fierce was the anger of their foes when they learned what had taken place. Fifty strong they surrounded the house of Joseph Knight, to which the Elders had retired, foaming with rage and threatening violence. But Joseph Smith was no coward; neither a physical weakling. Calmly confronting the mob he strove, though in vain, to pacify them. Finally they withdrew to mature their plans, and the Elders, deeming it prudent, departed also, going now to the house of Newel Knight.

That evening, just as they were about to confirm their converts, a constable appeared upon the scene and arrested the Prophet on the charge of being a disorderly person, for preaching the Book of Mormon and setting the country in an uproar. The officer, however, became friendly and informed Joseph that some men were in ambush, not far away, whose purpose was to get him into their power and maltreat him. He added that he was determined to defend him at all hazards. The statement proved true. A crowd of men surrounded the wagon in which the constable drove away with the Prophet, and would undoubtedly have taken him from custody had not the officer plied his whip, given his horse full rein and left them far behind. The two drove on rapidly to South Bainbridge, in Chenango County, where they put up at a tavern. The constable permitted his prisoner to occupy the bed in their room, while he slept with his feet against the door and a loaded musket at his side, ready to defend him against assault.

At the trial, next day, various charges were preferred against the Prophet. Some of them were of a very frivolous character. For instance, he was accused of obtaining from Josiah Stoal, his former employer, a horse, and from one Jonathan Thompson a yoke of oxen, by telling them that he had received revelations that he was to have them. Messrs. Stoal and Thompson, taking the witness stand, testified in the prisoner's favor, and he was promptly acquitted. On leaving the court-room, however, he was re-arrested on a warrant from Broome County, and taken back to Colesville for trial. This time he was in the custody of an officer who treated him with great harshness; subjecting him to the insults of the rabble, refusing him for many hours any refreshment, and finally allowing him for his supper only a diet of bread-crusts and water.

At the Colesville trial Newel Knight was put upon the stand and made to testify concerning the miracle reported to have been performed upon him.

"Did the prisoner, Joseph Smith, junior, cast the devil out of you?" asked the prosecuting attorney of the witness.

"No, sir," replied Mr. Knight.

"Why, have not you had the devil cast out of you?"

"Yes, sir."

"And had not Joe Smith some hand in its being done?"

"Yes, sir."

"And did not he cast him out of you?"

"No, sir. It was done by the power of God, and Joseph Smith was the instrument in the hands of God on the occasion. He commanded him out of me in the name of Jesus Christ."

"And are you sure that it was the devil?"

"Yes, sir."

"Did you see him after he was cast out of you?"

"Yes, sir; I saw him."

"Pray, what did he look like?"

Here the prisoner's counsel informed the witness that he need not answer the question. Mr. Knight, however, replied:

"I believe I need not answer your last question, but I will do it provided I be allowed to ask you one question first, and you answer me, namely: Do you, Mr. Seymour, understand the things of the spirit?"

"No," answered Mr. Seymour, "I do not pretend to such big things."

"Well then," rejoined Knight, "it would be of no use to tell you what the devil looked like, for it was a spiritual sight, and spiritually discerned; and of course you would not understand it were I to tell you of it."

A roar of laughter, at the lawyer's expense, shook the courtroom. Mr. Seymour then arose and addressing the court paid his respects in no gentle terms to the prisoner. Among other things he repeated the story of his having been a "money-digger." The defendant, however, was not on trial for money digging, and his counsel having returned the forensic fire of the prosecution, he was again set at liberty.

In the breasts of many, hitherto hostile, a revulsion of feeling now took place. Even the officer who had treated the prisoner so harshly came forward and apologized for his conduct, and offered to help him evade a mob that had assembled outside the court-room, to "tar and feather" the Prophet and ride him on a rail. Taking advantage of this opportunity to escape, Joseph, rejoining his anxious wife, returned with her to Pennsylvania.

A few days later Joseph and Oliver revisited Colesville for the purpose of confirming their converts; but the mob, again gathering, compelled them to forego their purpose and beat a hasty retreat, hotly pursued by the belligerent multitude. A subsequent visit was more successful. The inciters of this opposition were said to be prominent Presbyterians.

At his home in Harmony the Prophet now devoted some time to making a record of and arranging in their proper order the revelations he had from time to time delivered. At first Oliver Cowdery assisted him, but he soon departed for Fayette, and Emma Smith then acted as a scribe to her husband.

Hitherto the relations between Joseph and Oliver seem to have been of the most friendly character. Mutually helpful,—Oliver to Joseph by means of a better education, and Joseph to Oliver by reason of superior intelligence and strength of character,—they were congenial in spirit and united in purpose. The first intimation of a change of heart in Oliver was contained in a letter from him to the Prophet, calling in question certain words of one of the revelations, and demanding that they be changed. The First Elder replied to the Second that the revelation came from God, and must stand as it had been delivered until God should change it. A personal visit to Fayette followed, where Joseph found that some of the Whitmer family were in sympathy with Oliver. It required much pleading and persuasion on the part of the Prophet to finally convince them that they were in error. Even then the breach was closed only to be soon re-opened.

During August the persecutive spirit revived at Harmony, where the Methodists now conspired to create trouble for the hated founder of the rapidly growing rival Church. The influence brought to bear was such as to alienate from Joseph the friendship of his father-in-law, Isaac Hale, who joined the ranks of his opponents and became his bitter and relentless foe. Life at Harmony for Joseph and Emma, was now rendered intolerable. He therefore accepted a second invitation from the Whitmers to remove to Fayette, this time with his family, and take up his abode in their domicile. He arrived there during the last week in August.

Again, to his surprise and sorrow, the Prophet found the spirit of dissension among his followers. The trouble this time was over a certain stone in the possession of Hiram Page, one of the eight witnesses. From this stone, it was claimed, sundry mysterious communications had been received, of a tenor and purport at variance with revelations already on record. These communications Joseph pronounced spurious, but Elder Cowdery and some of the Whitmers still placed reliance in them. The Prophet then spoke to them in the name of the Lord. Oliver was reminded that while he was as Aaron to Israel—a spokesman to the Prophet—Joseph was as Moses, the mouthpiece of the Almighty. He alone had the right to voice revelations to the Church for its guidance. Oliver was required to use his influence with Hiram Page to induce him to discard the stone—the apple of discord—and was informed of an important mission in store for him, a mission to the Lamanites, upon which he should set out as soon as the differences then agitating the Church had been settled. Allusion was made in this revelation to a certain "city" that was to be built "on the borders by the Lamanites."

Subsequently, at a conference held early in September, Hiram Page and his associates renounced the stone and "all things connected therewith," and in common with the whole Church renewed their covenant of fealty to Joseph, as its supreme prophet, seer and revelator. Thus was "the imminent deadly breach" closed, and what threatened to be for Mormonism, in its infancy, a serious if not a fatal wound, healed. Immediately afterward preparations went forward for the departure of the mission to the Lamanites.

CHAPTER V.
1830-1831.

MORMONISM'S MISSION TO THE LAMANITES—ITS SIGNIFICANCE—OLIVER COWDERY, PARLEY P. PRATT, PETER WHITMER, JUNIOR, AND ZIBA PETERSON THE CHOSEN EVANGELISTS TO THE RED MEN—THEIR DEPARTURE FOR THE WEST—THE CATTERAUGUS INDIANS— KIRTLAND AND THE CAMPBELLITES—SIDNEY RIGDON—HIS CONVERSION TO MORMONISM—EDWARD PARTRIDGE—NEWEL K. WHITNEY—SUCCESS OF THE ELDERS IN OHIO—THEIR PILGRIMAGE RESUMED—ELDER PRATT'S ARREST AND ESCAPE—SIMEON CARTER—AMONG THE WYANDOTS—STORMS AND PRIVATIONS—ARRIVAL AT INDEPENDENCE, MISSOURI—PREACHING TO THE DELAWARES—GOVERNMENT AGENTS AND CHRISTIAN MISSIONARIES—THE ELDERS ORDERED OUT OF THE INDIAN COUNTRY.

THE significance of the missionary movement inaugurated by the Prophet, in sending forth Elders to evangelize the American Indians and distribute among the dusky tribes copies of the Book of Mormon, is only to be fully comprehended by those who have made careful study of the contents of that record, and of the various revelations voiced to the world by Joseph Smith. Indeed, the only key to the real history of Mormonism, from Cumorah to Carthage, and from Carthage to Deseret, is a knowledge of the aims and motives of its founders and disciples, as learned from their own lips or reflected from the pages of the records esteemed by them divine. Neither the enemies of a people, nor the disinterested, uninitiated observers of that people, however fair and honest, are trustworthy oracles and reliable exponents of their views and doctrines. Methodism, Catholicism, Mormonism, or any other ism, in order to be properly understood, must be permitted, like Paul before Agrippa, to speak for itself. In this light let us take a brief general glance at Mormonism.

First of all it must be borne in mind, as a basic fact, upon which to found all further argument or theory in relation to the

Saints and their religion, that they sincerely believe themselves to be literally of the blood of Israel; children of Abraham, Isaac and Jacob,—mostly of Joseph through the lineage of Ephraim. The loss of their tribal identity, and their scattered state among the nations,—whence the gospel, they say, has begun to gather them,—is explained to them by the scriptures, which declare that Ephraim hath "mixed himself with the people;" that is, with other nations, presumably from the days of the Assyrian captivity. They believe, moreover, that in this age, "the dispensation of the fullness of times,"—a figurative spiritual ocean, into which all past dispensations of divine power and authority like rills and rivers run,—it is the purpose of Jehovah, the God of Israel, to gather His scattered people from their long dispersion among the nations, and weld in one vast chain the broken links of the fated house of Abraham. They quote from Jeremiah: "Hear the word of the Lord, O ye nations, and declare it in the isles afar off, and say, He that scattered Israel will gather him, and keep him as a shepherd doth his flock." This gathering of Israel, they claim, is a step preparatory to the "gathering together in one" of "all things in Christ," both in heaven and on earth, as spoken of by Paul the Apostle. Mormonism, to its disciples, is no more nor less than primitive Christianity restored; and Christianity in its primitive state, unpaganized, unapostate, no more nor less than the restored religion of Adam, Enoch, Noah, Melchisedek, Abraham, Moses and other ancient worthies who received the same from God, successively, all down the dispensations.

Israel's gathering in the "last days,"—the closing period of our planet's mortal probation,—is a cardinal doctrine with the Latter-day Saints, accounting as it does for their world-wide proselytism, the wanderings abroad of their Apostles and Elders in quest of the seed of Ephraim, their fellows, and their migrations from the ends of the earth to the American continent, believed by them to be the land of Zion.* Upon this land, which they hold to be the inherit-

---

* This in a general sense; specifically their "land of Zion" is Jackson County, Missouri.

ance of Joseph,—given him by the Almighty in the blessings of Jacob and Moses,* and occupied for ages by his descendants, the Nephites and Lamanites,—is to arise the latter-day Zion, New Jerusalem, concerning which so many of the prophet-poets of antiquity have sung. It was for this purpose, say the Saints, that the land was held in reserve, hidden for ages behind Atlantic's waves—the wall of waters over which, in Lehi and his colony, climbed Joseph's "fruitful bough." Next came the Gentiles, with Columbus in their van, to unveil the hidden hemisphere; then a Washington, a Jefferson and other heaven-inspired patriots to win and maintain the liberty of the land,—a land destined to be "free from bondage." And all this that Zion might here be established, and the Lord's latter-day work founded and fostered on Columbia's chosen soil. Yes, these Latter-day Saints,—false and fanatical as the view may seem to most,—actually believe that the greatest and most liberal of earthly governments, that of the United States, was founded for the express purpose of favoring the growth of what the world terms Mormonism.

Ephraim and Manasseh, the half tribes of Joseph, are to combine for the up-building of Zion, which is to become, in due time, "the joy of the whole earth," the glorious head and front of the world's civilization. "And the Gentiles shall come to thy light, and kings to the brightness of thy rising." Much of the seed of Ephraim is mixed with the Gentiles; therefore is he to be gathered from among them. Manasseh is largely to be found among the Lamanites, the American Indians, and the dark-hued dwellers of the neighboring ocean islands. Though cursed of God and smitten by the Gentiles, the red men are yet to be reclaimed and the curse lifted from off them. Then will they become "white and delightsome," as of yore. The Book of Mormon and its believers declare that these Lamanites—Manasseh—will yet build the Zion of God, the Jerusalem of America, in which work they will be joined—some say

---

* Genesis xlix: 22–26. Deuteronomy xxxiii: 13–17.

assisted, some directed—by the Latter-day Saints, the children of Ephraim.

But the gathering of Israel is to include the whole house of Jacob; not merely the half tribes of Ephraim and Manasseh. It involves the restoration of the Jews and the re-building of old Jerusalem, prior to the acceptance by Judah of the gospel and mission of the crucified Messiah; also the return of the lost Ten Tribes from "the north country" and their re-establishment in Palestine, their ancient Canaan.

The preliminary work of founding Zion, as well as a greater spiritual mission to follow, when the Ten Tribes from the north will receive in Zion their blessings under his hands, devolves upon Ephraim, the "first-born," empowered by a restored gospel and priesthood unto this very end and purpose. Hence, say the Saints, the mission and calling of Joseph Smith, the Prophet of Ephraim, who claimed to be a lineal descendant of Joseph who was sold into Egypt.

Again, the message borne by Ephraim in the last days, reversing the order of ancient-day evangelism, is first to the Gentiles, and then, when "the fullness of the Gentiles" has "come in," to the whole house of Israel. Perhaps it was a type, designed to foreshadow the anticipated fulfillment, this sending of the Elders, in the fall of 1830, after several months proselyting among the Gentiles of New York and Pennsylvania, to Lamanitish Israel, mostly inhabiting the wilderness beyond the nation's western frontier. The mission of these Elders was to preach the Gospel to the red men, as contained in the Bible and the Book of Mormon,—the sticks of Judah and of Joseph now "in the hand of Ephraim,"—* deliver to them the record of their forefathers, and inasmuch as they received their teachings to establish the Church of Christ among them. In other words, to prepare Manasseh for his part of the work of building up Zion. Such, from a Mormon standpoint, was the significance of that Lamanite mission, and such in general is the Mormon view of Mormonism.

---

* Ezekiel xxxvii: 16–20.

The Elders chosen for this service were Oliver Cowdery, Peter Whitmer, junior, Parley P. Pratt and Ziba Peterson.

A word here in relation to Parley P. Pratt, the future poet-Apostle of Mormonism, whose personal history interweaves at this point with several important events of that period. He was a native of the state of New York, and was now in his twenty-fourth year. Prior to his baptism by Oliver Cowdery in Seneca Lake about the 1st of September, 1830, he had been connected with a religious society called Reformed Baptists, or Campbellites, which he had joined two years before in the wilds of northern Ohio. In fact he had been a preacher of the Campbellites, who numbered among their leading men Alexander Campbell, the founder of the sect, and Sidney Rigdon, the latter, like Parley, an eloquent and gifted expounder of the scriptures. The magnet which had drawn Parley into the Campbellite fold was the scriptural nature of their doctrines, which included not only faith, repentance and baptism by immersion, —which, as a good Baptist, he believed in already,—but baptism for the remission of sins and the promise of the Holy Ghost, tenets not taught by the orthodox sects of Christendom. These doctrines had been preached by Sidney Rigdon in Parley's neighborhood; he being then a colonizer on the shores of Lake Erie. Soon after embracing the Campbellite faith, in August, 1830, he resolved to devote himself entirely to the work of the ministry. Selling out at a sacrifice, and abandoning his home in the wilderness, he traveled eastward to his native state; his young wife, *nee* Thankful Halsey, accompanying him. Near the city of Rochester, leaving his wife to pursue the journey homeward, Parley felt impelled to stop and preach, and walked ten miles into the country for that purpose. There, at the house of an old Baptist deacon named Hamlin, he first heard of and first saw the Book of Mormon. Deeply interested in its perusal,—particularly in that part descriptive of the personal ministry of the Savior to the Nephites,—he decided to visit the young man who claimed to have translated the record from plates of gold. Arriving at Manchester, the parental home of the Smiths, he learned that

the Prophet was then living in Pennsylvania. He met Hyrum Smith, however, who entertained him kindly, presented him with a copy of the Book of Mormon and subsequently accompanied him to Fayette. There, being fully converted to the new faith, he was baptized, as stated, confirmed and ordained an Elder. He then revisited his old home in Canaan, Columbia County, where he converted and baptized his brother Orson, then a youth of nineteen years; destined like himself to achieve fame as a Mormon Apostle, and as one of the pioneer founders of Utah. Returning westward, Parley met for the first time Joseph Smith, who had returned from Pennsylvania and was visiting his parents at Manchester. Soon afterward, being called to accompany Elders Cowdery, Whitmer and Peterson upon their mission, he set out for the land of the Lamanites.

It was late in October, 1830, that the four Elders departed for the west. As was customary then with itinerants, unable to afford a nag or vehicle, or to pay coach and steamboat fares, they started afoot, husbanding their scanty means and trusting in Providence to "open up the way." They first visited the Catteraugus Indians, near Buffalo, New York. By them they were kindly received, much interest being manifested by the red men in the strange things told them by the Elders. Presenting them with copies of the Book of Mormon, for the perusal of such of the Indians as could read, the missionaries bade them farewell and continued their journey westward.

The scene now changes to northern Ohio, a region at that time almost if not quite a wilderness, in the midst of which, among the hills and dales and glens and groves and streams that beautify the shores and give back the echoing music of Erie's rolling waves, not only these Mormon Elders,—who were merely the vanguard of a general migratory movement having westward as its watchword and religion as its guiding star,—but Mormonism itself, their parent church, was destined soon to plant its pilgrim feet.

Kirtland, a few miles inland from Lake Erie, was a picturesque and flourishing little town of one or two thousand inhabitants, doing business across the lakes with the fur-trapping regions of Michigan and some of the principal cities of the east. The leading "store" of the town, and indeed in all that region, was owned and conducted by Messrs. Gilbert and Whitney, who had formerly been in business at Painesville.

In this vicinity the Campbellites, or Disciples, as they called themselves, had made many converts. Among those now associated with them were Edward Partridge, of Painesville, and Newel K. Whitney, of Kirtland, both merchants,—the former a native of Pittsfield, Berkshire County, Massachusetts, and the latter of Marlborough, Windham County, Vermont. Like Parley P. Pratt, these men, who became the first two Bishops of the Mormon Church, were converts in the Campbellite faith of Sidney Rigdon's.

The prominent part played by this notable man in the affairs of Mormonism entitles his past record to some mention. Sidney Rigdon was born in St. Clair Township, Allegheny County, Pennsylvania, on the 19th of February, 1793. Connecting himself in his twenty-fifth year with the regular Baptist Church, he became, in March, 1819, a licensed preacher of that persuasion. Two months afterward he removed to Trumbull County, Ohio, where he subsequently married. Called in 1821 to the pastorate of the First Baptist Church of Pittsburg, he there became a very popular minister. Less than three years later, becoming dissatisfied with the doctrines of the Baptists, he conscientiously resigned his pastorate and withdrew from the society. During the next two years he labored in a tannery for a livelihood. Again removing to Ohio,—this time to Bainbridge, in Geauga County,—he there re-entered the ministry. He now preached the Campbellite doctrines. It seems that the founder of that sect, Alexander Campbell, had been one of Rigdon's parishioners at Pittsburg. Following his pastor's example, he had left the Baptist Church, and with Mr. Walter Scott, and warmly supported by Mr. Rigdon, had founded the society of Reformed Baptists, or Campbellites. Rigdon's success, always pronounced, was now remarkable. The fame of his eloquence and reasoning powers spread far and wide.

After a year's effective service in and around Bainbridge, he accepted a call to Mentor, thirty miles distant. There, in the midst of much persecution, occasioned by his phenomenal success, he continued to flourish. He converted and baptized multitudes, and organized congregations in all the country round. One of these was near the mouth of Black River, where Parley P. Pratt was converted. Sidney Rigdon was at the summit of his fame and popularity as a Campbellite preacher when Oliver Cowdery and his confreres,—the first missionaries sent westward by the Latter-day Saints from the cradle of their Church,—set out for the land of the Lamanites.

It was to Kirtland, not far from Mentor, that those Elders now made their way; Parley P. Pratt being desirous of laying before his former friends and associates the principles he had recently espoused. As a reminder to the reader of what those principles comprised, the Articles of Faith of the Church of Jesus Christ of Latter-day Saints, as formulated a few years later by the Prophet, are here presented:

1. We believe in God, the Eternal Father, and in His Son Jesus Christ, and in the Holy Ghost.

2. We believe that men will be punished for their own sins, and not for Adam's transgression.

3. We believe that through the atonement of Christ all men may be saved, by obedience to the laws and ordinances of the gospel.

4. We believe that these ordinances are: First, faith in the Lord Jesus Christ; second, repentance; third, baptism by immersion for the remission of sins; fourth, laying on of hands for the gift of the Holy Ghost.

5. We believe that a man must be called of God by "prophecy, and by the laying on of hands," by those who are in authority, to preach the Gospel and administer in the ordinances thereof.

6. We believe in the same organization that existed in the primitive church, viz.: apostles, prophets, pastors, teachers, evangelists, etc.

7. We believe in the gift of tongues, prophecy, revelation, visions, healing, interpretation of tongues, etc.

8. We believe the Bible to be the word of God, as far as it is translated correctly; we also believe the Book of Mormon to be the word of God.

9. We believe all that God has revealed, all that He does now reveal, and we believe that He will yet reveal many great and important things pertaining to the Kingdom of God.

10. We believe in the literal gathering of Israel and in the restoration of the Ten

Tribes. That Zion will be built upon this continent. That Christ will reign personally upon the earth, and that the earth will be renewed and receive its paradisic glory.

11. We claim the privilege of worshiping Almighty God according to the dictates of our conscience, and allow all men the same privilege, let them worship how, where or what they may.

12. We believe in being subject to kings, presidents, rulers and magistrates, in obeying, honoring and sustaining the law.

13. We believe in being honest, true, chaste, benevolent, virtuous, and in doing good to *all men;* indeed we may say that we follow the admonition of Paul, " We believe all things, we hope all things," we have endured many things, and hope to be able to endure all things. If there is anything virtuous, lovely or of good report or praiseworthy, we seek after these things.

Such were the doctrines that Parley P. Pratt desired to present to his former friends in and around Kirtland. The commission of the Elders being to "preach the gospel to every creature," regardless of creed or color, they were nothing loth to tarry for a season within the confines of civilization and "thrust in their sickles and reap," wherever the field of souls appeared "white unto the harvest." Calling on Mr. Rigdon, they presented him with the Book of Mormon, at the same time relating to him its history. This was his first knowledge of the record which, a few years later, he was accused of assisting Joseph Smith to create out of the materials of the Spaulding story. He entertained the Elders hospitably, and promised to read the book carefully. The result was his conversion to Mormonism. After due deliberation he offered himself to the Elders as a candidate for baptism. Many of his flock were likewise converted. Within three weeks after their arrival at Kirtland, the Elders baptized one hundred and twenty-seven souls. Among these were Sidney Rigdon, Newel K. Whitney, Frederick G. Williams, Isaac Morley, Lyman Wight, John Murdock and others whose names became more or less notable in the annals of Mormonism. Edward Partridge was also converted, but was not immediately baptized.

But the Elders must not tarry too long at Kirtland. The season is far advanced, the storms of winter will soon burst forth, and a vast journey still lies before them. They now prepare for departure. Ordaining Sidney Rigdon and others to the priesthood, and setting them apart to minister for the rest, the four Elders reported by letter to the Prophet, and bidding their new-found brethren and sisters adieu, resumed their westward pilgrimage. Frederick G. Williams accompanied them.

Near the mouth of Black River, in the neighborhood of Parley P. Pratt's former home, they stopped one night at the house of Simeon Carter. Here Parley was arrested on some trivial charge and held in durance till morning. Escaping by strategy he rejoined his companions, and they trudged on through mud and rain toward the interior. Everywhere they found that their fame had preceded them. Though ill-treated by some, they preached to crowded congregations, and sowed the seed broad-cast of a future bounteous harvest. Simeon Carter, at whose home Parley, on the night of his arrest, had left a copy of the Book of Mormon, perused it carefully, was converted, and walked fifty miles to Kirtland, where he was baptized and ordained an Elder. Returning, he began himself to preach and baptize, and built up a branch of the Church in his neighborhood numbering sixty members.

At Sandusky, Elder Cowdery and his companions came upon another Indian nation, the Wyandots, with whom they spent several days very agreeably. Like the Catteraugus Indians, they warmly welcomed the missionaries, listened with interest to their teachings, and at parting gave them God-speed. They also requested the Elders to write to them regarding their success among the tribes farther west. Proceeding to Cincinnati, the Elders tarried certain days, preaching, and in the latter part of December took passage on a steamboat bound for St. Louis. The mouth of the Ohio River being blocked with ice, their boat could proceed no farther. At that point, therefore, they landed and continued their journey afoot. Two hundred miles traveled in this manner brought them to the vicinity of St. Louis. Heavy storms of rain and snow now detained them for over a week, during which they were kindly cared for by hospitable people in that section.

With the opening year—1831—they resumed their journey,

passing through St. Louis and St. Charles. Then out over the bleak and storm-swept prairies, through wintry winds and stinging hail and driving sleet, at times half frozen, often fatigued, but never disheartened. Their frequent diet was frozen bread and raw pork, munched by the wayside, as they trudged along weary and foot-sore through deep and drifting snows, looking in vain for house or sign of shelter. Three hundred miles were thus traversed. Finally, after much privation and some suffering, they reached Independence, Jackson County, Missouri, then on the extreme western frontier of the United States. Their pilgrimage was now practically ended. Beyond lay the trackless wilderness,—trackless indeed save for the foot-prints of wild beast or savage, hovering in friendliness near the border, or roaming at will the vast plains stretching westward to the unexplored regions of the Rocky Mountains.

The country in which they found themselves was settled, or partly settled by whites, mostly ignorant and half civilized, with Indians and negroes interspersed,—a typical frontier population. Renegades and refugees from justice, who had fled from the older states to this out-of-the-way region, formed at that time no inconsiderable portion of the inhabitants of western Missouri. Civilization, however, was advancing; schools had been introduced and were beginning to thrive, and to offset the reckless criminal element many intelligent, upright and respectable people were numbered among the citizens. The curse of the country was the political demagogue, playing as ever for personal ends behind the mask of patriotism,—proverbially "the last refuge of a scoundrel." Missouri, only nine years a state,—having been admitted to the Union under the celebrated pro-slavery compromise of 1821,—was just the field where such characters might flourish, and flourish they did, to the infinite sorrow of their betters.

Jackson County, named for General Andrew Jackson—then President of the United States—was settled principally by people from Tennessee and farther south. Clay County, immediately north, and separated from Jackson County by the Missouri River, had been named for Henry Clay, Jackson's opponent in the presidential contest of 1828. Its settlers were mostly Kentuckians. Independence, the county seat of Jackson, was a new town prettily situated on a piece of rising ground, about three miles south of the river, and twelve miles east of the state boundary line. It contained a courthouse built of brick, two or three merchants' stores, and a score or more of private dwellings. The houses generally were log cabins, without glass windows or floors, and many of the settlers, women as well as men, dressed entirely in skins. Their food was also of the coarsest, consisting usually of wild meat, wild honey, pork and corn bread, prepared in the most primitive manner. These conditions prevailed among the poor. The rich and those well-to-do of course had things in much better style. The settlers of Jackson County, as said, were mostly from the south, and were either slaveholders or advocates of slavery. Christian churches had their representatives there, as elsewhere, and the general government its Indian agents and other functionaries. West of Jackson County was the Indian Territory, now the State of Kansas.

Leaving their companions at Independence, where two of them obtained temporary employment as tailors, Oliver Cowdery and Parley P. Pratt crossed over the line into Indian Territory, entering the country of the Shawnees and Delawares. The Delaware chief was the sachem of ten tribes. He was also a polygamist, having several wives. He welcomed his white visitors cordially, and though averse to missionaries in general, after some hesitation called a council of his leading men and permitted Elder Cowdery to address them. The Elder explained through an interpreter the import of his visit, and the mission of himself and his brethren to that land; gave an account of the coming forth of the Book of Mormon, with a brief statement of its contents, and closing presented the aged chief with one of the volumes. The gift was graciously accepted, the sachem testifying his appreciation of the efforts of the Elders in behalf of him and his people, and promising that in the spring they would build a large council house wherein they might be taught more fully. Several days elapsed, during which the two Elders continued to instruct the aged sachem and his people. They lodged meanwhile at the house of Mr. Pool, a blacksmith employed for the Indians by the government. He became a believer in the Book of Mormon, and served the Elders as an interpreter. The Indians manifested great interest in what was told them, insomuch that considerable excitement began to prevail among them. This coming to the ears of Christian missionaries, excited their jealousy, and inspired by them the agents of the government ordered the Elders to quit the Indian country. Threatened with the military if they failed to comply, Elders Cowdery and Pratt reluctantly recrossed the border and rejoined their companions. During the remainder of their sojourn in that land, they confined their proselyting labors mainly to the white settlers of Jackson County, some of whom were converted and baptized. And so ended this mission to the Lamanites.

CHAPTER VI.
1830-1833.

THE CHURCH REMOVES TO OHIO—THE UNITED ORDER—ORGANIZATION OF THE BISHOPRIC—JOSEPH SMITH'S FIRST VISIT TO MISSOURI—JACKSON COUNTY THE CHOSEN SITE OF THE CITY OF ZION—THE LAND DEDICATED FOR THE GATHERING OF ISRAEL AND THE BUILDING OF THE NEW JERUSALEM—THE RETURN TO KIRTLAND—THE PROPHET AND ELDER RIGDON AT HIRAM—A VISION OF HUMAN DESTINY—THE MOBBING OF JOSEPH AND SIDNEY—A SECOND VISIT TO MISSOURI—THE WAR OF THE REBELLION PREDICTED—THE FIRST PRESIDENCY ORGANIZED—THE KIRTLAND TEMPLE PROJECTED.

MEANTIME, in Ohio and in the east the cause of Mormonism had been steadily, even rapidly progressing. The Prophet and his co-laborers, after the departure of the Lamanite mission, had been kept busy preaching, baptizing and building up the Church in the states of New York and Pennsylvania. Among those who had recently become associated with the Mormon leader were Thomas B. Marsh, the future President of the Twelve Apostles, and Orson Pratt, another member of that council.

In December, 1830, there came to Fayette on a visit to the Prophet, Sidney Rigdon and Edward Partridge, from Kirtland, Ohio. Sidney, as seen, had been baptized, and was now an Elder of the Church. His companion, though converted, had not yet entered the fold, but was baptized by Joseph in Seneca River, a few days after his arrival at Fayette. Both these men, Sidney Rigdon and Edward Partridge, whose acquaintance with the Mormon leader here began, afterwards attained high positions in the Church.

A work now engaging the attention of the Prophet was a revision of the Scriptures. In the absence of Oliver Cowdery in the west, and of John Whitmer, who had been sent to preside over the

Saints in Ohio, he had need of an expert scribe to assist him in his literary labors. Such an assistant he found in Sidney Rigdon, who now became his secretary and near associate. In a revelation recorded about this time, Sidney is likened unto John the Baptist,—referring to his former labors as a Campbellite preacher, whereby, he was informed, he had prepared the way unwittingly for a greater one to follow.

It now became evident to the Prophet, whose mind had already conceived the idea that the west, and not the east, was the field of Mormonism's greater destiny, that the season was ripe for a general movement of his people in the direction of their promised Zion. The site of the future city had not yet been definitely declared, though it was understood in general terms to be "on the borders by the Lamanites." Thither Oliver Cowdery and his companions were now wending their way. But the success of those Elders in northern Ohio had indicated an eligible spot for the founding of a "stake of Zion," a temporary gathering place, where, pending further movements toward the building up of their central city, the Saints might assemble.* Accordingly, ere the month of December had expired, the word went forth from the Prophet to his followers in the eastern states to dispose of their possessions, migrate westward and "assemble together at the Ohio."

Not that the east was to be relinquished as a field for proselytism. Not that the Prophet and his people, as might be imagined, had become dispirited and lost confidence in the cause with which they were identified. On the contrary, never had the sun of hope beamed for them more brightly; never had their thorny pathway seemed so thickly bestrewn with flowers. True, they were hated and opposed on every hand, their leader's life was threatened, and secret plots, he had been warned, were even then forming for his destruction. But such had been their experience heretofore, and

---

* The distinction between Zion and the Stakes of Zion should be borne in mind by he reader who desires to properly understand Mormon history.

these were not the impelling causes of the migratory movement now in contemplation. Joseph Smith's character has not been read aright, nor the record of his people from the beginning, if it be imagined that fear for his personal safety or the hope of immunity from further persecution were the motives that then actuated them. No; it was to them the beginning of Israel's latter-day gathering, an initiatory step toward the building up of Zion; and though the reason may have been, in part, that Mormonism,—hated, defamed, and struggling against apparently overwhelming odds,—might gain a firmer foot-hold for its fight of faith than seemed possible amid the warring spiritual elements of the more thickly populated portions of the land, it was far from being the chief purpose and principal end in view. These Latter-day Saints believed they were fulfilling a God-given destiny in thus flocking Zionward,—in fleeing, as Isaiah had said Israel should, "upon the shoulders of the Philistines toward the west." They were destined to make literal these words of the ancient seer to an extent little dreamed of at that time in their philosophy.

A farewell conference was held at Fayette on the 2nd of January, 1831. The affairs of the Church in the eastern parts were settled, or left in the hands of trusty agents to wind up as speedily as possible, and the Prophet, accompanied by his wife, and by Sidney Rigdon, Edward Partridge, Ezra Thayre and Newel Knight, toward the latter part of the month set out for Kirtland.

They arrived there about the 1st of February. Driving his sleigh through the streets of the little town, the Prophet drew up at the mercantile door of Messrs. Gilbert and Whitney. Alighting from his vehicle he entered the store and introduced himself as "Joseph the Prophet," to Newel K. Whitney, the junior partner of the firm. By him and his household, Joseph and his wife, pending other arrangements for their reception, were cordially received and entertained.

The first step taken by the Prophet, after setting in order the Church at Kirtland,—the affairs of which, after the departure of

Elder Cowdery and his confreres, had become somewhat demoralized spiritually,—was to lay the foundation of what is known to Latter-day Saints as the United Order. A brief exposition of this principle of their religion will here be necessary.

Some of the views of the Saints relative to the up-building of Zion have already been dwelt upon. Of the United Order, or the Order of Enoch, as it is otherwise named, it may be said it is a religio-social system involving the methods whereby that "up-building" is to be accomplished. Said Joseph Smith: "It is not given that one man should possess that which is above another." This is the key-note of the United Order.

Co-operative or communistic schemes the world had known before. Saint Simon and Fourier in France, Owen in England and in America, each ere this had launched his bark of philanthropic thought and theory upon the waters of social reform. As early as 1825 Robert Owen and his associates had established industrial communities on both sides of the Atlantic. There was even at this time, in the vicinity of Kirtland—though not of Owen's origin—a small community called "the family," which, following the example of some of the early Christians, held their temporal possessions in common. But the United Order introduced by Joseph Smith probably went further toward realizing, or foreshadowing, the Millennarian dream of the prophet, poet and philanthropist, than anything the world had before witnessed.

Nor are these idle words, words of unmerited eulogy. A Millennium without a God is impossible. A communistic scheme, a plan for social reconstruction, without a religious basis, the love of God and man as its central idea, is born but to perish, howsoever for a season it may thrive. And even with religion,—the highest and strongest motive that can impel selfish humanity,—will it not be found a stupendous and all but impossible task? Instance the failures of those would-be social reformers, secularists, who have thought to leave God and religion out of their otherwise grand schemes for society's reconstruction and regeneration. Deity must be recognized, must be at the head and helm of all plans for man's perfecting. Otherwise they cannot endure. The "natural man" is too much an enemy to God, too much the enemy of his fellow man, to conquer covetousness and love his neighbor as himself, save God be with him. And without self-conquest, without love of humanity, no Millennium, no universal brotherhood, no reign of peace and righteousness is possible.

Herein lay the superiority of Joseph Smith's concept over those of the eminent social reformers, his predecessors and cotemporaries. The United Order was not a mere financial scheme, not a co-operative, joint-stock mercantile concern; not a mere plan for social reconstruction, involving only a community of temporal interests. It was all these and more. It was religious, not secular in its character; spiritual, not temporal in its genius; and yet, being spiritual, it comprehended and circumscribed the temporal. How and where Joseph Smith obtained it is not the question to be here determined. He declared that it was revealed to him by the Almighty. Impartial history can neither affirm nor deny it. The province of the historian is the field of facts, and it is a fact that Joseph Smith so stated. At all events, God was recognized as its author, its laws as His laws, its aim and purpose His. Its avowed object was to glorify God by lifting up man, mentally, physically, morally, spiritually. It was to the Saints the Millennial lever that was to move the world, gradually but effectually, toward the glorious goal of universal brotherhood and good will. It was as the voice of Elias,—the voice of one crying in the wilderness: "Prepare ye the way of the Lord." "Make His paths straight." "Every valley shall be exalted, and every mountain and hill shall be made low; and the crooked shall be made straight, and the rough places plain." In other words, it meant the leveling of class distinctions,—the bringing down of the mountains of pride, the exalting of the valleys of humility; the extirpation of fraud and crookedness, and the eventual triumph of true culture and civilization. By means of it Zion was to "arise and shine," the "joy of the whole earth," ere the coming of Him whose peaceful and righteous reign has been the theme of prophet tongues and poet pens in all ages.

It was an order of industry, too, and not of idleness; a rule of law and not of anarchy, wherein each soul, having consecrated his all, and being assigned his stewardship, was to labor faithfully for the common weal in that field or pursuit for which he proved best fitted and designed. "Every man seeking the interest of his neighbor, and doing all things with an eye single to the glory of God." Such was the theory of the United Order.

More practically speaking, the system meant that each individual, on entering the Order, was to deed to the Church, or its authorized representative, his or her property *in toto*, utterly relinquishing its possession. It might be a farm, a workshop or a sum of money, much or little, that was thus "consecrated." But whatever it was, it thenceforth belonged to the Order, and not to the individual. All would then be owners alike, and equality in temporal things be inaugurated.

A deed would then be given by the Church, or its representative, to each member of the Order, conveying to him or her a certain portion of the general property, probably the same farm or workshop that the individual had before consecrated. This was a "stewardship," thenceforth possessed by the individual, but to be used for the general good; all gains reverting to a common fund or store, whence each steward should derive his or her support. All were required to labor diligently—there were to be no drones in the hive —and to deal fairly and justly with one another. Apostasy from the Church was equivalent to withdrawal from the Order. The individual might then retain his stewardship, but not reclaim the residue of property, over and above that portion, which he had consecrated to the common cause. Unity and equality were the watchwords of the Order; man's salvation and God's glory the ends to be kept constantly in view.

According to the faith of the Saints, it was just such a system as this that sanctified in antediluvian times the City of Enoch and prepared it for translation, when, according to the record, "the Lord called his people Zion, because they were of one heart and one mind and dwelt in righteousness, and there was no poor among them;" a system established in after ages by the Apostles at Jerusalem, when "the multitude of them that believed were of one heart and of one soul,—neither said any of them that ought of the things which he possessed was his own; but they had all things common;" a system which, according to the Book of Mormon, prevailed upon this land among the Nephites for nearly two centuries after the coming of Christ. An order of unity and equality, a system of consecrations and stewardships, the abolition of fraud and monopoly in all their phases, a sinking of individual interests into and for the purpose of the common good, the sacrifice of self at the shrine of principle—of pure religion—whose incense, call it charity, philanthropy, or what we will, is the pure love of God and humanity.

It was to the establishment of such an order,—one object of which, in the arcana of the faith, was to pave the way for the return of the Zion of Enoch, which the Saints believe will yet descend to earth, the planet whence it was taken,—that Joseph Smith, as early as February, 1831, more than fifty years before Edward Bellamy and his ingenious book "Looking Backward" were heard of, directed his thoughts and labors.

A movement to that end was the organization of the Bishopric, representing the temporal wing of the Mormon Church government. The Apostleship, which pertains to the Priesthood of Melchisedek, though possessing general powers has a special calling to minister in spiritual things; while the Bishopric, which is the presidency of the Priesthood of Aaron, administers, under the direction of the higher authority, in things temporal.

The first call to the Bishopric was that of Edward Partridge, who received his appointment on the fourth day of February. He was required "to leave his merchandise and spend all his time in the service of the Church," for which he was to receive his support, or a just remuneration. Two other Elders were called to officiate as his counselors. The duties of this Bishopric were outlined as follows:*

And behold, thou wilt remember the poor, and consecrate of thy properties for their support, that which thou hast to impart unto them with a covenant and a deed which cannot be broken.

And inasmuch as ye impart of your substance unto the poor, ye will do it unto me, and they shall be laid before the bishop of my church and his counselors, two of the Elders, or High Priests, such as he shall or has appointed and set apart for that purpose.

And it shall come to pass, that after they are laid before the bishop of my church, and after that he has received these testimonies concerning the consecration of the properties of my church, that they cannot be taken from the church agreeable to my commandments; every man shall be made accountable unto me, a steward over his own property, or that which he has received by consecration, inasmuch as is sufficient for himself and family.

* * * * * * * * *

Wherefore let my servant Edward Partridge, and those whom he has chosen, in whom I am well pleased, appoint unto this people their portion, every man equal according to their families, according to their circumstances, and their wants and needs.

And let my servant Edward Partridge, when he shall appoint a man his portion, give unto him a writing that shall secure unto him his portion, that he shall hold it, even this right and this inheritance in the church, until he transgresses and is not accounted worthy by the voice of the church, according to the laws and covenants of the church, to belong to the church;

And if he shall transgress and is not accounted worthy to belong to the church, he shall not have power to claim that portion which he has consecrated unto the bishop for the poor and needy of my church; therefore, he shall not retain the gift, but shall only have claim on that portion that is deeded unto him.

And thus all things shall be made sure, according to the laws of the land.

* * * * * * * * *

And again, let the bishop appoint a storehouse unto this church, and let all things both in money and in meat, which is more than is needful for the want of this people, be kept in the hands of the bishop.

And let him also reserve unto himself for his own wants, and for the wants of his family, as he shall be employed in doing this business.

And thus I grant unto this people a privilege of organizing themselves according to my laws;

And I consecrate unto them this land for a little season, until I, the Lord, shall provide for them otherwise, and command them to go hence;

And the hour and the day is not given unto them, wherefore let them act upon this land as for years, and this shall turn unto them for their good.

---

* Doctrine and Covenants, Sec.. 42, verses 30–32; Sec. 51, verses 3–6 and 13–17.

Such was the general outline of the United Order, which the Mormon Prophet sought to establish, and did introduce, among his people in Ohio and in Missouri. That it was not permanently established was due partly to persecution, and partly to the innate selfishness of human nature. It is still with the Saints one of the problems of the future, as they hold that Zion cannot be built up without it.

The fourth general conference of the Church of Jesus Christ of Latter-day Saints convened at Kirtland on the 6th of June, 1831. Nearly two thousand Saints assembled, including those who had followed the Prophet from New York and Pennsylvania. Among the Elders present was Parley P. Pratt, who had returned in February to report the labors of himself and his confreres in Missouri. There Elder Cowdery and the others yet remained. Several High Priests, the first known to the Church, were ordained at this conference. Most of the Elders were now commissioned to go forth two by two, after the manner of the Apostles anciently, proclaiming that the kingdom of heaven was at hand, preaching and baptizing. The appointed destination of the majority of them was the Missouri frontier, toward which they were directed to travel by different routes. It was decided that the next conference of the Church should be held upon that land. The burden of the message the Elders were to bear as they wended their way, was as follows:*

Wherefore I, the Lord, have said, gather ye out from the eastern lands, assemble ye yourselves together ye elders of my church; go ye forth into the western countries, call upon the inhabitants to repent, and inasmuch as they do repent, build up churches unto me;

And with one heart and with one mind, gather up your riches that ye may purchase an inheritance which shall hereafter be appointed unto you,

And it shall be called the New Jerusalem, a land of peace, a city of refuge, a place of safety for the saints of the most High God;

And the glory of the Lord shall be there, and the terror of the Lord also shall be there, insomuch that the wicked will not come unto it, and it shall be called Zion.

And it shall come to pass, among the wicked, that every man that will not take his sword against his neighbor, must needs flee unto Zion for safety.

* Doctrine and Covenants, Sec. 45, verses 64–71.

And there shall be gathered unto it out of every nation under heaven; and it shall be the only people that shall not be at war one with another.

And it shall be said among the wicked, Let us not go up to battle against Zion, for the inhabitants of Zion are terrible; wherefore we cannot stand.

And it shall come to pass that the righteous shall be gathered out from among all nations, and shall come to Zion, singing with songs of everlasting joy.

Among the Elders thus commissioned were Joseph Smith, junior, Sidney Rigdon, Lyman Wight, John Corrill, John Murdock, Hyrum Smith, Thomas B. Marsh, Ezra Thayre, Isaac Morley, Ezra Booth, Edward Partridge, Martin Harris, David Whitmer, Harvey Whitlock, Parley P. Pratt, Orson Pratt, Solomon Hancock, Simeon Carter, Edson Fuller, Jacob Scott, Levi Hancock, Zebedee Coltrin, Reynolds Cahoon, Samuel H. Smith, Wheeler Baldwin, William Carter, Newel Knight, Selah J. Griffin, Joseph Wakefield, Solomon Humphrey, A. S. Gilbert, William W. Phelps, and Joseph Coe. Newel Knight and the Colesville branch of the Church, formerly of Broome County, New York, but now at Thompson, Ohio, were instructed to migrate in a body to Missouri.

On the 19th of June the Prophet set out from Kirtland on his first visit to Missouri. He was accompanied by Sidney Rigdon, Martin Harris, Edward Partridge, William W. Phelps, Joseph Coe and A. S. Gilbert and wife. Journeying by wagon, stage and canal-boat to Cincinnati, they there took steamer for Louisville, Kentucky; whence, after a brief delay, they proceeded by water to St. Louis. From that point Sidney Rigdon and the Gilberts continued by steamer up the Missouri river, while the Prophet and the rest of his party walked across the state of Missouri, reaching Independence, Jackson County, about the middle of July. The meeting with Elder Cowdery and his companions was one of great rejoicing.

Immediately after the Prophet's arrival the site of the City of Zion, the central gathering place, where the Saints, according to their faith, will yet assemble to await Messiah's coming, was for the first time definitely designated. Independence and its vicinity was the chosen spot. Here lands were to be purchased by the Saints, and the soil dedicated for the gathering of Israel and the building of the New

Jerusalem. Here Bishop Edward Partridge was to take his stand as "a judge in Israel," to receive the consecration of properties, assign stewardships and apportion to the Saints their inheritance. Martin Harris, who, had before contributed so generously for the publication of the Book of Mormon, was selected as "an example to the Church," in laying his monies at the feet of the Bishop.

It may interest the reader to know what form of conveyance was used in connection with the consecration of properties. It was as follows:

BE IT KNOWN, THAT I, ———— ————, Of Jackson county, and state of Missouri, having become a member of the Church of Christ, organized according to law, and established by the revelations of the Lord, on the 6th day of April, 1830, do, of my own free will and accord, having first paid my just debts, grant and hereby give unto Edward Partridge of Jackson county, and state of Missouri, bishop of said church, the following described property, viz:—Sundry articles of furniture valued fifty five dollars twenty seven cents,—also two beds, bedding and extra clothing valued seventy three dollars twenty five cents,—also farming utensils valued forty one dollars,—also one horse, two wagons two cows and two calves valued one hundred and forty seven dollars.

For the purpose of purchasing lands in Jackson County Mo. and building up the New Jerusalem, even Zion, and for relieving the wants of the poor and needy. For which I the said ———— ———— do covenant and bind myself and my heirs forever, to release all my right and interest to the above described property, unto him the said Edward Partridge bishop of said church. And I the said Edward Partridge bishop of said church, having received the above described property, of the said ———— ———— do bind myself, that I will cause the same to be expended for the above mentioned purposes of the said ———— ———— to the satisfaction of said church; and in case I should be removed from the office of bishop of said church, by death or otherwise, I hereby bind myself and my heirs forever, to make over to my successor in office, for the benefit of said church, all the above described property, which may then be in my possession.

IN TESTIMONY WHEREOF, WE have hereunto set our hands and seals this ———— day of ———— in the year of our Lord, one thousand eight hundred and thirty —

IN PRESENCE OF ————

The legal document securing to the individual his stewardship, was in this form:

BE IT KNOWN, THAT I, Edward Partridge of Jackson county, and state of Missouri, bishop of the church of Christ, organized according to law, and established by the revelations of the Lord, on the 6th day of April, 1830, have leased and by these presents, do lease unto ———— ———— of Jackson county, and state of Missouri, a member of said church, the following described piece or parcel of land, being a part of section No. three township No. forty nine range No. thirty two situated in Jackson county, and state of Missouri, and is bounded as follows, viz:—beginning eighty rods E, from the S. W. corner of Sd Sec, thence N. one hundred and sixty rods thence E. twenty seven rods 25 L, thence S. one hundred and sixty rods, thence W. twenty seven rods 25 L, to the place of beginning, containing twenty seven & ½ acres be the same more or less subject to roads and highways. And also have loaned the following described property, viz:—Sundry articles of furniture valued fifty five dollars twenty five cents,—also two beds, bedding and clothing valued seventy three dollars twenty seven cents,—also sundry farming utensils valued forty one dollars,—also one horse, two cows, two calves and two waggons valued one hundred forty seven dollars TO HAVE AND TO HOLD the above described property, by him the said ———— ———— to be used and occupied as to him shall seem meet and proper. And as a consideration for the use of the above described property, I the said ———— ———— do bind myself to pay the taxes, and also to pay yearly unto the said Edward Partridge bishop of said church, or his successor in office, for the benefit of said church, all that I shall make or accumulate more than is needful for the support and comfort of myself and family. And it is agreed by the parties, that this lease and loan shall be binding during the life of the said ———— ———— unless he transgress, and is not deemed worthy by the authority of the Church, according to its laws, to belong to the church. And in that case I the said ———— ———— do acknowledge that I forfeit all claim to the above described leased and loaned property, and hereby bind myself to give back the lease, and also pay an equivalent for the loaned, for the benefit of said church, unto the said Edward Partridge bishop of said church, or his successor in office. And further, in case that said ———— ———— or family's inability in consequence of infirmity or old age, to provide for themselves while members of this church, I the said Edward Partridge bishop of said church, do bind myself to administer to their necessities out of any fund in my hands appropriated for that purpose, not otherwise disposed of, to the satisfaction of the church. And further, in case of the death of said ———— ———— his wife or widow, being at the time a member of said church, has claim upon the above described leased and loaned property, upon precisely the same conditions that her said husband had them, as above described; and the children of said ———— ———— in case of the death of both their parents, also have claim upon the above described property, for their support, until they shall become of age, and no longer; subject to the same conditions yearly that their parents were; provided however, should the parents not be members of said church, and in possession of the above described property at the time of their deaths, the claim of the children as above described, is null and void.

IN TESTIMONY WHEREOF, WE have hereunto set our hands and seals this ———— day of ———— in the year of our Lord, one thousand eight hundred and thirty ————

IN PRESENCE OF ————

The dual duty of dedicating the land of Zion and writing a description of it for the benefit of the Church, was devolved upon Sidney Rigdon. William W. Phelps, assisted by Oliver Cowdery, was to establish himself as the Church printer in that land, and A. S.

Gilbert, senior partner of the firm of Gilbert and Whitney, was given a mission to open a store at Independence, and act as an agent for the Church in purchasing lands in the surrounding region.

The first formal step toward the founding of the city of Zion was taken on the 2nd of August, 1831. In Kaw Township, twelve miles west of Independence, in which locality the newly arrived Colesville Saints were settling, the first log of the first house was that day borne to its place by twelve men, representing the twelve tribes of Israel. The Prophet was one of the number. The same day Elder Rigdon dedicated the land of Zion. On the day following, the site of the future temple, near Independence, was consecrated by the Prophet. Then came the appointed conference. It was held at the house of Joshua Lewis, in Kaw Township, all or most of the Saints in that region being present.

On the 9th of August the Prophet and ten other Elders set out to return to Kirtland. From Independence Landing a fleet of sixteen canoes carried them and their provisions down the Missouri. Three days they rowed and drifted. The Prophet, with Elders Cowdery and Rigdon, then left the canoes in charge of their companions, and continued the journey by land. They reached Kirtland on the 27th of August.

Having thus planted a colony of his people in their "land of promise," and set in motion a migratory stream of the Saints in that direction, the Prophet resumed his task of revising the scriptures,—a work suspended since the previous December. For this purpose he and Elder Rigdon retired to the little town of Hiram, in Portage County, thirty miles south-east of Kirtland, where, on September 12th, Joseph took up his abode at the home of John Johnson, a member of the Church there residing. Emma Smith accompanied her husband, taking with her two infants, twins, the children of John Murdock, which she had adopted in lieu of twins of her own that had died. John Johnson was the father of Luke S. and Lyman E. Johnson, two of the future Twelve Apostles, and father-in-law to Orson Hyde, who also became one of that council. Orson had recently been a clerk in the store of Gilbert and Whitney, at Kirtland. At Hiram the Prophet continued his literary labors, and from time to time took active part in the ministry, attending frequent conferences and issuing verbal or written instructions to the Church at large. Many of these were in the form of revelations, now of record in the book of Doctrine and Covenants. It was about this time that William E. McLellin, a prominent Elder, lost some prestige with the Saints by attempting, in a spirit of rivalry, to write revelations similar to those uttered by the Prophet.

Kirtland as a Stake of Zion continued to grow and prosper, her numbers increasing as converts multiplied, despite the constant drain upon her population by the Missouri emigrations. The Ohio Saints, like those in Missouri, being required to enter "the Order," an accession to the Bishopric now became necessary. On December 4th, 1831, Newel K. Whitney was called to be the Bishop of Kirtland; two counselors being chosen to assist him. The powers and duties of the Bishopric of Kirtland were similar to those of the Bishopric in Missouri.

It was during his sojourn at Hiram that the Prophet enunciated the doctrine of universal salvation. He declared that all men would be saved except a certain few called "sons of perdition,"—shedders of innocent blood and sinners against the Holy Ghost,—but that souls would be saved upon principles of justice and mercy, according to their merits, in different degrees of glory. There was hope, he said, for the heathen, who had never heard the name of Christ; hope even for the wicked, who were "thrust down to hell," after they had paid the "uttermost farthing" and suffered sufficiently for their sins.* No soul, he maintained, could escape merited punishment, designed to purge away uncleanness, simply by confessing Christ. As for little children, there was no damnation for them. They were irresponsible innocents redeemed by the blood of Christ from the

---

* Joseph Smith taught that "eternal punishment" did not mean never-ending punishment, but punishment inflicted by Him who is Eternal.

foundation of the world. A few excerpts from the "Vision" of February 16th, 1832, wherein are set forth the Prophet's views relating to the various states of man hereafter, will here be appropriate:*

We, Joseph Smith, jun., and Sidney Rigdon, being in the Spirit on the sixteenth of February, in the year of our Lord, one thousand eight hundred and thirty-two,
By the power of the Spirit our eyes were opened and our understandings were enlightened, so as to see and understand the things of God –
Even those things which were from the beginning before the world was, which were ordained of the Father, through his Only Begotten Son, who was in the bosom of the Father, even from the beginning;
Of whom we bear record, and the record which we bear is the fullness of the gospel of Jesus Christ, who is the Son, whom we saw and with whom we conversed in the heavenly vision;

*　*　*　*　*　*　*　*　*

And this we saw also, and bear record, that an angel of God who was in authority in the presence of God, who rebelled against the Only Begotten Son, whom the Father loved, and who was in the bosom of the Father – was thrust down from the presence of God and the Son,
And was called Perdition, for the heavens wept over him—he was Lucifer, a son of the morning.

*　*　*　*　*　*　*　*

And we saw a vision of the sufferings of those with whom he made war and overcame, for thus came the voice of the Lord unto us.
Thus saith the Lord, concerning all those who know my power, and have been made partakers thereof, and suffered themselves, through the power of the devil, to be overcome, and to deny the truth and defy my power—
They are they who are the sons of perdition, of whom I say that it had been better for them never to have been born.
For they are vessels of wrath, doomed to suffer the wrath of God, with the devil and his angels in eternity;

*　*　*　*　*　*　*　*

And the only ones on whom the second death shall have any power;
Yea, verily, the only ones who shall not be redeemed in the due time of the Lord, after the sufferings of his wrath:
For all the rest shall be brought forth by the resurrection of the dead, through the triumph and the glory of the Lamb, who was slain, who was in the bosom of the Father before the worlds were made.

*　*　*　*　*　*　*　*

And again, we bear record, for we saw and heard, and this is the testimony of the gospel of Christ, concerning them who come forth in the resurrection of the just:

---

* Doctrine and Covenants. Section 76.

They are they who received the testimony of Jesus, and believed on his name and were baptized after the manner of his burial, being buried in the water in his name, and this according to the commandment which he has given.

That by keeping the commandments they might be washed and cleansed from all their sins, and receive the Holy Spirit by the laying on of the hands of him who is ordained and sealed unto this power,

And who overcome by faith, and are sealed by the Holy Spirit of promise, which the Father sheds forth upon all those who are just and true.

They are they who are the church of the first born.

They are they into whose hands the Father has given all things—

They are they who are Priests and Kings, who have received of his fullness, and of his glory,

And are Priests of the Most High, after the order of Melchisedek, which was after the order of Enoch, which was after the order of the Only Begotten Son;

Wherefore, as it is written, they are Gods, even the sons of God—

Wherefore all things are theirs, whether life or death, or things present, or things to come, all are theirs and they are Christ's and Christ is God's.

* * * * * * * * *

These are they whose bodies are celestial, whose glory is that of the sun, even the glory of God, the highest of all, whose glory the sun of the firmament is written of as being typical.

And again, we saw the terrestrial world, and behold and lo, these are they who are of the terrestrial, whose glory differs from that of the church of the first born, who have received the fullness of the Father, even as that of the moon differs from the sun in the firmament.

Behold, these are they who died without law.

And also they who are the spirits of men kept in prison, whom the Son visited, and preached the gospel unto them, that they might be judged according to men in the flesh,

Who received not the testimony of Jesus in the flesh, but afterwards received it.

These are they who are honorable men of the earth, who were blinded by the craftiness of men.

These are they who receive of his glory, but not of his fullness.

These are they who receive of the presence of the Son, but not of the fullness of the Father;

Wherefore they are bodies terrestrial, and not bodies celestial, and differ in glory as the moon differs from the sun.

These are they who are not valiant in the testimony of Jesus; wherefore they obtain not the crown over the kingdom of our God.

* * * * * * * * *

And again, we saw the glory of the telestial, which glory is that of the lesser, even as the glory of the stars differs from that of the glory of the moon in the firmament.

These are they who received not the gospel of Christ, neither the testimony of Jesus.

These are they who deny not the Holy Spirit.

These are they who are thrust down to hell.

These are they who shall not be redeemed from the devil, until the last resurrection, until the Lord, even Christ the Lamb shall have finished his work.

These are they who receive not of his fullness in the eternal world, but of the Holy Spirit through the ministration of the terrestrial;

* * * * * * *

And the glory of the celestial is one, even as the glory of the sun is one.

And the glory of the terrestrial is one, even as the glory of the moon is one.

And the glory of the telestial is one, even as the glory of the stars is one, for as one star differs from another star in glory, even so differs one from another in glory in the telestial world;

* * * * * * * * *.

For they shall be judged according to their works, and every man shall receive according to his own works, his own dominion, in the mansions which are prepared.

And they shall be servants of the Most High, but where God and Christ dwell they cannot come, worlds without end.

Joseph Smith here virtually declares that God is man made perfect, and that man in his highest estate, resurrected and glorified,—the child developed to the status of the parent,—is nothing less than Deity. The idea of "Lords many and Gods many," a celestial brotherhood, a divine United Order, is also plainly set forth. Whatever may be thought of such views, one thing is certain, the charge that Mormonism teaches a narrow salvation here falls to the ground. Nor is the thought that man by development becomes God,—retaining his individuality, while doffing his mortal nature and blossoming into an eternal being,—a groveling concept of human destiny. The Nirvana of Buddhism pales before it, as do the mystical views of most Christian divines.

About the time of the Prophet's removal to Hiram, Ezra Booth, one of the Elders who had accompanied him to Missouri, apostatized, and in a series of letters published in the Ohio *Star* was now assailing the system and principles he had once accepted and advocated as divine. He succeeded in creating considerable prejudice against the Prophet, and through his influence several others turned from the Church. A feeling of intense hostility was awakened at Hiram, where, on the night of March 25th, a violent assault was committed upon the Prophet and Elder Rigdon. Joseph and his wife had been watching at the bedside of the twins, who were dangerously ill, and weary and worn from loss of sleep he had thrown himself down and was slumbering heavily. Suddenly the door was burst open, and in rushed a mob of ten or a dozen men, who, surrounding the sleeper, seized him and attempted to drag him from the house. His wife's screams aroused him, and he struggled desperately with his assailants. His hands being held, he felled one man to the floor with a vigorous kick. Enraged at his resistance, they threatened to kill him if he did not desist, and suiting the action to the word seized him by the throat and choked him until he was insensible.

Father Johnson, whom the mob had locked in a room prior to attacking his guest, regaining his liberty, pursued them, club in hand. Encountering another party who had captured Elder Rigdon, he knocked one of them down, and was about to fell another when the crowd turned upon him and held him at bay.

Joseph, recovering consciousness, found himself lying upon the ground surrounded by his captors, about a mile from the house where his weeping and half frantic wife still watched beside the sick babes, one of whom was now death-stricken. Near him lay the motionless form of Elder Rigdon, whom the mob had dragged by his heels over the hard frozen earth until life was almost extinct. Joseph supposed him dead. He himself was now hurried into a meadow, a mile farther away, where the mob stripped off his clothes, cursing and beating him meanwhile, and coated his naked form with tar. They forced a tar paddle into his mouth, and a phial containing *aqua fortis* between his lips. The phial broke against his tightly clenched teeth, and the deadly acid was spilled. One of the mob then fell upon him like a wild-cat, tearing his flesh and shrieking in his ear: "That's the way the Holy Ghost falls on folks." Having sated their fury, they departed, leaving their bleeding victim to find his way, as best he might, through the cold and darkness back to Father Johnson's. At sight of his lacerated form, covered with tar, his wife screamed and fainted, supposing him to have been horribly mangled. He spent the rest of the night cleansing the tar from his bruised and bleeding body.

Next day was the Sabbath, and the Saints in that vicinity assembled for their usual worship. Methodists, Baptists, Campbellites and Mormon apostates came also. Some of them had helped compose the mob party of the previous night. Scarred and wounded the Prophet appeared before them, bore a ringing testimony to the truth of his mission, and that day baptized three more into the Church.

But the mobocratic spirit was now rampant, not only at Hiram, where fresh plots were at once formed against the Mormon leader, but also at Kirtland, and throughout the surrounding region. Elder Rigdon, after recovering from the effects of the ill-treatment he had received, fled with his family from Hiram to escape further outrage.

Joseph and Emma remained another week, during which one of the sick twins died. He then sent his wife to Kirtland, and set out upon his second visit to Missouri. He was accompanied by Sidney Rigdon, Bishop Whitney and others, who joined him at different points along the way. A circuitous route was taken, to evade mobocratic ambush and pursuit. The party reached Independence late in April.

The affairs of the Church in Missouri were found to be prospering, though some prejudice had been created against the Saints by certain persons who had misinterpreted their motives in settling there. A series of petty persecutions had resulted. Stones and brick-bats were thrown through their windows, and they were otherwise insulted and annoyed. It was the beginning of sorrows, the precursor of the coming storm, the first, faint sparks of a furious conflagration, destined ere many months to burst forth as a besom of fire, sweeping before it into exile the whipped and plundered Saints of Jackson County.

Early in May the Prophet started back to Kirtland. Elder Rigdon and Bishop Whitney accompanying him. Near Greenville, Indiana, the Bishop had his leg broken, while jumping from a runaway stage-coach. This delayed him and the Prophet for a month at a public house in Greenville. Elder Rigdon meanwhile proceeding on to Kirtland. During the stay at Greenville an attempt was made to murder the Prophet by mixing poison with his food at dinner. He narrowly escaped death. Next morning he and his friend departed from the dangerous neighborhood, and sometime in June arrived at Kirtland. The birth of the Prophet's son Joseph, the present leader of the sect known as Josephites, or, as they call themselves, the Reorganized Church of Jesus Christ of Latter-day Saints, occurred on November 3rd of this year, just prior to the return of his father and Bishop Whitney from a hasty trip to the east.

On Christmas Day, 1832, was recorded the following "revelation and prophecy on war:"*

Verily, thus saith the Lord, concerning the wars that will shortly come to pass, beginning at the rebellion of South Carolina, which will eventually terminate in the death and misery of many souls.

The days will come that war will be poured out upon all nations, beginning at that place;

For behold, the Southern States shall be divided against the Northern States, and the Southern States will call on other nations, even the nation of Great Britain, as it is called, and they shall also call upon other nations, in order to defend themselves against other nations; and thus war shall be poured out upon all nations.

And it shall come to pass, after many days, slaves shall rise up against their masters, who shall be marshalled and disciplined for war;

And it shall come to pass also, that the remnants who are left of the land will marshal themselves, and shall become exceeding angry, and shall vex the Gentiles with a sore vexation;

And thus, with the sword, and by bloodshed, the inhabitants of the earth shall mourn; and with famine, and plague, and earthquakes, and the thunder of heaven, and the fierce and vivid lightning also, shall the inhabitants of the earth be made to feel the wrath, the indignation and chastening hand of an Almighty God, until the consumption decreed hath made a full end of all nations.

The Saints claim that this prediction began to be fulfilled on April 12th, 1861, when the Confederate batteries at Charleston, South Carolina, opened fire on Fort Sumter.

* Doctrine and Covenants, Section 87.

During the winter of 1832-3, the Mormon leader organized at Kirtland the School of the Prophets, designed for the instruction of the Elders in the "things of the Kingdom." He also completed his revision of the scriptures.

On the 18th of March, 1833, was organized the First Presidency, the highest depository of authority in the Church. This council consists of three High Priests after the order of Melchisedek, chosen and sustained by the whole body, over which they preside. The personnel of the Presidency at this first organization was as follows: Joseph Smith, junior, President; Sidney Rigdon, First Counselor; Frederick G. Williams, Second Counselor.

It was now decided to purchase lands in and around Kirtland, surnamed "the land of Shinehah," and build up and beautify the city while awaiting further developments in Missouri, "the land of Zion." Farms were accordingly purchased, work-shops and mills erected, and various industries established. During the early part of 1833 a temple at Kirtland was projected.

CHAPTER VII.
1833.

THE JACKSON COUNTY EXPULSION AND ITS CAUSES—MOBOCRATIC MASS MEETINGS AT INDEPENDENCE—DESTRUCTION OF THE OFFICE OF THE "EVENING AND MORNING STAR"—BISHOP PARTRIDGE TARRED AND FEATHERED—THE MORMONS REQUIRED TO LEAVE THE COUNTY FORTHWITH—A TRUCE AGREED UPON—THE MOB BREAK THEIR PLEDGE—RENEWAL OF DEPREDATIONS—THE MORMONS APPEAL TO GOVERNOR DUNKLIN—HE ADVISES THEM TO SEEK REDRESS IN THE COURTS—LEGAL PROCEEDINGS INSTITUTED—THE MOB ENRAGED—THE OCTOBER AND NOVEMBER RIOTS—A BATTLE ON THE BIG BLUE—LIEUTENANT-GOVERNOR BOGGS CALLS OUT THE MILITIA—THE MORMONS DISARMED AND DRIVEN—CLAY COUNTY RECEIVES THE REFUGEES—JACKSON COUNTY, MISSOURI, STILL "THE LAND OF ZION."

TWELVE to fifteen hundred Latter-day Saints now inhabited Jackson County, Missouri. They had purchased lands and improved them, built houses—mostly log cabins—and were occupying them, sowed their farms and fields and reaped repeated harvests. A store had been established by them at Independence, a printing press and type had been procured from the east, and a periodical called the *Evening and Morning Star*, edited by William W. Phelps, was being issued. A school of Elders, numbering sixty members, with Parley P. Pratt as its president and preceptor, had been instituted, and preaching to the Missourians was continued with success.

Plans for the city and temple of Zion had been forwarded by the Prophet from Kirtland, but so far little had been done toward the building of the New Jerusalem. The Book of Commandments, or revelations, had also been sent from Ohio to be published in Missouri. The United Order, though still in its incipiency, was being established as fast as circumstances would allow.

The Saints, as a rule, were poor, but were sober, moral, honest and industrious; attending strictly to their own affairs, and not meddling with the concerns of their neighbors. Indeed, so thoroughly did they "mind their own business" as to lay themselves open to the charge of exclusiveness.

They were far from being a perfect people—an ideal Zion. On the contrary, they manifested many of the faults that are the common heritage of weak humanity. But those faults were chiefly manifested among themselves, and were violative of the precepts of their religion rather than of the laws of the land. Seldom were they subversive of the rights of the Missourians. But in an Order such as theirs, demanding strict unselfishness of its members, it could not be but some would slip and frequently break the rigid rules that bound them. They were repeatedly warned by the Prophet of dire consequences that would follow these infractions, and were especially admonished against covetousness and disunion.

But with the esoteric views of the Saints, as to divine punishments visited upon them for transgressing the rules of their Order, the historian has naught to do. He has only to consider here their every-day dealings with their fellow-men. So considering, it must be admitted by those cognizant of the truth, that not to their misdeeds against the Missourians—though some misdeeds there may have been—but to their social and religious peculiarities, are we to look for the main causes of the calamities that now befell them. These peculiarities, which have ever rendered the Mormons unpopular with other sects and parties, were made doubly obnoxious by the misrepresentations of those politically, religiously or pecuniarily interested in decrying them.

Allusion has been made to the fact that the motives of the Mormons in migrating to Missouri had been misinterpreted by the older settlers. Some of these actually supposed, and others affected to believe, that it was the purpose of the Prophet's followers, when they became strong enough, to take forcible possession of the country, unite with the Indians across the border and drive the Gentiles from the land. That this fear, wherever sincerely felt, was due in part to ill-advised and vain-glorious utterances of persons connected with the Church,—whose views were as much at variance with truth and the teachings of authority as the deductions of the ignorant and inflammable masses around them,—is more than probable. That it was also due to misrepresentation by Mormon apostates, political and religious opponents of the Saints, bent upon furthering their own ends and playing for that purpose upon the credulity of the common people, is not only probable, but an established fact.

The teachings of the Book of Mormon and the Church authorities upon these points were as follows: That God had given into the hands of the Gentiles this land; had inspired them to discover it and maintain it as a land of liberty; that the Gentiles, such as embraced the faith, were to assist Ephraim and Manasseh in building up Zion and would share in her glory; and that the duty of the Saints in relation to the Gentiles was to preach to them the gospel of peace, and honestly purchase every inch of ground to be used or occupied in the rearing of the New Jerusalem.

True, the Book of Mormon contains certain prophecies of retribution upon the Gentiles, such as rejected the Gospel and oppressed the Lamanites. But the Lamanites themselves were to avenge their own wrongs, and that without aid or instigation from Ephraim. The queerest phase of the subject, and it would be extremely funny but for the terrible tragedy to which it led, was that the Missourians, who like most people scoffed at the Book of Mormon and scouted the idea of "Joe Smith" being a prophet, should have allowed these predictions to so alarm them. Perhaps it was their effect upon the Saints that was feared. In that event the hapless Mormons were punished, not for crimes committed, but for crimes they were expected to commit.

Besides the charge of "tampering with the Indians," the Mormons were accused by the Missourians of being abolitionists—anti-slavery advocates—which charge, supported only by the fact that they were mostly eastern and northern people, was sufficient at that time, and in that region, to blacken their characters irredeemably.

Their United Order theories were dubbed "Communism," and were said to involve a community, not only of goods and chattels, but of wives. Also,—though the reader may smile incredulously at the statement,—the fact that they were poor was urged as an accusation of evil against them. This charge, unlike the rest, had the merit of being strictly true.

A man named Pixley, local agent for a Christian missionary society, took an active and initiative part in circulating these reports, which were caught up by others and sown broad-cast until well-nigh all Jackson County with the anti-Mormon spirit was aflame. As early as April, 1833, meetings were held to consider the most effective means of ridding the county of the unpopular Mormons. Lawful methods were not considered, for obvious reasons. The Mormons were law-abiding and peaceable. Poverty, superstition, unity, unpopular doctrines,—these were their crimes. What law, in a land of civil and religious liberty, could reach them? No; law could not, but mob violence, trampling on law, strangling liberty in her very sanctuary, could and would, and did.

Three hundred men assembled one day in April, at Independence, and endeavored to unite upon a plan for the proposed Mormon extirpation. Too much liquor having been imbibed beforehand, the meeting, after much cursing and quarreling, broke up in confusion.

Other attempts, in July, were more successful. On the 20th of that month a mass meeting of five hundred convened, presided over by Colonel Richard Simpson. James H. Flournay and Colonel Samuel D. Lucas acted as secretaries. A declaration against the Saints, embodying charges similar to the foregoing, was unanimously adopted, and it was resolved that they be required to leave the county forthwith, and that no Mormon be permitted in future to settle there. It was demanded that the publication of the *Evening and Morning Star* be at once suspended. A committee of thirteen was sent to confer with the local Mormon leaders, acquaint them with the decision made concerning them and their people, and report to the mass meeting within two hours. The committee having executed its errand returned, reporting that the Mormons requested sufficient time to fully consider the matter and consult their leaders in Ohio.

A furious yell was the only answer vouchsafed, and forth rushed the mob to begin its work of outrage and destruction. A red flag led them on. Surrounding the house of William W. Phelps, editor of the *Star*, they razed it to the ground, confiscating the printing press, type and other materials found upon the premises. The editor's family, including his wife with a sick child in her arms, were brutally thrust into the street, and the household furniture, books, etc., destroyed or carried away by the rabble. The editor himself was captured, but escaped through the crowd.

The Church store was next assailed, but the mob soon desisted from their work of plunder and gathered upon the public square. Thither, Bishop Edward Partridge had been dragged from his fireside. Refusing to at once leave the county, he was stripped of most of his apparel, covered with tar, and feathers were thrown over him. Elder Charles Allen suffered similar treatment. Mixed with the tar was a powerful acid which severely burned their flesh. Other Mormons were threatened and abused. Night coming on, the mob dispersed.

These lawless acts were committed, not alone by the rabble, ignorant, easily inflamed, and perhaps not wholly accountable for their frenzy, but by men of prominence and position. Clergymen, magistrates, state and county officials, who had sworn to honor and sustain the law, looked on approvingly while the law was being violated, and even participated in its infraction. It is said that the leaders of the mob, prior to engaging in these acts of vandalism, in imitation of the patriot founders of the nation pledged to each other "their bodily powers, their lives, fortunes and sacred honor." Shortly after the affair, Lilburn W. Boggs, Lieutenant-Governor of Missouri, said to some of the Mormons: "You now know what our Jackson boys can do, and you must leave the county."

Three days after the assault upon Bishop Partridge and his brethren, the mobocratic mass-meeting again convened, this time in greater numbers than before. The recent acts of violence had seemingly sated in part their anger. At all events they were a little more reasonable than before. A new committee was appointed to confer with the leading Mormons, and the result was a mutual agreement between the two parties. By the terms of this compact, one half the Saints were to be permitted to remain in the county until the 1st of January, 1834, and the other half until the 1st of April. It was agreed that the *Star* should not again be published, nor a printing press set up by any Mormon in Jackson County. Their immigration thither was at once to cease. In return for these concessions by the Saints, the committee gave a pledge that no further attacks should be made upon them. This agreement the mass meeting ratified and then adjourned.

Oliver Cowdery now carried to Kirtland a full account of what had taken place in Missouri. Affairs in Ohio at that time were far from peaceable. The Prophet was harassed with law-suits, and frequently threatened with violence. Yet the Kirtland Stake was progressing. The corner-stone of the Temple was laid on the very day that the Jackson County mob issued its decree of expatriation against the Saints. It was decided, after Elder Cowdery's arrival, to purchase a new printing press and continue the publication of the *Evening and Morning Star* at Kirtland; also that another paper called the *Latter-day Saints' Messenger and Advocate* be published there. The latter was succeeded by the *Elders' Journal*.

About the middle of September the Prophet sent Orson Hyde and John Gould to Missouri, with a message of comfort and instruction to his people in that State. By this time the mob troubles in Jackson County had resumed. It was Punic faith in which the Saints had trusted. The pledge given by the mass meeting in July had been broken. Two months had not elapsed before the mob renewed hostilities. Some of the Saints then moved into adjoining counties, hoping thereby to allay excitement and secure peace and tranquility. Vain hope. They had no sooner settled there than they were threatened with expulsion from these newly acquired homes. "The Mormons must go!" was now the prevailing sentiment south of the Missouri river.

An appeal was next made to the Executive of the State. Daniel Dunklin was then Governor of Missouri. A document setting forth the wrongs the Saints had suffered from their fellow-citizens of Jackson County, describing the situation, and asking for military aid and protection while seeking redress in the courts, was carried to Jefferson City and delivered at the Governor's mansion by William W. Phelps and Orson Hyde. This document was dated September 28th, 1833. A reply was received late in October. The Governor declined to give the military aid requested, but advised the petitioners to make a trial of the efficacy of the laws, and promised that if they failed to obtain a proper execution of the same he would then take steps for their relief.

Pursuant to the Governor's advice, though not without some apprehension as to the result, the Mormons, having secured for the sum of a thousand dollars the services of four lawyers, instituted legal proceedings against their oppressors. It was as the application of the lighted match to the mine. An explosion of popular fury followed, before which, like stones and timbers of some huge building blown to atoms, the entire Mormon community, men, women and children, were driven in every direction from Jackson County.

It was about the last of October. Night attacks by armed mobs were made simultaneously at several points. Beyond the Big Blue river, in the western part of the county, houses were unroofed, men beaten, and women and children driven screaming into the wilderness. Similar scenes were enacted elsewhere. For three consecutive nights the work of rapine and ruin went on. At Independence houses were attacked and the expelled inmates whipped and pelted with stones. The Church store was broken open and plundered, its goods strewing the streets. One man, caught in the act of robbing the store, was taken before Justice of the Peace Samuel Weston, who refused to issue a warrant for his arrest. The robber was thus turned loose to rejoin his companions. Later, the Mormons who had arrested him were taken into custody, charged with assaulting their prisoner. Being fired at while under arrest, they were placed in jail to save them from the fury of the rabble. Every effort of the Mormons to obtain justice was unavailing. The officers of the law were either too timid to come to their rescue, or were in league with the mob against them. The circuit judge at Lexington, being applied to for a peace warrant, refused to issue one, but advised the Mormons to arm themselves and shoot down the outlaws who came upon them.

To the Saints such advice was most repugnant. Their religion forbade strife, and strictly prohibited the needless shedding of blood. To meet violence with violence, however, now seemed their only recourse. The mob, emboldened by their policy of non-resistance, were hourly becoming more aggressive. The Mormons must either defend themselves, or supinely submit to wholesale outrage, plunder and massacre. Preferring the former course, they followed the advice of the Lexington judge and armed themselves, and the next onslaught of their foes found them ready to receive them.

On the 4th of November a marauding band fired upon some of the settlers beyond the Big Blue. A battle ensued. Several Mormons were wounded, one fatally, and it was found that two of the banditti had bitten the dust. The Mormon mortally wounded was a young man named Barber. He died next day. Philo Dibble, who was thought to be fatally shot, recovered and is still living, an aged and respected citizen of Utah.

A "Mormon uprising" was now widely heralded. The purpose of the Missourians had been accomplished. They had goaded their victims to desperation, and at length blood had been shed. The rest of the program was comparatively easy. On November 5th Lieutenant-Governor Boggs ordered out the militia to suppress the alleged insurrection. Colonel Thomas Pitcher, a radical anti-Mormon, was placed in command. He permitted the mobocrats, who had caused the trouble, to enroll themselves among the troops called out to put down the "uprising." He required the Mormons to lay down their arms, and deliver up to be tried for murder certain men who had taken part in the previous day's battle. The rest of the community were required to leave the county forthwith.

The first two behests being obeyed, Colonel Pitcher, to enforce speedy compliance with the other, turned loose his mob militia to work their will upon the disarmed and helpless Saints. Scenes beggaring description were now enacted. Armed bands of ruffians ranged the county in every direction, bursting into houses, terrifying women and children and threatening the defenseless people with death if they did not instantly flee. One of these bands was led by a Christian minister heading, like another Peter the Hermit, this holy crusade. Out upon the bleak prairies, along the Missouri's banks, chilled by November's winds and drenched by pouring rains, hungry and shelterless, weeping and heart-broken, wandered forth the exiles. Families scattered and divided, husbands seeking wives, wives husbands, parents searching for their children, not knowing if they were yet alive. Such was the sorrowful scene—a veritable Acadian tableau—enough, it might be thought, to melt a heart of stone. But alas, the human heart, inhumanized by hate, is harder than stone.

Most of the refugees, after much suffering from hunger and exposure, found an asylum in Clay County, on the opposite shore, where they were kindly received and their woes compassionated. All the other counties to which the Mormons had fled followed the example of Jackson and expelled them from their borders. Ten settlements were now left desolate.

But the exiles did not despair. It was a lawless mob that had driven them from their homes and robbed them of their possessions. Surely in a land of law and order there was recompense and redress for such wrongs. The Governor, Judges and other state officials were in turn appealed to, and even the President of the United States was memorialized in relation to the Jackson County tragedy. Courteous replies came back, deprecating and deploring what had taken place, but that was all. Governor Dunklin held that he could not lawfully extend military aid to maintain the Mormons in possession of their homes, and the reply of the President, by the Secretary of War, was to the same effect. The mob then was supreme. So seemed it to these homeless and plundered American citizens, suing in vain for redress at the feet of the highest civil and military authority in the land.

President Jackson, as well as Governor Dunklin, doubtless sincerely desired to right the wrongs of the exiles. It was not like "Old Hickory,"* with his "anti-nullifying" record, to hesitate or falter in the presence of what he deemed a duty unperformed. He evidently thought, as most Democrats would think, that the Jackson County episode was a local wrong to be locally rectified, and that he was powerless, unless requested by the Governor or the Legislature of the State, to interfere and take action against the Missouri mob, as he had formerly against the South Carolina nullifiers.

As to Governor Dunklin, a well-meaning though rather weak official, he perhaps did all that a man of his calibre and stamina could be expected to do under the circumstances. At his instance a court of inquiry was held, and Colonel Pitcher for his conduct was court-martialed. It was decided that there had been no Mormon uprising, and that the calling out of the troops and the enforced surrender of arms by citizens defending themselves against unrighteous aggression, was therefore unnecessary and unlawful. The Governor commanded the officers of the militia to restore to the Mormons their arms. This order they ignored. Further efforts for the relief of the Saints were made by fair-minded citizens,—who regarded the Jackson County affair as a grave crime, a stain upon the fair fame of the State,—but owing to popular prejudice, and the difficulty of enforcing in a mobocratic community the edicts of law and order, no adequate recompense was ever given, and the Mormons remain dispossessed of their lands in that locality to this day.

Nearly sixty years have passed since then, yet Jackson County,

* A surname of Andrew Jackson's.

Missouri, to the Latter-day Saints, is still "the land of Zion." Stakes of Zion have multiplied, and the people have flocked thereto; but "the place for the city" has remained unchanged. Zion has not been "moved out of her place, notwithstanding her children are scattered." The generation which once possessed the land—whose descendants still possess it—after repeated mobbings and massacres, endured for conscience-sake, have nearly all fallen asleep. But their aims and aspirations survive in the hearts of their children, who as confidently look forward as did ever their exiled sires, who followed Joseph Smith to Nauvoo and Brigham Young into the wilderness, to the eventual return of the Saints to Jackson County, and the rearing upon its sacred soil, consecrated by their fathers for that purpose, of the glorious Zion of their hopes.

CHAPTER VIII.
1833-1837.

BRIGHAM YOUNG, THE FOUNDER OF UTAH, EMBRACES MORMONISM—HEBER C. KIMBALL ENTERS THE FOLD—WILFORD WOODRUFF—GEORGE A. SMITH—JEDEDIAH M. GRANT—ERASTUS SNOW—THE FIRST HIGH COUNCIL ORGANIZED—ZION'S CAMP—THE TWELVE APOSTLES CHOSEN—THE SEVENTIES SELECTED—A REVELATION ON PRIESTHOOD—MORMONISM AND EDUCATION—THE KIRTLAND TEMPLE DEDICATED—LORENZO SNOW—THE MISSOURI MORMONS—THEIR REMOVAL FROM CLAY COUNTY TO CALDWELL—THE FOUNDING OF FAR WEST.

JUST prior to the Jackson County expulsion, the main incidents of which tragic event were narrated in the preceding chapter, there arrived at Kirtland two men, both destined to become prominent and powerful in the future of Mormonism, and one of whom was fated to win a place in fame's pantheon among the most remarkable men of history. That man was Brigham Young. His companion was Heber C. Kimball.

It was not their introduction to Mormonism, nor indeed their first visit to the head-quarters of the Saints. Twice before had Brigham, and once before had Heber been to Kirtland. Both had espoused the cause at Mendon, Monroe County, New York, from which place they had now permanently removed, to take up their abode in the bosom of the Church and thenceforth follow the fortunes of their people.

Both these men were natives of Vermont; Brigham Young having been born at Whitingham, in Windham County, June 1st, 1801, and Heber C. Kimball at Sheldon, Franklin County, on June 14th of the same year. At the time that Mormonism was taking root in western New York and northern Pennsylvania they were dwelling in the town of Mendon. Heber was by trade a potter; Brigham a carpenter and joiner, painter and glazier. Though not highly educated,—a common school training, and a limited amount of that, being all that either could boast,—they were men of gifted minds, possessing unusual intelligence and strength of character.

Brigham Young was a man of undoubted genius,—a master mind, well balanced and powerful, thoroughly practical in thought and method, and of Napoleonic energy and intuition. Heber C. Kimball was a natural prophet,—a poet he would have been, had education lent his genius wings. A deep spiritual thinker, a great yet simple soul, replete with eccentricity. In religion Heber, when Mormonism found him, was a Baptist; while Brigham, like Joseph Smith in his boyhood, leaned toward Methodism.

Brigham Young first saw the Book of Mormon in the spring of 1830, at the home of his brother Phineas in Mendon. It had been left there by Samuel H. Smith, brother to the Prophet. Two years later a party of Mormon Elders from Pennsylvania came preaching in that neighborhood. Being converted to the faith, Brigham was baptized by Eleazer Miller on the 14th of April, 1832. Heber C. Kimball was baptized by Alpheus Gifford on the day following. John Young, senior, Phineas H., Joseph and Lorenzo D. Young, John P. Greene, Israel Barlow and a score of others with their families, in and around Mendon, also embraced Mormonism about the same time. Ordained to the ministry, Brigham, Heber and others rendered the Church efficient service in that region.

Not long afterward Brigham and Heber, accompanied by Joseph Young, visited Kirtland and became acquainted with the Prophet. It was the summer or fall of 1832. This was the first meeting of Joseph Smith with the man who was destined to be his successor. It is said that Joseph predicted about this time that Brigham Young would yet preside over the Church.

Returning east the three visiting Elders re-engaged in the work of the ministry. Brigham and Joseph Young visiting Upper Canada, whence the former, in July, 1833, led several families of converts to Kirtland. Again returning to Mendon, where his wife had died the year before, Brigham and his two motherless daughters dwelt for a season under the roof-tree of his friend Heber, and in the fall of that year accompanied him and his family to Kirtland.

Other notable stars were likewise dawning or were about to dawn upon Mormonism's cloud-hung horizon. Wilford Woodruff, afterwards an Apostle and the fourth President of the Church, was baptized by Zera Pulsipher at Richland, Oswego County, New York, on December 31st, 1833. He was a native of Farmington—now Avon—Hartford County, Connecticut, and was born March 1st, 1807. George A. Smith, a cousin of the Prophet's, had come to Kirtland with his parents from Potsdam, St. Lawrence County, New York, in May, 1833. Jedediah M. Grant, of Broome County, New York, had joined the Church in March, and Erastus Snow, in February, had espoused the faith in his native State of Vermont. George A. and Jedediah were then youths of sixteen and seventeen respectively, and Erastus only a lad of fourteen.

It was about this time that D. P. Hurlburt was severed from the Church for immoral conduct. He felt his disgrace keenly. He first threatened the Prophet's life,—for which he was tried and put under bonds at Chardon,—and then set diligently to work to stir up strife and prejudice against the Mormons and their leader. He was quite successful in this, and the Prophet was guarded night and day by trusty friends, who feared his attempted assassination. We have already seen how Hurlburt, after his expulsion from the Church, originated the theory identifying the Book of Mormon with the Spaulding story.

On the 17th of February, 1834, was organized at Kirtland the first High Council of the Church of Jesus Christ of Latter-day Saints. It was composed of twelve High Priests, presided over by three of the same order. A few words here in relation to High Councils and Mormon religious tribunals in general.

It is pretty well known by this time that the Mormon leaders do not favor litigation among their followers; that "brother going to law against brother" is an offense against the precepts and regulations of the Church. To obviate the need of such things there are instituted among the Saints tribunals called Bishops' Courts and High Councils, the members of which serve gratuitously and labor much in the capacity of peace-makers; adjusting difficulties between Church members in such a way as to save expense and prevent ill-feeling at the same time.

The Teacher is the peace-maker proper of the Church, but if he finds it impossible to reconcile the parties disagreeing, it is his duty to report the case to the Bishop,—whose officer he is,—together with any iniquity he may discover from time to time in visiting among the Saints of his "district." There may be many districts and many teachers,—two of whom usually act together,—in the "ward" over which the Bishop and his two counselors as High Priests preside.

The Bishop's Court hears evidence pro and con and decides accordingly. An appeal from its decision may be taken, if the gravity of the case warrants, to the High Council of the Stake in which the Bishop's ward is located. A Stake may have many wards, as the Church at large has many Stakes. Each Stake has its High Council, consisting of twelve High Priests, presided over by three other High Priests who are known as the Stake Presidency. This presidency, to whom the ward Bishops are accountable, are amenable themselves to the First Presidency. The High Councils are the appellate courts of the Church, having also original jurisdiction.

Each party to a case before the High Council has a right to be represented by half the members of that body,—one or more on either side being appointed to defend him,—and the matter in dispute having been thoroughly ventilated, the President renders his decision, which, if sustained by a majority of the Council, is the end of controversy, unless a rehearing is ordered by the First Presidency on a review of the evidence.

The greatest punishment inflicted by the Bishop's Court is disfellowshipment,—suspension from all privileges of Church membership.*

* This applies to persons holding the Melchisedek Priesthood. Members not holding that Priesthood may be excommunicated by the Bishop's Court.

The extreme penalty adjudged by the High Council is excommunication from the Church. All its members are amenable for transgression to these tribunals, one of the main objects of which is to prevent expensive and strife-breeding litigation among the Saints. They were not designed, though it is often alleged, to supersede or in any way interfere with the operations of the civil courts. According to Mormon doctrine, offenders against the laws of the land are amenable to those laws, as interpreted by legally constituted tribunals.

The twelve High Priests composing the first High Council, organized in February 1834, were Oliver Cowdery, Joseph Coe, Samuel H. Smith, Luke Johnson, John S. Carter, Sylvester Smith, John Johnson, Orson Hyde, Jared Carter, Joseph Smith, senior, John Smith and Martin Harris. The presidency of this council was identical with the First Presidency of the Church, namely: Joseph Smith, junior, Sidney Rigdon and Frederick G. Williams.

In the latter part of February, the Prophet began organizing at Kirtland, an expedition for the relief of his people in Missouri. This organization is known in Mormon history as Zion's Camp. It consisted when complete of two hundred and five men, nearly all Elders, Priests, Teachers and Deacons, organized as a military body, with Joseph Smith as their general. They took with them twenty wagons, well laden with supplies. The object of the expedition was to "redeem Zion;" in other words to regain possession of the lands in Jackson County from which the Saints had been driven. It subsequently transpired that the Prophet had another purpose in view: that of proving the mettle of the men who were to be his future Apostles.

One hundred of the Camp left Kirtland on the 5th of May, 1834. The remainder reinforced them on the way. They crossed the Mississippi early in June, and in the latter part of the month pitched their tents between two forks of Fishing River, Missouri, between Richmond, Ray County, and Liberty, the county seat of Clay. There they were joined by some of their brethren of those parts, and from them learned particulars of further outrages upon the few remaining Saints in Jackson County.

The news of the coming of Zion's Camp, with exaggerated rumors concerning their numbers and the purpose of the expedition, created considerable excitement in western Missouri. Armed bands went out to meet them, and dire threats were uttered as to their doom. They were saved from attack one night on Fishing River by a terrible storm which beat back their foes and rendered the raging stream impassable. Colonel Sconce, of Ray County, Sheriff Gilliam, of Clay, and other prominent men of that vicinity then visited the camp and conversed with the Mormon leader. Having learned from him that his design was merely to secure an amicable adjustment of the difficulties between his despoiled disciples and the people of Jackson County, they were soon placated and became friendly.

Certain dissensions had broken out in Zion's Camp while on the way from Kirtland, and the Prophet, it is said, severely reprimanded some of his followers and predicted that a scourge would come upon the camp in consequence. Certain it is that a scourge did come, in the form of cholera, appearing among them about the 22nd of June. Sixty-eight were attacked by the malady, and thirteen or fourteen died. Among those who fell victims was Algernon S. Gilbert, who had kept the Church store at Independence.

During the plague the camp removed from Fishing River to within a few miles of Liberty. There they were met by General David R. Atchison and others, who in a friendly spirit requested that they come no nearer the town, as the excitement caused by the sensational rumors concerning them had not yet abated. This request was complied with, the Camp changing its course to Rush Creek, where some of the Mormons had settled. In order to show still further that his motives were not hostile, the Prophet disbanded his force and apprised General Atchison of the fact, requesting him to inform Governor Dunklin, whose ears were being filled with all sorts of tales from Jackson County regarding "Joe Smith and his army."

Negotiations, already begun, now continued between the Mormon leaders and the men of Jackson County. The latter proposed to purchase the possessions of the Saints in that locality. To this the Mormons would not listen, deeming it sacrilege to sell their "sacred inheritance." On their part they submitted a proposition to buy out all residents of Jackson County who did not desire to dwell as their near neighbors. This offer their opponents rejected. It was evident that upon no condition would the Mormons be permitted to return. Samuel C. Owens, a prominent mobocrat, advised the Mormons to "cast an eye back of Clinton"—a distant county—and seek a new home in the wilderness. Believing that further effort would be vain, at all events for the present, the Prophet concluded to return to Kirtland.

Before starting, however, he organized a High Council among his followers in Clay County, and set apart a presidency to take charge of the Church in Missouri. David Whitmer, William W. Phelps and John Whitmer were that presidency. The twelve high councilors were as follows: Simeon Carter, Parley P. Pratt, William E. McLellin, Calvin Beebe, Levi Jackman, Solomon Hancock, Christian Whitmer, Newel Knight, Orson Pratt, Lyman Wight, Thomas B. Marsh and John Murdock. This High Council was organized early in July, 1834. On the 9th the Prophet and his friends set out for Kirtland. And so ended the Zion's Camp expedition.

Work on the Kirtland Temple was now zealously prosecuted. The Saints, as before stated, were poor, and of late their numbers in Ohio had been much diminished by the Missouri emigrations. But all united with a will,—the Prophet and other Elders setting the example by laboring in the quarry or upon the building, while the women sewed, knit, spun and made clothing for the workmen. The walls of the edifice, which were only partly reared when the Missouri expedition took from Kirtland nearly all the bone and sinew of the Church, now that the laborers had returned climbed rapidly toward completion.

The next notable event in Mormon history was the choosing of the Twelve Apostles, the council next in authority to the First Presidency. It took place at Kirtland on Saturday, February 14th, 1835. The survivors of Zion's Camp were that day called to assemble, and the Twelve were selected from their numbers. The choosing was done by the Three Witnesses to the Book of Mormon, after which each Apostle was blessed and set apart by the First Presidency.

The Twelve Apostles were equal in authority, but the order of precedence in council was determined by their ages. According to seniority they ranged as follows: Thomas B. Marsh, David W. Patten, Brigham Young, Heber C. Kimball, Orson Hyde, William E. McLellin, Parley P. Pratt, Luke Johnson, William Smith, Orson Pratt, John F. Boynton, Lyman E. Johnson.

The same month witnessed the selection of the Seventies—assistant Apostles—who were likewise chosen from the ranks of the survivors of Zion's Camp. Two quorums of Seventies were ordained. Their names are here given:

PRESIDENTS.	Alden Burdick,	Alex. Whitesides,
Hazen Aldrich,	Hiram Winters,	George W. Brooks,
Joseph Young,	Hiram Blackman,	Michael Griffith,
Levi W. Hancock,	William D. Pratt,	Royal Barney,
Leonard Rich,	Zera S. Cole,	Libbeus T. Coons,
Zebedee Coltrin,	Jesse Huntsman,	Willard Snow,
Lyman Sherman,	Solomon Angell,	Jesse D. Harmon,
Sylvester Smith.	Henry Herriman,	Heman T. Hyde,
MEMBERS.	Israel Barlow,	Lorenzo D. Barnes,
Elias Hutchings	Jenkins Salisbury,	Hiram Stratton,
Cyrus Smalling,	Nelson Higgins,	Moses Martin,
Levi Gifford,	Harry Brown,	Lyman Smith,
Stephen Winchester,	Jezaniah B. Smith,	Harvey Stanley,
Roger Orton,	Lorenzo Booth,	Almon W. Babbitt,
Peter Buchanan,	Alexander Badlam,	William F. Cahoon,
John D. Parker,	Zerubbabel Snow,	Darwin Richardson,
David Elliot,	Harpin Riggs,	Milo Andrus,
Samuel Brown,	Edson Barney,	True Glidden,
Salmon Warner,	Joseph B. Noble,	Henry Shibley,
Jacob Chapman,	Henry Benner,	Harrison Burgess,
Charles Kelley,	David Evans,	Jedediah M. Grant,
Edmund Fisher,	Nathan B. Baldwin,	Daniel Stevens,
Warren Parrish,	Burr Riggs,	Amasa M. Lyman,
Joseph Hancock.	Lewis Robbins.	George A. Smith.

SECOND QUORUM.

Elijah Fordham,	Samuel Phelps,	Robert Rathburn,
Hyrum Dayton,	Joel McWithy,	Giles Cook,
Joel H. Johnson,	Selah J. Griffin,	John E. Page,
Daniel Wood,	Shadrach Roundy,	William Tenney,
Reuben McBride,	Zera Pulsipher,	Edmund Marvin,
Jonathan Holmes,	King Follett,	Marvel C. Davis,
Lorenzo D. Young,	Joseph Rose,	Almon Shearman,
Wilford Woodruff,	Robert Culbertson,	Isaac H. Bishop,
Jonathan Crosby,	John Young,	Elijah Reed,
Truman O. Angell,	James Foster,	Rufus Fisher,
Chauncey G. Webb,	Salmon Gee,	Dexter Stillman,
Solon Foster,	Nathaniel Millikin,	Thomas Gates,
Erastus Snow,	Gad Yale,	Uriah B. Powell,
Nathan Tanner,	Josiah Butterfield,	Amasa Bonney,
John Gould,	Elias Benner,	Ebenezer Page,
Stephen Starks,	Ariel Stephens,	Loren Babbitt,
Levi Woodruff,	William Perry,	Levi S. Nickerson,
William Carpenter,	Milton Holmes,	Edmund Durfee, jr.
Francis G. Bishop,	James Dalay,	Henry Wilcox,
William Gould,	Arvin A. Avery,	Edmund M. Webb,
Sherman A. Gilbert,	Charles Thompson,	William Miller,
William Redfield,	Joshua Grant,	Stephen Post,
John Herrit,	Andrew J. Squires,	William Bosley.
Jonathan Hampton.		

From the following paragraphs of a revelation on Priesthood the reader may derive all desired information regarding the duties and powers of the various councils and quorums in the Church:*

> There are, in the church, two Priesthoods, namely, the Melchisedek, and Aaronic including the Levitical priesthood.
> Why the first is called the Melchisedek Priesthood, is because Melchisedek was such a great High Priest.
> Before his day it was called *the Holy Priesthood, after the order of the Son of God.*
> But out of respect or reverence to the name of the Supreme Being, to avoid the too frequent repetition of his name, they, the church, in ancient days, called that Priesthood after Melchisedek, or the Melchisedek Priesthood.
> All other authorities or offices in the church are appendages to this Priesthood:
> But there are two divisions or grand heads—one is the Melchisedek Priesthood, and the other is the Aaronic, or Levitical priesthood.

---

* Doctrine and Covenants, Section 107.

The office of an elder comes under the Priesthood of Melchisedek.

The Melchisedek Priesthood holds the right of Presidency, and has power and authority over all the offices in the church in all ages of the world, to administer in spiritual things.

The Presidency of the High Priesthood, after the order of Melchisedek, have a right to officiate in all the offices of the church.

High Priests after the order of the Melchisedek Priesthood, have a right to officiate in their own standing, under the direction of the Presidency, in administering spiritual things; and also in the office of an elder, priest, (of the Levitical order,) teacher, deacon and member.

An elder has a right to officiate in his stead when the High Priest is not present.

The High Priest and elder are to administer in spiritual things, agreeable to the covenants and commandments of the church; and they have a right to officiate in all these offices of the church when there are no higher authorities present.

The second priesthood is called the priesthood of Aaron, because it was conferred upon Aaron and his seed, throughout all their generations.

Why it is called the lesser priesthood, is because it is an appendage to the greater or the Melchisedek Priesthood, and has power in administering outward ordinances.

The bishopric is the presidency of this priesthood and holds the keys or authority of the same.

No man has a legal right to this office, to hold the keys of this priesthood, except he be a literal descendant of Aaron.

But as a High Priest of the Melchisedek Priesthood has authority to officiate in all the lesser offices, he may officiate in the office of bishop when no literal descendant of Aaron can be found, provided he is called and set apart and ordained unto this power by the hands of the Presidency of the Melchisedek Priesthood.

The power and authority of the Higher or Melchisedek Priesthood, is to hold the keys of all the spiritual blessings of the church—

To have the privilege of receiving the mysteries of the kingdom of heaven—to have the heavens opened to them—to commune with the general assembly and church of the first born, and to enjoy the communion and presence of God the Father, and Jesus the Mediator of the new covenant.

The power and authority of the lesser, or Aaronic priesthood, is to hold the keys of the ministering of angels, and to administer in outward ordinances, the letter of the gospel—the baptism of repentance for the remission of sins, agreeable to the covenants and commandments.

Of necessity there are presidents, or presiding offices growing out of, or appointed of or from among those who are ordained to the several offices in those two priesthoods.

Of the Melchisedek Priesthood, three Presiding High Priests, chosen by the body, appointed and ordained to that office, and upheld by the confidence, faith, and prayer of the church, form a quorum of the Presidency of the church.

The Twelve traveling counselors are called to be the Twelve apostles, or special witnesses of the name of Christ in all the world; thus differing from other officers in the church in the duties of their calling.

And they form a quorum, equal in authority and power to the three Presidents previously mentioned.

The seventy are also called to preach the gospel, and to be especial witnesses unto the Gentiles and in all the world. Thus differing from other officers in the church in the duties of their callings;

And they form a quorum equal in authority to that of the Twelve special witnesses or apostles just named.

And every decision made by either of these quorums, must be by the unanimous voice of the same; that is, every member in each quorum must be agreed to its decisions, in order to make their decisions of the same power or validity one with the other.

(A majority may form a quorum, when circumstances render it impossible to be otherwise.)

* * * * * * * * *

The Twelve are a traveling presiding High Council, to officiate in the name of the Lord, under the direction of the Presidency of the church, agreeable to the institution of heaven; to build up the church, and regulate all the affairs of the same in all nations; first unto the Gentiles, and secondly unto the Jews.

The seventy are to act in the name of the Lord, under the direction of the Twelve or the traveling High Council, in building up the Church and regulating all the affairs of the same in all nations—first unto the Gentiles and then unto the Jews;

The Twelve being sent out, holding the keys, to open the door by the proclamation of the gospel of Jesus Christ—and first unto the Gentiles and then unto the Jews.

* * * * * * * * *

Verily, I say unto you, says the Lord of hosts, there must needs be presiding elders to preside over those who are of the office of an elder;

And also priests to preside over those who are of the office of a priest;

And also teachers to preside over those who are of the office of a teacher; in like manner, and also the deacons;

Wherefore, from deacon to teacher, and from teacher to priest, and from priest to elder, severally as they are appointed, according to the covenants and commandments of the church.

Then comes the High Priesthood, which is the greatest of all;

Wherefore it must needs be that one be appointed of the High Priesthood to preside over the Priesthood, and he shall be called President of the High Priesthood of the church;

Or, in other words, the Presiding High Priest over the High Priesthood of the church.

From the same comes the administering of ordinances and blessings upon the church, by the laying on of the hands.

Wherefore the office of a bishop is not equal unto it: for the office of a bishop is in administering all temporal things;

Nevertheless a bishop must be chosen from the High Priesthood, unless he is a literal descendant of Aaron;

For unless he is a literal descendant of Aaron he cannot hold the keys of that priesthood.

Nevertheless, a High Priest that is after the order of Melchisedek, may be set apart unto the ministering of temporal things, having a knowledge of them by the Spirit of truth,

And also to be a judge in Israel, to do the business of the church, to sit in judgment upon transgressors upon testimony as it shall be laid before him according to the laws, by the assistance of his counselors, whom he has chosen, or will choose among the elders of the church.

This is the duty of a bishop who is not a literal descendant of Aaron, but has been ordained to the High Priesthood after the order of Melchisedek.

* * * * * * * * *

But a literal descendant of Aaron has a legal right to the presidency of this priesthood, to the keys of this ministry, to act in the office of bishop independently, without counselors, except in a case where a President of the High Priesthood, after the order of Melchisedek, is tried, to sit as a judge in Israel.

* * * * * * * * *

And again, verily I say unto you, the duty of a president over the office of a deacon is to preside over twelve deacons, to sit in council with them, and to teach them their duty —edifying one another, as it is given according to the covenants.

And also the duty of the president over the office of the teachers is to preside over twenty-four of the teachers, and to sit in council with them, teaching them the duties of their office, as given in the covenants.

Also the duty of the president over the priesthood of Aaron is to preside over forty-eight priests, and sit in council with them, to teach them the duties of their office, as is given in the covenants.

This president is to be a bishop; for this is one of the duties of this priesthood.

Again, the duty of the president over the office of elders is to preside over ninety-six elders, and to sit in council with them, and to teach them according to the covenants.

This presidency is a distinct one from that of the seventy, and is designed for those who do not travel into all the world.

And again, the duty of the President of the office of the High Priesthood is to preside over the whole church, and to be like unto Moses.

* * * * * * * * *

And it is according to the vision, showing the order of the seventy, that they should have seven presidents to preside over them, chosen out of the number of the seventy;

And the seventh president of these presidents is to preside over the six;

And these seven presidents are to choose other seventy besides the first seventy, to whom they belong, and are to preside over them;

And also other seventy, until seven times seventy, if the labor in the vineyard of necessity requires it.

And these seventy are to be traveling ministers unto the Gentiles first, and also unto the Jews;

Whereas other officers of the church, who belong not unto the Twelve, neither to the seventy, are not under the responsibility to travel among all nations, but are to travel as their circumstances shall allow, notwithstanding they may hold as high and responsible offices in the church.

Early in May the Twelve Apostles started upon their first mission. They traveled through the Eastern States and Upper Canada, preaching, baptizing, advising the scattered Saints to gather westward, and collecting means for the purchase of lands in Missouri and the completion of the Kirtland Temple. They went two by two, but met together in councils and conferences at various points. Late in September they returned to Kirtland.

It is often asserted by opponents of Mormonism that the founders of the Church were coarse and illiterate men, and that the system itself fosters ignorance and is opposed to education. The assertion is for the greater part groundless. That many of the early Elders were at the outset of their careers uncultured and unlearned, is true. No Latter-day Saint disputes it. But that Mormonism fosters or favors ignorance, or in any way opposes education, they emphatically deny. "It is impossible to be saved in ignorance." "A man is saved no faster than he gets knowledge." "The glory of God is intelligence." "Seek ye out of the best books words of wisdom; seek learning even by study and also by faith." Sample precepts, these, of Joseph Smith's. No teacher ever taught more plainly that knowledge in any sphere, in or out of the world, is power.

Reference has already been made to the establishment of the School of the Prophets at Kirtland, and its counterpart the School of Elders in Missouri. These were instituted mainly for spiritual culture. Other schools were founded by the Prophet for secular instruction. A grammar school at Kirtland, taught by Sidney Rigdon and William E. McLellin, was supplemented by a school of science and languages, presided over by learned preceptors engaged for that purpose. Professor Seixas, a finished scholar, was one of these. The Prophet and many other Elders attended these schools.

At the age of thirty Joseph Smith was no longer an illiterate youth, but had become, if not a ripe and rounded scholar, at least a proficient student, uniting with the lore of ancient languages the far-seeing wisdom of a statesman and a social philosopher. Later he added to these acquirements a knowledge of law. It was about this time that he translated, from papyrus found upon some mummies brought from the catacombs of Egypt, the record known as the Book of Abraham.

The views of the Prophet and his people on civil government and its relationship with religion are set forth in the following pronunciamento of August, 1835: *

We believe that governments were instituted of God for the benefit of man, and that he holds men accountable for their acts in relation to them, either in making laws or administering them, for the good and safety of society.

We believe that no government can exist in peace, except such laws are framed and held inviolate as will secure to each individual the free exercise of conscience, the right and control of property, and the protection of life.

We believe that all governments necessarily require civil officers and magistrates to enforce the laws of the same, and that such as will administer the law in equity and justice, should be sought for and upheld by the voice of the people (if a republic,) or the will of the sovereign.

We believe that religion is instituted of God, and that men are amenable to him, and to him only, for the exercise of it, unless their religious opinions prompt them to infringe upon the rights and liberties of others; but we do not believe that human law has a right to interfere in prescribing rules of worship to bind the consciences of men, nor dictate forms for public or private devotion; that the civil magistrate should restrain crime, but never control conscience; should punish guilt, but never suppress the freedom of the soul.

We believe that all men are bound to sustain and uphold the respective governments in which they reside, while protected in their inherent and inalienable rights by the laws of such governments; and that sedition and rebellion are unbecoming every citizen thus protected, and should be punished accordingly; and that all governments have a right to enact such laws as in their own judgment are best calculated to secure the public interest, at the same time, however, holding sacred the freedom of conscience.

We believe that every man should be honored in his station: rulers and magistrates as such, being placed for the protection of the innocent, and the punishment of the guilty; and that to the laws, all men owe respect and deference, as without them peace and harmony would be supplanted by anarchy and terror; human laws being instituted for the express purpose of regulating our interests as individuals and nations, between man and man, and

---

* Doctrine and Covenants, Section 134.

divine laws given of heaven, prescribing rules on spiritual concerns, for faith and worship, both to be answered by man to his Maker.

We believe that rulers, states, and governments, have a right, and are bound to enact laws for the protection of all citizens in the free exercise of their religious belief; but we do not believe that they have a right in justice, to deprive citizens of this privilege, or proscribe them in their opinions, so long as a regard and reverence are shown to the laws, and such religious opinions do not justify sedition nor conspiracy.

We believe that the commission of crime should be punished according to the nature of the offence; that murder, treason, robbery, theft, and the breach of the general peace, in all respects, should be punished according to their criminality, and their tendency to evil among men, by the laws of that government in which the offence is committed; and for the public peace and tranquility, all men should step forward and use their ability in bringing offenders against good laws to punishment.

We do not believe it just to mingle religious influence with civil government, whereby one religious society is fostered, and another proscribed in its spiritual privileges, and the individual rights of its members as citizens, denied.

We believe that all religious societies have a right to deal with their members for disorderly conduct according to the rules and regulations of such societies, provided that such dealings be for fellowship and good standing; but we do not believe that any religious society has authority to try men on the right of property or life, to take from them this world's goods, or to put them in jeopardy of either life or limb, neither to inflict any physical punishment upon them, they can only excommunicate them from their society, and withdraw from them their fellowship.

We believe that men should appeal to the civil law for redress of all wrongs and grievances, where personal abuse is inflicted, or the right of property or character infringed, where such laws exist as will protect the same; but we believe that all men are justified in defending themselves, their friends, and property, and the government, from the unlawful assaults and encroachments of all persons, in times of exigency, where immediate appeal cannot be made to the laws, and relief afforded.

We believe it just to preach the gospel to the nations of the earth, and warn the righteous to save themselves from the corruption of the world; but we do not believe it right to interfere with bond servants, neither preach the gospel to, nor baptize them, contrary to the will and wish of their masters, nor to meddle with or influence them in the least, to cause them to be dissatisfied with their situations in this life, thereby jeopardizing the lives of men; such interference we believe to be unlawful and unjust, and dangerous to the peace of every government allowing human beings to be held in servitude.

The Kirtland Temple was dedicated on the 27th of March, 1836. Part of the interior at the time, was in an unfinished state. It had occupied three years in construction, and had cost between sixty and seventy thousand dollars. The dimensions of the edifice were eighty by sixty feet; the walls being fifty-seven feet high to the eaves. It comprised two stories and an attic; the whole surmounted by a tower. The building, which was chiefly of stone, stood upon a hill, and was the most conspicuous object visible for miles.

The main purpose of the temple was the administration of religious ordinances, but it was also designed and used for schools, meetings and councils of the Priesthood. Unlike all temples since erected by the Saints, there was no baptismal font in this building; the ordinance of baptism for the dead—for which such fonts are principally used—not yet being practiced in the Church. We will here state, for the benefit of the uninformed, that the Mormons believe that vicarious work, such as baptisms, confirmations, ordinations, marriages, etc., may be performed by the living for the dead; for their friends and progenitors who died without a knowledge of the gospel. This is one of their chief objects in temple building.

Accounts of many miraculous manifestations are recorded in connection with the Kirtland Temple; among them the following by Joseph Smith and Oliver Cowdery, dated April 3rd, 1836: *

The vail was taken from our minds, and the eyes of our understanding were opened.

We saw the Lord standing upon the breastwork of the pulpit, before us, and under his feet was a paved work of pure gold in color like amber.

His eyes were as a flame of fire, the hair of his head was white like the pure snow, his countenance shone above the brightness of the sun, and his voice was as the sound of the rushing of great waters, even the voice of Jehovah, saying—

I am the first and the last, I am he who liveth, I am he who was slain, I am your advocate with the Father.

Behold, your sins are forgiven you, you are clean before me, therefore lift up your heads and rejoice.

Let the hearts of your brethren rejoice, and let the hearts of all my people rejoice, who have, with their might, built this house to my name.

For behold, I have accepted this house, and my name shall be here, and I will manifest myself to my people in mercy in this house.

Yea, I will appear unto my servants, and speak unto them with mine own voice, if my people will keep my commandments, and do not pollute this holy house.

Yea the hearts of thousands and tens of thousands shall greatly rejoice in consequence of the blessings which shall be poured out, and the endowment with which my servants have been endowed in this house;

---

* Doctrine and Covenants, Section 110.

And the fame of this house shall spread to foreign lands, and this is the beginning of the blessing which shall be poured out upon the heads of my people. Even so. Amen.

After this vision closed, the heavens were again opened unto us, and Moses appeared before us, and committed unto us the keys of the gathering of Israel from the four parts of the earth, and the leading of the ten tribes from the land of the north.

After this, Elias appeared, and committed the dispensation of the gospel of Abraham, saying, that in us, and our seed, all generations after us should be blessed.

After this vision had closed, another great and glorious vision burst upon us, for Elijah the prophet, who was taken to heaven without tasting death, stood before us, and said—

Behold, the time has fully come, which was spoken of by the mouth of Malachi, testifying that he (Elijah) should be sent before the great and dreadful day of the Lord come,

To turn the hearts of the fathers to the children, and the children to the fathers, lest the whole earth be smitten with a curse.

Therefore the keys of this dispensation are committed into your hands, and by this ye may know that the great and dreadful day of the Lord is near, even at the doors.

Among those who came to Kirtland during this period, attracted thither not by the religion of the Saints, but by the advantages for lingual training in the Hebrew school founded by the Prophet, was Lorenzo Snow, a native of Mantua, Portage County, in that State, who had been pursuing his studies at Oberlin College. Lorenzo was then a youth of twenty-two. His sister, Eliza R. Snow, the poetess, had joined the Church in April, 1835, and at the time that her brother came to Kirtland was living in the Prophet's household. Lorenzo was baptized in June, 1836, by Apostle John F. Boynton.

Returning now to the Mormons in Missouri. Expelled with fire and sword from Jackson County in the fall of 1833, they had dwelt since then among the hospitable and kindly disposed people of Clay County. Nearly three years they had dwelt there in peace and amity. Though that section was regarded by them as only a temporary abiding place, where they awaited the day when law and justice should restore them to their former homes, they had nevertheless secured lands, purchased or erected dwellings, workshops, etc., and were receiving constant accessions to their numbers by immigration. With these peaceful and legitimate pursuits little or no fault had hitherto been found.

But now a change had come. The people of Clay County had

partaken in a measure of the anti-Mormon spirit which reigned in Jackson. The Saints were on the eve of another exodus, another general abandonment of their homes; though not threatened, as before, with "fire and brand and hostile hand," with robbery and expulsion from the roofs which of late had sheltered them. They had been requested, however, to remove as a community from Clay County, and "seek some other abiding place, where the manners, the habits and customs of the people would be more consonant with their own." Such was the action taken regarding them by a mass meeting of reputable citizens which convened at Liberty on the 29th of June, 1836.

No charge of crime had been preferred against the Mormons. It was not claimed that they had infringed upon the rights of their fellow citizens, broken the laws of the land, or been wanting in respect and loyalty to the local or the general government. True, the old charges were afloat of what they intended doing, what their opinions were on the negro and Indian questions, etc., and these, with their continuous immigrations into the county, were doubtless among the chief reasons for the change of sentiment concerning them. The men of Jackson County too, were constantly sowing the seeds of ill-will between the old settlers of Clay County and the Mormons. Doubtless some of the latter,—for there are cranks and criminals among all peoples,—warranted the adverse opinions formed respecting them. But this, despite the fly-in-the-ointment proverb, ought not to have condemned the whole community.

Yet they were not accused of crime, of any overt act against peace and good order. It was argued merely that "they were eastern men, whose manners, habits, customs and even dialect, were essentially different" from those of the Missourians; that they were "non-slaveholders, and opposed to slavery;" and that their religious tenets were "so different from the present churches of the age" that they "always had, and always would, excite deep prejudices against them in any populous country where they might locate." Such a prejudice, it was claimed, had taken root in Clay County, and had grown into "a feeling of hostility that the first spark might ignite into all the horrors and desolations of a civil war."

Hence, in the spirit of mediation, with an earnest desire to avert such a calamity for the sake of all, had the mass meeting spoken. Such was its candid and no doubt truthful claim. "We do not contend," said these citizens of Clay County, "that we have the least right, under the constitution and laws of the country to expel them (the Mormons) by force. * * * We only ask them, for their own safety and for ours, to take the least of the two evils." The "least evil" in question was that no more Mormons should settle in Clay County, and that those already there should remove to some other place at as early a period as possible.

Though perfectly aware that in complying with this request they would surrender some of their dearest rights as American citizens, and that if they saw fit they might entrench themselves behind the bulwark of the Constitution and defy their opponents to legally dislodge them, for the sake of peace and through a sense of gratitude for former kindness, the Mormons decided to make the required sacrifice and leave the county. First, however, they determined to put upon record their denial of the charges afloat concerning them.

At a meeting held on July 1st, presided over by William W. Phelps, a preamble and resolutions were reported by a committee previously appointed for the purpose. Therein the Mormons expressed gratitude and good will toward the people of Clay County for past kindness; denied having any claim to lands further than they purchased with money, or more than they were allowed to possess under the Constitution and laws of the country; denied being abolitionists, or that they were holding communications with the Indians, and affirmed their fealty to the government, its laws and institutions. They agreed, however, for the sake of peace and friendship, to comply with the requisitions of the mass meeting held in June.

Within three months they were on their way, migrating, after selling out at a sacrifice, to the spot selected as the site of their new home. It was known as the Shoal Creek region, comprising the upper part of Ray County, north and east of Clay. It was a wilderness, almost entirely unoccupied, seven men only inhabiting its solitudes. These were bee-hunters. The Mormons purchased their possessions, pre-empted other lands in the vicinity, and were left the sole occupants of that region. Here, in this isolated spot, where the question of social and religious differences could not well arise, at least for the present, they hoped to dwell unmolested, worshiping God in their own way,—in the way that they believed He had commanded.

In December, 1836, in response to their petition, the Legislature of Missouri incorporated the Shoal Creek region and some adjoining lands containing a few settlers, as a separate county, to which was given the name of Caldwell. The Mormons were permitted to organize the county government and select its officers. Here the Saints settled in large numbers, and founded during the winter of 1836-7 the city of Far West.

CHAPTER IX.
1836-1838.

THE KIRTLAND APOSTASY—THE TEMPORAL AT WAR WITH THE SPIRITUAL—FINANCIAL DISASTERS—"SOMETHING NEW MUST BE DONE TO SAVE THE CHURCH"—OPENING OF THE BRITISH MISSION—HEBER C. KIMBALL AND HIS CONFRERES IN LANCASHIRE—MARVELOUS SUCCESS OF MORMONISM ABROAD—AFFAIRS AT KIRTLAND CONTINUED—A DARK HOUR—BRIGHAM YOUNG'S FIDELITY—JOHN TAYLOR—SETTING IN ORDER THE CHURCH—FLIGHT OF THE PROPHET AND HIS FRIENDS FROM KIRTLAND—THE CHURCH REMOVES TO MISSOURI—EXCOMMUNICATIONS—NEW CALLS TO THE APOSTLESHIP—THE LAW OF TITHING INSTITUTED.

WHILE the events last narrated were occurring in Missouri, affairs at Kirtland had been hastening to a crisis. A spirit essentially antagonistic to the genius of religion,—opposed to the success of any great spiritual movement such as Mormonism, had crept into the Church and was playing havoc with the faith and once fervent zeal of many of its members.

The spirit of speculation, then so prevalent throughout the nation; the greed of worldly gain, so fatal to religious enthusiasm in all ages, was rapidly permeating the Mormon community at Kirtland, cooling the spiritual ardor of the Saints, and diverting the minds of many followers of the Prophet from the aims and purposes for which they had renounced "the world" to become his associates and disciples.

Even some of the leading Elders,—Apostles, High Priests and Seventies,—whose especial mission, unless otherwise directed by their superiors, was to administer in spiritual things, were neglecting the duties enjoined upon them and plucking greedily the golden fruit that hung so temptingly from the tree of mammon. Reproved for their remissness by the Prophet, they became angry, and falling away from their fealty to Joseph, sowed the seeds of disaffection among their friends and sympathizers.

Thus occurred the first serious apostasy in the Church. Before it was over, about half the council of the Apostles, one of the First Presidency and many other prominent Elders had become disaffected, and some of them bitterly hostile to the Prophet and all who adhered to him. Outside enemies were not slow to take advantage of this situation, and unite with the Church's internal foes in various schemes for its destruction.

The Kirtland "boom"—as it would now be styled—began in the summer or fall of 1836, and during the following winter and spring went rushing and roaring on toward the whirlpool of financial ruin that soon swallowed it. The all-prevailing desire to amass wealth did not confine itself to mercantile pursuits, real estate dealings, and other branches of business of a legitimate if much inflated character, but was productive of "wild-cat" schemes of every description, enterprises in every respect fraudulent, designed as traps for the unwary.

An effort was made by the Prophet, who foresaw the inevitable disaster that awaited, to stem the tide of recklessness and corruption now threatening to sweep everything before it. For this purpose the Kirtland Safety Society was organized, the main object of which was to control the prevailing sentiment and direct it in legitimate channels. The Prophet and some of his staunchest supporters became officers and members of this association.

The career of the Kirtland Bank was very brief. Unable to collect its loans, victimized by counterfeiters, and robbed by some of its own officials—subordinates having charge of the funds—it soon collapsed. A heroic effort was made to save it. Well-to-do members of the Church beggared themselves to buy up the bank's floating paper and preserve its credit.* But in vain. In common with many other banks and business houses throughout the country,—for it was a

---

* Isaac Decker, a prosperous farmer, was one of these.

year of general financial disaster,—it went down in the ruinous crash of 1837.

Another opportunity was thus given to heap censure upon the Prophet; an opportunity of which his enemies, in and out of the Church, quickly availed themselves. As a matter of fact Joseph had withdrawn from the Society some time before, not being satisfied with the way events were shaping. It mattered not. Someone had done wrong, and someone must be blamed. As usual the most prominent target was the one fired at. Before this, however, so intense had become the feeling against the Prophet at Kirtland, that it was almost as much as one's life was worth to defend him against his accusers. Affairs with Mormonism had reached a culminating point, where it was evident—to use the Prophet's own words—that "something new must be done for the salvation of the Church."

Joseph Smith believed,—as all men must, into whose ideas the philosophy of the divine Nazarene enters,—that the spiritual must save the temporal; that life alone can redeem from death. Consequently, he knew that in the crisis now reached,—a stagnation of the spiritual life-blood of the Church,—a strong reactionary movement was essential to its resuscitation. Too much care for the temporal, with a corresponding neglect of the spiritual, had nearly proved the ruin of Mormonism. The supremacy of the spiritual over the temporal,—the basic and crowning principle of the salvation offered by Jesus Christ,—must needs be emphasized and reasserted. At this period, therefore, the Prophet planned and executed a project as a measure of rescue from the ruin which seemed impending. It was to send his Apostles across the sea and plant the standard of Mormonism upon the shores of Europe.

Hitherto the labors of the Elders had been confined to various parts of the United States and Upper Canada. Into that province such men as Brigham and Joseph Young, Orson Pratt, Parley P. Pratt and even the Prophet himself had penetrated and made many converts. Parley P. Pratt's missions to Canada had been especially productive. Among his converts in the city of Toronto, in the spring or summer of 1836, was John Taylor, afterwards an Apostle, and the third President of the Church. But as yet no foreign mission had been attempted. Indeed, at that time, when the age of steamships and railways was in its infancy, and months instead of days were consumed in crossing the Atlantic, the idea of a voyage over the ocean was to ordinary minds little less awe-inspiring and miraculous than a projected flight to the moon. To send the Elders to Great Britain, however, and "open the door of salvation to that nation," was the plan conceived by the Prophet early in the summer of 1837.

The Apostle chosen to stand at the head of this important mission was Heber C. Kimball, a staunch friend of Joseph's, a man unlettered, but possessed of much native ability and mental and physical force. His companion Apostle was Orson Hyde, better educated and considerable of an orator. Orson was a native of Oxford, New Haven County, Connecticut, where he was born on the 8th of January, 1805. Another of the party was Elder Willard Richards, a cousin to Brigham Young, late of Berkshire County, Massachusetts, who had but recently joined the Church. Willard was the pioneer of the numerous and distinguished Richards family in Mormonism.

The other members of the mission were Joseph Fielding, a Canadian convert, Isaac Russell, John Goodson and John Snider. The last three were now in Canada.

Apostle Kimball and the others left Kirtland on the 13th of June. Being joined by the Canadian party in New York, they sailed from that port July 1st, on board the packet *Garrick* bound for Liverpool.

It is not our purpose in these pages to give a detailed account of the rise and progress of the British Mission,—the first and so far greatest foreign mission established by the Latter-day Saints,— nor of the various missions which radiated from and grew out of it. Such a work would necessarily fill volumes. Only the main incidents of that wonderfully successful missionary movement,—which was destined to bring into the Church and emigrate to America, from

Great Britain alone, between fifty and seventy-five thousand souls,—can here be touched upon.

Landing at Liverpool on July 20th, 1837, the day that Queen Victoria ascended the throne, Apostle Kimball and his confreres tarried two days in that city, and then repaired by coach to Preston, thirty miles distant. There Joseph Fielding had a brother, the pastor of a church, who had previously been informed by letter from Joseph and other relatives in Canada, of the rise and spread of Mormonism in America. He opened his church—Vauxhall Chapel—to the Elders, who, the day after their arrival at Preston, it being the Sabbath, preached from his pulpit the first sermons delivered by Mormon Elders on the eastern hemisphere.

Baptisms soon followed, then the usual opposition,—though of a much less violent character than had been experienced in some parts of America. The Reverend James Fielding, the first to welcome the Elders and extend to them ministerial courtesy, was also the first to withdraw from them the hand of friendship. Learning that some of his flock had been converted by their preaching, and had applied to them for baptism, he quickly closed his pulpit against the Elders and was thenceforth their bitter opponent. Later, the Reverend Robert Aitken, a famous minister of that period, entered the lists against them. Nothing daunted, for they were inured to such treatment, the Elders betook themselves to the streets and public squares, preaching in the open air to vast crowds—tradesmen, laborers, factory hands, farmers, etc.,—that thronged from all sides to hear them. They also addressed audiences in private houses, that were opened for their accommodation. More opposition ensued, and greater success followed.

From Preston, having there gained a foothold, the missionaries, separating, passed into other counties. Richards and Goodson went to the city of Bedford, Russell and Snider to Alston, in Cumberland, while the two Apostles with Joseph Fielding remained to spread the work in Preston and introduce it into other towns and villages of Lancashire.

Everywhere success attended them,—success nothing short of marvelous. Whole villages were converted at a sweep, and fresh friends flocked round them almost daily. The people as a rule were very poor, and the Elders, themselves penniless, preaching "without purse or scrip," and most of the time laboring arduously, suffered many privations. But there was no dearth of warm hearts and willing hands, and though the fare was often less than frugal, the shelter never so scant, the guests whom these poor people delighted to honor were ever welcome to the best and most of it.

Sunday, July 30th, 1837—the tenth day of the Elders on British soil—witnessed their first baptisms, nine in number, in the river Ribble, which runs through Preston. Sunday, April 8th, 1838, a little over eight months afterward, at a conference held there prior to the return of the Apostles to America, their total following in that land was reported at about two thousand souls. Three-fourths of these had been converted by one man,—the unlettered but magnetic Apostle, Heber C. Kimball. Twenty-six branches of the Church were represented. Thus was laid the foundation of the British Mission.

Apostles Kimball and Hyde with Elder Russell on the 20th of April sailed from Liverpool aboard the *Garrick*, homeward bound. Joseph Fielding was left to preside over the British Mission, with Willard Richards and William Clayton as his counselors. Clayton was an English convert. Goodson and Snider—the former being disaffected—had returned to America some months before.

On the 12th of May the returning Apostles landed at New York. There they met Orson Pratt, who, with his brother Parley, had succeeded after much labor in raising up a branch of the Church in that city. Parley's celebrated work, the *Voice of Warning*, which was destined to convert thousands to Mormonism, had been published there the year before. Two days after landing, the Kimball party proceeded on to Kirtland, arriving there on the 22nd of May.

Returning now to the summer of 1837. While Mormonism had been prospering abroad, what had been its fortunes in America? The tidal wave of disaffection still swept over Kirtland. The Mormon leader was denounced as "a fallen prophet" by men who had been his trusted friends and associates. A plot was formed to depose him from the Presidency and put another in his stead. Concerned in this conspiracy were several of the Apostles and some of the witnesses to the Book of Mormon. Their choice for Joseph's successor was David Whitmer, one of the Three Witnesses.

Heber C. Kimball, when appointed to his foreign mission, had asked the Prophet if Brigham Young might go with him. The answer was: "No; I want him to stay with me. I have something else for him to do."

Doubtless it was well for Joseph and for Mormonism in general that he decided to keep by him at that time the lion heart and intrepid soul of Brigham Young. Firm as a rock in his fealty to his chief, he combined sound judgment, keen perception, with courage unfaltering and sublime. Like lightning were his intuitions, his decisions between right and wrong; like thunder his denunciations of what his soul conceived was error. A man for emergencies, far-sighted and inspirational; a master spirit and natural leader of men.

Well might Joseph,—brave almost to rashness,—whose genius, though lofty and general in its scope, was pre-eminently spiritual, while Brigham's was pronouncedly practical, wish to have near him at such a time, just such a man. In that dark hour,—the darkest perhaps that Mormonism has seen,—when its very foundations seemed crumbling, when men supposed to be its pillars were weakening and falling away, joining hands secretly or openly with its enemies, the man Brigham never faltered, never failed in his allegiance to his leader, never ceased defending him against his accusers, and as boldly denouncing them betimes for falsehood, selfishness and treachery. His life was imperilled by his boldness. He heeded not, but steadily held on his way, an example of valor and fidelity, a faithful friend, *sans peur et sans reproche*.

Among others who stood loyal to the Prophet was John Taylor.

the future Apostle and President, who arrived at Kirtland from his home in Canada in the latter part of 1837. It was in Toronto, during August of that year, that Joseph Smith and John Taylor had first met. Seven years later they stood side by side in an Illinois dungeon, facing an infuriate mob, together receiving the bullets,—fatal to Joseph, well-nigh fatal to John,—which reddened with their mingled life-blood the floor of Carthage jail.

Soon after the Prophet's return from Canada, a return rendered barely possible by mobs lying in wait to attack him, a conference was held at Kirtland and steps taken to purge the disaffected element from the various councils of the Priesthood. It was Sunday, September 3rd, 1837. On that day the Church voted with uplifted hands to sustain in office the following named Elders: Joseph Smith, junior, as President of the Church; Sidney Rigdon as his first counselor; Oliver Cowdery, Joseph Smith, senior, Hyrum Smith and John Smith, as assistant counselors; Thomas B. Marsh, David W. Patten, Brigham Young, Heber C. Kimball, Orson Hyde, Parley P. Pratt, Orson Pratt, William Smith and William E. McLellin as members of the council of the Apostles; John Gaylord, James Foster, Salmon Gee, Daniel S. Miles, Joseph Young, Josiah Butterfield and Levi Hancock, as Presidents of Seventies, and Newel K. Whitney as Bishop of Kirtland, with Reynolds Cahoon and Jared Carter as his counselors.

Frederick G. Williams, one of the First Presidency; Luke S. and Lyman E. Johnson and John F. Boynton, three of the Apostles, and John Gould, one of the Presidents of Seventies, were rejected. Five members of the High Council were also objected to by the people, and new ones appointed in their stead.

Affairs of a similar nature, with other business pertaining to the settlement of the Saints in their new gathering place, now summoned the Prophet to Missouri. In company with Elder Rigdon and others he left Kirtland on September 27th, and reached Far West about the 1st of November. On the 7th of that month a conference was held there, at which the general and local Church authorities were presented, as usual, to the congregation. Frederick G. Williams, being rejected as one of the First Presidency, Hyrum Smith, the Prophet's brother, was chosen in his stead. The local presidency, David Whitmer, John Whitmer and William W. Phelps, after some consideration were retained in office, as were also the members of the High Council. Bishop Edward Partridge and his counselors, Isaac Morley and Titus Billings, were likewise sustained. It was decided, during the Prophet's stay, to enlarge the plat of Far West to two miles square. About the 10th of November he started back to Kirtland, arriving there a month later.

During his absence Warren Parrish, John F. Boynton, Joseph Coe and others had dissented from the Church, and aided and abetted by prominent Elders in Missouri, were now conspiring for its overthrow. In every way possible they sought to induce others to join them. Brigham Young's only reply was to denounce them. Wilford Woodruff, likewise approached, remained immovable. John Taylor stood staunchly by Joseph. As for Heber C. Kimball, Orson Hyde and Willard Richards, they had given their answer in June, when they accepted a call to cross the Atlantic and herald on Europe's shores the advent of a restored Gospel, and a latter-day Prophet in the person of Joseph Smith. The Pratt brothers, Bishop Whitney and many more threw in their lot with the Prophet, while others equally prominent forsook him.

Soon after his return from Missouri, the dissenters at Kirtland boldly came out, proclaiming themselves the Church of Christ, "the old standard," and denouncing Joseph and his followers as heretics. Then came the climax. Threatened with assassination, their lives in imminent jeopardy, the Church leaders were finally compelled to flee. Brigham Young, to escape the fury of a mob which had sworn to kill him, left Kirtland on the 22nd of December. He directed his course toward Missouri. Less than three weeks later the Prophet and Elder Rigdon fled also. Their flight being discovered, they were pursued by armed men a distance of two hundred miles, narrowly escaping capture. The Prophet and his party, including Brigham Young and others who had joined him, reached Far West about the middle of March, 1838.

Several weeks before, a general assembly of the Saints had convened there for the purpose of setting in order the Church in Missouri. David Whitmer, John Whitmer and William W. Phelps, the local presidency, whose conduct for some time had not been satisfactory to the people, were now suspended from office. Subsequently they were severed from the Church. William W. Phelps soon returned, but the Whitmer brothers were never again connected with the cause.

The Prophet having arrived, the work of "setting in order" continued. Evidently a clean sweep had been determined on. The Church, so nearly brought to ruin by apostates in Ohio, insomuch that a general exodus of the Saints from that state was now necessary, could no longer afford to harbor within its fold the disaffected element, indifferent to or bent upon its destruction. The tree, in order to live, must be pruned of its dead branches.

Doubtless this end was in view when, at the April conference of 1838, Thomas B. Marsh, Brigham Young and David W. Patten were chosen to preside over the Church in Missouri. Under their administration the work of pruning went vigorously on. Neither high nor low were spared, except they speedily brought forth "fruits of repentance." The excommunicating axe even lopped some of the loftiest limbs. Oliver Cowdery, David Whitmer, Martin Harris, Luke S. and Lyman E. Johnson, John F. Boynton and William E. McLellin were all deprived of membership in the Church during this period. Luke Johnson afterwards returned, and became one of the Utah pioneers of 1847. Oliver Cowdery and Martin Harris also rejoined the Church many years later, but the others were never again identified with Mormonism. The vacancies in the council of the Twelve caused by the excommunication of Elders Boynton, McLellin and the Johnson brothers, were filled by the calling of John Taylor, John E. Page, Wilford Woodruff and Willard Richards to the Apostleship.

The departure of the Church leaders from Kirtland had been the signal for a general migration of the Mormons from Ohio to

Missouri. Far West was now their gathering place,—not their Zion, but only a stake of Zion, as Kirtland had been before. All during the spring and summer of 1838 the exodus continued, until the Saints remaining at Kirtland were very few. Apostles Kimball and Hyde, arriving there from Europe in May, tarried only long enough to arrange their affairs and make suitable preparations for their journey to Missouri. About the 1st of July the two Apostles, accompanied by Erastus Snow, Winslow Farr and others, with their families, set out for Far West. Among those remaining at Kirtland were Bishop N. K. Whitney and Oliver Granger, who had charge of the Church property in Ohio.

At Far West, on the 8th of July, the law of tithing was instituted as a standing law of the Church. Hitherto it had been practiced only by individuals. Its observance was now obligatory upon all, officers as well as members.

This event signalized the discontinuance of the United Order, which had practically been dissolved some time before. According to that system, which, as has been shown, the Saints yet hope to establish, the members of the community consecrated their all, and each, being given a stewardship, with his or her support, labored unitedly for the common weal. The law of tithing, which bears about the same relation to the Order of Enoch as the Mosaic law to the gospel of Christ, required of them as individual possessors, (1) all their surplus property, to be placed in the hands of the Bishop and by him cared and accounted for; (2) one tenth of all their interest annually.

The fund thus created was for the support of the Priesthood,—such as devoted their whole time to the service of the Church,—the building of temples and for public purposes in general. From the first, however, much of the tithing fund, together with special offerings for that purpose, was expended to support the helpless poor. Such was and is the law of tithing, instituted in July, 1838, and observed by the Church of Jesus Christ of Latter-day Saints to this day.

CHAPTER X.
1838-1839.

THE MORMONS IN MISSOURI—FAR WEST, DIAHMAN AND DEWITT—A SLUMBERING VOLCANO—CELEBRATING THE NATION'S BIRTHDAY—THE STATE ELECTION—ATTEMPT TO PREVENT MORMONS FROM VOTING—THE GALLATIN RIOT—THE VOLCANO AWAKES—DAVIESS COUNTY IN ARMS—JOSEPH SMITH AND LYMAN WIGHT ARRESTED—THE MOB ARMY THREATENS DIAHMAN—THE MORMONS ARM IN SELF-DEFENSE—GENERALS ATCHISON, PARKS AND DONIPHAN—THE SAINTS EXONERATED—SIEGE AND BOMBARDMENT OF DEWITT—GOVERNOR BOGGS APPEALED TO—HE DECLINES TO INTERFERE—DEWITT EVACUATED AND DIAHMAN AGAIN THREATENED—GILLIAM'S GUERILLAS—THE MORMON MILITIA MAKE WAR UPON THE MOB—THE DANITES—BATTLE OF CROOKED RIVER—DEATH OF DAVID W. PATTEN—GOVERNOR BOGGS ESPOUSES THE CAUSE OF THE MOBOCRATS—THE MORMONS TO BE "EXTERMINATED OR DRIVEN FROM THE STATE"—THE HAUN'S MILL MASSACRE—FALL OF FAR WEST—THE MORMON LEADERS IN CHAINS—LIBERTY JAIL—THE EXODUS TO ILLINOIS.

THE Mormons in Missouri in the summer of 1838 numbered in the neighborhood of twelve thousand souls. All were not located in Caldwell County. Lands had been purchased or pre-empted by them in other places as well. In two of the counties contiguous to Caldwell, namely: Daviess on the north, and Carroll on the east, in parts previously unoccupied or but thinly peopled, they had founded flourishing settlements. In Daviess County, as in Caldwell, a stake of Zion was organized.

Their chief settlement in Daviess County was Adam-ondi-Ahman,*—abbreviated to Diahman; the one in Carroll County, Dewitt. Good order, sobriety and industry prevailed, and peace and prosperity were everywhere manifest. "Heaven smiles upon the Saints in Caldwell," wrote the Prophet at the time, and even in parts where they were

---

* So named, said the Prophet, because Adam, who dwelt there after being driven from Eden, would there sit, as Ancient of Days, fulfilling the vision of Daniel. The Garden of Eden, Joseph Smith declared, was in Jackson County, Missouri.

not, as there, politically dominant, they were thriving and dwelling in amity with their neighbors.

But all this must soon change. The old fires were but smouldering. The volcano only slept. Beneath the fair frail crust of outside seeming lurked the burning lava streams,—the pitiless torrent of human hate,—about to be belched forth in whelming ruin upon the hapless Saints. Missouri, in spite of every promise and fair prospect,—whatever the far future might develop,—was not yet to be their permanent abiding place. Inexorable fate with iron finger pointed elsewhere. Destiny, for these sons and daughters of the Pilgrims, had other fortunes in store. History,—the history of religion in quest of liberty, wading in its search through rivers of blood and tears,—for the hundredth time was preparing to repeat itself.

July 4th, that day of days, in the year 1838 was celebrated at Far West with great rejoicings. Thousands of the Saints assembled from the surrounding districts to witness and participate in the proceedings in honor of the nation's birthday. Yes, these "disloyal" Mormons,—for disloyal even then they were deemed,—many of whom might trace their life-stream back to its parent lake in the bosom of patriots of the Revolution, came together, erected a liberty-pole, unfurled the stars and stripes, sacred emblem of the success and sufferings of their heroic ancestors, and worshiped gratefully beneath its glorious folds the God of truth and freedom.

True, it was but their custom so to do, as it has continued their custom ever since. But such had been their past experience, deprived as many of them had been of that liberty for which their forefathers contended, and such was their present situation, as to render the occasion one of peculiar interest. Robbed of their rights, despoiled and trampled on, for daring to believe as conscience dictated, and exercise as American freemen the privileges guaranteed by a Constitution which they believed to be God-inspired, instituted for their especial protection, small wonder that some of the sentiments uttered that day, a day on which patriotism is prone to take unusual and oft-times extravagant flights, did not smack entirely of saintly meekness.

"We take God to witness," cried Sidney Rigdon, in a burst of heated eloquence, "and the holy angels to witness THIS DAY, that we warn all men in the name of Jesus Christ to come on us no more forever. The man or the set of men who attempt it do it at the expense of their lives; and the mob that comes on us to disturb us, there shall be between us and them a war of extermination, for we will follow them till the last drop of their blood is spilled, or else they will have to exterminate us."

Censure such sentiments, Christian reader, if you will. Fault-finding is easy, and human nature, the world over, weak and censurable. But the provocation, in such cases, should in all fairness be considered.

The foundations of a temple at Far West were likewise laid that day; the Saints thus emphasizing their determination to establish in that place a permanent stake of Zion. Why that temple was not built, nor another temple, projected at Diahman, we have yet in detail to explain.

Among the numerous charges preferred against the Mormon people, by those who seek to justify or extenuate the harsh treatment to which they have at various times been subjected, is that of "meddling in politics." Parallel with this runs the charge of "voting solidly" for the candidates of their choice.

If by meddling in politics is meant—as we assume it must mean —practicing or participating in politics, the science of government, there is little doubt that the defendant community, if arraigned on such a charge, would promptly plead guilty. Moreover, they would very likely inquire if the right of any class of American citizens, no matter to what creed or church attached, to wield the ballot and peacefully strive to put in office the persons of their choice, could legally or morally be called in question? As to "voting solidly," they would probably plead guilty again, but they might ask who was responsible for it in their case,—for the unity and compactness of an oppressed people at the polls? Outside pressure, they would maintain,—the principle that even in an urchin's hands forms from a few loose feathery flakes the snow-ball and moulds it into a lump of ice,—was so responsible. A common peril, they would argue, will unite and ought to unite any people, any nation, savage or civilized.

To this extent the Mormons would admit having "meddled in politics." They would doubtless freely concede that they had generally "voted solid" to insure the election of their friends and the defeat of their enemies.

But, some will say, it is not the right of the Mormon people, as American citizens, to engage in politics that is questioned. It is the right of their leaders to control their political actions that is disputed. It is believed that their Apostles and Bishops wield undue influence over them in such matters; that there is a union of Church and State among them, and that the people are not left free to vote as they please.

These allegations the Mormons emphatically deny. They maintain that their leaders have never sought to wield more influence over them in political affairs than prominent men in every community exercise over the masses who naturally look to them for guidance and instruction. They deny that a union of Church and State has ever existed among them, but they affirm that it has practically existed among those who find fault with them on that score,—the priests and politicians who have repeatedly joined hands, on the stump, and even in the halls of Congress, to create anti-Mormon legislation.

They admit that their Apostles and Bishops have sometimes given political advice, though not as Apostles and Bishops, but as American citizens, with a free opinion and the right to voice that opinion. They admit, too, that in Mormon communities Church officials have often been elected to civil offices; yet not because they were Church officials, but simply the best men that could be found in whom the people had confidence; men who knew how to be just and fair, and would separate their civil from their ecclesiastical functions.

In the Mormon Church, it should be remembered, nearly every man is an Elder, and it would be next to impossible to nominate from among them a man who did not hold some order of priesthood.

They claim that while in communities strictly Mormon, Mormons have necessarily held all the offices, that in mixed communities where they predominated they have allowed the minority a fair representation. They admit that in places where they themselves were in the minority they have asked the same privilege, demanding it as a right, and when necessary have banded together to secure that right. They admit having used the balance of power, which at times they have found themselves possessed of, to put in office, regardless of party affiliations, men of capacity and integrity, their friends in lieu of their enemies.

If this be "meddling in politics" the Mormons, like all other American citizens, have undoubtedly so meddled; and they do not deny it.

It was just such an event as this,—their voting or trying to vote for their friends and against their foes,—that formed the prologue to the appalling tragedy, which, beginning with outrage, robbery and rapine, ended in murder, massacre, and the eventual expulsion—a mid-winter exodus—of the entire Mormon community from Missouri.

It was the 6th of August, 1838, and the state election was in progress. To Gallatin, the principal town of Daviess County, went twelve Mormon citizens for the purpose of casting their ballots. Colonel William P. Peniston was a candidate in that district for representative to the Legislature. Having been prominent in the anti-Mormon agitation, preceding the moderate action of the mediators, in Clay County, he had good reason to believe that the people whom he would have driven from their homes did not design aiding him with their suffrages. He had therefore organized a mob, and now harangued them at the polls, to prevent the Mormons from voting. Mounting a barrel, he poured out upon them a torrent of abuse, styling them "horse-thieves and robbers" and proclaiming his opposition to their settling in that region or being allowed to vote. He admitted having headed a mob to drive them from Clay County, and declared that he would not now interfere to prevent a similar fate befalling them. He also attacked their religion, denouncing as "a d———d lie" their profession of healing the sick by the laying on of hands.

What all this had to do with the right of the Mormons to vote, and to vote if they wished against William P. Peniston, is not very apparent at this time, nor was it, we opine, even then. But the tirade had its desired and designed effect. The Mormons, pronouncing his charges false, insisted upon their right to vote. Immediately Peniston's party, crazed with drink and furious with rage, set upon them. The twelve Mormons, attacked by over a hundred men, stoutly defended themselves. Clubs, stones and fists were freely used, and even knives were unsheathed by some of the assailants. In the melee, though no lives were lost, some on both sides were wounded, and several mobocratic heads were broken. The Mormons withdrew from the scene, and the election proceeded.

This event, supplemented by incendiary speeches and articles in the local press, caused a general anti-Mormon uprising. All Daviess County was aroused, and even in parts adjacent, as ran the exaggerated rumor of the riot at Gallatin, the Missourians began arming and organizing. For what? They scarcely knew,—ignorant dupes as most of them were, tools of designing demagogues, of men without principle, who saw, as such characters quickly see, in a popular movement against an unpopular people, opportunities for plunder and promotion.

Social and religious as well as political lines were sharply drawn. Old charges, oft-denied, were reiterated, and new ones brought forth and made to do yeoman service in the cause of the coming crusade. The priest, the politician and the apostate again joined hands, like the three weird sisters in Macbeth, each putting in his quota of terrible tales to make the cauldron of the people's hatred "boil and bubble."

As the excitement grew and hostilities began, hordes of red-handed desperadoes, refugees from justice,—a class commonly found on the frontier,—scenting the conflict from afar, came pouring into Daviess and Caldwell counties, like vultures flocking to the shambles. Some of these painted and disguised themselves as Indians,—the better, no doubt, to escape detection for past and future crimes. The leader of these pseudo savages was Cornelius Gilliam, formerly sheriff of Clay County, who styled himself "the Delaware chief."

Efforts were early made to avert the bloody crisis that was felt to be approaching. Good and wise men on both sides met and signed a covenant of peace, agreeing to maintain the right and use their influence to allay the unwarrantable agitation. Among these were Lyman Wight, John Smith, Vinson Knight and Reynolds Cahoon, who signed for the Mormons of Daviess County; and Joseph Morin, senator-elect, John Williams, representative-elect, James P. Turner, clerk of the circuit court, and others representing the older settlers.

But all in vain. The Missourians, misled and thoroughly prejudiced, were for war, not peace. The excitement continued to increase, until finally nothing but bloodshed or the banishment of the hated Mormons would suffice.

Adam Black, an illiterate politician, though a justice of the peace for Daviess County, was visited on the 8th of August, two days after the election, by Joseph Smith and Lyman Wight, and requested, as other prominent men had been, to sign an agreement of peace. He acceded to their request, writing and signing a document amicable in tone, if well-nigh illegible in character, and immediately afterwards circulated the report that his signature had been secured by threats of violence.

On the complaint of Colonel Peniston, the mob leader at Gallatin, Joseph Smith and Lyman Wight were arrested, charged not only with intimidating Judge Black, but with collecting a large body of armed men in Daviess County, to drive out the older settlers and despoil them of their lands. Tried before Judge Austin A. King, at Gallatin, early in September, nothing was proven against the two defendants. Judge King, they claimed, admitted as much to them in private, but deemed it politic to bind them over in the sum of $500.

That the Mormons in Daviess County had been arming themselves, was doubtless true. True also that they had been receiving reinforcements from other places. The Missourians, their neighbors, had been doing precisely the same things, and threatening them daily with attack. Already had they driven some Mormons from their homes and compelled them to seek safety with their friends at Diahman. Remembering their experience in Jackson County, when, being unarmed, they were trampled on without mercy by the mob, the Saints, as Sidney Rigdon had declared, did not propose to tamely submit to a repetition of such outrages. They were determined to maintain their rights, and defend to the death, if need be, their hard earned homes and the peace and safety of their families.

But this was their only purpose—self-defense; a fact subsequently affirmed by the chief officers of the State militia, sent to suppress the insurrection. To say that the Mormons contemplated wholesale robbery and expulsion—the infliction upon their fellow settlers of wrongs similar to what they themselves had suffered in Jackson County, and for which they were still hoping redress, and that too, at a time when confronted by foes eager for an excuse to attack and annihilate them, is to accuse them, not of criminal intent, but of madness, sheer idiocy.

Lilburn W. Boggs was now governor of Missouri. He was Lieutenant-Governor, the reader will remember, during the troubles of 1833, at which time he espoused the cause of the mob which drove the Saints from Jackson County. He was a rank Mormon-hater, as were nearly all the residents of that county, and probably owed to that, in part, his elevation to the executive chair. Learning of the situation in Daviess County, the Governor directed Major-General Atchison and other officers of militia to muster and equip men to put down the insurrection.

While this order was being executed, the mob army was making ready to attack Diahman. For this purpose reinforcements and supplies were being forwarded to them from other points. On the 9th of September a wagon load of guns and ammunition, on its way from Richmond, Ray County, to the mobocratic camp, was captured with those in charge of it by Captain William Allred and his men,—Mormons belonging to the State militia.

Notifying Judge King of his capture, and asking what disposition should be made of the prisoners, Captain Allred was ordered by that official to treat them kindly and set them at liberty. Whether or not they were promptly released does not appear. The probability is that Captain Allred, surprised at receiving such an order, still held them. At any rate Judge King, on the same day, wrote to General Atchison to send two hundred or more men to force the Mormons to surrender.

The militia of Ray and Clay Counties, commanded by Brigadier-Generals Parks and Doniphan, now came upon the scene. Parks proceeded to Gallatin, the county seat of Daviess, to survey the situation, while Doniphan went via Far West to Millport and Diahman. At Far West, which place he visited with a single aide, leaving his troops on Crooked River, General Doniphan was the guest of the Prophet, who was favorably impressed with his frank and friendly manner. This was the same General Doniphan who subsequently played a notable part in the Mexican War. He and his superior, General Atchison, were Joseph Smith's attorneys in the legal troubles following the military episode of the autumn of 1838. Under them also the Prophet and Elder Rigdon studied law.

Marching to the camp of the mobocrats near Millport, Doniphan ordered them to disperse. They protested that they were merely acting in self-defense. He then went to Diahman and conferred with Colonel Wight, commanding the Mormon force, "Host of Israel." He found them willing to disband, provided the enemy threatening them would disperse, and willing also to surrender any of their number accused of offenses against the laws to be dealt with by legal authority. The prisoners and weapons taken by the Mormons were delivered up at the demand of General Doniphan, who, on the 15th of September joined Generals Atchison and Parks at Gallatin.

The report of these officers to the Governor was substantially as follows: that affairs in Daviess County were not so bad as rumor had represented, and that his Excellency had been deceived by designing or half-crazy men; that the Mormons, so far as could be learned, had been acting on the defensive, showing no hostile intent, and evincing no disposition to resist the laws; that the officers, on their arrival there, had found a large body of men from other counties, armed and in the field, to assist the people of Daviess against the Mormons, without being called out by the proper authorities; and that the Daviess County men were still threatening, in the event of the failure of a certain committee on compromise to agree, to drive the Mormons with powder and lead.

Colonel Wight and a score of others, accused of various offenses, had previously given themselves up and been pledged to appear for trial on the 29th of September. It is noticeable that no Missourians were arrested, though many of them were guilty of riot and mobocracy, and that even those captured by the Mormons had been set at liberty. During the excitement of the past several weeks overt acts had doubtless been committed on both sides. The wonder is not that such was the case, but that the Mormons were the only ones called to account.

Most of the troops were now disbanded, it being supposed that the trouble was over. Only a few companies remained under arms to quell, if necessary, any further demonstrations of disorder.

The scene now changes to Dewitt, in Carroll County. Enraged at being thwarted in their designs upon Diahman, the mob army, a portion of which had previously threatened Dewitt, appeared in force before that place, and in the beginning of October began to bombard the town. A party from Jackson County, with a six-pounder, assisted in the assault. The besieged, compared with the besiegers, were a mere handful. Colonel George M. Hinkle was their commander. The leaders of the attacking force—which was partly composed of militia men lately disbanded—were a Doctor Austin, Major Ashley, a member of the Legislature, and Sashiel Woods, a Presbyterian clergyman. Later came Captains Bogart and Houston, the former a Methodist preacher, with two companies of militia. These, instead of operating against the mob, united with them against the Mormons. General Parks came also, but did nothing to restore order remaining a silent and apparently a helpless spectator of the scene. His troops were evidently in sympathy with the mob.

The first gun was fired upon Dewitt on the 2nd of October. Colonel Hinkle waited forty-eight hours, and then ordered the fire returned. The bombardment continued at intervals for nine days. During its progress the Prophet made his way through much difficulty and danger from Far West to the beleaguered settlement. He found his people there hemmed in by their foes, their provisions exhausted, their cattle and horses stolen, their houses burned, and themselves threatened with death if they attempted to leave the town.

Through the agency of non-Mormon friends in that vicinity an appeal was made to Governor Boggs, in behalf of the beleaguered Saints. He replied that the quarrel was between the Mormons and the mob, and that they might "fight it out."

Finally the Mormons were permitted to evacuate Dewitt, which they did on the 11th of October. Under the treacherous fire of their foes the homeless and plundered refugees fled to Far West.

Eight hundred strong the mob army now marched upon Diahman. General Doniphan informed the Prophet of this movement, and stated that no protection could be hoped for from the militia. Said he: "They are d———d rotten hearted." They were certainly in sympathy if not in league with the lawless element that now concentrated from every direction against Diahman. It was under these circumstances that General Doniphan advised the Mormon militia at Far West to organize and march to the relief of their friends in Daviess County. His advice was taken, the command of the Caldwell regiment being given to Colonel George M. Hinkle.

About this time was brought to Diahman the news of house-burnings, drivings and other depredations committed by Gilliam's guerillas upon some scattered families of Saints beyond Grand River. Women, children and even the sick were dragged from their beds and thrust out into the night, some wandering for days through a pitiless storm that prevailed in that region about the middle of October. One of these refugees was Agnes, wife of Don Carlos Smith, the Prophet's brother, who was then absent in Tennessee. Her house being burned she had fled with two babes in her arms and waded Grand River to get beyond the reach of her ruffian pursuers.

The Mormon blood was now thoroughly up. The Prophet no longer counseled peace and submission. He bade his followers arm and defend themselves; to die, if need be, protecting their homes, the virtue of their wives and daughters, and the lives of their little ones. General Parks, arriving at Diahman, against which the mob was fast gathering, permitted Colonel Wight, who held a commission under him in the 59th regiment of the militia, to organize his command and proceed against the robbers and house-burners.

Here apparently was the beginning of retaliative measures on the part of the Mormons in Missouri. Smarting under their wrongs they made vigorous war upon the marauding bands that now fled precipitately before them, and ceased not their efforts until Daviess County was well clear of them. If they went further, as alleged by the Missourians, and burned the towns—or hamlets—of Millport and Gallatin, it was not to be wondered at after the provocation given.

The Mormons, however, do not admit having burned the property of the Missourians; but allege that the mob set fire to the houses of their own friends, and then fled, scattering the false report that the Mormons were the incendiaries. Be this as it may, there is at least one Missourian now living who, while claiming that the Mormons did the burning, concedes that they were justified in what they did, as the Missourians had set the example.*

It was asserted by those who spread these reports that the design of the Mormons was next to sack and burn the town of Richmond. This rumor, being generally believed, or feared,—all the more readily since the Mormons had suffered just such outrages, and the law of retaliation is a recognized rule of human nature,—served to augment the reigning agitation and swell the discord of the hour.

About this time the rumor become current at Far West of a secret organization called Danites, or Destroying Angels, whose alleged purpose was to prey upon the Gentiles and avenge the Saints of their enemies.† The origin of the movement was accredited to the chiefs of the Church, especially Sidney Rigdon, who, it was said, had authorized the organization. It transpired, however, that the originator of the movement, which was indeed attempted, was Dr. Sampson Avard, a characterless fanatic then numbered among the Saints, whose scheme for blood and plunder, becoming known to the First Presidency, was repudiated and its author severed from the Church. In revenge for the exposure of his villainy, Avard declared that the Church leaders had authorized him to organize the death-dealing society called Danites.

The story of these preyers and avengers, which, barring the above, is a pure myth,—Joaquin Miller and other less reputable romancers to the contrary notwithstanding,—is still perpetuated by anti-Mormon writers and speakers, and has probably done the Saints more harm than any other of the numerous tales uttered

---

* Messrs. Andrew Jenson and Edward Stevenson, of Salt Lake City, state that during a visit to Daviess County, Missouri, in September, 1888, they conversed with one Major McGee, an old resident of Gallatin, who spoke to that effect. He said that he thought some of the Mormons were to blame for teasing the other inhabitants with the doctrine that they—the Saints—were the heirs to the whole country, but that he knew of no lawlessness committed by the Mormons prior to the troubles in 1838. He also stated that he was taken prisoner by the Mormons during those troubles and treated kindly. According to Major McGee, Gallatin at that time consisted of about four houses.

† Genesis xlix—17.

against them. The Danite Society, according to all but anti-Mormon authors, whose assertions against the Saints should be taken *cum grano salis*, was nipped in the bud, and had no after existence.

The battle of Crooked River was fought on the 25th of October. Captain David W. Patten, of the Far West militia, had been directed by Colonel Hinkle to proceed with a company of men to the ford of the river and disperse a band of marauders under Captain Bogart, who were committing depredations in that vicinity. They had captured three Mormons,—Nathan Pinkham, William Seely and Addison Green,—and had boasted of their intention to put them to death the next night. It was to rescue these men, as well as to put a stop to Bogart's operations that Captain Patten went forth. Leaving Far West about midnight, he and his company, seventy-five in number, came upon Bogart's band in ambush just at day-break. As the Mormons crossed the bluff above his camp, which was among the brush and willows in the river bottom, the mob leader ordered his men to fire. They obeyed, when young Patrick O'Banion, a Mormon, fell mortally wounded. Captain Patten then ordered his men to charge. Forward they dashed, returning the enemy's fire. After delivering a second volley Bogart's band broke and fled, crossing the river at the ford and abandoning their camp to the victorious Mormons. The three prisoners held by the mob were liberated, though one of them had been shot and wounded by his captors during the engagement.

But the victory had been dearly won. Captain Patten, like O'Banion, was mortally wounded, and Gideon Carter killed. Other Mormons were wounded, but not seriously. Bogart, whose force outnumbered the attacking party, lost one man.

David W. Patten died that night. He was a man much esteemed by his people, and his loss was deeply mourned. The Church regarded him as a martyr.

The excitement among the Missourians, already at fever heat over the troubles in Daviess County, now became intense. The Crooked River battle was heralded abroad as another "Mormon atrocity," and the public mind was more and more inflamed against the Saints.

The Mormon-hating Governor of Missouri now saw his opportunity. So long as it was only the Saints who were being worsted, he could afford to sit by, like Xerxes on his mountain throne at Salamis, and see the two sides "fight it out." But when the tables were turned, and the mob began to suffer some reverses, he came to the conclusion that it was high time for him to interfere for their protection. Besides the opportunity to wreak personal spite upon the Mormons, there was a chance to make political capital out of the situation.

On the 27th of October Governor Boggs issued an order to Major-General John B. Clark, giving him command of an overwhelming force of militia, with instructions to proceed at once against the Mormons. "Their outrages are beyond all description" said the Governor, "they must be exterminated or driven from the State." Other generals were ordered to take part, under Clark, in the military crusade.

General Atchison, upon whom the command rightfully devolved, had been ignored or relieved by the Governor,—apparently for the same reason that caused the wife of the newly fledged Thane of Cawdor to "fear the nature" of her lord. In General Clark, who was not so "full o' the milk of human kindness," but proved himself a pitiless tyrant, Boggs found a fitting instrument to execute his fell design. Another account states that Atchison, while raising troops to quell the disturbance, on learning of the Governor's exterminating purpose, exclaimed: "I will have nothing to do with so infamous a proceeding," and resigned.

Over two thousand troops, massed at Richmond under Major-General Samuel D. Lucas and Brigadier General Moses Wilson, both of Jackson County, during the closing days of October set out for Far West. General Clark, their commander, was elsewhere mustering another army for the same purpose. Lucas, on his march, captured two Mormons named Tanner and Carey. Tanner, an old man, was struck with a gun by one of the soldiers, and his skull laid bare. A similar blow dashed out Carey's brains. He was laid in a wagon, no aid being rendered him, and died within twenty-four hours. Thus the militia moved on toward the fated town of Far West.

Among the first fruits of the sanguinary edict of Missouri's executive was the Haun's Mill massacre. It occurred on the 30th of October. Haun's Mill was situated on Shoal Creek, about twenty miles south of Far West. Here dwelt, in the neighborhood of other lately arrived immigrants, all awaiting a lull in the warlike storm before proceeding farther, a few families of Latter-day Saints. Among them were Joseph Young and his family, lately from Kirtland.

About four o'clock in the afternoon a company of two hundred and forty men, commanded by one Nehemiah Comstock, fell upon the little settlement and butchered in cold blood, without warning or provocation, nearly a score of the unoffending Mormons. Men, women and children were shot down indiscriminately, their bodies stripped and mutilated, their camp plundered and their horses and wagons driven off by the murdering marauders. The dead bodies were thrown into an old well.

Among the victims was an aged man named Thomas McBride, a soldier of the Revolution who had served under General Washington. A Missourian named Rogers, after shooting the old man with his own gun, hacked him to pieces with a corn-cutter. Another victim was George Spencer Richards, aged fifteen, son of Phinehas Richards, and brother to Franklin D., the present Apostle. Franklin at that very time was making his way across the Alleghanies from his native town of Richmond, Berkshire County, Massachusetts, to join his people at Far West.

Among those who survived the awful butchery, though almost riddled with bullets from the assassins' rifles, was the late Isaac Laney, father of Judge H. S. Laney, of Salt Lake City; also the late Alma L. Smith, of Coalville, Summit County, brother of Hon. Willard G. Smith, of Morgan County. His father, Warren, and his brother Sardius were among the slain.

On the day of the massacre, the troops from Richmond, reinforced to nearly three thousand men, advanced upon and beleaguered Far West. General Clark was still at a distance, mustering his forces. The whole surrounding region was now being over-run by marauding bands, shooting, burning and pillaging wherever Mormons were to be found. As the survivors of these savage raids came fleeing into Far West for safety, their red-handed pursuers augmented the army of investment. Among those who thus joined the militia against the Mormons were Gilliam's painted guerillas and the perpetrators of the Haun's Mill massacre.

The inhabitants of the doomed city, their mails having been stopped, had not yet heard of the Governor's exterminating order, but supposed the army of General Lucas to be an overwhelming military mob. Though greatly outnumbered by the besieging force, they prepared to make a vigorous defense and sell their lives as dearly as possible. Hastily throwing up some rude fortifications, they awaited the onslaught of the foe.

A messenger was now sent from Lucas to announce that to three persons in the town—Adam Lightner, John Cleminson and wife—two of them non-Mormons, amnesty would be given, but that the design was to lay Far West in ashes and exterminate the rest. "Then we will die with them!" heroically answered the three, and rejected the proffered pardon.

Charles C. Rich went out from the city with a flag of truce, to confer with General Doniphan, who was with Lucas. As he approached the camp of the militia Captain Bogart fired upon him.

It was at this critical juncture that Colonel George M. Hinkle, commanding the defenders of Far West, entered into negotiations with General Lucas, and without consulting his associates agreed upon a compromise, the terms of which were as follows:

(1) The Mormon leaders were to be delivered up to be tried and punished.

(2) The Far West militia were to surrender their arms.

(3) An appropriation was to be made of the property of all

Mormons who had taken up arms, to indemnify for damages said to have been inflicted by them. This was afterwards construed to cover all the expenses of the militia in making war upon the Saints.

(4) The Mormons, as a body, excepting such as should be held as prisoners, were to forthwith leave the State. The prisoners were to include all Mormon participants in the Crooked River battle, who were to be tried for murder.

The observance of these conditions, it was promised, would avert bloodshed. The alternative was an immediate assault upon the city.

Under pretense of arranging a conference between the Mormon leaders and the besieging generals, and without notifying the former of the compact he had entered into, Colonel Hinkle, on the 31st of October, delivered up to General Lucas the following named persons, who had been demanded: Joseph Smith, junior, Sidney Rigdon, Parley P. Pratt, Lyman Wight and George W. Robinson. Later were added to the list, Hyrum Smith and Amasa M. Lyman. They were placed under a strong guard and treated as prisoners of war.

Some writers have palliated Colonel Hinkle's conduct in this affair, on the score of obedience to his superior officer, General Lucas, who demanded the prisoners; also because their delivery is supposed to have saved the lives of the other citizens. The Mormons, however, will always regard George M. Hinkle as a traitor, who to save himself betrayed his friends, in the most cowardly and contemptible manner possible.

Next day, the army having advanced nearer the city, the Mormon militia laid down their arms, and were then compelled at the point of the bayonet and the cannon's mouth to sign away their property to pay the expenses of the war waged upon them. They had made no agreement to do so, but Hinkle, forsooth, had made it for them. All the men, save those who had escaped, were held in temporary durance, and the town then given up to pillage. Nameless crimes were committed by the ruthless soldiery, and their yet more ruthless allies, the banditti. Women were abused, some of them till they died, within sight of their agonized husbands and fathers, powerless to protect them. Let imagination paint the horror from which the historian's pen recoils.

William E. McLellin and other apostate Mormons were in Far West at this time, taking part against their former brethren.

On the evening of November 1st, General Lucas convened a court-martial, consisting of the principal officers of his army, and no less than seventeen Christian preachers. By a majority of this religio-military tribunal, Joseph Smith and his fellow prisoners, none of whom were permitted to be present during their trial, were sentenced to be shot at eight o'clock next morning, in the public square at Far West, in the presence of their wives and children. Generals Doniphan and Graham refused their assent to this decision, the former denouncing it as "cold-blooded murder," and threatening to withdraw his brigade from the scene of the proposed massacre. This caused Lucas and his murderous colleagues to hesitate, and finally to reconsider their action. On the morning set for the execution they decided, in lieu of killing the prisoners, to parade them in triumph through the neighboring counties.

Prior to setting out from Far West, General Lucas allowed the prisoners to see for a few moments, in the presence of their guards, their weeping wives and children. Most of them were not permitted to speak, but merely look farewell to them, before being hurried away.

Mary Fielding Smith, wife of Hyrum Smith, a few days after this painful parting from her husband became a mother. The child thus born amid these warlike scenes, drinking in with his mother's milk a wholesome hatred of tyrants and mobs, and the courage to fearlessly denounce them, is known to-day as Joseph Fielding Smith, second counselor in the existing First Presidency.

Leaving a large portion of his troops at Far West, to await the arrival of General Clark, and having sent Gilliam and his banditti against the Mormons at Diahman, Lucas, with his confrere Wilson and a strong guard set out with the prisoners southward. As they neared the Missouri River orders were received from General Clark, demanding the return of the captives. Lucas, however, ignored the order, and pressed on with the prisoners to Jackson County.

They were now treated with some degree of consideration. Wilson assured them that their lives should be spared, and that they should be protected: "We only want to take you over the river and let our people see what a d——d fine looking set of fellows you are," said this typical son of Jackson County. He also told them that one of the reasons for bringing them along was to keep them out of the hands of General Clark, "a G——d d——d old bigot," said he, "so stuffed with lies and prejudice that he would shoot you down in a moment."*

The Prophet, on the day of their arrival at Independence—Sunday, November 4th—was permitted to preach to the multitude that thronged to gaze at him and his brethren. The feeling against them diminished daily, until it was almost in their favor. After four days' imprisonment at Independence, during which they were visited by curious thousands, the prisoners, in response to repeated demands from General Clark, were sent to Richmond for trial.

Clark, at the head of two thousand troops, had arrived at Far West on the 4th of November. He approved of all that Lucas had done, except the taking away of the Mormon leaders, whose persons he evidently desired as trophies of his own triumph. He solaced himself, however, by putting Bishop Partridge and fifty-five other prominent Mormons in chains and carrying them captive to Richmond.

Prior to departing, he sent a brigade of troops in the wake of Gilliam and his guerillas, to demand the surrender of Diahman, on the same terms as those enforced at Far West. He also delivered, before leaving, an address to the citizens of that place, of which the following was the substance:

*Wilson admitted, according to Parley P. Pratt, that in the reigning troubles, as well as those in Jackson County, the Mormons had not been the aggressors, but had been purposely goaded to resistance by the Missourians in order to furnish an excuse for their expulsion.

GENTLEMEN :

You whose names are not attached to this list of names, will now have the privilege of going to your fields, and of providing corn, wood, etc., for your families. Those who are now taken will go from this to prison, to be tried and receive the due demerit of their crimes ; but you (except such as charges may hereafter be preferred against), are at liberty as soon as the troops are removed that now guard the place, which I shall cause to be done immediately.

It now devolves upon you to fulfill a treaty that you have entered into, the leading items of which I shall now lay before you. The first requires that your leading men be given up to be tried according to law ; this you already have complied with. The second is, that you deliver up your arms ; this has been attended to. The third stipulation is that you sign over your properties to defray the expenses of the war. This you have also done. Another article yet remains for you to comply with,—and that is, that you leave the state forthwith. And whatever may be your feelings concerning this, or whatever your innocence, it is nothing to me. General Lucas (whose military rank is equal with mine), has made this treaty with you ; I approve of it, I should have done the same had I been here. I am therefore determined to see it executed.

The character of this state has suffered almost beyond redemption, from the character, conduct and influence that you have exerted ; and we deem it an act of justice to restore her character to its former standing among the states by every proper means. *The orders of the Governor to me were, that you should be exterminated, and not allowed to remain in the state. And had not your leaders been given up, and the terms of the treaty complied with, before this time you and your families would have been destroyed, and your houses in ashes.*

There is a discretionary power vested in my hands, which, considering your circumstances, I shall exercise for a season. You are indebted to me for this clemency. I do not say that you shall go now, but you must not think of staying here another season or of putting in crops ; for the moment you do this the citizens will be upon you ; and if I am called here again in case of a non-compliance of a treaty made, do not think that I shall do as I have done now. *You need not expect any mercy, but extermination, for I am determined the Governor's order shall be executed.*

As for your leaders, do not think, do not imagine for a moment, do not let it enter into your minds, that they will be delivered and restored to you again, for their fate is fixed, their die is cast, their doom is sealed.

I am sorry, gentlemen, to see so many apparently intelligent men found in the situation that they are; and oh! if I could invoke that Great Spirit, the Unknown God to rest upon and deliver you from that awful chain of superstition, and liberate you from those fetters of fanaticism with which you are bound—that you no longer do homage to a man.

I would advise you to scatter abroad and never again organize yourselves with Bishops, Presidents, etc., lest you excite the jealousies of the people and subject yourselves to the same calamities that have now come upon you. You have always been the aggressors—you have brought upon yourselves these difficulties by being disaffected, and not being subject to rule. And my advice is, that you become as other citizens, lest by a recurrence of these events you bring upon yourselves irretrievable ruin.

General Clark then proceeded with his captives to Richmond, where the Prophet and his fellow prisoners soon arrived. A protracted examination before Judge Austin A. King,—who, with the public prosecutor, Thomas Burch, had sat in the court-martial at Far West and sentenced these same men to be shot,—failed to fasten guilt upon any of them. Finally, all save Joseph Smith, Sidney Rigdon, Hyrum Smith, Lyman Wight, Parley P. Pratt, Caleb Baldwin, Alexander McRae, Morris Phelps, Luman Gibbs, Darwin Chase and Norman Shearer, were discharged. These were held for murder, arson, treason,—in fact nearly all the crimes in the calendar.

One evidence of their treason, as cited in open court, was their avowed belief in the prophecy of Daniel—Chapters II. and VII.—relative to the setting up of the latter-day kingdom of God. Their taking up arms in the late troubles was also construed as treason. Their murders were the battles and skirmishes they had had with the mob. The depredations and deeds of blood committed by the Missourians against the Mormons apparently cut no figure in the case. The Haun's Mill massacre was as completely ignored as if it had never occurred. Said General Doniphan to the defendants, whose attorney he was: "Offer no defense; for if a cohort of angels should declare your innocence it would be all the same. The judge is determined to throw you into prison."

Colonel Sterling Price had charge of the captives at this time. The yet to be noted Confederate general seems to have done all in his power to render their situation as miserable as possible. One method employed by their guards to entertain them was the recital in their hearing of the murders and rapes that they—the soldiers—boasted of having committed at and in the vicinity of Far West. Finally the Prophet, arising in his chains, in a voice of thunder rebuked the crime-stained wretches and commanded them to be still. So overpowering was his indignation, his metaphysical force, that the armed guards quailed before him and begged his pardon.*

---

* Says Parley P. Pratt of the Prophet on that occasion: "He ceased to speak. He stood erect in terrible majesty, chained and without a weapon. * * * *

Joseph and Hyrum Smith, Sidney Rigdon, Lyman Wight, Alexander McRae and Caleb Baldwin were now removed to Clay County, and immured in Liberty jail. The remainder of the prisoners were still held at Richmond. The Clay County captives were treated with great barbarity. Several times their food was poisoned, nearly causing their death, and they even declared that cooked human flesh, called by their guards "Mormon beef," was repeatedly served up to them.

Months passed. Various efforts were made by legal process to free the prisoners. Among those actively engaged in their behalf were Brigham Young and Heber C. Kimball, who, being comparatively unknown by the Missourians, had escaped arrest and incarceration. Stephen Markham was another faithful friend. Generals Atchison and Doniphan lent their aid, and Judge Hughes, of the Supreme Court of Missouri, also favored the release of the captives. It was conceded by many that they were illegally held, but owing to the prevailing prejudice, their friends were powerless to do much for them. Again and again they were put upon trial and nothing was proven against them, even after their own witnesses had all been driven from the State. Finally by proceedings in *habeas corpus* Sidney Rigdon was let out on bail. Threatened by the mob after his liberation he was compelled to flee for his life. His companions were remanded to prison, where they passed the winter of 1838-9.

Meantime such of the leading Mormons as had retained or regained their liberty addressed a memorial to the Missouri Legislature, reciting the wrongs and sufferings of the Saints in that State and praying for redress of grievances. The total loss of property sustained by the Mormons in Missouri was estimated at about two million dollars. The Legislature, after much delay, appropriated

---

I have seen the ministers of justice, clothed in magisterial robes and criminals arraigned before them, while life was suspended on a breath in the courts of England; I have witnessed a congress in solemn session to give laws to nations; * * * but dignity and majesty have I seen but once, as it stood in chains at midnight, in a dungeon, in an obscure village of Missouri."

some thousands of dollars to be distributed among the people of
Daviess and Caldwell counties, "the Mormons not excepted." Some
say that only two thousand dollars were thus appropriated; others
that two hundred thousand was the amount. The latter seems the
more reasonable, and the Missourians should be given the benefit of
the doubt.*

In the absence of the First Presidency—in prison—the authority
to direct the Church devolved upon the Twelve Apostles. Their
some time president, Thomas B. Marsh, had apostatized during the
Far West troubles, which event, with the death of David W. Patten, left Brigham Young the senior Apostle and consequently the
President of the Twelve. Being sustained as such by his brethren
Brigham now took charge of the Church and planned and directed
the exodus of the Saints to Illinois.

Late in January and early in February, meetings were held at
Far West, and the following committee appointed to arrange for the
exodus: John Taylor, Alanson Ripley, Brigham Young, Theodore
Turley, Heber C. Kimball, John Smith, Don C. Smith, Elias Smith,
Erastus Bingham, Stephen Markham and James Newberry. A subcommittee was also appointed. They were William Huntington,
Charles Bird, Alanson Ripley, Theodore Turley, Daniel Shearer,
Shadrach Roundy and Jonathan H. Hale. "On motion of President
Brigham Young," says the record, "it was resolved that we this day
enter into a covenant to stand by and assist each other to the utmost
of our abilities in removing from this State, and that we will never
desert the poor, who are worthy, till they shall be out of the reach of
the exterminating order of General Clark, acting for and in the name

---

* Heber C. Kimball thus describes the manner in which was distributed to the
Mormons their share of the appropriation: "Judge Cameron,"—who with one McHenry
had charge of the distribution,—"drove in the hogs belonging to the brethren (many of
which were identified) shot them down in the streets, and without further bleeding they
were half dressed, cut up and distributed by McHenry to the poor, charging four or five
cents per pound, which, together with a few pieces of refuse calicoes, at double and treble
price, soon consumed the appropriation."

of the State." This covenant, signed by several hundred persons, was faithfully kept.

That winter from ten to twelve thousand Latter-day Saints, men, women and children, still hounded and pursued by their merciless oppressors, fled from Missouri, leaving in places their bloody foot-prints on the snow of their frozen path-way. Crossing the icy Mississippi they cast themselves, homeless, plundered and penniless, upon the hospitable shores of Illinois. There their pitiable condition and the tragic story of their wrongs awoke wide-spread sympathy and compassion, with corresponding sentiments of indignation and abhorrence toward their persecutors.

The main body of the Mormons were now beyond the reach of the Missourians. But some of the Committee on Exodus and a few scattered families yet remained. These were now the objects of mobo-cratic malice. About the middle of April a lawless band, encouraged by Judge—once Captain—Bogart, assaulted and drove away the committee, threatened the lives of the remaining Mormons, and plundered and destroyed thousands of dollars' worth of property with which the committee were assisting the poor to remove.*

At Quincy, Adams County, Illinois, where most of the exiled Saints found refuge and a kindly welcome, they were joined late in April or early in May by the Prophet and his brother Hyrum, who had recently escaped with others of their captive companions from their imprisonment in Missouri.

---

* Says Heber C. Kimball: "One mobber rode up, and finding no convenient place to fasten his horse, shot a cow that was standing near while a girl was milking her, and as the poor animal was struggling in death he cut a strip of her hide from the nose to the tail to which he fastened his halter."

CHAPTER XI.
1839-1842.

NAUVOO—THE SAINTS IN ILLINOIS AND IOWA—DANIEL H. WELLS—THE APOSTLES DEPART FOR EUROPE—THE PROPHET LAYS THE GRIEVANCES OF HIS PEOPLE BEFORE THE GENERAL GOVERNMENT—PRESIDENT VAN BUREN'S REPLY—"YOUR CAUSE IS JUST, BUT I CAN DO NOTHING FOR YOU"—ILLINOIS POLITICS—WHIGS AND DEMOCRATS—THE MORMONS HOLD THE BALANCE OF POWER—A CLOUD ON THE HORIZON—MISSOURI DEMANDS OF ILLINOIS THE MORMON LEADERS AS FUGITIVES FROM JUSTICE—THE REQUISITION RETURNED UNSERVED—THE NAUVOO CHARTER—THE APOSTLES IN GREAT BRITAIN—THE BEGINNING OF MORMON IMMIGRATION FROM ABROAD—THE SAINTS CONCENTRATE AT NAUVOO—THE POLITICIANS ALARMED—RISE OF THE ANTI-MORMON PARTY—THE MISSOURI WRIT RE-ISSUED AND THE PROPHET ARRESTED—HABEAS CORPUS—JUDGE DOUGLAS—LIBERATION—JOHN C. BENNETT—THE SHADOW OF A COMING EVENT—THE PROPHET PREDICTS THE FLIGHT OF HIS PEOPLE TO THE ROCKY MOUNTAINS.

NAUVOO, the Beautiful. Such was the name of the fair city founded by Joseph Smith and his followers on the eastern shore of the Mississippi, after their flight and expulsion from Missouri. It was in Hancock County, Illinois, fifty miles above the town of Quincy.

Situated in a graceful bend of the majestic Father of Waters, on an eminence commanding a noble view of the broad and rolling river, here sweeping round it in a semi-circle, Nauvoo, even as the site of the lovely city it soon became, well merited the surname of Beautiful. The site of the city, prior to May, 1839, when the Mormons made their first purchase of lands in that locality, was the little town or village of Commerce, which title it continued to bear until about a year later, when it was rechristened by the Saints Nauvoo.

Among the landed proprietors from whom they made extensive purchases in and around Commerce was Daniel H. Wells, famous in

Utah history as General and as "Squire" Wells. He was a native of Trenton, Oneida County, New York, and was descended from Thomas Wells, the fourth Governor of Connecticut. He was now in his twenty-fifth year, and had resided in Illinois since he was eighteen. At first he had engaged in clearing land and farming, but before coming of age had entered upon his official career, being first elected constable and then justice of the peace. He also held an office in the first military organization of Hancock County. He was noted for courage and wisdom, and was a man of strict integrity and of broad and generous soul. He was not then connected with any religious society. In politics he was a staunch Whig, but was much esteemed by men of all creeds and parties.

A foe to oppression in all its forms, and a fearless champion of universal freedom, Squire Wells at once befriended the outcast Mormons upon their arrival in his neighborhood, and extended to them a cordial welcome. He might have speculated out of their necessities at that time, but would not. Platting his land into city lots he let them have it almost on their own terms—low rates and long-time payments. Though not a Mormon until after the Prophet's death, Daniel H. Wells was always his staunch and faithful friend.

Another land-owner from whom the Saints purchased largely in that locality was Dr. Isaac Galland, who also joined the Church. With him the Prophet had corresponded upon the subject while in Liberty jail.

Lands were likewise secured on the Iowa side of the river; about one hundred families settling in Lee County, opposite Nauvoo, in 1839. Brigham Young dwelt there, at a place called Montrose. The Iowa purchase included the town of Nashville, with twenty thousand acres of land adjoining, upon which was projected and partly built the Mormon town of Zarahemla.

Nauvoo was not altogether "a city set upon a hill." Some of it lay in the low lands, where the surface sloped down to the river. Here the soil was naturally moist and miry, superinducing malaria;

in consequence of which the locality was at first very unhealthy. Within a short time, however, under the energetic labors of the thrifty and industrious Saints,—whose mission seems to have been from the beginning to make the wilderness blossom,—the climate underwent a salutary change, regarded by the devout people as miraculous, and thenceforth it became a wholesome as well as a charming place of abode. But this was not until after some painful and protracted sieges of sickness, which at one time prostrated nearly all the inhabitants of Commerce, and many people in the neighboring towns.

It was during the reign of such an epidemic, in the latter part of 1839, that the Twelve Apostles of the Church—or a majority of them—started upon their first mission to foreign lands. They had been appointed to this mission in July, 1838, while the Saints were in Missouri. It had then been declared by the Prophet that they should meet upon the Temple grounds at Far West on the 26th of the ensuing April, and take formal leave of the city, prior to crossing the "great waters." What special significance was attached to this event we know not, but the Apostles and the Prophet seemed to regard it as very important and were determined to see the prophecy fulfilled.

The Missourians, however, who had been informed by their apostate allies of the prediction concerning the 26th of April, were just as firmly resolved to thwart it. Probably this was one reason why Bogart and his mob, as related, expelled the few remaining Mormons from Far West about the middle of April. It was their boast that if all others of "Joe Smith's prophecies" should be fulfilled, this one, now that he was in prison and his people driven from the State, should fail.

Before day-break, however, on the morning of April 26th, 1839, Apostles Brigham Young, Heber C. Kimball, Orson Pratt, John Taylor, John E. Page and others rode into Far West. Holding a meeting on the temple grounds, they ordained Wilford Woodruff and George A. Smith to the Apostleship, and having severed thirty-one persons from the Church, bade adieu to the half-deserted, half-ruined city and departed, ere their enemies had arisen to renew their oath that the words of the Mormon Prophet relating to this event should never be realized. Subsequently, the founding of Nauvoo and the labor of settling their people in that vicinity, with the terrible epidemic that swept over them that summer, unavoidably delayed the departure of the Apostles from America.

During August and September, however, seven of the Twelve, namely: Brigham Young, Heber C. Kimball, Parley P. Pratt, * Orson Pratt, John Taylor, Wilford Woodruff and George A. Smith, with Elders Theodore Turley, Reuben Hedlock and Hiram Clark, left Commerce for Europe. Most of them were weak and ailing, and some even arose from sick beds, burning with fever or shaking with ague to begin the journey. Their families, whom they were forced to leave behind, were also sick and well-nigh helpless. Penniless, as usual, and with swelling hearts, these devoted men went forth to perform their duty, trusting in Him who feedeth the sparrows and heareth the young ravens when they cry, to minister to their own needs, and to care for and comfort their wives and little ones.

Of such undaunted mettle and quenchless zeal were the men whom the Mormon Prophet had gathered round him as his Apostles, in whose destiny it was written that they should not only war with "principalities and powers," contending for their faith with the learned polemists of Christendom, but battle in the same strength and sturdiness of purpose with Nature's sterile elements, and conquering redeem a desert.

Reference has been made to the widespread sympathy and compassion for the Saints, coupled with abhorrence and detestation for their oppressors, felt by the generous people of Illinois when the homeless refugees first came among them. Indignation was rife that in a free land and in an enlightened age a community should thus be persecuted for their opinions; that a sovereign state of the American Union, instead of shielding its citizens from mobocracy, should

---

* Parley had but recently escaped from Richmond jail, Missouri.

actually join hands with the lawless element and assist in the work of wholesale plunder and expatriation. Upon Governor Boggs and his coadjutors censure was heaped unsparingly. Upon the hapless victims of their tyranny favors were abundantly bestowed. Said the Quincy *Argus* of March 16th, 1839:

> We have no language sufficiently strong for the expression of our indignation and shame at the recent transaction in a sister State, and that State Missouri, a State of which we had long been proud, alike for her men and history, but now so fallen that we could wish her star stricken out from the bright constellation of the Union. We say we know of no language sufficiently strong for the expression of our shame and abhorrence of her recent conduct. She has written her own character in letters of blood, and stained it by acts of merciless cruelty and brutality that the waters of ages cannot efface. It will be observed that an organized mob, aided by many of the civil and military officers of Missouri, with Governor Boggs at their head, have been the prominent actors in this business, incited, too, it appears, against the Mormons by political hatred, and by the additional motives of plunder and revenge. They have but too well put in execution their threats of extermination and expulsion, and fully wreaked their vengeance on a body of industrious and enterprising men who had never wronged nor wished to wrong them, but on the contrary had ever comported themselves as good and honest citizens, living under the same laws, and having the same right with themselves to the sacred immunities of life, liberty, and property.*

Professor Turner, of Illinois College, wrote:

> Who began the quarrel? Was it the Mormons? Is it not notorious, on the contrary, that they were hunted like wild beasts, from county to county, before they made any desperate resistance? Did they ever, as a body, refuse obedience to the laws, when called upon to do so, until driven to desperation by repeated threats and assaults from the mob? Did the State ever make one decent effort to defend them as fellow-citizens in their rights, or to redress their wrongs? Let the conduct of its governors, attorneys, and the fate of their final petitions answer. Have any who plundered and openly massacred the Mormons ever been brought to the punishment due to their crimes? Let the boasting murderers of begging and helpless infancy answer. Has the State ever remunerated even those known to be innocent, for the loss of either their property or their arms? Did either the pulpit or the press through the State raise a note of remonstrance or alarm? Let the clergymen who abetted and the editors who encouraged the mob answer.

To be sure, not all the people of Illinois shared these sentiments. The Mormons had enemies there as well as friends. These, it is

---

* Some of the Missouri papers of that period contained similar articles, denouncing the ill-treatment of the Mormons and censuring the Legislature for avoiding an investigation of the crimes committed against them.

almost needless to say, were largely of the religious element, who could neither forget nor forgive that Joseph Smith, whatever his innocence of crime, had been guilty of founding a new Church, which opposed theirs, and in spite of all that had been said and done against it, was fast becoming a power in the land.

Of course there were exceptions even here; but this was the general feeling among earnest Christians concerning Mormonism. They sincerely and heartily hated the system, and their hatred extended in most instances to all connected with it. It was this class, in conjunction with two others, its traditional allies—politicians and apostates—that finally encompassed the murder of the Mormon Prophet, and the driving of his people into the western wilderness.

As yet, however, there were no signs of such an issue. Illinois had opened her arms to the exiles. Her governor, Thomas Carlin, and other State officials, with editors, professors and prominent citizens in general had taken the lead in extending aid and sympathy to the outcast community. Thousands of dollars in money, clothing and provisions had been contributed for their relief by the citizens of Quincy and other places, and every effort made of which a humane and benevolent people seemed capable, to cause the Saints to forget their former sufferings in the assurance of present protection and promised peace.

Nor were the people of Iowa at all behind in friendly feeling for the Mormons. Robert Lucas, Governor of that Territory—a former governor of Ohio—treated them kindly, pledged to them the protection of the Constitution and the laws, and testified to their general repute as "industrious, inoffensive and worthy citizens."

One of the first steps taken by the Prophet, after planting the feet of his people in these places of refuge, was to lay their grievances before the general government. A committee, consisting of himself, Sidney Rigdon and Elias Higbee, was appointed at a conference held at Commerce, October 5th, 1839, to proceed to Washington for that purpose. They started on the 29th of October. Elder Rigdon, owing to ill health, did not go any farther than Columbus, Ohio. His companions reached the capital late in November.

On the way thither the Prophet met with an exciting adventure, in which the part he played doubtless saved the limbs if not the lives of several persons. The coach upon which they were traveling was descending a mountain pass of the Alleghanies. The driver having laid down his lines and got off at a wayside tavern, the horses, becoming frightened, ran away. Climbing from the inside of the vehicle to the driver's seat, while the horses were in furious motion, the Prophet secured the reins and skillfully guided the foaming steeds until they were brought to a stand-still. On the coach were several ladies and some members of Congress. The daring feat of their fellow-traveler, whose identity they were unaware of, was greatly admired and gratefully mentioned by all. Later they learned with much surprise that the one to whom they were so deeply indebted was no other than Joseph Smith, the Mormon Prophet.

He remained several months at the capital, forming many acquaintances among leading statesmen and politicians of the period, and pleading earnestly the cause of his plundered and exiled people. But beyond the personal interest that he excited his mission was apparently fruitless. The authority of the general government to interfere in the affairs of a State,—even when that State had acted as Missouri had done,—where not denied, was seriously doubted, especially by Democrats, and it was a Democratic administration that held the reins of power. Others, though holding different views, were unwilling, for political reasons, to champion the cause of the unpopular Mormons. Policy, the Prophet discovered, rather than principle, swayed the hearts and minds of the majority of his country's statesmen. The Committee on Judiciary, to whom the memorial of the Saints was referred, with claims against Missouri for about one-and-a-half million dollars, finally reported adversely upon the petition. This, however, was after the Prophet left Washington.

While there he had interviews with the President, Martin Van Buren, who said, after listening to his story: "Your cause is just, but I can do nothing for you." This frank democratic statement the Mormon leader might have excused,—though himself a Whig, and differing from the President on the "State Rights" question involved. But Van Buren unwisely added: "If I take up for you I shall lose the votes of Missouri,"—referring to the approaching presidential election. Personal ambition, quite as much as loyalty to his political principles, was thus shown to be his ruling motive. For such an admission Joseph Smith's fearless, uncalculating spirit was hardly prepared. Heartsick and disgusted at what he deemed a display of pusillanimity in high places, he now left Washington for home.

Passing through Chester County, Pennsylvania, he formed the acquaintance of Edward Hunter, a prosperous farmer and an influential man in that vicinity, who was already favorably impressed with Mormonism. He soon afterwards embraced the faith and removed to Illinois. Edward Hunter became Bishop of the Fifth Ward of Nauvoo, and in Utah the Presiding Bishop of the Church.

From Chester County the Prophet proceeded to Philadelphia, where a flourishing branch of the Church existed, and then returned to Illinois, arriving at Commerce on the 4th of March, 1840.

Hyrum Smith, in the absence of his associates, had had presidential charge of the Church. Stakes of Zion had been organized at Commerce and in Iowa. William Marks became President of the Commerce Stake, with Charles C. Rich and Austin Cowles as his counselors. The members of the High Council were G. W. Harris, Samuel Bent, Henry G. Sherwood, David Fullmer, Alpheus Cutler, William Huntington, Thomas Grover, Newel Knight, Charles C. Rich, David Dort, Seymour Brunson and Lewis D. Wilson. On the Iowa side John Smith was President of the Stake, and Reynolds Cahoon and Lyman Wight were his counselors. Members of the High Council: Asahel Smith, John M. Burk, A. O. Smoot, Richard Howard, Willard Snow, Erastus Snow, David Pettigrew, Elijah Fordham,

Edward Fisher, Elias Smith, John Patten and Stephen Chase. Alanson Ripley was Bishop in Iowa. Other stakes were in early contemplation.

At Commerce in November, 1839, Don Carlos Smith and Ebenezer Robinson had established a semi-monthly paper called the *Times and Seasons*. This was the organ of the Church. In its columns Hyrum Smith had published an account of the Missouri persecutions. The Prophet became the editor of this paper. The *Nauvoo Wasp*, edited by William Smith, and afterwards renamed the *Nauvoo Neighbor*, was a later publication.

On April 6th, 1840—the tenth anniversary of the Church—the Saints convened, according to custom, in general conference. During its session Apostles Orson Hyde and John E. Page were appointed to take a mission to Palestine. Orson Hyde accepted the call, and subsequently departed for the Holy Land. Elder Page failed to fulfill his mission. It was the beginning of his defection from Mormonism. President Joseph Smith detailed to the conference his recent visit to Washington, including his interview with Van Buren, of whom he expressed his opinion in plain terms. Resolutions were passed thanking the people of Illinois, their representatives in Congress, their governor, Thomas Carlin, and Governor Lucas, of Iowa, for aid, sympathy and protection.

Commerce now changed its name to Nauvoo. During their first year of occupancy, hundreds of houses had been erected by the Saints, who were fast flocking to their new gathering place, and the insignificant hamlet of a few months before was rapidly assuming the dimensions of a city. The bend in the Mississippi at this point gave the place three river fronts, with some of the streets terminating at the water's edge. The thoroughfares were wide, crossing each other at right angles; a model of healthfulness and beauty many times copied by the city-building Saints in laying out their settlements in the Rocky Mountains. The houses, embowered in groves and gardens, tastefully and securely fenced, ranged all the way from the neatly white-washed log-cabin, through buildings of brick and frame to the stately mansion of stone. When the Temple came to crown the noble hill upon which the city had already climbed, and the busy hum of industry from forge, mill and factory arose as incense from a hundred altars, Nauvoo, the home of twice ten thousand people, was not only the City Beautiful of the Saints, but bid fair to become, in the not far distant future, the pride and glory of Illinois.*

At the time of which we write, May, 1840, the town had from two to three thousand inhabitants, and was divided ecclesiastically into three wards—Upper, Middle and Lower—presided over severally by Bishops Edward Partridge,† Newel K. Whitney and Vinson Knight. As the place grew, these three wards became four, then ten, while in the farming districts, outside the city, three additional wards were created.

Thus were affairs at Nauvoo prospering. Thus, with that wonderful recuperative power which has ever characterized them as a people, were these whilom exiles of Missouri already recovering from the effects of the persecution which had robbed them of wellnigh their earthly all.

The Mormons now began to take part in Illinois politics. Perhaps it would have been well for them in a worldly sense, though not so well in a sense far wider and higher, had they refrained from exercising this right. Though not immediately apparent, it was the beginning for them of untold sorrow. Next to the rancor of religious hatred is the bitterness of political animosity. The Mormons ere this had experienced both. They were fated ere long to again experience them.

A great presidential election was approaching. The celebrated "log-cabin and hard cider" campaign was in progress, and Whigs and Democrats throughout the entire land were working arduously in the interests of their respective parties. William Henry Harrison was the Whig candidate for the Presidency, while Martin Van Buren had

---

* Nauvoo in 1844-5 was said to be the most populous city in the State.
† Bishop Partridge died on May 27th of that year.

again been put forward by the Democrats. In Hancock County, Illinois, the two great parties were almost equally divided. A handful of votes, thrown either way, would suffice to turn a local election. This balance of power was held by the Mormons. To secure and retain their favor, therefore, became an object with politicians of both sides.

Most of the Mormons were traditionally Democrats. In Ohio, in February, 1835, they had started a paper called the *Northern Times*, supporting democracy. But now, it seems, they mostly voted with the Whigs, casting their ballots for the Harrison electors. The reason probably was, not that Joseph Smith was a Whig, but that Martin Van Buren was a Democrat. At subsequent elections in Illinois the majority of the Mormons generally voted the democratic ticket.

They were quite naturally averse, however, to supporting their enemies on any ticket, or men whom they believed incompetent, corrupt and immoral. They insisted, not only upon representation for themselves, but that men of character and ability be put forward, if their vote was wanted to elect them. The politicians, not always able to furnish what was required, no doubt deemed this fastidious. Many thought it dictatorial. Misunderstandings occurred, and much ill-feeling was at times created. Men whom the Mormons thus rejected as nominees,—for at times they carried their point in caucus,—as well as those whom they defeated at elections, generally became their enemies.

Among their friends in political circles were Hon. Sidney H. Little and Hon. Stephen A. Douglas, the former a Whig and the latter a Democrat. Mr. Little, who was a State senator, died before the Mormon troubles in Illinois had fairly begun. Judge Douglas, who was Secretary of the State, though he eventually proclaimed against the Saints, was their friend for several years after the Prophet's death. Stephen A. Douglas and Joseph Smith each regarded the other as a master spirit. It was by means of the Mormon vote, during the Prophet's lifetime, that "the little giant" finally attained to the

United States Senate. His opponents styled him "the Mormon-made Senator."

In 1840, as said, the Saints supported the Whig party in the contest which resulted in the defeat of Martin Van Buren, and the election of General Harrison as President of the United States. The anxiety of the rival parties to attach the Mormons to their interests, was doubtless an important element in the peace and prosperity enjoyed by the Saints during this period.

But now a cloud, "a cloud no bigger than a man's hand," but that hand an inveterate foe to the Prophet and his people, appears upon their horizon. It is the forerunner of a storm, a storm which, though not bursting forth instanter, shall know no lull when once its fury breaks, till the blood of that Prophet has been shed, and another and a crowning exodus of that people—from the confines of civilization to the wilds of the savage west—shall have startled by its strangeness and awakened by its unparalleled achievement, a world's wonder.

On the 15th of September, 1840, the Governor of Missouri, Lilburn W. Boggs, made a demand upon Thomas Carlin, Governor of Illinois, for Joseph Smith, junior, Sidney Rigdon, Lyman Wight, Parley P. Pratt, Caleb Baldwin and Alanson Brown, as fugitives from justice. The demand, it seems, was retaliative in its character. On the 7th of July, preceding, a party of Missourians had kidnapped four Mormons, namely: James Allred, Noah Rogers, Alanson Brown and Benjamin Boyce, whom they carried over the river to Tully, Lewis County, Missouri, tied them to trees and whipped them unmercifully.

Their excuse for their lawlessness and barbarity was that the Mormons had stolen from them. The valley of the Mississippi, at that time, was infested with thieves and rogues of every description; preying upon all classes, the Saints included. Some of these thieves were probably Mormons, weak and wicked enough to thus retaliate upon those who had robbed them of their all. But the Mormon people were not given to thievery, nor was there any proof that the four men abducted and abused by the Missourians were guilty. They were in the river-bottom hunting horses, it is said, when the men of Tully, after recovering some stolen goods near Warsaw, twenty miles below Nauvoo, came upon and captured them.

The affair created considerable excitement at Nauvoo and throughout Hancock County; the general feeling of all classes, Mormon and non-Mormon, being against the Missourians. Governor Carlin, in response to popular demand, called upon Missouri to deliver up the kidnappers. It was then that Governor Boggs issued his requisition for Joseph Smith and his brethren, most of whom had escaped from captivity in that State nearly eighteen months before.

Possibly there was more than retaliation in this act of Governor Boggs. The conduct of Missouri in the bloody crusade inaugurated by her Executive against her Mormon citizens, had been widely condemned, and the charges alleged against the Saints in justification of that conduct were generally disbelieved. The fact that many months had passed since the escape of the Mormon leaders, during which no effort had been made to retake them, was being cited in proof of the falsity of those charges. Governor Boggs, therefore, after a Rip Van Winkle sleep of seventeen months, suddenly wakes up and returns to the assault, hoping perhaps to vindicate, or at least render consistent his former course, and rescue by a *coup d'etat* what remains of his besmirched and shattered reputation.

Besides, the state election is approaching, and it may be that he hopes for another term of office. What more brilliant a bribe, what more tempting a bait for ballots, in Mormon-hating Missouri, than Joseph Smith the Mormon leader in chains?

Many non-Mormon citizens of Illinois stoutly opposed the delivery of the persons named, even if guilty, to be dealt with by officials who had sanctioned and even assisted in the butchery, wholesale robbery and expulsion of their innocent co-religionists. But many did not believe them guilty. Said the Quincy *Whig*, a prominent journal of that period: "We repeat, Smith and Rigdon should not be given up. * * The law is made to secure the punishment of the guilty, and not to sacrifice the innocent. * * Compliance on the part of Governor Carlin would be to deliver them, not to be tried for crime, but to be punished without crime."

Other papers justified the Governor in observing the forms of law usual in such cases, and issuing his requisition for the arrest and delivery of the Mormon leaders to the officers of Missouri.

Carlin's writ was returned to him unserved; the sheriff of Hancock County, entrusted with its service, not being able to find the persons wanted. Having no faith in Missouri justice, like the wise man in the proverb they had probably "foreseen the evil" and "hid themselves."

Despite this unpleasant episode, fortune continued to rain favors upon the Mormons in Illinois. During the winter of 1840-41 the Legislature granted the Charter of the City of Nauvoo, one of the most liberal charters ever bestowed upon a municipality. It was planned by the Prophet and devised, as he said, "on principles so broad that any honest man might dwell secure under its protective influence without distinction of sect or party."

A few sections of the Charter are here inserted:

Sec. 4. There shall be a City Council to consist of Mayor, four Aldermen and nine Councilors, who shall have the qualifications of electors of said city, and shall be chosen by the qualified voters thereof, and shall hold their offices for two years, and until their successors shall be elected and qualified. The City Council shall judge of the qualifications, elections and returns of their own members, and a majority of them shall form a quorum to do business; but a smaller number may adjourn from day to day, and compel the attendance of absent members, under such penalties as may be prescribed by ordinance.

Sec. 5. The Mayor, Aldermen and Councilors, before entering upon the duties of their offices, shall take and subscribe an oath or affirmation, that they will support the Constitution of the United States and of this State, and that they will well and truly perform the duties of their offices to the best of their skill and abilities.

Sec. 11. The City Council shall have power and authority to make, ordain, establish and execute all such ordinances, not repugnant to the Constitution of the United States or of this State, as they may deem necessary for the benefit, peace, good order, regulation, convenience and cleanliness of said city; for the protection of property therein from destruction by fire or otherwise, and for the health and happiness thereof; they shall have power to fill all vacancies that may happen by death, resignation or removal, in any of the offices herein made elective; to fix and establish all the fees of the officers of said corporation not herein established; to impose such fines not exceeding one hundred dollars for each offense, as they may deem just, for refusing to accept any office in or under the corporation, or for misconduct therein; to divide the city into wards; to add to the number of Aldermen and Councilors, and apportion them among the several wards as may be most just and conducive to the interests of the city.

Sec. 13. The City Council shall have exclusive power within the city, by ordinance to license, regulate and restrain the keeping of ferries; to regulate the police of the city; to impose fines, forfeitures and penalties for the breach of any ordinance, and provide for the recovery of such fines and forfeitures, and the enforcement of such penalties, and to pass such ordinances as may be necessary and proper for carrying into execution the powers specified in this act: Provided, Such ordinances are not repugnant to the Constitution of the United States or of this State; and in fine, to exercise such other legislative powers as are conferred on the City Council of the city of Springfield, by an act entitled "An act to incorporate the city of Springfield," approved February third, one thousand eight hundred and forty.

Sec. 16. The Mayor and Aldermen shall be conservators of the peace within the limits of said city, and shall have all the powers of Justices of the Peace therein, both in civil and criminal cases, arising under the laws of the State; they shall, as Justices of the Peace within the limits of said city, perform the same duties, be governed by the same laws, give the same bonds and security as other Justices of the Peace, and be commissioned as Justices of the Peace in and for said city by the Governor.

Sec. 17. The Mayor shall have exclusive jurisdiction in all cases arising under the ordinances of the corporation, and shall issue such process as may be necessary to carry said ordinances into execution and effect; appeals may be had from any decision or judgment of said Mayor or Aldermen, arising under the city ordinances, to the Municipal Court, under such regulations as may be presented by ordinance, which Court shall be composed of the Mayor, or Chief Justice, and the Aldermen as Associate Justices, and from the final judgment of the Municipal Court to the Circuit Court of Hancock County, in the same manner as appeals are taken from the judgments of Justices of the Peace: Provided, That the parties litigant shall have a right to a trial by a jury of twelve men in all cases before the Municipal Court. The Municipal Court shall have power to grant writs of *habeas corpus* in all cases arising under the ordinances of the City Council.

Sec. 19. All processes issued by the Mayor, Aldermen or Municipal Court shall be directed to the Marshal, and in the execution thereof he shall be governed by the same laws as are or may be prescribed for the direction and compensation of constables in similar cases. The Marshal shall also perform such other duties as may be required of him under the ordinances of said city, and shall be the principal ministerial officer.

Sec. 24. The City Council may establish and organize an institution of learning within the limits of the city for the teaching of the arts, sciences and learned professions, to be called the "University of the City of Nauvoo;" which institution shall be under the control and management of a Board of Trustees, consisting of a Chancellor, Registrar, and twenty-three Regents, which Board shall thereafter be a body corporate and politic, with perpetual succession, by the name of the "Chancellor and Regents of the University of the City of Nauvoo," and shall have full power to pass, ordain, establish and execute all such laws and ordinances as they may consider for the welfare and prosperity of said University, its officers and students; Provided, That the said laws and ordinances shall not be repugnant to the Constitution of the United States or of this State; and, Provided, also, That the Trustees shall at all times be appointed by the City Council, and shall have all the powers and privileges for the advancement of the cause of education which appertain to the trustees of any other college or university of this State.

Sec. 25. The City Council may organize the inhabitants of said city subject to military duty into a body of independent military men, to be called the "Nauvoo Legion," the court-martial of which shall be composed of the commissioned officers of said Legion, and constitute the law-making department, with full powers and authority to make, ordain, establish and execute, all such laws and ordinances, as may be considered necessary for the benefit, government and regulation of said Legion; Provided, Said court-martial shall pass no law or act repugnant to or inconsistent with the Constitution of the United States or of this State; and Provided, also, That the officers of the Legion shall be commissioned by the Governor of the State. The said Legion shall perform the same amount of military duty as is now or may be hereafter required of the regular militia of the State, and shall be at the disposal of the Mayor in executing the laws and ordinances of the City Corporation, and the laws of the State, and at the disposal of the Governor for the public defense and the execution of the laws of the State, or of the United States, and shall be entitled to their proportion of the public arms; and, Provided, also, That said Legion shall be exempt from all other military duty.

Having passed both houses of the Legislative Assembly, the Charter of Nauvoo was signed by Governor Carlin and certified by Secretary Douglas on the 16th of December. It went into effect February 1st, 1841.

On that day occurred the first city election of Nauvoo, resulting in the choice of the following named officers: Mayor, John C. Bennett; Aldermen, William Marks, Samuel H. Smith, Daniel H. Wells and Newel K. Whitney; Councilors, Joseph Smith, Hyrum Smith, Sidney Rigdon, Charles C. Rich, John T. Barnett, Wilson Law, Don Carlos Smith, John P. Greene and Vinson Knight.

Among the first bills for ordinances presented to the city council, was one to prohibit the sale of liquor at retail within the corporate limits, and others providing for the freedom of all religious sects and of all peaceable public meetings within the city. These bills were presented by the Prophet, and ordinances passed accordingly. It was the purpose of the Saints, who greatly predominated at Nauvoo, to make of it a strictly moral and free city, as free from vice as from tyranny, a delight at once to its inhabitants and to the stranger within its gates.

The municipal election was followed by the organization of the University and of the Nauvoo Legion, as provided for in the Charter. At the military election, held on the 4th of February, Joseph Smith was chosen Lieutenant-General, John C. Bennett, Major-General, and Wilson Law and Don Carlos Smith, Brigadier-Generals of the Legion. It was modeled after the Roman legion, and consisted originally of six companies, divided into two brigades or cohorts. Subsequently other citizens of Hancock County joined the Legion, and it finally aggregated several thousand troops.

The Nauvoo University, for which a suitable edifice was to be erected, was officered as follows: Chancellor, John C. Bennett; Registrar, William Law; Regents, Joseph Smith, Sidney Rigdon, Hyrum Smith, William Marks, Samuel H. Smith, Daniel H. Wells, Newel K. Whitney, Charles C. Rich, John T. Barnett, Wilson Law, John P. Greene, Vinson Knight, Isaac Galland, Elias Higbee, Robert D. Foster, James Adams, Samuel Bennett, Ebenezer Robinson, John Snider, George Miller, Lenos M. Knight, John Taylor and Heber C. Kimball. Its faculty included the names of Sidney Rigdon, Orson Pratt, Orson Spencer and James Kelly; the latter two college graduates. Four common school wards, with three wardens to each, were connected with the University.

On January 24th of that year, a change had taken place in the personnel of the Church Presidency. Hyrum Smith, second counselor to the Prophet, having been called to succeed his deceased sire as Patriarch of the Church, William Law was chosen to fill the vacancy thus created in the Presidency. A few days later, Joseph Smith was chosen Trustee-in-Trust for the Church, to hold the legal title to its property agreeable to the laws of Illinois. The succession to this office was vested in the First Presidency. It was perpetuated for many years after the Mormons removed to Utah.

April 6th, 1841. A general conference convened this day at the chief city of the Saints. During the morning hours the corner stones of the Nauvoo Temple were laid and dedicated. On the third day of the conference, Lyman Wight was ordained an Apostle to fill a vacancy which had for some time existed in the council of the Twelve.

Apropos of the Apostles, let us now briefly advert to them and their mission abroad. After leaving Illinois, in the fall of 1839, the majority of the Twelve made their way to Kirtland, where a few families of Saints yet resided. Thence they journeyed to New York, preaching by the way and laboring for some time in that city and its vicinity. In the latter part of December, John Taylor, Wilford Woodruff, Hiram Clark and Theodore Turley sailed for Liverpool on board the *Oxford*. Three months later, Brigham Young, Heber C. Kimball, Parley P. Pratt, Orson Pratt, George A. Smith and Reuben Hedlock followed in their wake on the *Patrick Henry*.

Landing at Liverpool on the 6th of April, 1840, President Young and his party there found Apostle Taylor, with about thirty converts. He and his party had arrived at that port on the 11th of January. They were there welcomed by Mr. George Cannon, Apostle Taylor's brother-in-law, who resided at Liverpool. He was the father of George Q. Cannon, then a mere lad, and not yet connected with the cause in which he was destined to play, in after years, so prominent a part. Visiting Preston, Apostle Taylor had returned with Joseph Fielding to Liverpool, while Elders Woodruff and Turley had gone into Staffordshire, and Hiram Clark to Manchester. In that great town a branch of the Church had previously been built up by Elder William Clayton.

Immediately upon the arrival of President Young, a conference of the British Saints was called to convene at Preston on the 14th of April. That day Willard Richards was ordained to the Apostleship. It was decided to send for a score or more of the Seventies, to assist the Apostles in their ministry; to publish a hymn book for the use of the Saints, and to establish at Manchester a monthly periodical to be called *The Latter-day Saints' Millennial Star*.*

*The first number of the *Star*, edited by Parley P. Pratt, appeared in May, 1840. It is now a weekly issue and is published at Liverpool.

The Apostles and Elders then separated and went preaching into various parts of Great Britain. Their experience was a repetition of the success of Heber C. Kimball and his confreres in that land a few years before. The fruits of Apostle Woodruff's labors in Staffordshire and Herefordshire were especially abundant. He baptized hundreds, including over forty preachers of the sect known as United Brethren. Wales, Scotland, Ireland, the Isle of Man, and parts of England yet unvisited by the Elders, were all penetrated and many converts made of each nationality. The foundations for future missionary success, in the organization of conferences, the establishment of a publishing house and a shipping agency were now laid broad and permanently.

On June 6th, 1840, a company of forty-one Latter-day Saints—the first to emigrate from a foreign land, sailed from Liverpool on the ship *Britannia*, bound for Nauvoo, via New York. John Moon had charge of this company. About three months later two hundred more, in charge of Theodore Turley and William Clayton, were carried over in the *North America*. Several other companies sailed in 1841, the last one for that year going to Nauvoo by way of New Orleans, which then became the regular route. Each succeeding year added its quota; the work of proselyting more than keeping pace with the continuous drain of emigration. It is estimated that prior to the settlement of Utah nearly five thousand British converts to Mormonism had landed in America.

Thus was set in motion that great tide of immigration which, swelling the numbers of the Saints in the Mississippi Valley, peopled in later years with the skilled mechanics and hardy yeomanry of Britain, Scandinavia and other European countries, the mountain valleys of Utah; mingling their brave blood—brave to forsake native land, sunder all earthly ties and endure the scorn and odium heaped ever upon the adherents of an unpopular faith—with the life-stream of a race equally heroic, cradled in the lap of liberty. The result, the bone and sinew, character and intelligence of Utah to-day,—the promise of the present to the future.

When the Apostles landed at Liverpool, in April, 1840, the Church in Great Britain numbered less than two thousand souls. Twelve months later, when most of them returned to America, that figure had been more than trebled. Said Brigham Young: "It truly seems a miracle to look upon the contrast between our landing and departing at Liverpool. We landed in the spring of 1840, as strangers in a strange land, and penniless; but through the mercy of God we have gained many friends, established churches in almost every noted town and city of Great Britain; baptized between seven and eight thousand souls, printed five thousand Books of Mormon, three thousand hymn books, twenty-five hundred volumes of the *Millennial Star* and fifty thousand tracts; emigrated to Zion one thousand souls, established a permanent shipping agency, which will be a great blessing to the Saints, and have left sown in the hearts of thousands the seed of eternal life. And yet we have lacked nothing to eat, drink or wear."

Parley P. Pratt was left by his brethren to preside over the British Mission. Orson Hyde was in Palestine. The remainder of the Apostles who had gone abroad now returned home, some of them reaching Nauvoo early in July, 1841.

Anticipating their arrival by several weeks, our story now returns to the latter part of May. As already shown, it was a part of the plan of the Mormon leader, besides building up a central Stake of Zion at Nauvoo, to establish other stakes in that vicinity. Among these, which had now been organized for several months, were those of Ramus and Lima in Hancock County, Quincy and Mount Hope in Adams County, Geneva in Morgan County, and Zarahemla in Lee County, Iowa. One of the stake presidency at Quincy was Ezra T. Benson, afterwards an Apostle and a prominent Utah pioneer.

The stake at Kirtland, Ohio, had lately been reorganized, with Almon W. Babbitt, Lester Brooks and Zebedee Coltrin as its presidency. All or most of the stakes were being built up rapidly by the gathering of the Saints from various parts, including those from abroad.

On the 24th of May, 1841, President Smith announced through the *Times and Seasons* the discontinuance of all the stakes outside of Hancock County, Illinois, and Lee County, Iowa, and called upon the Saints residing in other parts " to make preparations to come in without delay." Said he: "This is important, and should be attended to by all who feel an interest in the prosperity of this, the corner stone of Zion. Here the temple must be raised, the university be built, and other edifices erected which are necessary for the great work of the last days; and which can only be done by a concentration of energy and enterprise." To this call the Saints responded with alacrity, and came pouring in from all parts outside the two counties mentioned, to engage in the work of building up and beautifying " the corner stone of Zion."

To the followers of the Prophet, as well as to the Prophet himself, this was all that the call really meant. Temple-building, with the Saints, we need scarcely inform the reader, amounts to what might be termed a divine passion; a work done by Time for Eternity. The sacred edifices they rear, with their solemn ceremonies and ordinances, represent to them so many links literally binding earth to heaven. No work in their estimation is so important,—not even their proselyting labors among the nations. Next to their religious mission of preaching, proselyting, and administering in their temples for the salvation of the living and the dead, is their penchant for founding institutions of learning. This fact Mormon history abundantly verifies, in spite of all that has been said and thought to the contrary. This explains in part that ready obedience,—wrongfully supposed to be a mere servile yielding to the dictum of a despot,—manifested by the Saints to the word and will of their leader. He was simply inviting them to engage in the work most congenial to their souls; and this, as we have said, was all that the call really meant.

But to the politicians it meant more,—or rather, meant something entirely different. It was construed by them as a shrewd political maneuver, foreshadowing the ultimate domination of Hancock County by the Mormons, and the relegation to the rear, as a hopeless minority, of the combined forces of Whigs, Democrats and whatever else, in spite of all that could be done to hinder. It was believed, in short, to be a "colonizing" scheme, a trick to increase and render supreme the local Mormon vote. Already jealous of the power wielded by the Saints at the polls, and professing to "view with alarm" the prospective increase of that power by means of the proposed concentration, some of the politicians now set about organizing in Hancock County a new party, the avowed object of which was to oppose and counteract the political influence of the Mormons in county and in state.

Public meetings to discuss the question were held at various points, and resolutions expressive of the anti-Mormon feeling passed by those assembled. The result was the rise of the Anti-Mormon Party, and the origin of the term "anti-Mormon," thenceforth in vogue in Illinois politics. Much bitterness was engendered by this party, not only against the Mormons, whom they finally compelled to leave the State, but against all who affiliated with or in any way befriended them. Such were denominated Jack-Mormons. The hatred of the Anti-Mormons for the Mormons, despite their resolutions and protestations to the contrary, expressed itself not only in politics, but in everything else, social, commercial and religious.

Of course there were exceptions to this rule; Joseph Smith himself styled some of the Anti-Mormons "good fellows." But they were mixed in politics,—which like adversity "makes strange bedfellows,"—with many characters that were positively disreputable. The party as a whole probably answered, far better than did Bacon, Pope's caustic description of England's great Lord Chancellor,—"the wisest, brightest, meanest of mankind."

The Anti-Mormon Party of Illinois was made up of all parties. Anyone with a grievance against the Saints,—from the apostate, expelled from the Church for adultery, to the common thief and counterfeiter, convicted and punished at Nauvoo for breaking the city ordinances,—forthwith became an anti-Mormon. Whigs and Democrats then, as Republicans and Democrats since, united to oppose and destroy the political power of the Mormons.

Whether or not the anti-Mormons conspired about this time with the Executive of Illinois, to effect a speedier solution of the problem than seemed possible by means of ordinary methods,—even to remove the Mormon leader from the midst of his people, thus paralyzing the gathering movement in progress,—may never be known. But the arrest of the Prophet, a few weeks after his proclamation had gone forth, on the identical writ first issued by Governor Boggs in September, 1840, with the part played by Governor Carlin in bringing about that arrest, almost warrants the suspicion. It occurred as follows: About the 4th of June, 1841, Joseph Smith, having accompanied as far as Quincy his brother Hyrum and William Law, who were starting east upon a mission, called upon Governor Carlin at his residence in that place. He was received with marked kindness and respect. In the extended interview which followed between the Governor and his visitor, nothing whatever was said of the writ formerly issued by Missouri, concerning which all excitement had long since abated. Taking leave of his Excellency, the Prophet set out for Nauvoo. He had not gone far when he was overtaken and arrested by Sheriff King of Adams County, and a *posse*, whom he believed the Governor had sent after him. Among them was an officer from Missouri, the bearer of the writ, who gloated exultingly over the prisoner and the prospect of carrying him back to his former captivity.

But Joseph Smith had studied law as well as theology, and knew how to defend his rights under the circumstances. Obtaining a writ of *habeas corpus* from C. A. Warren, Esq., master in chancery at Quincy, he had the hearing in the case set for the 8th of June, at Monmouth, Warren County, before Judge Stephen A. Douglas. Judge Douglas had arrived at Quincy on the night of the arrest. Next morning the Prophet, accompanied by Sheriff King and the Missouri officer, started for Nauvoo. On the way the Sheriff, who was in poor health, was taken seriously ill. The Prophet conveyed him to his own home and nursed him with the kindliest care.

The hearing at Monmouth came off in due order on the day appointed. Considerable excitement reigned, and an effort was made by the rabble to mob the Mormon leader as he entered the town. Sheriff King, however, faithfully stood by his prisoner and protected him from assault. A formidable array of attorneys assisted in the prosecution. The Prophet's counsel were C. A. Warren, Sidney H. Little, O. H. Browning, James H. Ralston, Cyrus Walker and Archibald Williams. Mr. Browning, in the course of an earnest and eloquent plea, pictured so vividly the sufferings of the Prophet and his people in Missouri, and the hopeless case of the prisoner if delivered over to his former persecutors, that nearly all present, including Judge Douglas himself, shed tears.*

The defense rested upon two propositions: (1) that the Missouri writ, having once been returned to the Executive unserved, was void; (2) that the entire proceeding on the part of Missouri was illegal. Judge Douglas, without going into the merits of the second proposition, decided that the writ was void and that the prisoner must be liberated. Amid the rejoicings of his friends, and to the chagrin of his enemies, the Prophet returned to Nauvoo.

But press and pulpit now took up the controversy, the tone of the former, once so favorable to the Saints, being now much modified. Some papers were openly hostile. Beneath the burning rays of political jealousy and religious hatred the flowers of friendship were fast fading. Even Judge Douglas was censured for his decision

---

* Said Browning: "Great God! have I not seen it? Yes, mine eyes have beheld the blood-stained traces of innocent women and children, in the drear winter, who had traveled hundreds of miles bare-foot through frost and snow, to seek a refuge from their savage pursuers. It was a scene of horror, sufficient to enlist sympathy from an adamantine heart. And shall this unfortunate man, whom their fury has seen proper to select for sacrifice, be driven into such a savage land, and none dare to enlist in the cause of justice? If there was no other voice under heaven ever to be heard in this cause, gladly would I stand alone, and proudly spend my latest breath in defence of an oppressed American citizen."

which had set the Mormon leader free. The Prophet's personal foes, the more radical anti-Mormons, sought in every way to prejudice the public mind against him. That they succeeded the tragic issue amply showed.

One charge preferred against the Mormons in Illinois was that of "spoiling the Philistines,"—in other words stealing from the Gentiles; a practice which it was said their leaders sanctioned. This accusation, being noised abroad and believed by many, was an effective weapon for the anti-Mormons. It was particularly gratifying to the thieving bands that continued plying their nefarious trade up and down the Mississippi. Screening them from suspicion, by placing the onus of their misdeeds upon others, it enabled them to pursue their dangerous vocation with greater security.

That some Mormons practiced thievery was doubtless true,—as true as that some anti-Mormons did,—but the allegation that the Mormon leaders sanctioned such a practice was totally false. On the contrary they denounced it, in public and in private, publishing, in December, 1841, their emphatic denial of the charge of teaching their followers that it was right and proper for them to prey upon "the Philistines." They made examples, too, of such of their community as were convicted of stealing. Two subordinate officers of the Nauvoo Legion, being found guilty of theft, were promptly cashiered and their names stricken from the rank roll.

With the return of the Apostles from Europe, the work of building up Nauvoo and the surrounding stakes was much accelerated. The Nauvoo Temple and the Nauvoo House—the latter designed for the entertainment of strangers—were now progressing favorably; also other edifices and public improvements. What gave the Temple a special impetus about this time was the enunciation by the Prophet of the tenet of baptism for the dead. A Masonic Temple was likewise projected at Nauvoo, and Joseph and Hyrum Smith, Brigham Young and many other leading Mormons became Free Masons.

Joseph Smith's fame was now the property of two hemispheres. He was styled, from his rank as Lieutenant General of the Nauvoo

Legion, "a military prophet," and referred to both in Europe and America as "the Western Mohamet." All sorts of rumors as to his alleged intended conquests, with the sword in one hand and his Koran—the Book of Mormon—in the other, began to fill the air.

Early in 1842 the great journals of the land, which had hitherto ignored or treated lightly the subject of Mormonism, began to send representatives to Nauvoo to write up the question, or solicit from the Prophet contributions to their columns touching that topic, which had become one of the most interesting of the hour. The first of these journals to give the Mormons a fair and full presentation to the public was the New York *Herald*, in which a series of letters appeared over the signature of James Arlington Bennett, of Long Island, who visited Nauvoo to see for himself, and as the representative of James Gordon Bennett, this Mecca and its Mohamet of the West. So pleased were the authorities at Nauvoo with the fair and impartial letters published in the *Herald* that the City Council passed resolutions thanking the editor for his courtesy and liberality, while upon the author of the articles was gratefully conferred the honorary title of Inspector-General of the Nauvoo Legion.

John Wentworth, Esq., proprietor of the Chicago *Democrat*—an influential journal—solicited from the Prophet's pen a concise sketch of his personal history with that of the Church from its inception to the year 1842. The sketch was furnished and published. It contained what are known as the Articles of Faith of the Church of Jesus Christ of Latter-day Saints. It stated, among other things, that the Prophet's followers at Nauvoo, were from six to eight thousand souls, with "vast numbers in the county around and in almost every county of the State." Other pens and tongues, of tourists and visitors, praised the hospitality, enterprise, industry, good order and morality of the City Beautiful and its inhabitants.

We have stated that Stephen A. Douglas regarded Joseph Smith as a master spirit. He was not alone in that opinion of the founder of Mormonism. James Arlington Bennett styled him "one of the greatest characters of the age." Josiah Quincy, who, in company with Charles Francis Adams, senior, was at Nauvoo shortly before the Prophet's death, said of him:

It is by no means improbable that some future textbook, for the use of generations yet unborn, will contain a question something like this: What historical American of the nineteenth century has exerted the most powerful influence upon the destinies of his countrymen? And it is by no means impossible that the answer to that interrogatory may be thus written: *Joseph Smith, the Mormon Prophet*. And the reply, absurd as it doubtless seems to most men now living, may be an obvious common-place to their descendants. History deals in surprises and paradoxes quite as startling as this. The man who established a religion in this age of free debate, who was and is today accepted by hundreds of thousands as a direct emissary from the Most High,—such a rare human being is not to be disposed of by pelting his memory with unsavory epithets. Fanatic, imposter, charlatan, he may have been; but these hard names furnish no solution to the problem he presents to us. Fanatics and impostors are living and dying every day, and their memory is buried with them; but the wonderful influence which this founder of a religion exerted and still exerts throws him into relief before us, not as a rogue to be criminated, but as a phenomenon to be explained. * * * * *

"A fine looking man," continues Mr. Quincy, "is what the passer-by would instinctively have murmured. But Smith was more than this, and one could not resist the impression that capacity and resource were natural in his stalwart person."

In May, 1842, the treachery and rascality of a man whom the Mormon leader had befriended and loaded with honors, became known to his benefactor. That man was Dr. John C. Bennett, Mayor of Nauvoo, Chancellor of its University, and Major-General of its Legion. He had become associated with the Saints soon after their exodus from Missouri. Though a great egotist, he was a man of education, address and ability. That he had little or no principle was not immediately apparent. Considerable of a diplomat and possessing some influence in political circles, he rendered valuable aid in securing the passage by the Illinois Legislature of the act incorporating the city of Nauvoo.* Hence the honors bestowed upon

---

* It was to such men as Senator Little and Judge Douglas that the Mormons were most indebted for the passage of the act. Abraham Lincoln, the future martyr President, then a member of the Illinois Legislature, voted, it is said, for the Nauvoo Charter and congratulated the Mormons on its passage. Lincoln was never an enemy to the Saints, and they much esteemed him.

him by the Mormon people. Prior to that, and subsequently, he was Quartermaster-General of Illinois. Bennett professed great sympathy for the Saints. He joined the Church and apparently was a sincere convert to the faith.

Governor Thomas Ford, in his history of Illinois, styles Bennett "probably the greatest scamp in the western country." But this was not until long after the Mormons, thrice victimized, had become aware of his villainy.

On the 7th of May the Nauvoo Legion, now consisting of twenty-six companies, aggregating two thousand troops, assembled for a grand parade and sham battle, which was witnessed by thousands of spectators. Among the visitors present, as guests of General Joseph Smith, were Judge Stephen A. Douglas and other legal lights, who had adjourned the circuit court at Carthage in order to attend the Mormon military review. Wilson Law and Charles C. Rich,—the latter successor to Don Carlos Smith, deceased,—were the Brigadier-Generals of the Legion. As such, it devolved upon them to lead the two cohorts in the battle. For some reason, however, Major-General Bennett tried hard to induce the Prophet to take part in the fight and lead one of the cohorts. Suspecting Bennett's motive, General Smith declined, and subsequently recorded his impression that the purpose was to have him treacherously slain, in such a way that none but the guilty might know who did the deed.

Bennett's after course gave color to the Prophet's suspicion. The same month he was convicted of seduction,—a crime which seems to have been common with him,—and expelled from the Mormon Church. He was also deprived of the various offices given him by the people of Nauvoo. Joseph Smith succeeded him as Mayor, Orson Spencer as Chancellor of the University, and Wilson Law as Major-General of the Legion.

Bennett, to subserve his licentious practices, had secretly taught that the Prophet sanctioned illicit relations between the sexes. Professing deep contrition after his exposure, he voluntarily went before Alderman Daniel H. Wells and made oath to the effect that Joseph

Smith had never taught him anything contrary to virtue and morality, and that so far as he knew the Prophet's private life was above reproach. These statements he repeated in public meetings. Finding, however, that he had become morally bankrupt in the eyes of the community, and could not, even if forgiven, regain their confidence, he withdrew from Nauvoo and joined the anti-Mormons.

He now repeated his former tale of Joseph Smith's licentious teachings and practices, claiming that his denial of the charge had been forced from him by threats of violence. He revived the story of the Danites, originated by Dr. Avard at Far West. Bennett declared that these "Avenging Angels," were following him to take his life, as they had previously taken other lives at the Prophet's command. He also wrote and published a book against Mormonism, and devoted himself assiduously to the task of bringing trouble upon his former friends. The more intelligent and reputable anti-Mormons despised Bennett and distrusted his story, but others believed and made use of it, and prejudice against the Saints increased correspondingly.* During August the Prophet sent out the Apostles and a large number of Elders to preach in the country round and refute the vile slanders of this vengeful apostate.

Coming events now cast their solemn shadows before. The Prophet foresaw the inevitable. He more than once had hinted at his own death, and, as seen, had singled out intuitively his successor. To him a mighty destiny was opening for his people, but the far West, and not the East, nor even the intermediary region was the fated arena of Mormonism's immediate future. On Saturday, August 6th, 1842, at Montrose, Lee County, Iowa, he uttered in the presence of several friends a prediction, recorded in his own words as follows:

"I prophesied that the Saints would continue to suffer much affliction, and would be driven to the Rocky Mountains. Many would

---

* Governor Carlin being informed by Joseph Smith of Bennett's conduct at Nauvoo, replied, "Bennett's meanness is in accordance with representations of his character made to me more than two years since, and which I felt constrained to believe were true, since which time I have desired to have as little intercourse with him as possible."

apostatize; others would be put to death by our persecutors, or lose their lives in consequence of exposure or disease; and some would live to go and assist in making settlements and building cities, and see the Saints become a mighty people in the midst of the Rocky Mountains."

CHAPTER XII.
1842-1843.

AGAIN IN THE TOILS—JOSEPH SMITH AND PORTER ROCKWELL ARRESTED, CHARGED WITH ATTEMPTED MURDER—EX-GOVERNOR BOGGS OF MISSOURI THE ALLEGED VICTIM—HOW THE DEED WAS DONE—THE PRISONERS RELEASED BY HABEAS CORPUS—THEY EVADE RE-ARREST —ROCKWELL KIDNAPPED AND CARRIED TO MISSOURI—GOVERNOR FORD SUCCEEDS GOVERNOR CARLIN—THE PROPHET SUBMITS TO A JUDICIAL INVESTIGATION—JUDGE POPE—THE MORMON LEADER AGAIN LIBERATED—ANOTHER REQUISITION—JOSEPH SMITH KIDNAPPED—HIS RESCUE AND RELEASE—ANTI-MORMON DEPREDATIONS AROUND NAUVOO.

TWO days after the delivery of the foregoing prediction the Prophet was again arrested. He was charged this time with being an accessory to an attempt to murder. The alleged victim was no other than Lilburn W. Boggs, ex-Governor of Missouri, who, on the night of May 6th, 1842, at his home in Independence, Jackson County, in that State, had indeed been shot and dangerously wounded by some person or persons unknown.

Lying near an open window in a pool of blood, with a ghastly wound in his head, the ex-Governor had been found by his little son, soon after the shooting. Footprints and a smoking pistol on the ground outside afforded the only clue to the perpetrator of the deed. Suspicion, however, at once rested upon the Mormons, whom Boggs had so persistently persecuted while in power, and without further ado the crime was laid at their door. It was said that Joseph Smith had predicted a violent death for Governor Boggs, and lo! here was an attempt at fulfillment. Could anything be plainer? The proof was positive—positive enough to suit the Missourians, eager for any excuse to get the Mormon leader back into their power—that he was in some way connected with the commission of the crime.

It was not contended that he had committed the assault in person.

The Missourians soon learned that Joseph Smith, if so accused, could prove an *alibi*. The date of the assault was just one day prior to the grand parade and sham battle at Nauvoo, already mentioned, and the distance between that place and Independence was at least two hundred miles; in those days a full week's journey. Besides it was pretty generally known that the Prophet had not been in Missouri since his escape from captivity in that State in the spring of 1839. But then he might have sent a "Danite"—say Porter Rockwell, or some "avenging angel,"—to do the deed of blood, after which the assassin had made good his escape. So reasoned among themselves the Missourians.

It was useless after that for Joseph Smith to deny—as he did—having ever made such a prediction about ex-Governor Boggs. Useless, also, that he denied sending Porter Rockwell, or anyone else into Missouri for such a purpose; or that Rockwell had been in that State during the year 1842. Such denials availed nothing. Suspicion had already decided his guilt. Neither would evidence the most conclusive now clear him. Were not the Mormons all falsifiers? Had they not slandered Missouri and rendered her name odious by declaring that she had persecuted them for their religious opinions? Here was a rare chance for revenge. The hated Prophet had lain himself liable, or had been laid liable to fall back into their power. Let them once but "get him on the hip," and they would "feed fat the ancient grudge" they bore him.

Boggs himself shared, or professed to share, in the general opinion regarding the Mormon leader's complicity in the crime. As soon, therefore, as he had recovered from his well-nigh fatal wound, and he and his friends had had time to mature their plans, he went before a justice of the peace—Samuel Weston—and swore out a complaint charging "Joseph Smith, commonly called the Mormon Prophet," with being "an accessory before the fact of the intended murder." The affidavit stated that "the said Joseph Smith" was "a citizen or resident of the State of Illinois."

Upon this complaint, application was made to the Governor of

Missouri, Thomas Reynolds, for the issuance of a writ demanding Joseph Smith of the authorities of Illinois. Governor Reynolds promptly responded, issuing the desired requisition. The writ, however, instead of following the language of the affidavit, described Joseph Smith, not as "a citizen or resident of the State of Illinois," but as a "fugitive from justice" who had "fled to the State of Illinois." It also went beyond the affidavit in stating that the assault was "made by one O. P. Rockwell." whose name, it appears, had been left out of the original complaint.

Governor Carlin, on receiving the requisition from Missouri, issued a warrant for Joseph Smith's arrest, stating therein—if Governor Ford's duplicate warrant upon which the case finally came up for trial was an exact copy of the original—that it had been "made known" to him "by the Executive authority of the State of Missouri, that one Joseph Smith stands charged by the affidavit of one Lilburn W. Boggs * * with being accessory before the fact to an assault with intent to kill, made by one O. P. Rockwell." etc., "and that the said Joseph Smith had fled from the justice of said State and taken refuge in the State of Illinois." Thus Carlin not only repeated the mis-statements of Governor Reynolds, but added one of his own, in saying that the Executive of Missouri had informed him that "Joseph Smith had fled from the justice of said State." It was these discrepancies between the Boggs affidavit and the writs of the two governors ostensibly based thereon, together with the insufficiency of the affidavit, that proved the mouse to gnaw the net and set the lion free.

The glaring illegality of the whole proceeding is further shown in the fact that an attempt was here made to transport to Missouri for trial a citizen of the State of Illinois, for an offense committed—if committed at all—in Illinois. Joseph Smith was not charged with assaulting ex-Governor Boggs, but with sending O. P. Rockwell from Illinois to Missouri for that purpose. Rockwell, on a proper showing, might indeed have been lawfully tried in Missouri; but not Joseph Smith, whose alleged offense was against the laws of Illinois.

Whether the two governors erred blindly or wilfully in the parts played by them in this legal burlesque, we know not. The probability is that Reynolds, perceiving the weakness of the affidavit, purposely overstated its contents in order to insure the success of the undertaking. Carlin, on his part, was either a co-conspirator with Reynolds, or, to give him the benefit of the doubt, ignorant or careless as to the outcome.

Anyway, Joseph Smith and Orrin Porter Rockwell were both arrested by the deputy sheriff of Adams County, at Nauvoo, on the 8th of August. Immediately after their arrest they obtained a writ of *habeas corpus*, and were discharged after a hearing before the Municipal Court of Nauvoo. The deputy sheriff and his assistants denied the jurisdiction of the Nauvoo Court, but leaving the prisoners, they returned to Governor Carlin for further instructions. Two days later they reappeared, having been instructed to "re-arrest at all hazards." But the persons wanted were nowhere to be found.

The authority under which the Municipal Court acted in discharging the prisoners was the following ordinance passed by the City Council on the day of the arrest:

An Ordinance regulating the mode of proceeding in cases of *habeas corpus* before the Municipal Court:

Sec. 1. Be it ordained by the City Council of the City of Nauvoo, That in all cases where any person or persons shall at any time hereafter be arrested or under arrest, in this city, under any writ or process, and shall be brought before the Municipal Court of this city, by virtue of a writ of *habeas corpus*, the Court shall in every case have power and authority, and are hereby required to examine into the origin, validity and legality of the writ or process, under which such arrest was made; and if it shall appear to the Court upon sufficient testimony, that said writ or process was illegal, or not legally issued, or did not proceed from the proper authority, then the Court shall discharge the prisoner from under said arrest; but if it shall appear to the Court that said writ or process had issued from proper authority, and was a legal process, the Court shall then proceed and fully hear the merits of the case upon which said arrest was made, upon such evidence as may be produced and sworn before said Court ; and shall have power to adjourn the hearing, and also issue process from time to time, in their discretion, in order to procure the attendance of witnesses, so that a fair and impartial trial and decision may be obtained in every case.

Sec. 2. And be it further ordained, That if upon investigation it shall be proven before the Municipal Court that the writ or process has been issued either through private pique, malicious intent, religious or other persecution, falsehood or misrepresentation, contrary to the Constitution of the United States or of this State, the said writ or process shall be quashed, and considered of no force or effect, and the prisoner or prisoners shall be released and discharged therefrom.

Sec. 3. And be it also further ordained, That in the absence, sickness, debility or other circumstances disqualifying or preventing the Mayor from officiating in his office, as Chief Justice of the Municipal Court, the Aldermen present shall appoint one from amongst them to act as Chief Justice or President *pro tempore*.

Sec. 4. This ordinance to take effect and be in force from and after its passage.

HYRUM SMITH,
Vice-Mayor and President *pro tempore*.

Passed August 8, 1842.
JAMES SLOAN, Recorder.

The Prophet, who was determined not to be taken back to Missouri, now retired for several weeks, concealing himself in the homes of trusted friends at and near Nauvoo. Rockwell, equally averse to being taken, absented himself for some months, during which he traveled to the eastern states. Returning thence and visiting St. Louis, he was captured and carried in chains to Jackson County. Nothing being proven against him, he was eventually set free and made his way back to Illinois.

The most strenuous efforts were put forth for the capture of the Prophet, but without avail. Besides the regular officers, John C. Bennett and others were in the field, seeking to kidnap and carry him to Missouri. Such an event, however, was not destined to be. The fates had not decreed his return to his former captivity.

From his secret retreat he sent forth epistles from time to time relative to the administration of the affairs of his various offices. In one of these, addressed to the Major-General of the Nauvoo Legion, he expressed his desires for peace and the supremacy of the law, but declared his determination to submit no more to mob violence and tyranny. Appeals were successively made to Governor Carlin by the Prophet, his wife Emma, and the ladies of the Nauvoo Relief Society, a benevolent institution that Joseph Smith had founded.[*] But all to no purpose. The Governor apparently was hand-and-

---

[*] The forerunner of the great Relief Society system now flourishing in Utah.

glove with the anti-Mormons, who were doing all in their power to foment trouble and bring affairs to a bloody crisis. Carlin insisted that Joseph give himself up to the officers. This the Prophet refused to do, as his friends feared his assassination or kidnapping.

Joseph Smith, as repeatedly averred, was no coward; but neither did he court death, nor a repetition of his experience in a Missouri dungeon. It would have been eminently characteristic of him,—for his was truly a martial spirit,—to have taken the field with his legion and fought like a lion to the death rather than tamely submit to what he had endured, or was now enduring. But other considerations restrained him. Because he declined to surrender himself, he was represented as being with his people in an attitude of defiance to the laws. Public feeling ran high against him, and men were daily offering their services to Governor Carlin to arm and march upon Nauvoo.

Meantime, the State election had come round. Joseph Duncan, an ex-Governor of Illinois, was put forward by the Whigs for re-election. The Democrats nominated Adam W. Snyder for Governor, but he dying, Judge Thomas Ford became a candidate in his stead. Duncan was regarded as a brave and able man, and under ordinary conditions might have been elected. But he was an anti-Mormon, and took the stump against the Saints, expecting, it is said, to be elected on that issue. This solidified the Mormon vote against him, and in favor of his opponent. The result was the election of Thomas Ford as Governor of Illinois. At the same time William Smith, the Prophet's brother, was chosen a representative from Hancock County to the Legislature. Jacob C. Davis—of whom more anon—was elected a state senator.

The Whigs were very angry at the outcome, and the papers of that party now teemed with accounts of the alleged iniquities of the Mormons at Nauvoo, and severely took to task the Democrats for deigning to accept support from the Prophet and his followers.

About the 1st of October Governor Carlin made public proclamation offering a reward of four hundred dollars for the persons of

Joseph Smith and Orrin Porter Rockwell. At the same time Governor Reynolds of Missouri increased his standing offer of a much larger sum for their capture.

In December, 1842, Carlin's term of office expired, and he was succeeded by Governor Ford. The new executive was reputed as a well-meaning man, though not a strong official; possessing some ability, but liable to be swayed from his convictions by the opinions of others. In his inaugural address to the Legislature, Ford recommended that the Charter of Nauvoo, as it was objectionable to other citizens of the State, be modified and restricted. This caused the Whigs to exult over the Mormons and ask them ironically what they thought of their democratic Governor.

Immediately after Governor Ford's installation, the Mormon leader, still in exile, appealed to him to recall the writs and proclamation of his predecessor. The case was fully presented to Ford by Justin Butterfield, Esq., the United States District Attorney. He, in common with several of the Judges of the Supreme Court, held that Carlin's writs were illegal. Ford, though sharing the same opinion, deemed it impolitic to interfere with the acts of his predecessor. He therefore advised the Prophet to submit his case to a judicial investigation.

This the latter finally concluded to do. Accordingly, on the 26th of December, he allowed himself to be arrested by General Wilson Law, and on the day following, in company with Hyrum Smith, John Taylor, Willard Richards and others, he set out for Springfield, the State capital. There, on the 4th of January, 1843, occurred his celebrated trial before Judge Pope, which resulted in his again being set at liberty.

The original warrant issued by Governor Carlin not being at hand, it was duplicated for the purpose of this trial by his successor. Judge Pope granted a writ of *habeas corpus*, and the case was argued by Josiah Lamborn, Attorney-General of Illinois, for the prosecution, and by Justin Butterfield, Esq., for the defense. The Judge gave as the grounds for his decision in the prisoner's favor the insufficiency of the Boggs affidavit and the mis-recitals and overstatements in the documents of the two Governors. This decision rendered void the proclamation as well as the writs issued against the Prophet, and he was once more a free man.

He now enjoyed a brief season of peace. On the 6th of February, 1843, recurred the city election of Nauvoo. The officers chosen for the ensuing two years were: Joseph Smith, Mayor; Orson Spencer, Daniel H. Wells, George A. Smith and Stephen Markham, Aldermen; Hyrum Smith, John Taylor, Orson Hyde, Orson Pratt, Sylvester Emmons, Heber C. Kimball, Benjamin Warrington, Daniel Spencer and Brigham Young, Councilors. Liberality without extravagance in public officials, the establishment of markets, and the regulation of prices to protect the poor against avarice and monopoly, were among the measures proposed by Mayor Smith to the new council.

On the 25th of March the Mayor issued the following proclamation:

Whereas it is reported that there now exists a band of desperadoes, bound by oaths of secrecy, under severe penalties in case any number of the combination divulges their plans of stealing and conveying properties from station to station up and down the Mississippi and other routes; And

Whereas it is reported that the fear of the execution of the pains and penalties of their secret oaths on their persons prevents some members of said secret association (who have, through falsehood and deceit, been drawn into their snares,) from divulging the same to the legally-constituted authorities of the land;

Know ye, therefore, that I, Joseph Smith, Mayor of the city of Nauvoo, will grant and insure protection against all personal mob violence to each and every citizen of this city who will come before me and truly make known the names of all such abominable characters as are engaged in said secret combination for stealing, or are accessory thereto in any manner. And I respectfully solicit the co-operation of all ministers of justice in this and the neighboring states to ferret out a band of thievish outlaws from our midst.

Immigration continued pouring in at Nauvoo. On the 12th of April two large companies, led by Parley P. Pratt, Lorenzo Snow and Levi Richards, landed there. Among these arrivals were the Cannon family from Liverpool. They had crossed the sea in the fall of 1842, but were ice-bound at St Louis, and had there spent the winter.

Mrs. Cannon, the mother, had died and been buried at sea. The father, George Cannon, with his sons, George Q., Angus M., David H. and three daughters, reached their destination in safety.

Another attempt, the final one, was now made to drag the Mormon leader back to Missouri. The charge this time was treason— treason against that State—a reiteration of the old charge upon which the Prophet had once suffered imprisonment. John C. Bennett was at the bottom of this new attempt upon the liberty and life of his former friend, and Samuel C. Owens and others in Jackson County assisted in the scheme. Governor Reynolds issued his writ, Governor Ford his warrant, and the ball was thus set rolling. Sheriff J. H. Reynolds of Jackson County was Missouri's officer to receive the prisoner, and Harmon T. Wilson of Carthage, Hancock County, the person authorized to make the arrest.

Late in June, 1843, they set out upon their errand. Learning that the Prophet was visiting with his wife at a Mrs. Wasson's— Emma Smith's sister—near Dixon, Lee County, Illinois, the two officers proceeded thither, passing themselves off as Mormon Elders. Arriving at Mrs. Wasson's, they inquired for "Brother Joseph." On his appearing, they covered him with cocked pistols, threatened him with death if he resisted, hurried him into a vehicle and were about to drive away. Stephen Markham, who was present, protested against this lawlessness,—Reynolds and Wilson having shown no warrant for their act,—but they threatened his life also and drove away with their prisoner toward Dixon. They compelled him to sit between them, and all along continued to threaten him, punching his sides with their pistols. The pain from these assaults was so excruciating that the Prophet finally begged them to cease torturing and kill him outright, whereupon they modified their abusive treatment.

Meanwhile Stephen Markham, mounting a horse, preceded the party to Dixon, where he secured legal counsel for his friend. Reynolds and Wilson, on their arrival, at first refused to allow the prisoner to confer with his attorneys, but finding the citizens of

Dixon opposed to them, demanding that their brutality cease, they finally consented.*

A writ of *habeas corpus* was obtained for the Prophet, returnable before Judge Caton, at Ottawa, but he being absent another writ was secured, returnable before the nearest tribunal in the fifth judicial district authorized to hear and determine writs of *habeas corpus*. This district included Quincy and Nauvoo. Reynolds and Wilson, who were now themselves under arrest for abuse, threatening and false imprisonment, obtained a writ of *habeas corpus*, made returnable before Judge Young at Quincy. Toward that place the whole party now proceeded, in charge of Sheriff Campbell, of Lee County.

Meeting a party of his friends from Nauvoo,—for the city had been alarmed and the whole surrounding region was being scoured by the Mormons in quest of their leader,—the Prophet asked permission of the sheriff to go to Nauvoo, instead of to Quincy, where he feared treachery. The attorneys present, one of whom was Cyrus Walker, Esq., giving it as their opinion that the hearing might legally be held there, the sheriff consented and to Nauvoo they went accordingly. Reynolds and Wilson fiercely protested against this change in the program, probably fearing violence at the hands of the Mormon citizens. The Prophet, however, took them to his own home and seated them at the head of his own table, thus heaping upon them, in a scriptural sense, "coals of fire." They were not in the least molested, but treated kindly by all.

A hearing before the Municipal Court followed,—the Prophet's case coming up on its merits,—and the defendant was again discharged. Reynolds and Wilson, denying the court's jurisdiction, applied to Governor Ford for the use of the militia to re-take their prisoner, but His Excellency, being fully informed of the matter, refused the request, and Sheriff Reynolds returned crest-fallen to Missouri.

---

* It is said that the Prophet, on being taken to the Dixon hotel, found a Masonic friend in the landlord, who rendered him timely succor.

Why he and his confrere Wilson,—against whom the prosecution for false imprisonment, etc., seems to have been dropped,—failed to show their warrant at the time of the Prophet's arrest, and acted, instead of as officers, in the role of kidnappers, has never been satisfactorily explained. Possibly kidnapping was their purpose, and not anticipating the intervention of officers and courts, they deemed the warrant superfluous and unnecessary.

Another election occurred. Cyrus Walker was the Whig candidate, and Joseph P. Hoge the Democratic candidate for Congress, from the district of which Hancock County was a part. The Whigs, it seems, had been counting upon, and fully expected to receive the Mormon vote; notwithstanding their former criticism of the Democrats for condescending to accept it. What gave the Whigs hope of securing it at this election was the fact that Mr. Walker, their candidate, had defended the Mormon leader in his latest legal difficulty and rescued him from the clutches of the would-be kidnappers, Reynolds and Wilson. Judge Pope, whose decision in January had liberated the Prophet, was also a Whig, as was Mr. Browning, the eloquent champion of the prisoner's cause on that occasion. These considerations, it was thought, would be of sufficient weight to turn the majority of the Saints in favor of Mr. Walker.

The Mormons, however, or the majority of them, stood by their democratic principles, and cast their ballots for Mr. Hoge; while a minority, including the Prophet, being Whigs, voted for Mr. Walker.*
Hoge was elected by a majority in the district of 455 votes.

The Whigs were now angry again; not only at the Mormons, for failing to solidify in favor of Mr. Walker, but also at the Democrats, for again accepting Mormon assistance.

It is not at all clear, however, that the Mormons were responsible for the defeat of Mr. Walker at this election. Many of the Whigs, being sincere anti-Mormons, were "highly indignant" at

---

* The Mormons in Adams County, being Whigs, voted at this election for Mr. O. H. Browning, the party candidate in that district.

their candidate for defending the Prophet in the Reynolds and Wilson affair.* It is not improbable, therefore, that the dissatisfied ones repudiated him at the polls. Still it cannot be doubted that this exhibition of anti-Mormon animus on the part of the Whigs was not likely to attract Mormon votes, and it may have accounted in part for the large majority rolled up at Nauvoo for the democratic candidate.

Naturally the Whigs were angry, but they ought not to have been surprised. After denouncing the Democrats for receiving on a former occasion Mormon support, and filling their journals with accounts of alleged Mormon atrocities at Nauvoo, they should have been prepared for what awaited them. A little queer, too, that the fox, having once pronounced the grapes sour, should make another desperate attempt to taste them, and be angry because they were still out of reach. It beats the original fable. But such is politics.

Jealousy of the political power of the Mormons was now much enhanced. In August, several of them, chosen for county offices at the late election, proceeded to Carthage, the county seat of Hancock, to qualify. They were there threatened by an armed mob, led by Constable Harmon T. Wilson, who swore that they should not be installed. The Mormons, however, filed their bonds and took the required oaths of office, while their opponents were deliberating upon how best to prevent them.

The anti-Mormon party, which for some time had been discontinued, was now reorganized, with "war to the knife"—figuratively speaking—as its motto. Not altogether figurative, either, was that motto, if what followed may be taken as a criterion. The party pledged itself to assist Missouri in any future attempt that she might make against the Mormon leader.

Nor was this all. Mobs began attacking and burning Mormon houses outside Nauvoo, and even threatened to come against the city. Governor Ford being appealed to for protection, answered much in

---

* Gregg's History of Hancock County, page 295.

the same vein as President Van Buren when visited by the Prophet on a former occasion. "You must defend yourselves," was the inference drawn from Ford's reply. The Nauvoo Legion was therefore held in constant readiness to repel any mobocratic assault that might be made upon the city or the surrounding settlements.

CHAPTER XIII.
1843-1844.

CELESTIAL MARRIAGE—WHY THE MORMONS PRACTICED POLYGAMY—THE PROPHET AND THE POLITICIANS—JOSEPH SMITH A CANDIDATE FOR PRESIDENT OF THE UNITED STATES—HIS PLATFORM OF PRINCIPLES—PLANNING THE WESTERN EXODUS—THE LAWS, FOSTERS, AND HIGBEES EXCOMMUNICATED—THE "EXPOSITOR" ABATEMENT—ARREST OF THE MAYOR AND CITY COUNCIL OF NAUVOO—A GATHERING STORM—NAUVOO UNDER MARTIAL LAW—GOVERNOR FORD DEMANDS THE SURRENDER OF THE MORMON LEADERS—THE PROPHET AND HIS FRIENDS START FOR THE ROCKY MOUNTAINS—THE RETURN—THE SURRENDER—CARTHAGE JAIL—MURDER OF THE PROPHET AND PATRIARCH.

THE question has probably occurred to the reader, was there really any ground for the charges of immorality and licentiousness hurled against the Mormon leaders by their enemies, personal, political and ecclesiastical. What of John C. Bennett's story to the effect that Joseph Smith sanctioned illicit relations between the sexes? Was the tale true or false? We propose to answer these queries.

First let us ask if it seems consistent,—except upon the theory that the Mormon leaders were double-dyed hypocrites, arrant knaves, who were wont to sacrifice on occasion one of their own number in order to throw a halo of virtue around the rest,—that such men as John C. Bennett, D. P. Hurlburt and others, expelled from the Mormon Church for unchastity, would have been so expelled if unchastity had been sanctioned by that Church or those leaders? Again, where was their cunning, that shrewdness for which their enemies gave them credit, to have thus alienated from their cause for such a purpose—their own preservation—men fully cognizant of their crimes?

Reader, the Latter-day Saints, with all their faults—for they have never pretended to be perfect—are a chaste and virtuous people. We speak of course of the generality of them. There are black sheep in every fold. No community on earth values virtue more highly. They require chastity in man, as well as in woman, and next in enormity to murder, in their minds and according to their doctrines, are the sins of seduction and adultery. Had they their way the adulterer and the seducer, no less than the murderer, should answer for his crime with his life. Those who do not know this, do not know the Latter-day Saints, and they who state to the contrary simply state what is not true.

Then why so much talk about Mormon immorality? It springs, aside from sheer falsehood, from this fact. The Mormons believed in a doctrine called by them Celestial Marriage, but by others named polygamy. Whatever may be thought of the propriety of the former term, the latter, strictly speaking, is a misnomer. Polygamy means "many marriages," and may imply a plurality of husbands as well as wives. That a woman should have more than one husband, living and undivorced at the same time, the Mormons have never believed, but that a man, upright and moral, might under proper regulations, and in conformity with religious principle, have more than one wife, they have believed and in times past have practiced according to that belief. Polygeny, meaning "many wives," and not polygamy, which may mean "many husbands," is a more correct term to use in this connection.

With the Mormons this was a religious principle,—a tenet of their faith. They ceased its practice after nearly half a century's observance, because of a manifesto issued by the President of their Church, indicating as the will of the Lord that it should be discontinued. Congress had previously passed laws against plural marriage, making it a crime, and the Supreme Court of the United States had declared those laws constitutional. Not immediately, however, did the Mormons cease the practice of polygamy. They thought that Congress was wrong in thus legislating against their religion; that the Supreme Court was wrong, and might yet see its error, as it did in the Dred Scott case, and reversing its former ruling declare the anti-polygamy laws unconstitutional. But finally, after much suffering, resulting from prosecutions, fines, imprisonments and some deaths, the manifesto was issued and the practice of Mormon polygamy was at an end.

Many, perhaps most of the Latter-day Saints, still believe in the plural-wife doctrine,—there being no law against their belief,—and consider that the former practice of the principle was eminently right and proper. Some, however, disbelieve the doctrine, while crediting those who accepted and practiced it with perfect sincerity. Only a small percentage of the Mormon people were ever practical polygamists, for the observance of the principle was not compulsory. But those who engaged in it—most of them at least—were actuated by high moral and religious motives. This, however difficult for some to believe, is nevertheless true. Their honesty of purpose was not questioned by those who knew them best, in or out of the Church. They proved their sincerity in many ways, suffering much as individuals and as a community rather than relinquish, even at the behest of the parent government, this tenet of their faith.

They were wont to give various reasons for the practice of this principle, among them the following: the right and privilege of every honorable woman to be a wife and mother, which in monogamy, under existing conditions, preponderance of women over men, disinclination of men to marry, etc., was virtually denied; the extirpation of the social evil; the production of a healthier posterity, and the physical, mental and moral improvement of the race. These were among the temporal or tangible reasons put forth. But they also believed, and this was the spiritual phase of the question, that those who faithfully obeyed this principle here would be exalted to the highest glory hereafter, as the ancient patriarchs, Abraham, Jacob, *et al*, and their plural wives had been. It was to the Latter-day Saints the key to the Celestial Kingdom, where, according to their faith, family relationships formed on earth according to divine law will be perpetuated. Hence the revelation enjoining Celestial Marriage was entitled: "Revelation on the Eternity of the Marriage

Covenant including Plurality of Wives." The more pertinent parts of it are here given:

Verily, thus saith the Lord unto you, my servant Joseph, that inasmuch as you have inquired of my hand, to know and understand wherein I, the Lord, justified my servants Abraham, Isaac and Jacob; as also Moses, David and Solomon, my servants, as touching the principle and doctrine of their having many wives and concubines:

Behold! and lo, I am the Lord thy God, and will answer thee as touching this matter:

Therefore, prepare thy heart to receive and obey the instructions which I am about to give unto you; for all those who have this law revealed unto them must obey the same;

For behold! I reveal unto you a new and an everlasting covenant; and if ye abide not that covenant, then are ye damned; for no one can reject this covenant, and be permitted to enter into my glory;

For all who will have a blessing at my hands, shall abide the law which was appointed for that blessing, and the conditions thereof, as were instituted from before the foundation of the world:

And as pertaining to the new and everlasting covenant, it was instituted for the fullness of my glory; and he that receiveth a fullness thereof, must and shall abide the law, or he shall be damned, saith the Lord God.

And verily I say unto you, that the conditions of this law are these:—All covenants, contracts, bonds, obligations, oaths, vows, performances, connections, associations, or expectations, that are not made, and entered into, and sealed, by the Holy Spirit of promise, of him who is anointed, both as well for time and for all eternity, and that too most holy, by revelation and commandment through the medium of mine anointed, whom I have appointed on the earth to hold this power, (and I have appointed unto my servant Joseph to hold this power in the last days, and there is never but one on the earth at a time, on whom this power and the keys of this Priesthood are conferred), are of no efficacy, virtue or force, in and after the resurrection from the dead; for all contracts that are not made unto this end, have an end when men are dead.

* * * * * * * * *

Therefore, if a man marry him a wife in the world, and he marry her not by me, nor by my word; and he covenant with her so long as he is in the world, and she with him, their covenant and marriage are not of force when they are dead, and when they are out of the world; therefore, they are not bound by any law when they are out of the world;

Therefore, when they are out of the world, they neither marry, nor are given in marriage; but are appointed angels in heaven, which angels are ministering servants, to minister for those who are worthy of a far more, and an exceeding and an eternal weight of glory;

For these angels did not abide my law, therefore they cannot be enlarged, but remain separately and singly, without exaltation, in their saved condition, to all eternity, and from henceforth are not Gods, but are angels of God, for ever and ever.

And again, verily I say unto you, if a man marry a wife, and make a covenant with her for time and for all eternity, if that covenant is not by me, or by my word, which is my law, and is not sealed by the holy spirit of promise, through him whom I have anointed and appointed unto this power—then it is not valid, neither of force when they are out of the world, because they are not joined by me, saith the Lord, neither by my word; when they are out of the world, it cannot be received there, because the angels and the Gods are appointed there; by whom they cannot pass; they cannot, therefore, inherit my glory, for my house is a house of order, saith the Lord God.

And again, verily I say unto you, if a man marry a wife by my word, which is my law, and by the new and everlasting covenant, and it is sealed unto them by the Holy Spirit of promise, by him who is anointed, unto whom I have appointed this power, and the keys of this Priesthood; and it shall be said unto them, ye shall come forth in the first resurrection; and if it be after the first resurrection, in the next resurrection; and shall inherit thrones, kingdoms, principalities, and powers, dominions, all heights and depths—then shall it be written in the Lamb's Book of Life, that he shall commit no murder whereby to shed innocent blood, and if ye abide in my covenant, and commit no murder whereby to shed innocent blood, it shall be done unto them in all things whatsoever my servant hath put upon them, in time, and through all eternity, and shall be of full force when they are out of the world; and they shall pass by the angels, and the Gods, which are set there, to their exaltation and glory in all things, as hath been sealed upon their heads, which glory shall be a fullness and a continuation of the seeds for ever and ever.

Then shall they be Gods, because they have no end; therefore shall they be from everlasting to everlasting, because they continue; then shall they be above all, because all things are subject unto them. Then shall they be Gods, because they have all power, and the angels are subject unto them.

* * * * * * * * *

I am the Lord thy God, and will give unto thee the law of my Holy Priesthood, as was ordained by me, and my Father, before the world was.

Abraham received all things, whatsoever he received, by revelation and commandment, by my word, saith the Lord, and hath entered into his exaltation, and sitteth upon his throne.

Abraham received promises concerning his seed, and of the fruit of his loins—from whose loins ye are, namely, my servant Joseph,—which were to continue so long as they were in the world; and as touching Abraham and his seed, out of the world they should continue; both in the world and out of the world should they continue as innumerable as the stars; or, if ye were to count the sand upon the sea shore, ye could not number them.

This promise is yours, also, because ye are of Abraham, and the promise was made unto Abraham; and by this law are the continuation of the works of my Father, wherein he glorifieth himself.

Go ye, therefore and do the works of Abraham; enter ye into my law, and ye shall be saved.

But if ye enter not into my law ye cannot receive the promise of my Father, which he made unto Abraham.

God commanded Abraham, and Sarah gave Hagar to Abraham to wife. And why did she do it? Because this was the law, and from Hagar sprang many people. This, therefore, was fulfilling, among other things, the promises.

Was Abraham, therefore, under condemnation? Verily, I say unto you, Nay; for I, the Lord, commanded it.

Abraham was commanded to offer his son Isaac; nevertheless, it was written, thou shalt not kill. Abraham, however, did not refuse, and it was accounted unto him for righteousness.

Abraham received concubines, and they bear him children, and it was accounted unto him for righteousness, because they were given unto him, and he abode in my law, as Isaac also, and Jacob did none other things than that which they were commanded; and because they did none other things than that which they were commanded, they have entered into their exaltation, according to the promises, and sit upon thrones, and are not angels, but are Gods.

David also received many wives and concubines, as also Solomon and Moses my servants; as also many others of my servants, from the beginning of creation until this time; and in nothing did they sin save in those things which they received not of me.

David's wives and concubines were given unto him, of me, by the hand of Nathan, my servant, and others of the prophets who had the keys of this power; and in none of these things did he sin against me, save in the case of Uriah and his wife; and, therefore he hath fallen from his exaltation, and received his portion; and he shall not inherit them out of the world; for I gave them unto another, saith the Lord.

I am the Lord thy God, and I gave unto thee, my servant Joseph, an appointment, and restore all things; ask what ye will, and it shall be given unto you according to my word:

And as ye have asked concerning adultery—verily, verily I say unto you, if a man receiveth a wife in the new and everlasting covenant, and if she be with another man, and I have not appointed unto her by the holy anointing, she hath committed adultery, and shall be destroyed.

If she be not in the new and everlasting covenant, and she be with another man, she has committed adultery;

And if her husband be with another woman, and he was under a vow, he hath broken his vow, and hath committed adultery.

* * * * * * * *

And again, as pertaining to the law of the Priesthood: If any man espouse a virgin, and desire to espouse another, and the first give her consent; and if he espouse the second, and they are virgins, and have vowed to no other man, then is he justified; he cannot commit adultery, for they are given unto him; for he cannot commit adultery with that that belongeth unto him and to no one else;

And if he have ten virgins given unto him by this law, he cannot commit adultery, for they belong to him, and they are given unto him, therefore is he justified.

But if one or either of the ten virgins, after she is espoused, shall be with another man; she has committed adultery, and shall be destroyed; for they are given unto him to multiply and replenish the earth, according to my commandment, and to fulfill the promise which was given by my Father before the foundation of the world; and for their exaltation in the eternal worlds, that they may bear the souls of men; for herein is the work of my Father continued, that he may be glorified.

Prior to the recording of this revelation the Prophet had taught the doctrine, privately, and he and other prominent Elders had practiced it. But this also was in secret, owing to the great prejudice it was foreseen it would evoke. It was not avowed, even to the masses of the Saints, until after their removal from Illinois.

Such a doctrine as plurality of wives—the patriarchal marriage system of the ancients—though practiced by an Abraham, a Jacob, a Moses, a Gideon, could not well be mooted, much less established in this monogamic age, without meeting opposition, even among the Saints, prepared in a measure by their peculiar religious training for startling innovations on the prescribed boundaries of tradition. Hence, as said, the secrecy with which it was at first carried on. It would have proved a terrible weapon in anti-Mormon hands, had it been openly proclaimed at Nauvoo in those dangerous days.

As it was, it became known to some extent on the outside through apostasy, and of course was deemed and denounced as immoral. John C. Bennett obtained an inkling of it before leaving Nauvoo, and it doubtless formed the basis of his vengeful assault upon those who had severed him from the Church for adultery, which to the Latter-day Saint differs as much from plural marriage as darkness differs from light. Other seceders from Mormonism, who fell away later, revamped the tales told by Bennett, until they became with other things a *casus belli* against the Prophet and his people, and no doubt helped to hasten his tragic end.

The first record of the revelation on Celestial Marriage was made by William Clayton, at the Prophet's dictation. It was on the 12th of July, 1843. A month later it was read by Hyrum Smith to the Stake Presidency and the High Council at Nauvoo. The majority of them accepted it. Emma Smith, the Prophet's wife, though at first averse to the doctrine, finally received it and gave other wives to her husband. Subsequently she is said to have destroyed the original document of the revelation. She positively denied, after the Prophet's death, that he had ever practiced polygamy. The revelation, as published, is from an exact copy of the original, taken by

Joseph C. Kingsbury for Bishop Newel K. Whitney, the day after it was recorded by William Clayton, the Prophet's secretary.

Joseph Smith's mind was largely the mind of a statesman. He had meditated much upon the political problems of his period, and sincerely sorrowed over the corruptions and degeneracy of the times. He thought, moreover, that he saw a way of escape from many of the evils then threatening his country. One of these was the slavery question, his plan for the solution of which, had it been adopted, would have saved the nation a million lives, millions of treasure and the terrible hatreds and heart-burnings that have ever since divided, far more effectually than Mason and Dixon's line, the North from the South. Joseph Smith's plan for the settlement of slavery was for the general government to purchase from the South their negroes and then liberate them.

During the winter of 1843-4, the Prophet corresponded with several eminent statesmen, such as Henry Clay, John C. Calhoun, Lewis Cass, Richard M. Johnson and Martin Van Buren, who were all known to be aspirants for the Presidency. Each was asked this question: "What will be your rule of action relative to us as a people, should fortune favor your ascension to the Chief Magistracy?" Clay and Calhoun were the only ones who replied. Their answers being politic and evasive, the Prophet administered to each a stinging reproof for what he deemed cowardice and lack of candor.

He also took to task, about this time, James Arlington Bennett, of New York, who in a rather bombastic letter to the "American Mohamet," had intimated his desire to become his "right-hand man;" at the same time making known his desire to run for high office in Illinois, and use the Mormon vote to lift himself into power. Said the Prophet to Bennett: "Shall I who have witnessed the visions of eternity, * * who have heard the voice of God, and communed with angels, * * shall I worm myself into a political hypocrite? Shall I who hold the keys of the last Kingdom * * * stoop from the sublime authority of Almighty God to be handled as a monkey's catspaw, and pettify myself into a clown to act the farce of political demagoguery? No, verily no. * * * I combat the errors of ages, I meet the violence of mobs, I cope with illegal proceedings from executive authority, I cut the Gordian knot of powers; and I solve mathematical problems of universities with *truth—diamond truth*; and God is my 'right-hand man.'"

The next announcement from Nauvoo was to the political world somewhat startling. It was the nomination of Joseph Smith, the Mormon Prophet, as a candidate for the Presidency of the United States. The nomination was made January 29th, 1844, and was duly sustained at a State convention held at Nauvoo on the 17th of May. This was followed by the public enunciation of Joseph Smith's views upon the powers and policy of the Federal Government. Therein he announced himself as favoring:

(1) The abolition of slavery, but upon the basis of a just remuneration of all slave-holders by the general government.

(2) The reduction of the numbers and pay of Congressmen; the money thus saved, together with the proceeds from the sale of public lands, to be used in reimbursing slave-holders for the negroes freed.

(3) The abolition of imprisonment for debt, and of imprisonment for every crime excepting murder; work upon public improvements to be made the penalty for larceny, burglary and like felonies. "Let the penitentiaries," said he, "be turned into seminaries of learning."

(4) The abolition of the practice, in army or navy, of court-martialing men for desertion. "If a soldier or marine runs away, send him his wages, with this instruction, that his country will never trust him again. * * * Make honor the standard with all men."

(5) The investment of power in the President to send armies to suppress mobs.

(6) The extension of the Union, with the consent of the red man, from sea to sea.

(7) The annexation of Texas, if she petitioned for it, and of Canada and Mexico, whenever they should desire to enter the Union.

Said the Prophet: "We have had Democratic presidents, Whig presidents, a pseudo-Democratic-Whig president, and now it is time to have a President of the United States." Such were the principal planks of the platform upon which Joseph Smith as a candidate for the Chief Magistracy went into the campaign of 1844. Henry Clay was the Whig candidate, and James K. Polk the Democratic candidate for President at the same time.

To promulgate these views through the eastern states and act as the Prophet's electioneerers in the campaign, went forth from Nauvoo, in April and May of that memorable year, Apostles Brigham Young, Heber C. Kimball, Orson Hyde, Parley P. Pratt, Orson Pratt, Wilford Woodruff, George A. Smith, Lyman Wight and many other Elders. Joseph kept with him his brother Hyrum and Apostles John Taylor and Willard Richards: Elder Taylor having succeeded the Prophet as editor of the *Times and Seasons*, and Willard Richards being Church historian. Sidney Rigdon, at this time, was living at Pittsburg, Pennsylvania, having lost faith in Mormonism, or at least in Joseph Smith, and retired from the troubles and turmoils of Nauvoo. William and Wilson Law with several other Elders had lately been severed from the Church and were now at the head of a local opposition movement designed for the Prophet's overthrow.

It may well be doubted that Joseph Smith, on entering the political arena as a presidential candidate, anticipated a successful issue of the campaign. Though his views in some places became very popular,—which we presume was his main object in running for the Presidency,—his thoughts at that time, judging from his acts and expressions, were dwelling upon another subject entirely. That subject was the exodus of the Saints to the west,—an event he had predicted in August, 1842, and a project which various notable personages, friendly to him and his people, had since advised him to carry into effect. Undoubtedly he would have done so had he lived, in which event Joseph Smith, in lieu of Brigham Young, would have been the founder of Utah.

In February, 1844, soon after his nomination for President, the Prophet had directed the organization of an exploring expedition to seek out a home for the Saints beyond the Rocky Mountains,—in California or Oregon. Among the men selected for this enterprise were Jonathan Dunham, Phineas H. Young, David D. Yearsley, David Fullmer, Alphonso Young, James Emmett, George D. Watt and Daniel Spencer. These formed the nucleus of the proposed expedition, to which volunteers were subsequently added. Says Samuel W. Richards, one of these volunteers: "The outfit for each man was to consist of a rifle and ammunition, a saddle-horse, a pack-horse, with a few provisions and cooking utensils, and for the rest of our support we were to kill game on the way. Each man was to have in his pocket five hundred dollars, to purchase lands for our people a home whenever we should find a place suitable. Our party was thoroughly organized, but never started from Nauvoo."

In March, Joseph Smith memorialized Congress and the President —John Tyler—relative to the passage of an act, drafted by himself, providing for the protection of American citizens "wishing to settle Oregon and other portions of the territory of the United States; also for the protection of the people of Texas against Mexico. He asked for the privilege of raising one hundred thousand men for these purposes.

Oregon at that time, it must be remembered, though rightfully possessed by the United States, was also claimed by Great Britain, and was jointly occupied by American settlers and British fur traders, pending final diplomatic settlement between the two countries. Oregon then included Washington, Idaho and portions of Montana and Wyoming. To the south were the Mexican provinces of California and New Mexico; California comprising Utah, Nevada and portions of Wyoming and Colorado, while New Mexico took in Arizona. Texas, formerly a part of Mexico, but now independent, was soon to be annexed to the United States,—the Democrats, who were about returning to power, having made that the issue of the presidential campaign. The annexation was much against Mexico's wish, and she threatened to regard it as equivalent to a declaration of war.

Such was the situation at the time that Joseph Smith sent his memorials to Washington: Orson Hyde and Orson Pratt being the bearers of the same to the nation's capital. From Apostle Hyde's reports to the Prophet in April, we excerpt the following:

"Judge Douglas has been quite ill, but is just recovered. He will help all he can; Mr. Hardin likewise. But Major Semple says he does not believe anything will be done about Texas or Oregon this session. * * * Congress * * is afraid of England, afraid of Mexico, afraid the Presidential election will be twisted by it. * * * The most of the settlers in Oregon and Texas are our old enemies, the mobocrats of Missouri. * * * Your superior wisdom must determine whether to go to Oregon, to Texas, or to remain in these United States."

Later: "We have this day (April 26th) had a long conversation with Judge Douglas. He is ripe for Oregon and California. He said he would resign his seat in Congress if he could command the force that Mr. Smith could, and would be on the march to that country in a month. 'In five years,' said he, 'a noble state might be formed, and then if they would not receive us into the Union, we would have a government of our own.'"

Thus we see that while the campaign for the Presidency gave the Prophet an excellent opportunity to present his political views to the nation, it was the contemplated exodus of his people to the Rocky Mountains that mostly occupied his thoughts. Said he, soon after the departure of the Apostles on their political mission: "I care but little about the presidential chair. I would not give half as much for the office of President of the United States, as I would for the one I now hold as Lieutenant-General of the Nauvoo Legion."

That Legion he doubtless designed as the nucleus of his army of one hundred thousand. At its head Joseph Smith, had he lived, would have moved westward to maintain the rights of his country against Great Britain and Mexico, and found another State for the Union in the midst of the Rocky Mountains. Fate, however, interposed at this juncture, not to defeat the design, which was eventually executed, but to change, as in the case of Moses and Joshua, the personality of the executor.

We come now to the last act in the drama, preceding the fulfillment of the Prophet's design. The winter of 1843-4 had witnessed the defection from Mormonism of several persons who for some years had been more or less prominent in its history. Among these, were William and Wilson Law, already mentioned. This twain were brothers. They were of Irish descent and natives of Mercer County, Pennsylvania. Francis M. and Chauncey L. Higbee, sons of Judge Elias Higbee, were numbered with the seceders, as were also Robert D. and Charles A. Foster. All or most of these had been excommunicated from the Church for dishonesty and immorality. They set up a church of their own, with William Law as its head, denounced Joseph Smith as "a fallen prophet," and proceeded to inaugurate another crusade against him. In secret sympathy with these men were Sidney Rigdon, William Marks and Austin A. Cowles.

Upon the testimony of William Law and others, Joseph Smith was indicted at Carthage for polygamy, in the latter part of May. He surrendered himself for trial, but the prosecution not being ready to proceed, the case was continued for the term. Charles Foster, temporarily friendly, disclosed to Joseph a plot of the seceders to murder him while at Carthage, which kindly service enabled him to baffle the conspirators and return to Nauvoo in safety.

But the design of the opposition was not merely to assail the Prophet. Nauvoo and its citizens generally were to be the objects of attack. To this end a paper was established there called the *Nauvoo Expositor*, of which the Laws, Fosters and Higbees with one Charles Ivins were the publishers, and Sylvester Emmons the editor. Emmons was a non-Mormon member of the City Council. One of the purposes of the *Expositor*, as announced in its prospectus issued

May 10th, 1844, was to advocate "the unconditional repeal of the Nauvoo City charter," efforts to which end had already been made in the Illinois Legislature. Its further design, as appeared later, was to libel and defame the leading Mormon citizens of Nauvoo,—possibly to incite mobocratic assaults upon the city. At all events such was the view taken by many citizens as to its purpose and policy.

The first and final number of the *Nauvoo Expositor*, reeking with filthy scandals, was issued on the 7th of June. Public indignation was at once aroused. Decency was shocked. Modesty had been made to blush. Potent to the people of Nauvoo as were such considerations, they were but secondary compared with the deep and deadly injury that was sought to be done the city. Mobs, incited by anti-Mormon politicians,—more than ever incensed at what they deemed the towering presumption of the Mormon leader in running for the Presidency,—were already threatening Nauvoo, and such scandalous reports, if accepted as true, might precipitate at any hour an attack upon the town. Such a fear was far from groundless to men and women upon whose minds were indelibly stamped the terrible memories of Far West and Haun's Mill. Besides, the charter of the city, the bulwark of their rights and liberties, was assailed. That swept away, and what evils might not follow, what vices flourish unchecked, in the midst of their peaceable, temperate and, for all that was said to the contrary, moral and virtuous community.

Such was the Mormon view of the situation. Yet not the Saints alone, but respectable people of all parties felt outraged. There were those who longed to take the law into their own hands, and raze the *Expositor* building to the ground.

The Mormon leaders, however, would not sanction mobocracy. They had suffered too much from it themselves to countenance it in their followers. Legal measures, in lieu of lawless force, were therefore employed against the *Expositor*. The City Council of Nauvoo convened in regular session on Saturday the 8th of June,

Mayor Joseph Smith presiding, and an adjourned session was held on Monday, the 10th. The character, aims and objects of the libelous sheet and its publishers were fully ventilated. Among those who spoke to the question were the Mayor, Aldermen George W. Harris, Samuel Bennett, Elias Smith, Stephen Markham, Orson Spencer, and Councilors Hyrum Smith, John Taylor, William W. Phelps, Edward Hunter, Levi and Phinehas Richards and Benjamin Warrington. Willard Richards was clerk of the Council. By an almost unanimous vote,—Councilor Warrington, a non-Mormon, alone dissenting,—the *Nauvoo Expositor* was declared a public nuisance, and the Mayor instructed to have it abated without delay. Councilor Warrington, it should be added, only opposed summary action. He considered the paper libelous, and was in favor of heavily fining its publishers. On the night of June 10th, by order of the Mayor, City Marshal John P. Greene and a force of police destroyed the printing press, pied the type, and burned the published sheets of the *Expositor* found upon its premises, in the streets of Nauvoo. The leaders of the opposition party immediately left the city.

On the 12th of June Constable David Bettisworth came from Carthage to Nauvoo and arrested on a charge of riot the following named persons: Joseph Smith, Samuel Bennett, John Taylor, William W. Phelps, Hyrum Smith, John P. Greene, Stephen Perry, Dimick B. Huntington, Jonathan Dunham, Stephen Markham, William Edwards, Jonathan Harmon, Jesse P. Harmon, John Lytle, Joseph W. Coolidge, Harvey D. Redfield, O. P. Rockwell and Levi Richards. The complaint was sworn to by Francis M. Higbee, and referred to the abatement of the *Nauvoo Expositor*.

The warrant required that the accused be brought before Justice Thomas Morrison, at Carthage, "or some other justice of the peace" in Hancock County. Taking advantage of this wording of the warrant they requested the privilege of going before one of the justices of Nauvoo. The constable, however, insisted on taking them to Carthage. They thereupon sued out writs of *habeas corpus* and were discharged, after a hearing, by the Municipal Court of Nauvoo.

Subsequently, at the advice of Judge Jesse B. Thomas, who was visiting the city, Mayor Smith and his friends went before Justice Daniel H. Wells, who was still a non-Mormon, and were again examined and discharged; it appearing that their course in relation to the *Expositor*, while summary, was strictly legal under the charter and ordinances of Nauvoo.

The same day—June 16th—Mayor Smith issued a proclamation, stating why the act of abatement had been deemed necessary and declaring that the city authorities were willing to appear, whenever the Governor should require it, before any high court in the State and answer for the correctness of their conduct. He also warned the lawless element, now reported to be gathering against Nauvoo, not to be precipitate in interfering with the affairs of that city. Governor Ford had previously been informed of the situation in detail, but no reply had been received from him.

The excitement caused by the abatement of the *Expositor* and the unwillingness of the Mormon leaders to be tried at Carthage, was intense. Armed men were now taking the field in deadly earnest. Carthage and Warsaw, the neighboring towns to Nauvoo, wore the aspect of military camps. Troops were training daily for the pending conflict. Fifteen hundred Missourians were reported to have joined the Warsaw forces, and five pieces of cannon and a supply of small arms had been forwarded to that point from Quincy and other places. The Warsaw *Signal*, edited by Thomas C. Sharp, was active in stirring up the spirit of mobocracy. It even advocated the massacre of the whole Mormon community.* The following is a sample of the mobocratic resolutions passed at Warsaw, published in the *Signal*, and afterwards adopted at Carthage by acclamation :

---

* Says Gregg's History of Hancock County: "There were at this time and even afterward while the Mormons remained, four classes of citizens in the county: 1. The Mormons themselves. 2. A class called Jack-Mormons. * * * 3. Old citizens who were anti-Mormons at heart, but who refused to countenance any but lawful measures for redress of grievances; and 4. Anti-Mormons who, now that the crisis had come, advocated ' war and extermination.' "

Resolved that the time, in our opinion, has arrived, when the adherents of Smith, as a body, should be driven from the surrounding settlements into Nauvoo. That the Prophet and his miscreant adherents should then be demanded at their hands, and if not surrendered a war of extermination should be waged to their entire destruction, if necessary for our protection.

The situation at Nauvoo was fast becoming serious. It was now the 18th of June, and no word had yet come from the Governor. Mobocratic threats were daily growing louder. Seeing no alternative, unless it were to quietly submit to the threatened assault and massacre, the Prophet, in his capacity of Mayor, now called out the Legion to defend the city, and proclaimed Nauvoo under martial law.*

" Will you stand by me," said he, as clothed in full uniform of Lieutenant-General of the Legion, he addressed his soldiers and fellow-citizens for the last time,—" Will you stand by me to the death, and sustain at the peril of your lives the laws of our country, and the liberties and privileges which our fathers have transmitted to us, sealed with their sacred blood? (" Aye," shouted thousands.) It is well. If you had not done it, I would have gone out there (pointing to the West) and would have raised up a mightier people. * * * (Drawing his sword and presenting it to heaven) " I call God and angels to witness that I have unsheathed my sword with a firm and unalterable determination that this people shall have their legal rights, and be protected from mob violence, or my blood shall be spilt upon the ground like water, and my body consigned to the silent tomb. While I live I will never tamely submit to the dominion of cursed mobocracy. * * * I do not regard my own life. I am ready to be offered a sacrifice for this people. * * * God has

---

* Governor Ford, in after years, wrote as follows regarding the designs of the mob upon Nauvoo: " I gradually learned, to my entire satisfaction, that there was a plan to get the troops into Nauvoo and then begin the war, probably by some of our own party, or some of the seceding Mormons, taking advantage of the night to fire on our own force and then laying it on the Mormons. I was satisfied there were those among us fully capable of such an act, hoping that in the alarm, bustle and confusion of a militia camp the truth could not be discovered, and that it might lead to the desired collision."

tried you. You are a good people; therefore I love you with all my heart. * * * You have stood by me in the hour of trouble, and I am willing to sacrifice my life for your preservation."

This was not the first time that the Prophet had predicted his own death. He felt that his enemies were thirsting for his blood, and that if once he fell into their power his days on earth were numbered. Neither, as seen, was it the first time that he had indicated the great West as the future home of his people. On the 20th of June he wrote for the immediate return of the absent Apostles.

Next day Governor Ford arrived at Carthage. Placing himself at the head of the troops there concentrated,—hitherto an armed mob, but now, by his act, transformed into regular militia, the Governor demanded that martial law at Nauvoo be abolished, and that the Mayor, the City Council and all persons concerned in the destruction of the *Expositor* press come to Carthage to be tried for riot.

The Governor's orders were obeyed. For a few hours only the Prophet hesitated. Life was still dear to him; if not for himself for the sake of his friends and family. On the night of the 22nd he crossed the Mississippi, and in company with his brother Hyrum, Apostles Richards, Taylor and a few other friends, started for the Rocky Mountains. Messages from home intercepted him, inducing him to reconsider his design, and he returned to meet his doom. "We are going back to be butchered," said he, and resigned himself to his fate.

Having delivered up, at the Governor's demand, the arms of the Nauvoo Legion, the Prophet and his friends, seventeen in number, on the evening of the 24th set out for Carthage.

It was about midnight when they arrived there. Though so late, the town was alive and stirring, in anticipation of their arrival. They were immediately surrounded with troops, who yelled their exultation at having them in their power. Some of the soldiers— notably the Carthage Greys—were very abusive and threatened to shoot the Prophet and his party, who were thus voluntarily surrendering themselves. Governor Ford pacified the would-be murderers and the threatened massacre was postponed.

Next day the Governor paraded the prisoners before the troops upon the public square, where the two principals were introduced as "Generals Joseph and Hyrum Smith." At this the Carthage Greys again became angry and violent, deeming too much honor was being done "the d———d Mormons" by bestowing upon them such titles. Soon afterward the Greys revolted against their commander, General Miner R. Deming, who, fearing his own assassination, left Carthage.* Again the Governor placated the hostiles by assuring them that they should have "full satisfaction," while to the prisoners he pledged his honor and the faith of the State of Illinois that they should be protected from violence and given a fair trial.

Before Justice Robert F. Smith, a captain in the Carthage Greys, the Prophet and his party were brought that afternoon and admitted to bail. Meanwhile Joseph and Hyrum Smith had been arrested for treason. This charge was based upon the calling out of the Legion and the placing of Nauvoo under martial law, proceedings construed into armed resistance to legal process. Nothing was done in this case until nightfall, when the accused, without a hearing, were thrust into Carthage jail by Justice Smith, now acting arbitrarily in his capacity of Captain of the Greys. Governor Ford sanctioned this illegal act, claiming afterwards that it was necessary for the safety of the prisoners, though the latter at the time protested against the incarceration. John Taylor, Willard Richards and a few other friends accompanied Joseph and Hyrum to prison.

It was the beginning of the end. The plot was fast consummating. Once more, and only once, did the two brothers emerge from that jail alive. Their doom was sealed. "The law cannot reach them," said their plotting murderers, "but powder and ball shall."

* General Deming is said to have suspected the murderous plot against the Mormon leaders, and being powerless to prevent its execution, determined to have nothing to do with the bloody deed.

Governor Ford, next morning, granted an interview to the Prophet, coming to the prison for that purpose. Colonel Geddes and others accompanied him. During their conversation the Prophet charged the Governor with knowing positively that he and his brother were innocent of treason, and that their enemies had begun the troubles which had culminated in the present situation.* He also claimed that Ford had advised him to use the Legion in the way that he had, in the event of a threatened mobocratic assault upon Nauvoo. As to the *Expositor* affair, the Prophet said that he was willing to be tried again, and if found guilty to make suitable reparation. That was a matter, he maintained, for courts to decide, and not for mobs to settle. Such was the main substance of the interview. The Governor, at parting, renewed his promise that the prisoners should be protected, and pledged his word that if he went to Nauvoo—as he contemplated doing—he would take Joseph with him. Both promises were unkept.†

In the afternoon the two brothers were arraigned before Justice Smith at the Court House on the charge of treason. They asked for time to obtain witnesses. The request was reluctantly granted, and the court was adjourned until noon next day, to enable the prisoners to send to Nauvoo—eighteen miles distant—for their witnesses. Subsequently the military justice, without notifying the prisoners, postponed the trial until the 29th of June.

The last night of the brothers Joseph and Hyrum on earth was

* Ford in his history thus disposes of this question of the alleged treason of the Mormon leaders: "Their actual guiltiness of the charge would depend upon circumstances. If their opponents had been seeking to put the law in force in good faith, and nothing more, then an array of military force in open resistance to the *posse comitatus* and the militia of the state, most probably would have amounted to treason. But if those opponents merely intended to use the powers of the law, the militia of the state, and the *posse comitatus* as cats'-paws to compass the possession of their persons for the purpose of murdering them afterwards, as the sequel demonstrated the fact to be, it might well be doubted whether they were guilty of treason."

† Governor Ford, who seems to have deferred utterly to his subordinates and the anti-Mormons at that time, failed to take the Prophet to Nauvoo because a council of his officers convinced him that it "would be highly inexpedient and dangerous."

shared with their friends John Taylor, Willard Richards, John S. Fullmer, Stephen Markham and Dan Jones. They occupied an up-stair room in the prison. Next day—the fatal 27th—Fullmer, Markham and Jones were excluded from the jail, and the four victims selected for the sacrifice were left alone. They cheered each other with sacred songs and by preaching in turn to their guards. Some of these were "pricked in their hearts," being convinced that the prisoners were innocent. Their feelings becoming known to their superiors, they were promptly relieved and men of sterner stuff put in their place. During the day Cyrus H. Wheelock was permitted to visit the prisoners. Before he left he managed secretly to slip a small pepper-box revolver into Joseph's pocket. This weapon, which belonged to John Taylor, and a single-barreled pistol left by John S. Fullmer, with two stout canes, were their sole means of defense against the horde of armed assassins that soon afterward descended upon the jail.

Governor Ford, that morning, regardless of his pledge, had gone to Nauvoo, leaving the Prophet, whom he had promised to take with him, in prison. He had done more. Disbanding most of the militia, he had taken with him the McDonough County troops,—of all the militia the best ordered and least vindictive against the Mormons,—and left the unruly and turbulent Carthage Greys, who had revolted against their own commander, and repeatedly threatened the lives of the prisoners, to guard the jail. Colonel Buckmaster, one of the officers who accompanied the Governor to Nauvoo, informed his Excellency of the threats that had been made against the prisoners, and expressed a suspicion that the jail might be attacked in their absence. But Ford seemed to have implicit confidence in the Carthage troops, and refused to believe that they would betray their trust. He had previously ignored similar warnings from the Prophet's friends at Carthage. "I could not believe," said he, "that anyone would attack the jail whilst we were in Nauvoo, and thereby expose my life and the lives of my companions to the sudden vengeance of the Mormons, upon hearing of the death of their

leaders." Captain Robert F. Smith, in the absence of General Deming, now commanded the Greys, who were encamped upon the public square, while Sergeant Frank A. Worrell, with eight men, had immediate charge of the prison.

Had the Governor connived at murder, or was he but the weak and pliant tool of men who undoubtedly had conspired against the lives of the prisoners? Let the Final Judgment answer. Suffice it that late in the afternoon of that day—June 27th, 1844—while the Governor was at Nauvoo, haranguing the Mormons on the enormity of the crimes committed in destroying the *Expositor* press and placing the city under martial law, a portion of the disbanded Warsaw troops, one or two hundred strong, led by Levi Williams, a Baptist priest and Colonel of militia, returned to Carthage, stormed the jail, and with the connivance of the guards shot to death Joseph and Hyrum Smith, and all but fatally wounded John Taylor. Of the four captives, Willard Richards alone escaped unhurt. The prisoners heroically defended themselves, the Prophet using his revolver and wounding several of the assassins, while Willard Richards and John Taylor beat up and down with their walking sticks the guns thrust in at the prison door-way, diverting as best they could the direction of the deadly missiles. But the unequal fight could not long be maintained. Hyrum Smith fell first, John Taylor next, and the Prophet last. Attempting to leap from the window, Joseph was fired upon, and fell to the ground outside, dead. His murderers, who had blackened their faces to prevent recognition, only paused long enough to pour a final volley into the lifeless body of their chief victim, and then broke and fled in every direction.

A horror of fear fell upon all the inhabitants of Carthage after the bloody deed was done. Dreading the vengeance of Nauvoo, when the news should reach that city, they fled pell-mell, panic-stricken, pursued by naught save the phantoms of their own fears.

The news did reach Nauvoo, that night,—the Governor and his escort having previously left the city,—and great beyond description was the grief of the betrayed and stricken people. But no retaliation was attempted. Vengeance was left to heaven,—to heaven indeed; for of that band of murderers who committed the crime, and that other band, equally guilty, who set them on, not one was ever brought to justice.

The day after the tragedy the bodies of the murdered brothers, accompanied by Willard Richards and Samuel H. Smith, were taken to Nauvoo for burial. John Taylor remained several days at Carthage, —too seriously wounded to admit of his immediate removal.

Of the absent Apostles, Parley P. Pratt was the first to return to Nauvoo. George A. Smith came next. Sidney Rigdon arrived a little later from Pittsburg. Brigham Young, Heber C. Kimball, Orson Hyde, Orson Pratt, Wilford Woodruff and Lyman Wight, who were in the Eastern States when the terrible tidings reached them, returned to Nauvoo on the 6th of August, forty days after the massacre.

CHAPTER XIV.
1844-1845.

BRIGHAM YOUNG SUCCEEDS JOSEPH SMITH—THE MAN FOR THE HOUR—SIDNEY RIGDON REJECTED AND EXCOMMUNICATED—FACTIONS AND FOLLOWINGS—THE PROPHET'S MURDER PROVES AN IMPETUS TO MORMONISM—THE CRUSADE RENEWED—THE APOSTLES DRIVEN INTO RETIREMENT—THE "BOGUS BRIGHAM" ARREST—REPEAL OF THE NAUVOO CHARTER—JOSIAH LAMBORN'S OPINION OF THE REPEAL—GOVERNOR FORD ADVISES A MORMON EXODUS—THE PROPHET'S MURDERERS ACQUITTED—THE ANTI-MORMONS CHANGE THEIR TACTICS—THE TORCH OF THE INCENDIARY IN LIEU OF THE WRIT OF ARREST—SHERIFF BACKENSTOS—THE MOBOCRATS WORSTED AND PUT TO FLIGHT—GOVERNOR FORD INTERPOSES TO RESTORE ORDER—GENERAL HARDIN AND THE COMMISSIONERS—THE MORMONS AGREE TO LEAVE ILLINOIS.

BRIGHAM YOUNG succeeded Joseph Smith as leader of the Latter-day Saints. Sidney Rigdon claimed the leadership. It was to secure it that he came from Pittsburg on learning of the Prophet's death. Being his first counselor in the Presidency,—though Joseph, distrusting his fidelity, had long since virtually cast him off,—Elder Rigdon believed, or affected to believe, that this entitled him to the succession. A small faction of the Saints felt likewise.

But the hearts of the people, as a rule, were not with Sidney. Though an eloquent orator, he was not a leader,—at least not such a leader as the Saints now required; a man to grapple with great emergencies. He had shown too plainly of late years the white feather, to insure him the full confidence of his people at this critical point in their history. Besides, Sidney's claim, though plausible, was not valid according to Church polity. The First Presidency to which he had belonged was no more. Death had dissolved that council. The Prophet in life had taught that "where he was not there was no First Presidency over the Twelve." Next in order stood the Twelve—the

Apostles—with Brigham Young as their President. Instinctively the people turned to Brigham, for they loved and trusted him, and by that "right divine," no less than of seniority and succession in the Priesthood, he became their President and spiritual guide.

Sidney Rigdon, after his rejection by the Saints, returned to Pittsburg. Soon afterward he was excommunicated. William Marks, William Smith, James J. Strang and others followed, being severed from the Church, some for immorality, others for refusing like Elder Rigdon to recognize the authority of the Apostles. Each prominent seceder had a limited following. There were Rigdonites, Smithites, Strangites, and later, Cutlerites, Millerites and Josephites. The last-named were followers of the Prophet's son "young Joseph." This sect, which still exists, and calls itself the "Reorganized Church of Jesus Christ of Latter-day Saints," did not spring into existence until many years later, and was then organized out of the remnants of the earlier factions. But the main body of the Nauvoo Saints adhered to Brigham and the Twelve.

The chief Apostle was now in his forty-fourth year,—in the full, ripe vigor of his mental and physical powers. Though his life, like those of most of his brethren, had been one of toil and trial, and sickness, resulting from hardship and exposure, had more than once preyed upon his matured and well-knit frame, still he was a man of iron mould, and of no less iron will, whose practical wisdom and temperate habits had perpetuated in him the strength and vitality of youth, and carried forward a reserve fund of energy into his prime. His mind, a master mind, far-sighted, keen, profound, born to direct, to counsel and command, was therefore fittingly enshrined. Nature had made him great. Experience had educated that greatness. Trials and afflictions to which weaker men had succumbed, had but developed this son of destiny and brought him to his plane and place.

He was unquestionably the man for the hour,—an hour big with events, whose birth would yet astonish the world. His colleagues, the Apostles, and the Saints in general regarded him as their divinely appointed leader,—quite as much so as the martyred Joseph before him. The exodus from Missouri, which he personally directed, and his subsequent management of the affairs of the British Mission, had shown something of his capacity and executive ability, but it remained for the exodus of his people to the Rocky Mountains, and the colonization of the great interior Basin, to fully demonstrate his rare genius as a leader and an organizer. A notable character in life's grand tragedy, one bloody scene of which had so lately closed, waiting at the wing he had caught his cue, and the stirring stage of Time was now ready for his advent.

The special meeting of the Saints, at which the claim of the Apostles to lead the Church had been recognized, and that of Elder Rigdon rejected, was held on the 8th of August, 1844. The same month witnessed the election of Brigham Young as Lieutenant-General of the Nauvoo Legion. Charles C. Rich was chosen Major-General. Amasa M. Lyman, previously ordained an Apostle, was admitted into the council of the Twelve, and that body then addressed an epistle to the Latter-day Saints in all the world, giving such advice and instruction as their situation and the times demanded. Wilford Woodruff was sent to Great Britain to preside over that important mission. With him went Elder Dan Jones, destined to head a very successful missionary movement in Wales. Parley P. Pratt was given charge of Church affairs in the Eastern States, and other Elders, besides many already in the field, were going forth to various parts of the Union. Among those now rising to prominence was Franklin D. Richards, the present Apostle and Church Historian.

Mormonism, its opponents discovered, was not dead, though the Church had sustained a heavy shock in the death of its Prophet and Patriarch. "The blood of the martyrs" is proverbially "the seed of the Church." The present case proved no exception. The murder of Joseph and Hyrum Smith undoubtedly gave a strong impetus to Mormonism. Short-sighted indeed the wisdom (?) which thought it would do otherwise.

Immigration continued arriving at Nauvoo, where the Saints.

under the direction of the Apostles, now hurried on the completion of the Temple. The exodus predicted and in a measure prepared for by their Prophet, was foreseen to be imminent, and it was their desire to finish this edifice,—another monument of religious zeal and self-sacrificing industry,—before taking up the cross of another painful pilgrimage and journeying toward the setting sun.

The anti-Mormons, their ranks now augmented by apostates, seemed bent upon compelling an early exodus. To this end they continued their former policy of trumping up charges against the chiefs of the Church. A murder, a theft, or any other crime,—and such things were frequent in that all but frontier region,—committed at or in the vicinity of Nauvoo, was at once laid to the Mormon leaders as principals or accessories, and forthwith the town would be inundated with sheriffs, constables and their *posses*, armed with writs of arrest, searching for the suspects. That some of these crimes were committed by citizens of Nauvoo is quite probable. But that all the stealing and killing in that region, or even the greater part of it was done by them, cannot be reasonably supposed, in spite of the awful examples set them.

Brigham and his brethren, with the memory of the murdered Joseph and Hyrum ever before them,—their Prophet and Patriarch, butchered in cold blood while in prison under the pledged protection of the State of Illinois,—determined not to be similarly ensnared. Instead of surrendering to the officers, therefore, they secreted themselves whenever apprised of their approach, only to reappear when they had departed and all danger was over. The celebrated "bogus Brigham" arrest occurred during this period. The Apostles and other Elders were at the Temple, then nearing completion, when some officers came to the door with a warrant for the arrest of Brigham Young. William Miller, who resembled the President, throwing on Heber C. Kimball's cloak—similar in size and color to Brigham's—crossed the threshold and mutely surrendered to the officers, who, thinking they had secured their man, drove away with him to Carthage. The *ruse* was not discovered until they reached

their journey's end, where "Bill Miller" was recognized, and it is safe to say anathematized. Meantime the real Brigham had got well out of the way and was laughing at the chagrin of his outwitted pursuers.

The lives of the Mormon leaders, no less than their liberties, were in constant jeopardy, and their houses and places of concealment were carefully guarded to prevent assassination. Foremost among their foes were men and women who had once been their brethren and sisters in the Church. Emma Smith, the Prophet's widow, was one of these. She refused to follow Brigham, whom she hated and regarded as a usurper. She taught her children that he, and not their father, introduced polygamy into the Church, and that the Prophet had never practiced it. Yet there are women still living in Utah who solemnly aver that they were Joseph Smith's plural wives, and they with others testify that Emma, to their personal knowledge, gave those wives to her husband in the sealing covenant.

In January, 1845, the Legislature of Illinois, yielding to long continued popular pressure, repealed the Nauvoo charter. Josiah Lamborn, Esq., Attorney-General of Illinois writing of this event to Brigham Young, said: "I have always considered that your enemies have been prompted by political and religious prejudices, and by a desire for plunder and blood, more than for the common good. By the repeal of your charter, and by refusing all amendments and modifications, our legislature has given a kind of sanction to the barbarous manner in which you have been treated.   *   *   *
It is truly a melancholy spectacle to witness the law-makers of a sovereign State condescending to pander to the vices, ignorance and malevolence of a class of people who are at all times ready for riot, murder and rebellion.

*   *   *   *   *   *   *   *   *

"Your Senator, Jacob C. Davis, has done much to poison the minds of the members against anything in your favor. He walks at large in defiance of law, an indicted murderer. If a Mormon was in his position the Senate would afford no protection, but he would be dragged forth to gaol or the gallows, or be shot down by a cowardly and brutal mob."

In April following, the Saints in general conference, attended by many thousands of people, voted to change the name Nauvoo to the City of Joseph, in honor of their martyred Prophet. A small portion of the city was afterwards incorporated as the town of Nauvoo.

Governor Ford, on the 8th of April, wrote to President Young, advising him to migrate with his people to California. In this letter the following passages occur:

If you can get off by yourselves you may enjoy peace; but, surrounded by such neighbors, I confess that I do not see the time when you will be permitted to enjoy quiet. I was informed by General Joseph Smith last summer that he contemplated a removal west; and from what I learned from him and others at that time, I think, if he had lived, he would have begun to move in the matter before this time. I would be willing to exert all my feeble abilities and influence to further your views in this respect if it was the wish of your people.

I would suggest a matter in confidence. California now offers a field for the prettiest enterprise that has been undertaken in modern times. It is but sparsely inhabited, and by none but the Indians or imbecile Mexican Spaniards. I have not enquired enough to know how strong it is in men and means. But this we know, that if conquered from Mexico, that country is so physically weak and morally distracted that she could never send a force there to reconquer it. Why should it not be a pretty operation for your people to go out there, take possession of and conquer a portion of that vacant country, and establish an independent Government of your own, subject only to the laws of nations? You would remain there a long time before you would be disturbed by the proximity of other settlements. If you conclude to do this, your design ought not to be known, or otherwise it would become the duty of the United States to prevent your emigration. If once you cross the line of the United States Territories, you would be in no danger of being interfered with."

Brigham Young, however, had already decided upon his course. It was in this, as in all else pertaining to the general conduct of Mormonism, to follow in the footsteps and build upon the foundation of his predecessor. Never, it is believed, during his entire administration did the President knowingly deviate from this fixed rule. It was one of the secrets of his great influence with the Saints. Let not lack of originality be imputed to him, however, because of this deference to the designs of the Prophet. Brigham believed Joseph to be inspired. He recognized the worth and wisdom of his plans, and his own genius and originality found ample play in their execution. As a designer Joseph Smith was without a peer among his fellows; as an executor Brigham Young without a parallel. Each was the other's complement, and neither career alone, in the eternal fitness of things would have been complete.

The Rocky Mountains was the place of refuge that Joseph had foretold. California, Texas, Oregon were but after-thoughts, vague and undetermined. To the Rocky Mountains, therefore, the Saints would go,—possibly pass beyond,—but precisely how far into that *terra incognita*, that unknown wilderness they might penetrate, they knew not, not even their leaders knew. It is a fact, however, that the region of the Great Basin, of which they had read in Colonel Fremont's reports, was in their thoughts, though not as a definite destination, when contemplating a removal from Illinois.*

It was not their destiny to colonize and people the Pacific coast; though undoubtedly they did much to hasten that great achievement. If not the first American settlers of California, they were the first to establish there a newspaper, among the first to turn up gold with their shovels at Sutter's Mill, and set agog the excitement which rolled, a mighty billow, over the civilized world, and staid not nor subsided till it had revolutionized the commerce of two hemispheres. If not the very point, therefore, they certainly were, as we shall see, a very important part of the entering wedge of western civilization.

Nor was it their design, in moving westward, to set up an independent government,—at least not in the sense that Governor Ford and Senator Douglas had suggested. Not knowing where they were going or what awaited them, whether the Union spreading

---

* The following is an extract from Heber C. Kimball's journal: "Nauvoo Temple, December 31st, 1845. Prest. Young and myself are superintending the operations of the day, examining maps with reference to selecting a location for the Saints west of the Rocky Mountains, and reading the various works which have been written and published by travelers in those regions."

Vancouver's Island was suggested to the Mormons about this time as a suitable place for them to settle.

westward would overtake them, or Mexican or British rule be their portion, how could they have formed any such definite design? It was certainly not their purpose to alienate themselves from that government which their forefathers had fought and bled to establish, whose starry standard they revered, whose glorious Constitution they believed to have been God-inspired. No; they were Mormons, hated, despised, defamed, but still Americans, loyal to their country and her cause: though that country now, they could not help but feel, was acting the part of a cold step-mother rather than of a tender parent to them. Some day, perchance, their countrymen would know them better, and for past contempt and cruelty would make amends. Perhaps they felt, as felt the poet,—"pilgrim of eternity."*

> "But I have lived, and have not lived in vain:
> My mind may lose its force, my blood its fire,
> And my frame perish even in conquering pain;
> But there is that within me which shall tire
> Torture and time, and breathe when I expire;
> Something unearthly, which they deem not of,
> Like the remembered tone of a mute lyre,
> Shall on their softened spirits sink, and move
> In hearts all rocky now the late remorse of love."

Till then, as pilgrims too—pilgrims of time and of eternity—they would retire into the wilderness, taking with them the starry flag, the traditions of Bunker Hill and Yorktown, and seeking some isolated spot behind the rocky ramparts of the Everlasting Hills, found a new state for the Union, foreseen to be spreading from sea to sea, and patiently wait the fulfillment of what had been predicted,—that the Saints should become a mighty people in the midst of the Rocky Mountains.

Before expatriating themselves, they resolved to make a last appeal to the country which they felt was casting them forth. To this end they addressed a memorial to the President of the United States—James K. Polk—and sent copies of the same to the Governors

---

* The poet Shelley so styled Lord Byron.

of all the States, excepting Missouri and Illinois. This memorial ran as follows:

Nauvoo, April, 24th, 1845.

His Excellency James K. Polk, President of the United States.

Hon. Sir: Suffer us, in behalf of a disfranchised and long afflicted people, to prefer a few suggestions for your serious consideration, in hope of a friendly and unequivocal response, at as early a period as may suit your convenience, and the extreme urgency of the case seems to demand.

It is not our present design to detail the multiplied and aggravated wrongs that we have received in the midst of a nation that gave us birth. Most of us have long been loyal citizens of some one of these United States, over which you have the honor to preside, while a few only claim the privilege of peaceable and lawful emigrants, designing to make the Union our permanent residence.

We say we are a disfranchised people. We are privately told by the highest authorities of the State that it is neither prudent nor safe for us to vote at the polls; still we have continued to maintain our right to vote, until the blood of our best men has been shed, both in Missouri and Illinois, with impunity.

You are doubtless somewhat familiar with the history of our expulsion from the State of Missouri, wherein scores of our brethren were massacred. Hundreds died through want and sickness, occasioned by their unparalleled sufferings. Some millions worth of our property was destroyed, and some fifteen thousand souls fled for their lives to the then hospitable and peaceful shores of Illinois; and that the State of Illinois granted to us a liberal charter, for the term of perpetual succession, under whose provision private rights have become invested, and the largest city in the State has grown up, numbering about twenty thousand inhabitants.

But, sir, the startling attitude recently assumed by the State of Illinois, forbids us to think that her designs are any less vindictive than those of Missouri. She has already used the military of the State, with the executive at their head, to coerce and surrender up our best men to unparalleled murder, and that too under the most sacred pledges of protection and safety. As a salve for such unearthly perfidy and guilt, she told us, through her highest executive officers, that the laws should be magnified and the murderers brought to justice; but the blood of her innocent victims had not been wholly wiped from the floor of the awful arena, ere the Senate of that State rescued one of the indicted actors in that mournful tragedy from the sheriff of Hancock County, and gave him a seat in her hall of legislation; and all who were indicted by the grand jury of Hancock County for the murder of Joseph and Hyrum Smith, are suffered to roam at large, watching for further prey.

To crown the climax of those bloody deeds, the State has repealed those chartered rights, by which we might have lawfully defended ourselves against aggressors. If we defend ourselves hereafter against violence, whether it comes under the shadow of law or otherwise (for we have reason to expect it in both ways), we shall then be charged with treason and suffer the penalty; and if we continue passive and non-resistant, we must certainly expect to perish, for our enemies have sworn it.

And here, sir, permit us to state that General Joseph Smith, during his short life, was arraigned at the bar of his country about fifty times, charged with criminal offences, but was acquitted every time by his country; his enemies, or rather his religious opponents, almost invariably being his judges. And we further testify that, as a people, we are law-abiding, peaceable and without crime; and we challenge the world to prove to the contrary; and while other less cities in Illinois have had special courts instituted to try their criminals, we have been stript of every source of arraigning marauders and murderers who are prowling around to destroy us, except the common magistracy.

With these facts before you, sir, will you write to us without delay as a father and a friend, and advise us what to do. We are members of the same great confederacy. Our fathers, yea some of us, have fought and bled for our country, and we love her constitution dearly.

In the name of Israel's God, and by virtue of multiplied ties of country and kindred, we ask your friendly interposition in our favor. Will it be too much for us to ask you to convene a special session of Congress, and furnish us an asylum, where we can enjoy our rights of conscience and religion unmolested? Or will you, in a special message to that body, when convened, recommend a remonstrance against such unhallowed acts of oppression and expatriation as this people have continued to receive from the States of Missouri and Illinois? Or will you favor us by your personal influence and by your official rank? Or will you express your views concerning what is called the "Great Western Measure" of colonizing the Latter-day Saints in Oregon, the north-western Territory, or some location remote from the States, where the hand of oppression shall not crush every noble principle and extinguish every patriotic feeling?

And now, honored sir, having reached out our imploring hands to you, with deep solemnity, we would importune you as a father, a friend, a patriot and the head of a mighty nation, by the constitution of American liberty, by the blood of our fathers who have fought for the independence of this republic, by the blood of the martyrs which has been shed in our midst, by the wailings of the widows and orphans, by our murdered fathers and mothers, brothers and sisters, wives and children, by the dread of immediate destruction from secret combinations, now forming for our overthrow, and by every endearing tie that binds man to man and renders life bearable, and that too, for aught we know, for the last time,—that you will lend your immediate aid to quell the violence of mobocracy, and exert your influence to establish us as a people in our civil and religious rights, where we now are, or in some part of the United States, or in some place remote therefrom, where we may colonize in peace and safety as soon as circumstances will permit.

We sincerely hope that your future prompt measures toward us will be dictated by the best feelings that dwell in the bosom of humanity, and the blessings of a grateful people, and many ready to perish, shall come upon you.

We are, sir, with great respect, your obedient servants,

BRIGHAM YOUNG,
WILLARD RICHARDS,
ORSON SPENCER,
ORSON PRATT, } Committee.
W. W. PHELPS,
A. W. BABBITT,
J. M. BERNHISEL,

In behalf of the Church of Jesus Christ of Latter-day Saints at Nauvoo, Illinois.

HISTORY OF UTAH.   243

P. S.—As many of our communications, post marked at Nauvoo, have failed of their destination, and the mails around us have been intercepted by our enemies, we shall send this to some distant office by the hand of a special messenger.

The appeals were unanswered save in a single instance, that of the Governor of Arkansas, who replied in a respectful and sympathetic epistle.

On the 19th of May, 1845, began the trial, at Carthage, of certain men who had been indicted for the murder of Joseph and Hyrum Smith. Sixty names had been presented to the Grand Jury of the Hancock Circuit Court in October, 1844, as being implicated in the assassination. Only nine, however, had been indicted. They were Levi Williams, Jacob C. Davis, Mark Aldrich, Thomas C. Sharp, William Voras, John Wills, William N. Grover, —— Gallagher, and —— Allen.

Of these, Levi Williams, as stated, was a Baptist preacher; Jacob C. Davis a State Senator, and Thomas C. Sharp the editor of the Warsaw *Signal*. Judge Richard M. Young presided at the trial, and James H. Ralston and Josiah Lamborn conducted the prosecution. The defense was represented by William A. Richardson, O. H. Browning, Calvin A. Warren, Archibald Williams, O. C. Skinner and Thomas Morrison. The panel of the trial jury was as follows: Jesse Griffits, Joseph Jones, William Robertson, William Smith, Joseph Massey, Silas Grifitts, Jonathan Foy, Solomon J. Hill, James Gittings, F. M. Walton, Jabez A. Beebe and Gilmore Callison.

The trial lasted until May 30th.* During its progress, Calvin A. Warren, Esq. of counsel for the defense, in the course of his plea is said to have argued that if the prisoners were guilty of murder, then he himself was guilty; that it was the public opinion that the Smiths ought to be killed, and public opinion made the laws, consequently it was not murder to kill them. Evidently this logic had

* "The Judge," says Governor Ford, "was compelled to admit the presence of armed bands to browbeat and overawe the administration of justice.   *   *   * The Judge himself was in duress, and informed me that he did not consider his life secure any part of the time. The consequence was that the crowd had everything their own way."

its weight with the jury, for they promptly returned a verdict of not guilty.*

Emboldened by the outcome of the trial, the tactics of the anti-Mormons now underwent a radical range. Trumping up charges against the Mormon leaders it was found would not effect the desired purpose. Extreme measures only would avail, and these the unconscionable crusaders were now prepared to execute, regardless of every consideration of right. Their own writers admit as much. Thomas Gregg, the historian of Hancock County, Illinois, whom none familiar with his work will accuse of partiality to the Mormons, is constrained to allow that the acts of their opponents now in question were absolutely unjustifiable. "Acts," says he, "which had no warrant in law or order, and which cannot be reconciled with any correct principles of reasoning, and which we then thought, and still think, were condemned by every consideration looking to good government; acts which had for their object, and which finally resulted in the forcible expulsion of the Mormon people from the county."

At a Mormon settlement called Morley, a few miles from Nauvoo, a band of incendiaries, on the night of September 10th, began operations. Deliberately setting fire to the house of Edmund Durfee they turned the inmates out of doors and threatened them with death if they did not at once leave the settlement. Durfee they subsequently killed. The mob continued its nefarious work until Morley was in ashes, and its people homeless. Green Plains and Bear Creek, localities also settled by the Saints, were next visited by the house-burners, and in like manner devastated.† Such scenes continued for

---

* Colonel John Hay, of the State Department at Washington, in the *Atlantic Monthly* for December, 1869, in an article reminiscent of the Prophet's murder and the trial of his assassins, says; "The case was closed. There was not a man on the jury, in the court, in the county, that did not know the defendants had done the murder. But it was not proven, and the verdict of Not Guilty was right in law."

† "At Lima and Green Plains," says Governor Ford, "the anti-Mormons appointed persons to fire a few harmless shots at their own meeting-house where services were in progress, whereupon the conspirators and their dupes rode all over the country and spread

a week, during which nearly two hundred houses, shops and sheds were destroyed and the people driven away. A hundred and thirty-five teams went out from Nauvoo to bring in the homeless refugees, with what grain had been saved from the flames.

Intense excitement now reigned, not only at Nauvoo, and the out-lying Mormon settlements that nightly anticipated attack, but throughout Hancock County. Non-Mormons not of the radical class disapproved of these deeds of vandalism,* and Sheriff Backenstos, of Carthage—to his honor be it said—did everything in his power to quell the riots and punish the guilty parties. He first issued a proclamation, demanding that they desist. This order they ignored. He then called upon the *posse comitatus*—the power of the County—to assist him in dispersing the rioters. But there was no response. Finally he applied to the Mormons for a *posse*, which was furnished him, and he proceeded at once against the house-burners.

In the encounters that ensued two mobocrats were killed. One of these was Frank A. Worrell, the same who, as sergeant of the Carthage Greys, had charge of the Jail when Joseph and Hyrum Smith were murdered. Worrell was shot by Porter Rockwell at the order of Sheriff Backenstos. Worrell at the time was approaching the Sheriff who, fearing for his own life, ordered Rockwell to fire. The two were tried for murder in this case, but were acquitted. The other man killed was Samuel McBratney, who was among the house-burners on Bear Creek. The Sheriff and his *posse*, after scattering the mob, surrounded Carthage and made several arrests. But most of

---

dire alarm. As a result a mob arose and burnt one hundred and seventy-five houses and huts belonging to Mormons, who fled for their lives in utter destitution, in the middle of the sickly season."

* The Quincy *Whig*, edited by a Mr. Bartlett, said: "Seriously, these outrages should be put a stop to at once; if the Mormons have been guilty of crime, why punish them, but do not visit their sins upon defenseless women and children. This is as bad as the savages. * * * It is feared that this rising against the Mormons is not confined to the Morley settlement, but that there is an understanding among the anties in the northern part of this and Hancock counties to make a general sweep, burning and destroying the property of the Mormons wherever it can be found."

the rioters had fled. The Mormon settlements around Nauvoo were now evacuated, the people, fearing pillage and massacre, gathering into the city for protection.

At this juncture Governor Ford put forth his hand to restore order. General John J. Hardin, with troops, was sent into Hancock County for that purpose. Accompanying him were J. A. McDougal, Attorney-General of Illinois; Senator Stephen A. Douglas, and Major W. B. Warren. Having issued a proclamation to the people of the county, enjoining peace, good order, and obedience to law and authority, General Hardin and his associates next held a consultation with the Mormon leaders at Nauvoo. The result was an agreement by the Latter-day Saints to leave Illinois; the exodus to begin in the spring. This demand came from a meeting of representatives of nine counties of the State, assembled at Carthage. The following correspondence, in relation to the proposed exodus, passed between General Hardin and his friends—representing Governor Ford and the anti-Mormons—and the Church leaders at Nauvoo:

Nauvoo, Oct. 1, 1845.

To the First President and Council of the Church at Nauvoo:

Having had a free and full conversation with you this day, in reference to your proposed removal from this county, together with the members of your Church, we have to request you to submit the facts and intentions stated to us in said conversation to writing, in order that we may lay them before the Governor and people of the State. We hope that by so doing it will have a tendency to allay the excitement at present existing in the public mind.

We have the honor to subscribe ourselves, respectfully yours, etc.,

JOHN J. HARDIN,
S. A. DOUGLAS.
W. B. WARREN,
J. A. McDOUGAL.

Nauvoo, October 1, 1845.

To Gen. John J. Hardin, W. B. Warren, S. A. Douglas, and J. A. McDougal:

MESSRS:—In reply to your letter of this date, requesting us to "submit the facts and intentions stated by us to writing, in order that you may lay them before the Governor and people of the State," we would refer you to our communication of the 24th ultimo, to the "Quincy Committee," etc, a copy of which is herewith inclosed.

In addition to this, we would say, that we had commenced making arrangements to remove from this county previous to the recent disturbances; that we now have four companies organized, of one hundred families each, and six more companies now organizing of the same number each, preparatory to removal. That one thousand families, including the Twelve, the High Council, the Trustees and general authorities of the Church, are fully determined to remove in the spring, independent of the contingency of selling our property, and that this company will comprise from five to six thousand souls.

That the Church, as a body, desires to remove with us, and will, if sales can be effected, so as to raise the necessary means.

That the organization of the Church we represent is such, that there never can exist but one head or presidency at any one time, and all good members wish to be with the organization; and all are determined to remove to some distant point where we shall neither infringe nor be infringed upon, so soon as time and means will permit.

That we have some hundreds of farms and some two thousand or more houses for sale in this city and county, and we request all good citizens to assist in the disposal of our property.

That we do not expect to find purchasers for our Temple and other public buildings; but we are willing to rent them to a respectable community who may inhabit the city.

That we wish it distinctly understood, that, although we may not find purchasers for our property, we will not sacrifice or give it away, or suffer it illegally to be wrested from us.

That we do not intend to sow any wheat this fall, and should we all sell we shall not put in any more crops of any description.

That as soon as practicable we will appoint committees for this city, La Harpe, Macedonia, Bear Creek, and all necessary places in the county, to give information to purchasers.

That if these testimonies are not sufficient to satisfy any people that we are in earnest, we will soon give them a sign that cannot be mistaken—*we will leave them!*

In behalf of the Council, respectfully yours, etc.,

BRIGHAM YOUNG, President.

WILLARD RICHARDS, Clerk.

CHAPTER XV.
1845-1847.

The Exodus—Brigham Young Leads his People Westward—Sugar Creek—Samuel Brannan and the Ship "Brooklyn"—Garden Grove and Mount Pisgah—The Saints Reach the Missouri River—The Mexican War and the Mormon Battalion—Elder Little and President Polk—Colonel Kane—More Anti-Mormon Demonstrations—The Battle of Nauvoo—Expulsion of the Mormon Remnant from the City—Colonel Kane's Description of Nauvoo—The Church in the Wilderness—Winter Quarters.

PURSUANT to the terms of the agreement, which satisfied General Hardin and his associate commissioners, and appeased for a time the anti-Mormons, preparations went forward all during the fall and winter for the spring exodus. Houses and lands in and around Nauvoo were sold, leased or abandoned. Wagons by hundreds were purchased or manufactured, and horses, mules, oxen, riding, draft and pack animals in general, procured in large numbers. Clothing, bedding, provisions, tents, tools, household goods, family relics and camp equipage composed the lading, wherewith animals and vehicles were packed and loaded until little or no room remained.

At length, all being ready for a start, on the 4th of February, 1846, the exodus of the Mormons from Illinois began. Charles Shumway, afterwards one of the original Utah pioneers, was the first to cross the Mississippi. Colonel Hosea Stout with a strong force of police had charge of the ferries, which were kept busy night and day until the river froze over. The companies then crossed on the ice. By the middle of February a thousand souls, with their wagons, teams and effects had been landed on the Iowa shore.

Sugar Creek, nine miles westward, was made the rendezvous and starting-point of the great overland pilgrimage. Here the advance companies pitched their tents, and awaited the coming of their leaders. The weather was bitter cold, the ground snow-covered and frozen, and the general prospect before the pilgrims so cheerless and desolate as to have dismayed souls less trustful in Providence, less inured to hardship and suffering than they. It was February 5th that the first camp formed on Sugar Creek. That night—a bitter night—nine wives became mothers; nine children were born in tents and wagons in that wintry camp. How these tender babes, these sick and delicate women were cared for under such conditions, is left to the imagination of the sensitive reader. How these Mormon exiles, outcasts of civilization, carrying their aged, infirm and helpless across the desolate plains and prairies, were tracked and trailed thereafter by the nameless graves of their dead, is a tale which, though often attempted, has never been and never will be fully told.*

On the 15th of February, Brigham Young, the leading spirit of the exodus, arrived at the camps on Sugar Creek. He was accompanied by Willard Richards and George A. Smith, with their families. Two days later Heber C. Kimball and Bishop Whitney joined them. Parley P. Pratt, who had returned from the east, was already there, but encamped at some distance from the main body. Other leading men, such as had not preceded these, soon followed. After the final departure of the Apostles from Nauvoo, Church affairs at that place

---

* "There is no parallel in the world's history to this migration from Nauvoo. The exodus from Egypt was from a heathen land, a land of idolaters, to a fertile region designated by the Lord for His chosen people, the land of Canaan. The pilgrim fathers in fleeing to America came from a bigoted and despotic people—a people making few pretensions to civil or religious liberty. It was from these same people who had fled from old-world persecutions that they might enjoy liberty of conscience in the wilds of America, from their descendants and associates, that other of their descendants, who claimed the right to differ from them in opinion and practice, were now fleeing. * * * Before this the Mormons had been driven to the outskirts of civilization, where they had built themselves a city; this they must now abandon, and throw themselves upon the mercy of savages."—Bancroft's History of Utah, page 217.

were left in charge of a committee consisting of Almon W. Babbitt, Joseph L. Heywood and John S. Fullmer.

Two days after Brigham's arrival on Sugar Creek,—during which interim he was busy with his brethren in organizing the camps for traveling,—he called together the Apostles who were with him and held a council. There were present Brigham Young, Heber C. Kimball, Orson Hyde, Orson Pratt, John Taylor, George A. Smith and Willard Richards. The subject considered by these leaders was as follows: It seems that about the time of the beginning of the exodus from Nauvoo, there had sailed from New York on the ship *Brooklyn* a company of Latter-day Saints bound for the Bay of San Francisco. They numbered two hundred and thirty-five souls, and were in charge of Elder Samuel Brannan. The company were well supplied with farming implements, and all tools necessary for the formation of a new settlement, which they proposed founding somewhere on the Californian coast. Elder Brannan believed that that would be the ultimate destination of the main body of his people. These Mormon colonists, who were probably the first American emigrants to land on the coast of California, carried with them a printing press, type, paper and other materials, with which was afterwards published the *California Star*, the pioneer newspaper of the Golden State. Elder Brannan, in New York, had edited a paper called *The Prophet*, published in the interests of the Latter-day Saints. He was a man of considerable energy and ability, but of speculative tendencies, and bent more to worldly ends than to spiritual aims.

Prior to sailing for San Francisco—then Yerba Buena—Brannan had entered into a peculiar compact with one A. G. Benson, representing certain politicians and financial sharpers at Washington, who, being aware of the contemplated Mormon exodus, proposed if possible to profit by it. This compact, which Brannan had sent to Nauvoo for the Church leaders to sign and then return to Mr. Benson, required that the Mormons transfer to A. G. Benson and Company, and to their heirs and assigns, the odd numbers of all the

lands and town lots they might acquire in the country where they settled. It was represented that ex-Postmaster Amos Kendall was one of the parties represented by Benson, and that no less a personage than the President of the United States was a "silent partner" in the scheme. If the Mormon leaders refused to sign the agreement, President Polk, it was stated, would forthwith proclaim that it was their intention to take sides with Great Britain or Mexico in the international controversies then pending between those countries and the United States, and send troops to intercept their flight, disarm and disperse them. In case they did sign, they and their people were to be protected and allowed to proceed on their journey unmolested. Such was the substance of Elder Brannan's letter, which, with a copy of this precious agreement, Brigham Young laid before his brethren, the Apostles, at their council on Sugar Creek, February 17th, 1846.

The proposition was treated with the contempt that it merited. Not only was it promptly rejected, but to Messrs. A. G. Benson and Company not even an answer was deigned. "Our trust is in God; we look to Him for protection," said Brigham and his brethren, too much inured to danger and deeds of violence to be frightened or tempted to thus dishonor themselves, even by threats of Federal bayonets.

That President Polk had really lent himself to the furtherance of such a rascally scheme, the general reader will be much inclined to doubt. We would prefer believing that the use of his name in this unsavory connection was without his consent and merely a shrewd trick of the sharpers, parties to the proposed land-grab, to give weight and cogency to their proposition.

A farewell visit to Nauvoo, where parting services were held in the all but completed Temple, and President Young and the Apostles again joined the camps on Sugar Creek. The temporary organization of the companies was now perfected. They comprised about four hundred wagons, all heavily loaded, with not more than half the number of teams necessary for a rapid journey. Most of the families were supplied with provisions for several months, but some were quite destitute, or had only sufficient to last for a few days. None, however, were permitted to lack food. The "share and share alike" principle and practice of the Mormon community prevented this. But the weather continuing very cold, some suffering was experienced on that score.

The "Camp of Israel" being organized, and the Governor of Iowa having been petitioned by the Saints for protection while passing through that Territory, President Young, on Sunday, March 1st, gave the order for a general advance. It was not the design, nor the subsequent practice of the Mormons to travel on Sundays. In all their migrations, except when necessity compelled, they were careful to keep the Sabbath day holy. But to get farther away from Nauvoo, which parties from the camps were frequently visiting, thus causing the anti-Mormons to suspect, or at least assert, that the exodus was not genuine, the President, on the opening day of spring, ordered the companies to move forward. Bishop George Miller's wagons had already departed. By noon all tents had been struck and the Camp began to move. In the van went Colonel Stephen Markham, with a hundred pioneers, to prepare the road before the main body. Colonel Hosea Stout with a company of riflemen—mounted police—guarded the wagons, and Colonel John Scott, with another hundred men, accompanied the artillery. William Clayton had been appointed clerk of the Camp, and Willard Richards, a graphic and ready writer, its historian.

Traveling five miles in a north-westerly direction, the Camp halted for the night,—still on Sugar Creek. Scraping away the snow, pitching their tents and corralling their wagons, quite a primitive little city soon sprang up, as if by magic, from the frozen earth. Large fires were built to dispel the gathering darkness, thaw out cold-benumbed fingers and features, and cook the evening meal. Despite the dreary situation and forbidding surroundings, a spirit of remarkable cheerfulness reigned throughout the Camp. Everybody seemed happy and determined to "make the best of it." In so doing, no people, under such circumstances, ever succeed better than the Mormons. Were it not the Sabbath, the merriest of songs would be sung, the jolliest of jokes cracked, the funniest of stories told, *ad infinitum.* Captain Pitts' Brass Band would tune their instruments, and awaken with soul-stirring, heart-cheering strains the prairie solitudes. At all events such was their custom during that long and dreary journey to the Missouri River and beyond. But at a seasonable hour all merriment would be hushed; heads and hearts bowed in reverent prayer, thanks returned to heaven for mercies already bestowed, and God's blessing invoked upon Israel,—these whose habitation was to be for many months the houseless plain and prairie, and the remnant left behind in the doomed city of Nauvoo.

Thus, from day to day, slowly and wearily traveling, went the exiled Saints across the undulating surface of snow-covered Iowa. The roads were very bad, the weather cold and stormy, and the streams, now frozen, now swollen by spring freshets, almost and at times quite impassable. Again and again they were obliged to double teams on the heavily loaded wagons, to drag them through deep streams and miry marshes on their line of travel. Some days three or four miles would be the extent of their journey. Many a halt was made, at times for weeks. Their able-bodied men often found employment at the nearest settlements, even crossing over the line into Missouri to obtain work, exchanging their labor with their old enemies for needed provisions and supplies.

On the 27th of March, on Shoal Creek, in the Chariton River region, where for three weeks they were delayed by the freshets, the Camp was more thoroughly organized. Companies of "hundreds," "fifties," and "tens" were formed, and captains appointed over them. Each company had its commissary, and there was a Commissary General. Henry G. Sherwood was that officer. David D. Yearsley, W. H. Edwards, Peter Haws, Samuel Gulley and Joseph Warburton were contracting commissaries. There were still others whose duty it was to distribute equitably among the various companies, grain, provisions and other commodities furnished for their use. The

Apostles, who had hitherto been acting as captains of companies were relieved of those commands and made presidents of divisions. The Camp consisted of two grand divisions, presided over by Brigham Young and Heber C. Kimball; the former as President and General-in-chief, directing the whole.

The laws of the Camp were strict without being oppressive. The President had said, while on Sugar Creek: "We will have no laws we cannot keep, but we will have order in the camp. If any want to live in peace when we have left this place, they must toe the mark." Honesty and morality were strictly enjoined; decency and decorum likewise. Thieving was not tolerated, either by Mormons or non-Mormons. In one or two instances where stolen property was found in camp,—some wayside trapper or farmer being the victim,—the thief was compelled to return it in person, and make due reparation. Profanity and irreverence were forbidden. Amusement and recreation, to a proper extent, were encouraged, as tending to divert the minds of the people from their past troubles and lighten their present toils, but excess of mirth and loud laughter were discountenanced.

At various points between the Mississippi and the Missouri the Mormons founded temporary settlements, or, as they called them, "traveling stakes of Zion," fencing the land, building log cabins, and putting in crops for their own use or for the benefit of their people who came after them. Two of these "stakes" were named Garden Grove and Mount Pisgah; the former on the east fork of Grand River, one hundred and forty-five miles from Nauvoo, and the latter near the middle fork of the Grand, twenty-seven miles farther west. Mount Pisgah was on the Pottawatomic Indian lands.

A thousand west-bound wagons of the Saints were now rolling over the prairies of Iowa. Amos Fielding, traveling back to Nauvoo, counted over nine hundred of their vehicles in three days. Many more were preparing to follow. Winter was past; the snow had disappeared, the icy streams had melted, the grass was growing, flowers blooming and birds singing. Summer had come, and all nature smiled in welcome. The vanguard of the migrating trains, under Brigham Young, reached the Missouri River about the middle of June. They were cordially welcomed by the Pottawatomie and Omaha Indians, upon whose lands the Saints temporarily settled.

Before reaching the Missouri the Mormon leaders had planned to leave the main body of their people there, and at the various settlements founded along the way, and while the remnants in the rear were gathering to those places, to push on that season, with a picked band of pioneers, and explore the Rocky Mountains. Apostle Woodruff, who was back from Europe, and had arrived at Mount Pisgah, received word from the President at Council Bluffs * to furnish one hundred mounted men for the expedition. Sixty had volunteered, and the muster was still in progress, when an event occurred to materially change the program, and delay the departure of the pioneers until the following spring. It was the call for the Mormon Battalion.

In April, 1846, war had broken out between the United States and Mexico. The original cause was the annexation of Texas in 1845, but the immediate *casus belli* was the occupation by United States troops, in March, 1846, of disputed territory on the Texan frontier, an act regarded by Mexico as a virtual declaration of war. She resented it as such, and in April began hostilities. The victories of Palo Alto and Resaca de la Palma, won by General Zachary Taylor on the 8th and 9th of May, drove the Mexicans across the Rio Grande, and here the war, in the opinion of many Americans, should have ended. But the majority of the nation, especially the South— bent upon extending slavery and preserving her balance of power— wished the strife continued, having set their hearts upon more. Nothing now would suffice but the extension of the boundaries of the Union to the Pacific Coast of California. This meant, in plain terms, the wresting from Mexico of her two provinces of New Mexico and

---

* So called from the fact that the Indian tribes of that region were in the habit of holding their councils there.

California, lying directly in the path of the Republic in its proposed march to the sea. Great Britain, still claiming Oregon, also coveted California, and it was to checkmate that power in her ambitious designs, as well as to acquire more territory for future states, that the war with Mexico was continued.

President Polk, having announced to Congress that war with Mexico existed by her own act, was authorized to issue a call for fifty thousand volunteers. At the same time ten million dollars were voted for war purposes. The plan was to strike Mexico in three places. General Stephen F. Kearney was to invade New Mexico and California, General Taylor to continue operations along the Rio Grande, and General Winfield Scott, commander-in-chief, to invade Mexico from the Gulf coast, carrying the war into the heart of the enemy's country. So much for the subject in general. The call for the Mormon Battalion was a portion of the plan matured at Washington for the invasion by General Kearney of the northern provinces of Mexico.

Let us now go back a little further. Shortly before the war broke out, and soon after the beginning of the exodus from Nauvoo, Elder Jesse C. Little, at the suggestion of President Young, visited Washington for the purpose of soliciting governmental aid for his people in their exodus. No gift of money or of other means was asked, but it was thought that the national authorities might wish to employ the Saints in freighting provisions and naval stores to Oregon or other points on the Pacific coast. Elder Little, who was in the east when he received his instructions from Nauvoo, carried with him to the capital letters of introduction from Governor Steele, of New Hampshire, and Colonel Thomas L. Kane, of Philadelphia; the former an old acquaintance of Elder Little's, and the latter—Colonel Kane—one of those brave and chivalric souls, too rarely met with in this world, ever ready to espouse, from a pure sense of justice and knightly valor, the cause of the oppressed. Such a class he believed the Mormons to be. Colonel Kane was brother to Dr. Kane, the famous Arctic explorer. Governor Steele's letter was addressed to

Secretary Bancroft, of the U. S. Navy; that of Colonel Kane to Vice-President George M. Dallas.

Through ex-Postmaster-General Amos Kendall, Elder Little obtained an introduction to President Polk and other distinguished personages, with whom he had several interviews, laying before them the situation and prospects of his people and their application for governmental aid. He was kindly received by the President, who referred to the Saints in favorable terms. He stated that he had no prejudice against them, but believed them to be good citizens and loyal Americans; as such he was "willing to do them all the good in his power, consistently." Elder Little, after his first interview with the President, addressed to him a petition which closed as follows:

> From twelve to fifteen thousand Mormons have already left Nauvoo for California, and many others are making ready to go; some have gone around Cape Horn, and I trust, before this time, have landed at the Bay of San Francisco. We have about forty thousand in the British Isles, all determined to gather to this land, and thousands will sail this Fall. There are also many thousands scattered through the States, besides the great number in and around Nauvoo, who will go to California as soon as possible, but many are destitute of money to pay their passage either by sea or land.
>
> We are true-hearted Americans, true to our native country, true to its laws, true to its glorious institutions; and we have a desire to go under the outstretched wings of the American Eagle; we would disdain to receive assistance from a foreign power, although it should be proffered, unless our Government shall turn us off in this great crisis, and compel us to be foreigners.
>
> If you will assist us in this crisis, I hereby pledge my honor, as the representative of this people, that the whole body will stand ready at your call, and act as one man in the land to which we are going; and should our territory be invaded, we will hold ourselves ready to enter the field of battle, and then like our patriotic fathers, make the battle-field our grave, or gain our liberty.

Just at this juncture the news reached Washington that the conflict for some time pending between the United States and Mexico had begun, General Taylor having fought his first two battles with the Mexicans. This news, which set all Washington aflame, determined President Polk upon the project of taking immediate possession of California, and of using the migrating Mormons for that purpose. His plan, as laid before his cabinet, was to send Elder Little direct to the Mormon camps in Iowa, to raise a thousand picked men "to make a dash into California and take possession of it in the name of the United States." This battalion was to be officered by its own men, with the exception of the commander, who was to be appointed by the President. They were to be armed and equipped by the government, and furnished with cannon and everything necessary to defend the country they conquered. A thousand more Mormons from the eastern states were to be sent via Cape Horn in a U. S. transport for the same purpose. The plan was fully matured, and about to be executed, when it was changed through the influence of Senator Thomas Benton, of Missouri. Then came the adoption of the general plan of operations, involving a call for five hundred Mormon volunteers to form a portion of General Kearney's force to invade New Mexico and California.

About the middle of June Elder Little left Washington for the west. He was accompanied by Colonel Thomas L. Kane, who had been commissioned by the President to carry special dispatches to General Kearney, at Fort Leavenworth, relative to the Mormon Battalion.

The commander of the Army of the West, who was about to start for Santa Fe, on receiving these dispatches, at once detailed Captain James Allen to proceed to the camps of the Saints, muster the battalion, and march them to Fort Leavenworth, where they would be armed and prepared for the field. Thence he was to lead them to Santa Fe, in the trail of General Kearney and the main army. Captain Allen, accompanied by three dragoons, reached Mount Pisgah on the 26th of June. Elder Little and Colonel Kane, who were on the way thither, had not yet arrived. Here we touch the point in our narrative from which digression was made in order to explain more fully the call for the Mormon Battalion.

At sight of the recruiting officer and his men, the Mormons at Mount Pisgah were at first somewhat alarmed, supposing them to be the vanguard of a United States army sent to intercept them. The threat of Messrs. Benson and Company, conveyed in Elder Brannan's letter, relative to disarming and dispersing the Saints if their leaders refused to sign away their rights, was probably known at Mount Pisgah, and its fulfillment now seemed imminent. But Captain Allen soon explained his errand to Apostle Woodruff and the High Council of the Stake,* and the first thrill of excitement subsided. The following "Circular to the Mormons" set forth more in detail the import of the officer's visit:

CIRCULAR TO THE MORMONS.

I have come among you, instructed by Col. S. F. Kearney of the U. S. army, now commanding the Army of the West, to visit the Mormon camp, and to accept the service for twelve months of four or five companies of Mormon men who may be willing to serve their country for that period in our present war with Mexico; this force to unite with the Army of the West at Santa Fe, and be marched thence to California, where they will be discharged.

They will receive pay and rations, and other allowances, such as other volunteers or regular soldiers receive, from the day they shall be mustered into the service, and will be entitled to all comforts and benefits of regular soldiers of the army, and when discharged, as contemplated, at California, they will be given gratis their arms and accoutrements, with which they will be fully equipped at Fort Leavenworth. This is offered to the Mormon people now. This year an opportunity of sending a portion of their young and intelligent men to the ultimate destination of their whole people, and entirely at the expense of the United States, and this advanced party can thus pave the way and look out the land for their brethren to come after them.

Those of the Mormons who are desirous of serving their country, on the conditions here enumerated, are requested to meet me without delay at their principal camp at the Council Bluffs, whither I am going to consult with their principal men, and to receive and organize the force contemplated to be raised.

I will receive all healthy, able-bodied men of from eighteen to forty-five years of age.

J. ALLEN, Captain 1st Dragoons.

Camp of the Mormons, at Mount Pisgah, one hundred and thirty-eight miles east of Council Bluffs, June 26th, 1846.

NOTE.—I hope to complete the organization of this battalion in six days after my reaching Council Bluffs, or within nine days from this time.

Carrying letters of introduction from the authorities at Mount Pisgah to the leaders at Council Bluffs, Captain Allen hurried on to the Missouri, whither he was preceded by a special messenger, sent by Apostle Woodruff to inform the President of his coming.

---

* These "traveling Stakes of Zion," like other stakes, had their High Councils and all needful equipment, spiritual and temporal.

The surprise, almost dismay, with which the main body of the Mormons received the startling news—startling indeed to them—that the United States government had demanded five hundred of their best men, to march to California and take part in the war against Mexico, may well be imagined. What! the nation which, according to their view, had virtually thrust them from its borders, permitted mobs to plunder them, rob them of their homes, murder their prophets, and drive them into the wilderness, now calling upon them for aid? Had that nation ever helped them in their extremity? Had not their appeals for succor and protection, addressed to Governors, Judges and Presidents invariably been ignored or denied? Five hundred able-bodied men, the pick and flower of the camp, wanted. And that, too, in an Indian country, in the midst of an exodus unparalleled for dangers and hardships, when every active man was needed as a bulwark of defense and a staff for the aged and feeble. Even delicate women, thus far, in some instances had been driving teams and tending stock, owing to the limited number of men available. And had they not already buried, in lonely prairie graves, many of their sick and helpless ones, who had perished from sheer lack of needed care impossible to bestow? Such was the subject as it presented itself to them. Such were among their thoughts and reflections at that hour.

And yet it was their country calling; that country to which their pilgrim ancestors had fled; for which their patriot sires had fought and suffered, whose deeds of heroism were among their highest and holiest traditions. America, land of liberty, land of Zion, the place for the Holy City which they or their children must yet uprear upon her chosen and consecrated soil! Such also were among their reflections.

What was to be done? What would their leaders decide to do? Queries, these, that flew like lightning, as the news of the coming of the government's agent sped from place to place, and from tent to tent, through all the "Camps of Israel." Not long were they left unanswered.

"You shall have your battalion, Captain Allen," said Brigham Young; that officer having arrived at the Bluffs, met the Mormon leaders, and made known to them his errand in person. It was the 1st of July. There were present, besides the Captain and the President, Heber C. Kimball, Orson Hyde, Orson Pratt, Willard Richards, George A. Smith, John Taylor, John Smith and Levi Richards. "You shall have your battalion," said Brigham determinedly, "and if there are not young men enough, we will take the old men, and if they are not enough, we will take the women," he added, a touch of grim humor tempering the sternness of his resolve. There not being enough able-bodied men on the Missouri to meet the requisition, back went three of the Apostles—Brigham Young, Heber C. Kimball and Willard Richards—to Mount Pisgah, in the role of recruiting sergeants. There they met Colonel Kane and Elder Little, the former, chaperoned by the latter, having come to visit the camps. From them they learned more fully of the avowed purpose of the government in calling for the Mormon volunteers.

The leaders were not convinced, however, that the call was not designed as a test of Mormon loyalty; nor were they converted from that view on hearing later, from a source esteemed reliable, that their inveterate foe, Senator Benton, of Missouri, had obtained from President Polk after the call was issued, a pledge that if the Mormons refused to respond, United States troops should be sent to cut off their route, disarm and disperse them. Of this they were yet unaware. Still they regarded the demand for the troops—"demand" they styled it—as designed to test their loyalty, and the opportunity to prove their fealty and stultify their traducers, who were insisting that they were traitors and aliens to their country, was one not to be lost.

Volunteers were enrolled at Mount Pisgah, and messengers sent to Garden Grove and other places, as far back as Nauvoo, to summon to head-quarters young men, old men and boys, to fill up the gaps in camp created by the enlistment of the Battalion. Men were detailed especially to look after the families of the volunteers in their absence. The President and his party then returned to Council Bluffs, Colonel Kane going also, and on the arrival there of the Pisgah volunteers the muster was completed. Colonel Kane thus speaks of the event: "A central mass meeting for council, some harangues at the more remotely scattered camps, an American flag brought out from the store-house of things rescued and hoisted to the top of a tree-mast, and in three days the force was reported, mustered, organized and ready to march."

What were the Mormons doing with that "American flag?" What use had they for the Stars and Stripes, and why were they bringing with them into the wilderness—into Mexico—the sacred banner of their sires, if they were indeed traitors and aliens, as their enemies so persistently asserted? Was it all a trick, a political and hypocritical master-stroke? Had they foreseen this test of their fealty, and prepared that banner as a proof of their patriotism beforehand, as calcium light and red-fire are prepared and held in readiness for a theatrical tableau? If as much were to be asserted in relation to that event, it would be no more than the Mormons have had to meet ever since that hour from their accusers. Such of these as are honest and sincere in their assertions have never understood the Mormons aright.

"I want to say to every man," said Brigham Young, in his farewell address to the Battalion,—"the Constitution of the United States, as framed by our fathers, was dictated, was revealed, was put into their hearts by the Almighty, * * and I tell you in the name of Jesus Christ it is as good as ever I could ask for. I say unto you, magnify the laws. There is no law in the United States, or in the Constitution, but I am ready to make honorable." He had before remarked to Colonel Kane—re-uttering an idea formerly advanced by Joseph Smith—that the time would come when the Saints would "have to save the Government of the United States, or it would crumble to atoms." A people who cherish such sentiments may seem fanatical, but they certainly are not disloyal.

HISTORY OF UTAH.   263

After a farewell ball in Father Taylor's "bowery,"* where to the music of violin, horn, triangle, bells and tamborine, the glowing hours of a midsummer afternoon were cheerily, merrily chased and consumed, the advance companies of the Battalion set out for Fort Leavenworth. The date of the enlistment was the 16th of July. In all, the Battalion numbered five hundred and forty-nine souls. As many of these volunteers had much to do with the early settlement of Utah and were virtually among the pioneers of the Territory, we deem it but proper to here preserve the record of their names. The various companies and the personnel of each were as follows:

LIST OF NAMES IN THE MORMON BATTALION.

COMPANY A.
Officers.

Jefferson Hunt, Captain.
George W. Oman, 1st Lieutenant.
Lorenzo Clark, 2nd Lieutenant.
William W. Willis, 3rd Lieutenant, (1st Sergeant at Muster In.)
James Ferguson, Sergeant Major.
Phinehas R. Wright, 1st Sergeant (Private at Muster Out.)
Ebenezer Brown, 2nd Sergeant.
Reddick N. Allred, 3rd Sergeant.

Alexander McCord, 4th Sergeant.
Gilbert Hunt, 1st Corporal.
Lafayette N. Frost, 2nd Corporal.
Thomas Weir, 3rd Corporal (Private at M. O.)
William S. Muir, 4th Corporal (Private at M. I., 1st Sergeant at Muster Out.)
Elisha Everett, Musician.
Joseph W. Richards, Musician, (Died at Pueblo.)

---

* Says Colonel Kane: "It was the custom, whenever the larger camps rested for a few days together, to make great arbors, or boweries, as they called them, of poles, and brush, and wattling, as places of shelter for their meetings of devotion or conference. In one of these, * * was gathered now the mirth and beauty of the Mormon Israel.

"If anything told that the Mormons had been bred to other lives, it was the appearance of the women as they assembled here. Before their flight they had sold their watches and trinkets as the most available recourse for raising ready money; and hence like their partners, who wore waistcoats cut with useless watch pockets, they, although their ears were pierced and bore the marks of rejected pendants, were without earrings, chains or broaches. Except such ornaments, however, they lacked nothing most becoming the attire of decorous maidens. The neatly darned white stockings, and clean white petticoat, the clear-starched collar and chemisette, the something faded, only because too well washed lawn or gingham gown, that fitted modishly to the waist of its pretty wearer —these, if any of them spoke of poverty, spoke of a poverty that had known better days."

Privates.

1 Allen, Rufus C.
2 Allred, James R.
3 Allred, James T. S.
4 Allred, Reuben W.
5 Allen, Albern
6 Brown, John
7 Butterfield, Jacob K.
8 Bailey, James
9 Brunson, Clinton D.
10 Brass, Benjamin
11 Blanchard, Mervin S.
12 Beckstead, Gordon S.
13 Beckstead, Orin M.
14 Bickmore, Gilbert
15 Brown, William W.
16 Beran, James
17 Bryant, John S.
18 Curtis, Josiah
19 Cox, Henderson
20 Chase, Hiram B.
21 Calkins, Alva C.
22 Casper, William W.
23 Calkins, James W.
24 Calkins, Sylvanus
25 Calkins, Edwin R.
26 Colman, George
27 Clark, Joseph
28 Clark, Riley G.
29 Decker, Zechariah B.
30 Dobson, Joseph
31 Dodson, Eli
32 Earl, James C.
33 Egbert, Robert C.
34 Fairbanks, Henry
35 Frederick, David
36 Glines, James H. (Q. M. Sergeant at M. I., Private at M. O.)
37 Garner, David
38 Gordon, Gilman
39 Goodwin, Andrew
40 Hulett, Schuyler
41 Holden, Elijah E.
42 Hampton, James (died at camp on Rio Grande.)
43 Hawkins, Benjamin
44 Hickenlooper, William F.
45 Hunt, Martial
46 Hewett, Eli B.
47 Hudson, Wilford
48 Hoyt, Timothy S.
49 Hoyt, Henry P.
50 Ivy, Richard A.
51 Jackson, Charles A.
52 Johnson, Henry
53 Kelly, William
54 Kelley, Nicholas
55 Kibley, James
56 Lemon, James W.
57 Lake, Barnabas
58 Moss, David
59 Maxwell, Maxie
60 Mayfield, Benjamin F.
61 Naile, Conrad
62 Oyler, Melcher
63 Packard, Henry, (M. C. as Corporal.)
64 Persons, Ebenezer
65 Roe, Cariatal C.
66 Riter, John
67 Steele, George E.
68 Steele, Isaiah C.
69 Sessions, Richard
70 Shepherd, Lafayette, (M. O. as Corporal.)
71 Swartout Hamilton
72 Sexton, George
73 Sessions, John
74 Sessions, William B.
75 Taylor, Joseph
76 Thompson, John
77 Vrandenburg Adna
78 Weaver, Miles
79 Wriston, John P.
80 Wriston, Isaac N.
81 Weaver, Franklin
82 Wilson, Alfred G.
83 Wheeler, Merrill W.
84 White, Samuel S. (Samuel F. in original)
85 Webb, Charles Y.
86 Winn, Dennis
87 Woodworth, Lysander
88 White, Joseph
89 Willey, Jeremiah

COMPANY B.

Officers.

Jesse D. Hunter, Captain.
Elam Luddington, 1st Lieutenant.
Ruel Barrus, 2nd Lieutenant.
Philemon C. Merrill, 3rd Lieutenant.
William Coray, 1st Orderly Sergeant.
William Hyde, 2nd Orderly Sergeant.
David P. Rainey, 1st Corporal.
Thomas Dunn, 2nd Corporal.
John D. Chase, 3rd Corporal.
William Hunter, Musician.
George W. Taggart, Musician.
Albert Smith, 3rd Orderly Sergeant.

HISTORY OF UTAH. 265

Privates.

1 Allen, George
2 Allen, Elijah
3 Alexander, Horace M.
4 Allen, Franklin
5 Bush, Richard
6 Bird, William
7 Bingham, Thomas
8 Bingham, Erastus
9 Billings, Orson
10 Bigler, Henry W.
11 Boley, Samuel (died on Missouri River)
12 Barrowman, John
13 Brackenberry, Benj. B.
14 Brown, Francis
15 Bliss, Robert S.
16 Bybee, John
17 Clark, George S.
18 Colton, Philander
19 Cheney, Zacheus
20 Callahan, Thomas W.
21 Church, Haden W.
22 Camp, J. G.
23 Carter, P. J.
24 Curtis, Dorr P.
25 Carter, R.
26 Dayton, William J.
27 Dutcher, Thomas P.
28 Dolton, Henry S.
29 Dunham, Albert
30 Evans, Israel

31 Evans, William
32 Eastman, Marcus N.
33 Freeman, Elijah N.
34 Follett, William A.
35 Fife, Peter
36 Green, Ephraim
37 Garner, William A.
38 Garner, Phillip
39 Hawk, Nathan
40 Huntsman, Isaiah
41 Hoffheins, Jacob
42 Hanks, Ephraim R.
43 Hawk, William
44 Hinkley, Arza E. (Ezra on original)
45 Hunter, Edward
46 Haskell, George
47 Harris, Silas
48 Jones, David H.
49 Keyser, Guy M.
50 King, John M.
51 Kirk, Thomas
52 Lawson, John
53 Morris, Thomas
54 McCarty, Nelson
55 Mount, Hiram B.
56 Martin, Jesse B.
57 Murdock, John R.
58 Murdock, Price
59 Myers, Samuel
60 Miles, Samuel

61 Noler, Christian
62 Owens, Robert
63 Pearson, Ephraim
64 Persons, Harmon D.
65 Prouse, William
66 Park, James 1st
67 Park, James 2nd
68 Richards, Peter F.
69 Rogers, Samuel H.
70 Study, David
71 Smith, Azariah
72 Stevens, Lyman
73 Stoddard, Rufus
74 Simmons, William A.
75 Sly, James C.
76 Steers, Andrew J.
77 Stillman, Dexter
78 Workman, Andrew J.
79 Walker, William
80 Willis, Ira
81 Workman, Oliver G.
82 Willis, W. S. S.
83 Watts, John
84 Whitney, Francis T.
85 Wright, Charles
86 Wilcox, Edward
87 Wilcox, Henry
88 Wheeler, John L.
89 Winters, Jacob
90 Zabriskie, Jerome

COMPANY C.

Officers.

James Brown, Captain.
George W. Rosecrans, 1st Lieutenant.
Samuel Thompson, 2nd Lieutenant,
Robert Clift, (Promoted from Orderly Sergeant to 3rd Lieutenant.)
Orson B. Adams, 1st Sergeant at M. I., 2nd Sergeant at M. O.
Elijah Elmer, 2nd Sergeant at M. I., 1st Sergeant at M. O.

Joel J. Terrill, 3rd Sergeant, (Private at M.O.)
David Wilken, 4th Sergeant; (Private at M. O.)
Jabez Nowlin, 1st Corporal; (Private at M. O.)
Alexander Brown, 2nd Corporal.
Edward Martin, 3rd Corporal; (2nd Sergeant at M. O.
Daniel Tyler, 4th Corporal; (3rd Sergt. at M.O.)
Richard D. Sprague, Musician.
Russell G. Brownell, Musician; (Corp'l at M.O.)

HISTORY OF UTAH.

Privates.

1 Adair, Wesley
2 Boyle, Henry G. (Henry B. Miller on original)
3 Burt, William
4 Barney, Walter
5 Babcock, Lorenzo
6 Brown, Jesse J.
7 Bailey, Addison
8 Bailey, Jefferson
9 Beckstead, William E.
10 Brimhall, John
11 Blackburn, Abner
12 Bybee, Henry G.
13 Clift, James
14 Covil, John Q. A.
15 Condit, Jeptha
16 Carpenter, Isaac
17 Carpenter, William H.
18 Calvert, John
19 Catlin, George W.
20 Donald, Neal
21 Dunn, James
22 Dalton, Harry
23 Dalton, Edward
24 Durphy, Francillo
25 Dodge, Augustus E.
26 Forbush, Lorin
27 Fellows, Hiram W.
28 Fife, John
29 Fifield, Levi
30 Gould, John C.

31 Gould, Samuel
32 Gibson, Thomas
33 Green, John
34 Hatch, Meltiah
35 Hatch, Orin
36 Holt, William
37 Harmon, Ebenezer
38 Harmon, Lorenzo F.
39 Holdaway, Shadrach
40 Hendrickson, James
41 Hancock, Charles
42 Hancock, George W.
43 Ivie, Thomas C.
44 Johnston, William J.
45 Johnston, Jesse W.
46 Johnson, Jarvis
47 Layton, Christopher
48 Larson, Thurston
49 Landers, Ebenezer
50 Lewis, Samuel
51 Myler, James
52 McCullough, Levi H.
53 Morey, Harley
54 Maggard, Benjamin
55 Mowrey, John T.
56 Mead, Orlando F.
57 More, Calvin W.
58 Olmstead, Hiram
59 Perkins, David
60 Perkins, John
61 Pickup, George

62 Peck, Thorit, (Corporal at M. O.)
63 Peck, Isaac
64 Pulsipher, David
65 Persons, Judson
66 Richie, Benjamin
67 Rust, William W.
68 Richmond, Benjamin
69 Reynolds, William
70 Riser, John J.
71 Smith, Milton
72 Smith, Richard
73 Shupe, James
74 Shupe, Andrew J.
75 Shipley, Joseph
76 Squires, William, (Corporal at M. O.)
77 Shumway, Aurora
78 Thompson, James L.
79 Thomas, Nathan T.
80 Thomas, Elijah
81 Tuttle, Elanson
82 Truman, Jacob M.
83 Tindell, Solomon
84 Wade, Edward W.
85 Wade, Moses
86 Wood, William
87 White, John J.
88 Wilcox, Matthew
89 Welsh, Madison
90 Wheeler, Henry

COMPANY D.

Officers.

Nelson Higgins, Captain.
George P. Dykes, 1st Lieutenant.
Sylvester Hulett, 2nd Lieutenant.
Cyrus C. Canfield, 3rd Lieutenant.
Nathaniel V. Jones, 1st Sergeant; (Private at M. O.)
Thomas Williams, 2nd Sergeant.
Luther T. Tuttle, 3rd Sergeant.

Alpheus P. Haws, 4th Sergeant.
Arnold Stephens, 1st Corporal.
John Buchanan, 2nd Corporal.
William Coon, 3rd Corporal.
Lewis Lane, 4th Corporal; (Private at M. O.)
Willard Smith, Musician.
Henry W. Jackson, (Henry J. on original.) Musician.

Privates.

1 Abbott, Joshua
2 Averett, Juthan
3 Brown, James 1st
4 Brown, James S
5 Badlam, Samuel
6 Button, Montgomery
7 Brizzee, Henry W.
8 Boyd, George W.
9 Boyd, William
10 Barger, William W.
11 Compton, Allen
12 Cole, James B.
13 Casto, William
14 Casto, James
15 Curtis Foster
16 Clawson, John R.
17 Cox, Amos
18 Collins, Robert H.
19 Chase, Abner
20 Davis, Sterling
21 Davis, Eleazer
22 Davis, James
23 Douglas, Ralph
24 Douglas, James
25 Flecther, Philander
26 Frazier, Thomas
27 Fatoute, Ezra
28 Forsgreen John
29 Finlay, Thomas
30 Gilbert, John
31 Gifford, William W.
32 Gribble, William
33 Hoagland, Lucas
34 Henry, Daniel
35 Hirons James
36 Huntington, Dimick B.
37 Hendricks, Wm. D.
38 Holmes, Jonathan
39 Higgins, Alfred
40 Hunsaker, Abraham, (1st Sergt. at M. O.)
41 Jacobs, Sanford, (Corporal at M. O.)
42 Kenny, Loren E.
43 Lamb, Lisbon
44 Laughlin, David S.
45 Maxwell, William
46 Meeseck, Peter J.
47 Meacham, Erastus
48 Bingham, Erastus
49 Merrill, Ferdinand
50 McArthur, Henry
51 Oakley, James
52 Owen, James
53 Peck, Edwin M.
54 Perrin, Charles
55 Pettegrew, James P.
56 Rollins, John
57 Rawson, Daniel B.
58 Roberts, Benjamin
59 Runyan, Levi
60 Rowe, William
61 Richmond, William
62 Robinson, William
63 Raymond, Almon P.
64 Smith, John G.
65 Stephens, Alexander
66 Spencer, William W.
67 Stewart, Benjamin
68 Stewart, James
69 Stewart, Robert B.
70 Sargent, Abel M.
71 Savage, Levi
72 Stillman, Clark
73 Swarthout, Nathan
74 Sharp, Albert
75 Sharp, Norman
76 Shelton, Sebert C.
77 Sanderson, Henry W.
78 Steele, John
79 Thompson, Henry
80 Thompson, Miles
81 Tanner, Myron
82 Twitchel, Anciel
83 Tubbs, William
84 Treat, Thomas
85 Hayward, Thomas
86 Tippets, John
87 Walker, Edwin
88 Woodward, Francis
89 Whiting, Almon
90 Whiting, Edmond

COMPANY E.

Officers.

Daniel C. Davis, Captain.
James Pace, 1st. Lieut.
Andrew Lytle, 2d. Lieut.
Samuel L. Gully, 3rd. Lieut.
Samuel L. Brown, 1st. Sergt.
Richard Brazier, 2nd. Sergt.
Ebenezer Hanks, 3rd. Sergt.
Daniel Browett, 4th. Sergt.
James A. Scott, Corp. (died at Pueblo)
Levi W. Hancock, Musician.
Jesse Earl.

Privates.

1 Allen John, (drummed out of service, non-"Mormon")
2 Allen, George
3 Bentley, John
4 Beers, William
5 Brown, Daniel
6 Buckley, Newman
7 Bunker, Edward
8 Caldwell, Matthew
9 Campbell, Samuel
10 Campbell, Jonathan
11 Cazier, James
12 Cazier, John
13 Clark, Samuel
14 Clark, Albert
15 Chapin, Samuel
16 Cox, John
17 Cummings, George
18 Day, Abraham
19 Dyke, Simon
20 Dennett, Daniel Q.
21 Earl, Jacob
22 Ewell, Wm.
23 Ewell, Martin F.
24 Earl, Justice C.
25 Findlay, John
26 Follett, William T.
27 Glazier, Luther W.
28 Harmon, Oliver N.
29 Harris, Robert
30 Harrison, Isaac
31 Hart, James S.
32 Harrison, Israel
33 Hess, John W.
34 Hickmot, John
35 Hopkins, Charles
36 Hoskins, Henry
37 Howell, T. C. D.
38 Howell, William
39 Jacobs, Bailey
40 Judd, Hiram
41 Judd, Zadock K.
42 Jimmerson, Charles
43 Knapp, Albert
44 Kelley, George
45 Karren, Thomas
46 Lance, William
47 McLelland, Wm. C.
48 Miller, Daniel
49 McBride, Haslam
50 Miller, Miles
51 Park, Wm. A.
52 Pettegrew, David
53 Pixton, Robert
54 Phelps, Alva, (died on the Arkansas)
55 Porter, Sanford
56 Pugmire, Jonathan, jun.
57 Rollins ——
58 Richardson, Thomas
59 Richards, L.
60 Roberts, L.
61 Sanders, Richard T.
62 Scott, Leonard M.
63 Scott, James R.
64 Skein, Joseph
65 Spidle, John
66 Slater, Richard
67 Snyder, John
68 Smith, Lot
69 Smith, David
70 Smith, Elisha
71 Smith, John
72 St. John, Stephen M.
73 Stephens, Roswell
74 Standage, Henry
75 Strong, William
76 Tanner, Albert
77 West, Benj.
78 Wilson, George
79 Woolsey, Thomas
80 Williams, James V.
81 Whitworth, Wm.

Several families of women and children accompanied their husbands and fathers in the Battalion, and these, with the officers' servants, brought the full number up to five hundred and forty-nine.

Captain James Allen, whose brave and generous spirit had from the first endeared him to every soul in the Battalion, to the great grief of all fell sick and died at Fort Leavenworth on the 23rd of August. Lieutenant A. J. Smith, an officer not so highly esteemed by them, then took command of the Battalion and marched them to Santa Fe, which town had already been captured by General Kearney.

On October 13th, by order of the General, Colonel Philip St. George Cooke, a brusque and eccentric though brave and manly officer, assumed command of the Mormon Battalion. Then began their arduous and heroic march across the burning plains and rugged mountains of New Mexico to southern California. In all, the Battalion marched, from the Missouri to the Pacific, a distance of over two thousand miles, pioneering much of the way through an untrodden wilderness, braving dangers and enduring hardships compared with which fighting would have been mere sport. Said Colonel Cooke, their commander: "History may be searched in vain for an equal march of infantry."

Short rations, lack of water, excessive toil in road-making, well-digging and over-marching, caused much suffering, sickness and some deaths among the Battalion. Even before reaching Santa Fe their sufferings were severe, and many were disabled and prevented from proceeding farther. These disabled detachments, with most of the women of the Battalion, were placed in charge of Captain James Brown and ordered to Pueblo on the head-waters of the Arkansas River, while their comrades, the main body, including four women* who accompanied their husbands, pushed on to the Pacific coast. They arrived near San Diego late in January, 1847.

General Kearney had reached California some time before, but with only a few men, having disbanded most of his force on being informed en route that California was already in the possession of the United States. Colonel John C. Fremont, who with sixty men was exploring west of the Sierras when the war broke out, had rallied the American settlers of Sacramento Valley—a few hundred strong—and with the co-operation of Commodores Sloat and Stockton, all but subdued the country before Kearney came. A few skirmishes then took place, and the conquest was complete. The war in California being virtually over before Colonel Cooke's command

---

* These four women were Mrs. Melissa Burton Coray, wife of Sergeant Coray; Mrs. Captain Davis, Mrs. Captain Hunter (who died in California) and Mrs. Ebenezer Brown.

could reach the coast, the Mormon Battalion did not take part in any engagement. Fort-building and garrison service were about all that was required of them. Nevertheless they did much work as mechanics and laborers. They performed their duties in such a manner as to elicit the commendation of their military superiors, and win the sincere esteem of the native Californians.* Fremont and some of his men were their foes.† But General Kearney, Governor Mason and others in authority spoke in high praise of the patience, subordination and general good conduct of the Mormon soldiers.‡

Prior to Kearney's arrival Colonel Fremont—authorized, it is said, by Commodore Stockton—had made himself military governor of California. As such he refused to recognize Kearney's authority. Thereupon the latter, backed by Colonel Cooke and the Mormon Battalion—the principal force then at his command—had Fremont arrested for insubordination and taken to Washington, where he was court-martialed.

While some of these events were taking place on the Pacific coast, other scenes of a military character were being enacted on the distant shores of the Mississippi. After the departure of the Mormon leaders from Nauvoo in February, 1846, the exodus of their people

---

* Says Henry G. Boyle, one of the Battalion: " I think I whitewashed all San Diego. We did their blacksmithing, put up a bakery, made and repaired carts, and, in fine, did all we could to benefit ourselves as well as the citizens. We never had any trouble with the Californians or Indians, nor they with us. The citizens became so attached to us that before our term of service expired they got [up a petition to the Governor to use his influence to keep us in the service. The petition was signed by every citizen in the town."

† Fremont was son-in-law to Senator Benton of Missouri.

‡ Governor R. B. Mason, General Kearney's successor as military commandant of California, in his report to the Adjutant-General September 18th, 1847, wrote : " Of the services of the Battalion, of their patience, subordination and general good conduct you have already heard, and I take great pleasure in adding that as a body of men they have religiously respected the rights and feelings of this conquered people, and not a syllable of complaint has reached my ear of a single insult offered or outrage done by a Mormon volunteer. So high an opinion did I entertain of the Battalion and of their special fitness for the duties now performed by the garrisons in this country, that I made strenuous efforts to engage their services for another year."

continued without cessation. The Saints were anxious that their enemies should have no ground upon which to base an accusation of bad faith, and no excuse for committing further outrages upon them. Major W. B. Warren, who with a small force of militia remained in Hancock County to preserve order, and doubtless to help on the exodus, thus reported to the Quincy *Whig* on May 20th: "The Mormons are leaving the city with all possible dispatch. During the week four hundred teams have crossed at three points, or about 1,350 souls. The demonstrations made by the Mormon population are unequivocal. They are leaving the State, and preparing to leave, with every means God and nature have placed in their hands. This ought to be satisfactory." The Warsaw *Signal*, the anti-Mormon organ, published similar reports from Major Warren.

As the Major says, this ought to have been satisfactory, but it was not. Men who were not sated at having imbrued their hands in blood to gratify political and religious animosities, are hard to satisfy. There was too good plundering at Nauvoo to permit the Mormons to dispose of their property and depart in peace, as they desired. Major Warren's reports, confirmed by events that were taking place daily, should have convinced reasonable men that the Mormons were in earnest in their exodus. But if convinced, the anti-Mormons failed to act upon their convictions. On the contrary, they continued to assert the falsehood that the Mormons did not intend to leave the State, and even raised troops at Carthage to march against Nauvoo. Governor Ford in his writings refers to these early settlers of Hancock County as "hard cases."[*] No fair-minded person, cognizant of the facts, will dispute the correctness of his estimate. A meeting between the leaders of the military mob and a committee of "new citizens" of Nauvoo—persons who had purchased Mormon properties and moved into the city—averted, but only for a little season, the threatened assault.

[*] The Governor's comment is as follows: "I had a good opportunity to know the early settlers of Hancock County, and to my certain knowledge the early settlers, with some honorable exceptions, were, in popular language, hard cases."

In July a party of Mormons from Nauvoo, ignoring a mobocratic edict ordering all of their faith to remain in the city except when leaving for the west, went into the country near a place called Pontoosuc, to help some of their brethren harvest a field of grain. While there they were set upon by a larger party of anti-Mormons, severely whipped and driven away. The last act in the drama of Mormonism in Illinois was thus begun. Several persons were arrested for this assault and taken to Nauvoo. The anti-Mormons retaliated by taking several of the Saints prisoners and holding them as hostages. The men held at Nauvoo, regaining their liberty, sued out writs against their captors for false imprisonment, which writs were placed in the hands of a deputy sheriff, one John Carlin of Carthage, to serve. Meeting some difficulty in executing these processes, he called out the *posse comitatus*, and having raised two regiments of troops started for Nauvoo.

Governor Ford, being apprised of this movement, ordered Major John R. Parker to muster a force of volunteers and defend the city. Parker and Carlin were thus placed in direct antagonism. Each styled the other's force "a mob." A treaty of peace between Major Parker and Colonel Singleton—in immediate command of the *posse*—being rejected by the Colonel's men as too favorable to the Mormons, Singleton in disgust resigned, and Carlin appointed Colonel Brockman in his stead. Governor Ford describes Brockman as "a Campbellite preacher, nominally belonging to the Democratic party, a large, awkward, uncouth, ignorant, semi-barbarian, ambitious of officer, and bent upon acquiring notoriety." On assuming command, Brockman and his "regulators"—as the *posse* was styled—advanced upon Nauvoo, and on the 10th of September began to bombard the town.

The citizens, though such as bore arms were greatly outnumbered by the attacking force, banded together for defense, and hastily fortifying the approaches to the city, returned the enemy's fire with spirit. Having no artillery, while Brockman's force was well supplied with cannon, they converted some old steam-boat

HISTORY OF UTAH.   273

shafts into guns, and placing them in position compelled the enemy to retire.

Major Parker for some reason had left Nauvoo, and Colonel Johnson was now in command of the citizen force, which numbered about four hundred men. Brockman is conceded by anti-Mormon estimates to have had twice that many. The main stay of the defense was a select body of riflemen called the "Spartan Band," of which William Anderson and Alexander McRae were first and second captains.

On the 12th of September occurred the battle of Nauvoo, a spirited action of an hour and a quarter's duration, between Brockman's force, which now renewed the attack with fury, and the overmatched but gallant defenders of the city. Colonel Johnson having fallen sick, Lieutenant-Colonel William E. Cutler directed the defense, with Daniel H. Wells as his aide. During the fight, which resulted in another repulse for the "regulators," Captain Anderson, his son Augustus and Isaac Morris were killed, and several others of the defenders wounded. On his side Brockman reported none killed, but twelve wounded. The siege lasted for several days. Finally, through the mediation of a citizen's committee from Quincy, a treaty was agreed upon between the forces militant. This treaty was as follows:

1. The City of Nauvoo will surrender. The force of Colonel Brockman to enter and take possession of the city tomorrow, the 17th of September, at 3 o'clock p. m.

2. The arms to be delivered to the Quincy Committee, to be returned on the crossing of the river.

3. The Quincy Committee pledge themselves to use their influence for the protection of persons and property from all violence; and the officers of the camp and the men pledge themselves to protect all persons and property from violence.

4. The sick and helpless to be protected and treated with humanity.

5. The Mormon population of the city to leave the State, or disperse, as soon as they can cross the river.

6. Five men, including the trustees of the Church, and five clerks, with their families (William Pickett* not one of the number) to be permitted to remain in the city for the disposition of property, free from all molestation and personal violence.

---

* Pickett's offense consisted in taking from one of the mob party— Major McCalla —a gun stolen from one of the Mormons who had been whipped and robbed at Pontoosuc.

7. Hostilities to cease immediately, and ten men of the Quincy Committee to enter the city in the execution of their duty as soon as they think proper.

We, the undersigned, subscribe to, ratify and confirm the foregoing articles of accommodation, treaty and agreement, the day and year first above written.

Signed by: Almon W. Babbitt, Joseph L. Heywood, John S. Fullmer, Trustees in Trust for the Church of Jesus Christ of Latter-day Saints; Andrew Johnson, Chairman of the Committee of Quincy; Thomas S. Brockman, commanding *posse*; John Carlin, Special Constable.

The terms of the treaty were outrageously violated by Brockman and his regulators, as soon as they found themselves in full possession of the city. "A grim and unawed tyrant," says Ford of the mob leader; "a self-constituted and irresponsible power," he styles the so-called *posse*, who, now that Nauvoo was prostrate at their feet, proceeded to work their will upon the helpless inhabitants. Mormons and non-Mormons, all who had defended the city or otherwise incurred the displeasure of the lawless horde, were treated with every indignity. Some of the "new citizens" were mockingly baptized in the river in the name of Brockman and other leaders of the mob, and then driven out of town. Houses were plundered, and the aged and infirm abused and threatened. Finally, all the Mormons, [such as had not already fled, were forced from their homes at the point of the bayonet, and thrown, men, women and children, sick, dying and shelterless, upon the western shore of the Mississippi. And this—shades of the patriots!—while their brethren of the Mormon Battalion were marching to fight their country's battles on the plains of Mexico.

Colonel Thomas L. Kane, who was now returning east from his visit to the Mormon camps on the Missouri, touched at Nauvoo just after this final expulsion. What he saw there he graphically and eloquently told in a lecture delivered a few years later before the Historical Society of Pennsylvania. An extract from his lecture is here inserted:

A few years ago, ascending the Upper Mississippi, in the autumn, when its waters were low, I was compelled to travel by land past the region of the rapids. My road lay through the half-breed tract, a fine section of Iowa which the unsettled state of its land-titles had appropriated as a sanctuary for coiners, horse thieves, and other outlaws. I had left my steamer at Keokuk, at the foot of the lower fall, to hire a carriage, and to contend for some fragment of a dirty meal with the swarming flies, the only scavengers of the locality. From this place to where the deep waters of the river return, my eye wearied to see everywhere sordid vagabonds and idle settlers; and a country marred, without being improved, by their careless hands.

I was descending the last hill-side upon my journey, when a landscape in delightful contrast broke upon my view. Half-encircled by the bend of the river, a beautiful city lay glittering in the fresh morning sun; its bright new dwellings, set in cool, green gardens, ranging up around a stately dome-shaped hill which was crowned by a noble marble edifice whose high tapering spire was radiant with white and gold. The city appeared to cover several miles; and beyond it, in the back-ground, there rolled off a fair country, chequered by the careful lines of fruitful husbandry. The unmistakeable marks of industry, enterprise and educated wealth everywhere, made the scene one of singular and most striking beauty.

It was a natural impulse to visit this inviting region. I procured a skiff, and rowing across the river, landed at the chief wharf of the city. No one met me there. I looked and saw no one. I could hear no one move, though the quiet everywhere was such that I heard the flies buzz, and the water-ripples break against the shallow of the beach. I walked through the solitary streets. The town lay as in a dream, under some deadening spell of loneliness, from which I almost feared to wake it; for plainly it had not slept long. There was no grass growing up in the paved ways; rains had not entirely washed away the prints of dusty footsteps.

Yet I went about unchecked. I went into empty workshops, ropewalks and smithies. The spinner's wheel was idle; the carpenter had gone from his work-bench and shavings, his unfinished sash and casing. Fresh bark was in the tanner's vat, and the fresh-chopped lightwood stood piled against the baker's oven. The blacksmith's shop was cold; but his coal heap, and ladling pool, and crooked water-horn were all there as if he had just gone off for a holiday. No work people anywhere looked to know my errand. If I went into the gardens, clinking the wicket-latch after me, to pull the marigolds, heart's-ease and lady slippers, and draw a drink with the water-sodden water bucket and its noisy chain, or knocking off with my stick the tall, heavy-headed dahlias and sunflowers, hunting over the beds for cucumbers and love-apples; no one called out to me from any open window, or dog sprang forward to bark an alarm. I could have supposed the people hidden in their houses, but the doors were unfastened; and when at last I timidly entered them, I found dead ashes white upon the hearths, and had to tread a-tip-toe, as if walking down the aisle of a country church, to avoid rousing irreverent echoes from the naked floors.

On the outskirts of the town was the city graveyard; but there was no record of plague there; nor did it in anywise differ much from other Protestant American cemeteries. Some of the mounds were not long sodded; some of the stones were newly set, their dates recent, and their black inscriptions glossy in the mason's hardly dried letter-ink. Beyond the graveyards, out in the fields, I saw on a spot hard by where the fruited boughs of a young orchard had been roughly torn down, the still smouldering remains of a barbecue fire, that had been constructed of rails from the fencing round it. It was the latest sign of life there. Fields upon fields of heavy headed yellow grain lay rotting ungathered upon the ground. No one was at hand to take in their rich harvest. As far as the eye could reach, they stretched away—they sleeping, too, in the hazy air of autumn.

Only two portions of the city seemed to suggest the import of this mysterious solitude. On the southern suburb, the houses looking out upon the country showed, by their splintered woodwork, and walls battered to the foundation, that they had lately been the mark of a destructive cannonade. And in and around the splendid temple which had been the chief object of my admiration, armed men were barracked, surrounded by their stacks of musketry and pieces of heavy ordnance. These challenged me to render an account of myself, and why I had had the temerity to cross the water without a written permit from a leader of their band.

Though these men were generally more or less under the influence of ardent spirits, after I had explained myself as a passing stranger, they seemed anxious to gain my good opinion. They told the story of the dead city; that it had been a notable manufacturing and commercial mart, sheltering over 20,000 persons; that they had waged war with its inhabitants for several years, and been finally successful only a few days before my visit, in an action brought in front of the ruined suburb, after which they had driven them forth at the point of the sword. The defence, they said, was obstinate, but gave way on the third day's bombardment. They boasted greatly of their prowess, especially in this battle as they called it; but I discovered that they were not of one mind as to certain of the exploits that had distinguished it; one of which, as I remember, was, that they had slain a father and his son, a boy of fifteen, not long residents of the fated city, whom they admitted had borne a character without reproach.

They also conducted me inside the massive sculptured walls of the curious temple, in which they said the banished inhabitants were accustomed to celebrate the mystic rites of an unhallowed worship. They particularly pointed out to me certain features of the building, which having been the peculiar objects of a former superstitious regard, they had, as a matter of duty, sedulously defiled and defaced. The reputed sites of certain shrines they had thus particularly noticed; and various sheltered chambers, in one of which was a deep well, constructed, they believed, with a dreadful design. Besides these, they led me to see a large and deep chiseled marble vase or basin, supported by twelve oxen, also of marble, and of the size of life, of which they told some romantic stories. They said the deluded persons, most of whom were emigrants from a great distance, believed their deity countenanced their reception here of a baptism of regeneration, as proxies for whomsoever they held in warm affection in the countries from which they had come. That here parents went into the water for their spouses, and young persons for their lovers. That thus the great vase came to be for them associated with all dear and distant memories, and was, therefore, the object of all others in the building to which they attached the greatest degree of idolatrous affection. On this account the victors had so diligently desecrated it, as to render the apartment in which it was contained too noisome to abide in.

They permitted me also to ascend into the steeple to see where it had been lightning-struck on the Sabbath before, and to look out east and south, on wasted farms like those I had seen near the city, extending till they were lost in the distance. There, in the face of the pure day, close by the scar of divine wrath left by the thunderbolt, were fragments of food, cruises of liquor, and broken drinking vessels, with a brass drum and a steamboat signal-bell, of which I afterwards learned with pain.

It was after nightfall when I was ready to cross the river on my return. The wind had freshened since the sunset, and the water beating roughly into my little boat, I hedged higher up the stream than the point I had left in the morning, and landed where a faint glimmering light invited me to steer.

There, among the dock and rushes, sheltered only by the darkness, without roof between them and sky, I came upon a crowd of several hundred human creatures, whom my movements roused from uneasy slumber upon the ground.

Passing these on my way to the light, I found it came from a tallow candle in a paper funnel shade, such as is used by street venders of apples and peanuts, and which, flaming and guttering away in the bleak air off the water, shone flickeringly on the emaciated features of a man in the last stage of a bilious remittent fever. They had done their best for him. Over his head was something like a tent, made of a sheet or two, and he rested on a partially ripped open old straw mattress, with a hair sofa cushion under his head for a pillow. His gaping jaw and glaring eye told how short a time he would monopolize these luxuries; though a seemingly bewildered and excited person, who might have been his wife, seemed to find hope in occasionally forcing him to swallow awkwardly sips of the tepid river water, from a burned and battered, bitter-smelling tin coffee-pot. Those who knew better had furnished the apothecary he needed; a toothless old bald-head, whose manner had the repulsive dullness of a man familiar with death scenes. He, so long as I remained, mumbled in his patient's ear a monotonous and melancholy prayer, between the pauses of which I heard the hiccup and sobbing of two little girls who were sitting upon a piece of driftwood outside.

Dreadful, indeed, was the suffering of these forsaken beings, bowed and cramped by cold and sunburn, alternating as each weary day and night dragged on. They were, almost all of them, the crippled victims of disease. They were there because they had no homes, nor hospital, nor poor house, nor friends to offer them any. They could not satisfy the feeble cravings of their sick; they had not bread to quiet the fractious hunger-cries of their children. Mothers and babes, daughters and grandparents, all of them alike, were bivouacked in tatters, wanting even covering to comfort those whom the sick shiver of fever was searching to the marrow.

These were Mormons in Lee County, Iowa, in the fourth week of the month of September, in the year of our Lord 1846. The city—it was Nauvoo, Illinois. The Mormons were the owners of that city, and the smiling country around. And those who had stopped their plows, who had silenced their hammers, their axes, their shuttles, and their workshop wheels; those who had put out their fires, who had eaten their food, spoiled their orchards, and trampled under foot their thousands of acres of unharvested bread— these were the keepers of their dwellings, the carousers in their temple, whose drunken riot insulted the ears of the dying.

I think it was as I turned from the wretched night watch of which I have spoken, that I first listened to the sounds of revel of a party of the guard within the city. Above the distant hum of the voices of many, occasionally rose distinct the loud oath-tainted exclamation, and the falsely intonated scrap of vulgar song; but lest this requiem should go unheeded, every now and then, when their boisterous orgies strove to attain a sort of ecstatic climax, a cruel spirit of insulting frolic carried some of them up into the high belfry of the Temple steeple, and there, with the wicked childishness of inebriates, they whooped, and shrieked, and beat the drum that I had seen, and rang, in charivaric unison, their loud-tongued steamboat bell.

There were, all told, not more than six hundred and forty persons who were thus lying upon the river flats. But the Mormons in Nauvoo and its dependencies had been numbered the year before at over twenty thousand. Where were they? They had last been seen, carrying in mournful train their sick and wounded, halt and blind, to disappear behind the western horizon, pursuing the phantom of another home. Hardly anything else was known of them; and people asked with curiosity, what had been their fate—what their fortune.

Returning now to the Mormons on the Missouri. With the departure of the Battalion in the summer of 1846, went every prospect, for that season, of the pioneer journey to the Rocky Mountains. The "Camp of Israel" now prepared to go into winter quarters. Apostles Orson Hyde, Parley P. Pratt, John Taylor, Elder Franklin D. Richards and others had been sent to England, the first three to set in order the affairs of the British Mission, now greatly demoralized through certain financial operations of Elder Reuben Hedlock and others. They had inaugurated a Joint Stock Company, the chief object of which was to assist in emigrating the Saints to America. Through mismanagement the scheme, originally a good one, had become a sad failure.* The residue of the Twelve—Ezra T. Benson now being one of their number—remained with their people in the wilderness. During the sojourn upon the Missouri, Alpheus Cutler and Bishop George Miller fell away from the Church, each being followed by a small faction, thenceforth known as Cutlerites and Millerites.

Some of the Mormons had early crossed to the west side of the river, constructing a ferry-boat for that purpose, and settled, by permission of the Indians—Omahas—upon the lands set apart for

---

* The original project was devised by Joseph Smith, in conjunction with Brigham Young and Newel K. Whitney, at Nauvoo, early in 1842.

their use by the Federal Government. These lands, which are now included in the State of Nebraska, were a portion of the vast tract once known as the Province of Louisiana, ceded by France to the United States in 1803. A very friendly feeling existed between the Pottawatomie and Omaha Indians and their Mormon "brothers"*— probably from the fact that both felt aggrieved at the treatment they had received from their white neighbors farther east. The Indians complained bitterly of being removed from their pleasant lands beyond the Mississippi to the damp and unhealthy bottoms of the Missouri. In return for permission from the Omahas—who were west, while the Pottawatomies were east of the river—to temporarily settle upon their lands and use what timber they required, the Mormons assisted the Indians to harvest and build, besides trading with them to mutual advantage. Major Harvey, the Indian Superintendent, did not approve of this arrangement, and tried to have the Mormons ejected; but President Polk, being appealed to through Colonel Kane, gave full permission for them to remain. Out of gratitude to Colonel Kane, the Saints afterwards named a settlement which they established on the east side of the river, Kanesville.

As the season advanced the settlers on the west side were instructed to congregate in one place, and a site being chosen for that purpose they there founded their celebrated Winter Quarters. This place is now Florence, Nebraska, five miles above the city of Omaha. It then consisted of seven hundred houses of log, turf, and other primitive materials, neatly arranged and laid out with streets and byways, with workshops, mills, etc., and a tabernacle of worship in the midst; the whole arising from a pretty plateau overlooking the river, and well fortified with breast-work, stockade and block-houses, after the fashion of the frontier. Such was Winter Quarters. The settlement was divided into twenty-two wards, with a Bishop over each. There was also a High Council. The population of the place was about four thousand. A ward east of the river contained a little

---

* Several Pottawatomie chiefs, and delegations from the Sacs and Foxes had visited Joseph Smith at Nauvoo.

over two hundred souls. Garden Grove and Mount Pisgah were also still inhabited; their numbers now swelled by the refugees from Nauvoo. Here in these humble prairie settlements, surrounded by Indians, hopeful and even happy, though enduring much sickness and privation, which resulted in many deaths, the pilgrim Mormons passed the winter of 1846-7.

HISTORY OF UTAH.   281

CHAPTER XVI.
1540-1847.

THE BEGINNING OF UTAH HISTORY—WHY THE MORMONS DID NOT COLONIZE THE PACIFIC COAST—THE GREAT BASIN—UTAH'S PHYSICAL FEATURES—DANIEL WEBSTER ON THE "WORTHLESS WEST"—EARLY SPANISH EXPLORATIONS—ESCALANTE IN UTAH VALLEY—LA HONTAN'S HEARSAYS—AMERICAN TRAPPERS ON THE SHORES OF THE GREAT SALT LAKE—COLONEL BRIDGER—CAPTAIN BONNEVILLE—COLONEL FREMONT—EARLY EMIGRATIONS FROM THE MISSOURI TO THE PACIFIC—THE DONNER DISASTER.

WE HAVE now traced the history of the Mormon people from the birth of their Prophet and the inception of their religious organization down to that point where their record as founders of Utah is about to begin. These preliminary chapters, dealing with early Mormonism, have been deemed indispensable to the proper understanding of a subject at once so unique and complex, so interesting and important as the history of our Territory. As premised at the opening, one cannot completely describe a lake or large body of water without giving some account of the origin, course and character of the streams flowing into and forming it; nor fully and faithfully narrate the history of a country and its inhabitants, if ignoring utterly their antecedents.

This is the author's explanation,—and he feels assured that the thoughtful reader will appreciate his motive and labors in this connection,—for entering more or less into detail with early Mormon annals. From this point begins the history of Utah proper; the narrative of early explorations in this region, and the settlement and formation of the Territory.

The opening of the year 1847 at the camps of the Saints east and west of the Missouri, saw preparations in progress for the contemplated pioneer journey to the mountains. And not only for this, but for the continued exodus of the entire Church, so soon as a place of refuge suitable for their reception could be found.

It was pretty well decided in the minds of the Mormon leaders, by this time, that the Pacific coast,—to which it was generally supposed they were migrating,—in spite of its many natural advantages, was no place for the main body of their people to settle. It might do for a colony, such as that of the ship *Brooklyn*, to make its way to California and there found a settlement,—as Elder Brannan and his company were now doing,—and other Mormon towns might spring up on the Pacific slope. But for the headquarters of the Church, and a permanent abiding place for the majority of the Saints, California proper or any part of the coast was exceedingly undesirable.

The reasons were these: that toward that favored land, that *El Dorado*,—though gold in California had not yet been discovered,—large numbers of emigrants, from Missouri and other border states, were now wending their way. Many had gone and were still going to Oregon, which Great Britain had finally relinquished, while others, as early as 1841, had bent their course to the future land of gold. Colonel Fremont, as seen, at the out-break of the Mexican war, had found enough American settlers in the Sacramento Valley to form, with his exploring party, a small army. And now that California, like Oregon and Texas, was a part of the American domain,—only awaiting the formality of its cession to the great Republic,—emigration thither was bound to increase manifold.

For the Mormons to have mingled with or settled any where near their old enemies, the Missourians, or people holding similar prejudices against their religious views and social customs, would simply have been to invite a repetition, sooner or later, of the very evils which had caused them so much suffering, and from which they were then fleeing. So thought Brigham Young. So thought his fellow chiefs of the migrating Church. Who, from their standpoint, can question the wisdom of their decision?—a decision to halt midway, if possible, between the Missouri and the Pacific, in some spot undesired, uncoveted by others, where they might be free to worship God in their own way, and work out their religious and social problems unmolested.

It was not for gold and silver, broad acres and teeming fields that these Latter-day Saints had left their homes, in this or in foreign lands. "After such things do the Gentiles seek," and the Saints, according to their faith, were no longer Gentiles, but of Israel. The children of Japheth perhaps had a mission in temporal things. If so, let them work it out, as best they might, before Him to whom all men are accountable. But as for Israel—for Ephraim—his mission was in spiritual things; comprehending indeed the temporal, but not to be absorbed and swallowed up by it. Religious liberty, freedom to worship God and prepare themselves for their future work of building up Zion,—these were the prime objects the migrating Mormons had in view. Gold and silver, houses and lands, flocks, herds, orchards, vineyards—though to all mortals more or less desirable—were but as dust beneath their feet by comparison.

Nor is this an exaggeration. The Mormons were essentially a religious people, deeply, earnestly religious, as much so as were the Albegois of France, the Covenanters of Scotland or the Pilgrims of New England. Unquestionably such were the motives and feelings of the vast majority of the Saints in their exodus. They had proved it by that exodus, in which many had forsaken, not for the first, but for the fourth and fifth times, for conscience' sake, their earthly possessions.

Zion, not Babylon, was in their thoughts. They had not relinquished their hopes concerning Jackson County. Many, perhaps most of those who had lived upon that land had sacredly kept the deeds to the homes from which they had been driven; while the few who had disposed of their possessions "in Zion," were believed by the others to have practically denied the faith.*

They were but going into the wilderness for a season, where, free from contact with those who understood them not, or persisted

---

* See remarks of Lyman Wight at a conference in Far West, February 5th, 1838, in relation to selling lands in Jackson County.

in misinterpreting their motives, they might peaceably prepare themselves for the time when, unless Joseph Smith was a false prophet and Brigham Young a blind leader of the blind, they or their children must needs return and build up Zion. Isolation, therefore, was what they sought, was what they must have, if they were to have peace, and fit and prepare themselves for what they believed was in their destiny.

True, there was the alternative, ever open, of relinquishing their religious faith, and becoming in every respect homogeneous with the Gentiles. But this was utterly out of the question. Friendly with the Gentiles they would gladly have been, mingling with them, so far as need be, in society, in business and in politics. But to relinquish their religion for the sake of peace,—the very thought were treason. It would have made of their high professions a mockery, of their past experience, written in blood and tears, a farce. The life-stream of their martyred Prophet would have smoked to heaven in vain. No; come what would, they must cling to their principles, however unpopular, and stand or fall with them.

Such were their thoughts and feelings. Such were the motives that impelled them westward. Such were their reasons for not settling, as a people, on the Pacific coast, and for isolating themselves, instead, in the tops of the Rocky Mountains, a thousand miles from civilization.

While the Saints are preparing to prosecute their journey, and their vanguard is making ready for its memorable march across the vast prairies and desolate plains lying west of the Missouri River, will be an appropriate time to pioneer the way before them into the region they are about to enter.

Beyond the Rocky Mountains, the so-called "back-bone of the American continent,"—the great water-shed dividing the streams flowing toward the Pacific from those which seek the Atlantic through the Mississippi and the Gulf of Mexico,—lies the region known in topographical parlance as the "Great Basin." It is a vast inter-mountain plateau, extending four or five hundred miles from east to west, and about the same distance from north to south. Its eastern

HISTORY OF UTAH.   285

edge does not touch the Rocky Mountains proper, but is rimmed by a smaller and almost parallel range called the Wasatch, between which and the great spinal column—the Rockies—is the region through which flow the Green and Grand Rivers. These, uniting with other streams, form the Colorado. The western rim of the Basin is the Sierra Nevada range, nearly parallel with, but much longer than the Wasatch, and separating the great plateau from the Pacific coast.

The Basin on the north converges toward the Blue Mountains of Oregon, and on the south in the direction of the Colorado plateau. It is traversed north and south by numerous mountain ranges, some of which are as high as those composing the rim. For this reason the term "Basin," bestowed by the famous explorer, Colonel Fremont, on a partial acquaintance with the region, is now deemed a misnomer. Instead of being one basin it is many, a group of basins, each containing a "sink," or lake, whose waters have no visible outlet to the sea. The more prominent of these are the basin of the Great Salt Lake, whose lowest point of altitude is 4,170 feet above the sea level; Sevier Lake basin, with an altitude of 4,690 feet; Humboldt River basin, 4,147 feet; Carson River basin, at Carson Lake, 3,840 feet; and the Walker River basin, the lowest point of which is 4,072 feet above the ocean.

It is supposed by many, and the supposition is confirmed by geological signs, such as ripple-marks on the mountain sides, shells on the slopes and summits, etc., that this great elevated plateau was once a broad inland sea communicating with the Pacific. At that time these mountain tops were so many islands, laved or lashed by its briny waves. These sinks, or some of them, are believed to be the remains of that pre-historic sea, which for some reason disappeared centuries before the foot of the European pressed the soil of the new world.

The great drawbacks to this otherwise rich and valuable region are scarcity of timber and fresh water. The former is only to be found in the mountains or along the water courses, and these, in this arid region, are few and far between. Though artesian wells and irrigation have done much of late years to redeem the desert land, vast tracts of country still remain *in statu quo*, bare and unproductive. But the mountains are full of minerals, from the precious metals down, and the term "treasure house of the nation" has not been inaptly bestowed upon this portion of the public domain.

Among the remarkable features of the Great Basin, which comprises the western part of what is now Utah Territory, and nearly the entire State of Nevada, are the Great Salt Lake and its neighboring desert. The lake is wholly in Utah, and the desert lies along its western shore, stretching away to the south and west a hundred miles or more. This lake—the famous "Dead Sea of America"—is one of the most wonderful natural objects in all the West. Laving the base of the Wasatch range in northern Utah, it extends north and south for seventy-five miles, having a mean breadth of about thirty. Its extreme depth is sixty or seventy feet. Jutting up from its briny bosom are no less than eight mountain islands, lifting their craggy crests almost level with the rugged ranges surrounding them. Though constantly augmented by fresh rivers and streams, the waters of the lake remain ever intensely salt. As said, it has no outlet—at least none visible—its waters, far brinier than those of the ocean, and wonderfully buoyant withal, either evaporating to the clouds, sinking mysteriously in subterranean depths, or solidifying under the sun's rays and banking up in bright crystals and glittering incrustations along its shores. These waters were once supposed to be absolutely lifeless, but of late years some species of *animalculæ* have been discovered therein. Fish cannot live in the Great Salt Lake, but several varieties abound in the fresh lakes and streams of this region. One of the main affluents of the Salt Lake is the river Jordan, the outlet of Lake Utah, forty miles southward.

As stated, the Wasatch Mountains are the eastern rim of the Great Basin,*—at least they form the main portion of that rim.

---

* Specifically the Coal Range, a portion of the Wasatch system twenty or thirty miles east of Salt Lake Valley, is the eastern rim.

Traversing Utah from north-east to south-west, they divide the Territory into two unequal parts. Through the eastern section, which is not included in the Great Basin, run the Green and Grand Rivers and their tributaries. Eastward from and forming a spur of the Wasatch, near the Wyoming line, extends the Uintah range. West of the Wasatch, and running parallel therewith, are the Oquirrh hills, and west of them the Onaquis. To the south-east and through southern Utah generally are other ranges and broken ridges, diversified with valleys and plateaus.

Utah's lakes are mostly in the north, the principal one being the Great Salt Lake, previously mentioned. Of the fresh water lakes the Utah and the Bear—the last-named partly in Idaho—are the more notable. Sevier Lake is a shallow, brackish body fifty or sixty miles south of Lake Utah. Parowan Lake, formerly known as Little Salt Lake, is a small salt water sheet still farther south. The rivers feeding these lakes are formed principally of smaller streams, owing their origin to the snows of winter packed in the mountain tops and gradually melted by the rays of summer.

Along the bases of the mountains, wherever these streams descend,—often spilling from the brims of little lakes among the summits, tumbling over high cliffs, forming beautiful cascades, and emerging into the valleys through deep gorges called canyons,— the soil as a rule is fertile, and if irrigated, susceptible of high cultivation. In other parts, where not pure desert, hopelessly barren, it is so devoid of moisture and so strongly impregnated with salt and alkali, as to be all but irredeemable. Hot and warm sulphur springs, the waters of which are highly curative, also gush forth from the bases of these mighty hills.

The rainfall of Utah averages twenty inches for the year, four-tenths coming in the spring, one-tenth in summer, three-tenths in autumn, and the rest during the winter. Owing to its scarcity in summer, irrigation is resorted to for crop-raising. The ground, during the heated term, is fairly parched and blistered by the sun, and the climate, though ordinarily temperate and delightful—the atmospheric rarity counteracting to a great extent the heat—is at times almost tropical. The climate of south-western Utah—the Santa Clara region—is well nigh tropical the whole year round.

In the canyons along the water-courses spring groves of quaking-asp, maple and pine, and in spring and early summer rich grasses and wild flowers cover the sides of the ravines. But the valleys, when Utah was first settled, save for the slight symptoms of verdure following the trail of winding streams in their weary pilgrimage across barren plains, had neither groves nor grass to hide their nakedness. Like the brown and sun-burnt hill-sides above them, they were either utterly bare, or clothed with sagebrush, sun-flowers and other wild and worthless growths springing prolifically on every hand.

Such is or was Utah, in the year 1847, a land of mountains, valleys, lakes, rivers and sandy wastes; directly in the path of early overland emigration from the Missouri to the Pacific, but shunned by all passers because of its sterile and forbidding aspect. The "Great American Desert,"—such was its name upon the maps and in the school books of that period.

Its only human dwellers at that time,—save here and there a few trappers or mountaineers, exiles of civilization, consorting with savages, and dwelling in some isolated fort or cave or hut among the hills,—were roving bands of Indians, some of them the most degraded of their race. These savages, who subsisted by fishing, hunting, root-digging and insect-eating, shared with wild beasts and venomous reptiles the then barren and desolate, but now fruitful and lovely land of Utah.

The popular estimate of this whole western region, including the Pacific Coast, at that early day, is expressed in the following words of a speech by Daniel Webster on the floor of the United States Senate. He was denouncing a proposition to establish a mail route from Independence, Missouri, to the mouth of the Columbia River. Says the great orator and statesman: "What do we want with this vast, worthless area? This region of savages and wild beasts, of deserts, of shifting sands and whirlwinds of dust, of cactus and prairie dogs? To what use could we ever hope to put these great deserts, or those endless mountain ranges, impenetrable, and covered to their very base with eternal snow? What can we ever hope to do with the western coast, a coast of 3,000 miles, rock-bound, cheerless, uninviting, and not a harbor on it? Mr. President, I will never vote one cent from the public treasury to place the Pacific Coast one inch nearer to Boston than it now is."

Yet it was to the very heart of this inhospitable region, "a thousand miles from anywhere," that Brigham Young, America's greatest colonizer, led his exiled people; and by his genius and energy, and their united industry, under the blessing of divine providence, subdued the desert, made the wilderness to blossom, and became the founder of a hundred cities.

So far as known, the first white men, moderns, to approach and partly penetrate the Utah region, were a small band of Spaniards, a detachment of the army of Francisco Vazquez de Coronado, the famous explorer of New Mexico. Being at Zuni—then Cibola—in 1540, and having heard of a great river to the north-west, Coronado despatched Captain Garcia Lopez de Cardenas with twelve men to explore it. This party is supposed to have proceeded by way of the Moquis villages—previously captured by the Spaniards—to the banks of the Colorado, just within Utah's southern boundary. They did not cross the river, but returned soon to report to Coronado at Cibola.

In July, 1776,—that immortal month of an immortal year,—two Franciscan friars, Francisco Antanasio Dominguez and Silvester Velez de Escalante, Spanish officials of New Mexico, with seven men set out from Santa Fe in quest of a direct route to Monterey on the Californian sea-coast. Pursuing a devious, north-westerly course, Escalante and his comrades traversed what is now western Colorado and crossed White River, flowing west, near the Utah line. White River was called by them San Clemente. They then passed Green River— San Buenaventura—and following up the Uintah and crossing the mountains came to a stream which they at first named Purisima, probably from the purity of its waters. This was no other than the Timpanogos or Provo River, which they followed down to Utah Lake.

The Spaniards were kindly received by the native Utahs—dwelling in willow huts in the valley—from whom they derived considerable information regarding that and adjacent parts. But they could learn nothing of a route to the sea, nor of Spanish settlers in all that region. Among other things they were told of a valley to the northward, in which there was a large salt lake, covering many leagues, with which their own fresh lake—Timpanogos—communicated. The waters of the larger lake were described as extremely salt and injurious,—a fact many times since proven by the hapless bather unfortunate enough to swallow much of the saline liquid. The Utahs, or, as Escalante styles them, "Timpanois" further said that he who wet any part of his body with this water immediately felt an itching in the wet part. Near this lake dwelt the Puaguampe, or Sorcerers, "a numerous and quiet nation," speaking the language of, but not otherwise emulating the hostile Comanches, whom the Utahs greatly dreaded. The Puaguampe dwelt in "little houses of grass and earth" and drank from "various fountains or springs of good water" which were "about the lake."

Escalante describes Utah Valley—north of which his party did not go—as extending from north-east to south-west sixteen Spanish leagues, and having a width of ten or twelve leagues. It was quite level, and, excepting the marshes on the lake-shore, arable. Provo River they renamed San Antonio. To the Jordan they gave the name of Santa Ana, and christened other streams in the vicinity. The Indians subsisted then, as later, by fishing and hunting. Bear, deer and buffalo ranged the region freely, and the bounding jack-rabbit, still so plentiful, was not lacking. The streams were filled with fish, and the marshes with wild fowl.

Late in September the Spaniards, accompanied by two native guides, resumed their journey, turning now to the south-west in the direction of Monterey. Passing down the Sevier, which river they named Santa Isabel, they skirted the eastern shore of the lake and crossed Beaver River. They then visited the valley now bearing the name of Escalante. There, owing to the exhaustion of their food supplies, and the prospect of a long and arduous journey to the seacoast—for still they could learn of no open route to the Pacific—they reluctantly abandoned the expedition. Turning eastward they traveled toward the Colorado, purchasing from the natives, as they went, seeds with which to make bread. Reaching the river, they found, after much difficulty, a ford in latitude 37°,—near where Utah and Arizona now divide. Passing thence by way of the Moquis villages they reached Zuni and in due time Santa Fe. They arrived there January 2nd, 1777.

To establish beyond dispute the identity of the discoverer of the Great Salt Lake would prove a difficult if not an impossible task. The first to hear of it—if credence may be given to his very fanciful narrative—was Baron La Hontan, lord-lieutenant of the French colony at Placentia, Newfoundland. La Hontan, whose narrative was first published in English in 1735, tells how in 1689 he sailed for six weeks up a certain affluent of the Mississippi called Long River, passing through various savage tribes till he came near the nation of the Gnacsitares. There he met four Mozeemlek slaves, captives of the Gnacsitares, who gave him a description of the country from which they originally hailed. Their villages, they said, stood upon a river springing out of a ridge of mountains, whence Long River likewise derived its source. The Mozeemleks were numerous and powerful. The slaves informed La Hontan that at a distance of a hundred and fifty leagues from where he then stood their principal river emptied itself into a salt lake, three hundred leagues in circumference by thirty in breadth, the mouth of the river being two leagues broad. The lower part of the stream was adorned with "six noble cities," and there were above a hundred towns, great and small, "round that sort of sea." The lake was navigated with boats. The government of the land was despotic, and was "lodged in the hands of one great head" to whom the rest paid "trembling submission," etc. So much for La Hontan and his hearsays.

Now, as to the actual discovery of the Great Salt Lake. Many are the rival claims and accounts concerning it. Some of these are easily disposed of in the negative. Others must stand for what they are worth until disproved or more thoroughly established. Colonel John C. Fremont claimed the honor of discovery as late as 1843; he having that year passed the Rocky Mountains on his second exploring expedition to the West. The year before he had gone only as far as South Pass, that great gateway of overland travel, which he elaborately described in his report to Congress. He now penetrated to the Great Basin, accompanied by the noted scout Kit Carson and other daring spirits, and on the 6th of September, from the crest of an elevated peninsula* a little north of Weber River, caught his first glimpse of America's Dead Sea.

Launching his rubber boat upon the briny waters, he explored the island now known as Fremont Island—so named by Captain Stansbury in 1849—but which Fremont himself called Disappointment Island, from failing to find there the fertile fields and abundant game he had anticipated. Fremont supposed himself to be the first white man, not only to embark upon, but to see the Great Salt Lake. In both conjectures he was in error. The lake had been discovered, and boats launched upon it by American trappers nearly twenty years before the advent of the "Pathfinder" into the Great Basin. As early as the "twenties," if not before, this whole region was overrun by American and British fur-hunters, trapping, exploring, building forts, trading and fighting with the Indians, from British America to Mexico. The celebrated Hudson's Bay Company and the scarcely less famous North American Fur Company, were among the earliest, if not the very earliest organizations to engage in these lucrative though perilous pursuits.

Bancroft, the Pacific States historian, is disposed to accord the

---

* This peninsula is known in Weber County as Little or Low Mountain.

honor of discovering the Lake to Colonel James Bridger, founder of the once celebrated fort, bearing his name, situated on Black's Fork of Green River. Bridger, it is said, who in 1825 was trapping in the Bear River region, in Cache or Willow Valley, in order to decide a wager among his men as to the probable course of the Bear, followed that stream through the mountains till he stood upon the shores and tasted of the briny waters of the great inland sea. In the spring of 1826 four men, it is said, explored the lake in skin boats, and reported that it had no outlet. So little was known of the great West at that time, even by the adventurous spirits who traversed it, that they thought it quite probable this lake was an arm of the Pacific ocean.

Other claims, not so well authenticated as Bridger's, place the time of probable discovery at about 1820. A trapper named Provost—for whom Provo River presumably was named—is said to have been in this vicinity during that year. By some, William N. Ashley is thought to have preceded Bridger. Mr. Ashley, in 1825-6, led a large company from St Louis through South Pass and founded on Utah Lake, Fort Ashley*. He is said to have named the Sweetwater and Green rivers,—the latter after one of his party. His own name still clings to Ashley's Fork.

Among the notable characters traversing the Great Basin about this time was Peter Skeen Ogden, of the Hudson's Bay Company, who gave his name to the Ogden or Humboldt river.† Another was Jedediah S. Smith, of the Rocky Mountain Fur Company, who, in 1826-7 penetrated with a party from the shores of the Great Salt Lake to California; thence recrossing the Sierras and returning to this region. Smith and his associates, William L. Sublette and David E. Jackson, are reputed to have taken the first wagons from the Missouri River to the Rocky Mountains. Their wagons, however, were left at Wind River, and did not pass the Rockies.

In 1832-3, came the renowned Captain Bonneville, whose

---

* Utah Lake was formerly called Lake Ashley.
† Weber River was also named for a trapper in that region.

adventures in this region were afterwards immortalized by Washington Irving. His name has been given to the great fossil lake or prehistoric sea supposed to have once existed in the Great Basin. Bonneville was by birth a Frenchman, but at that time a United States army officer on leave.* His wagons, twenty in number, laden with Indian goods, provisions and ammunition, are believed to have been the first to roll down the western slope of the Rockies. He is thought to have been the first also to use ox-teams upon this line of travel.

From 1834 to 1839 parties of missionaries, men and women, crossed the Rocky Mountains to the shores of the Pacific. Mrs. Narcissa Whiteman and a Mrs. Spalding are reputed to have been the first white women to perform this long and perilous pilgrimage.

And all this and more before Colonel Fremont stood upon these desolate, brine-washed shores, and imagined himself a second Balboa discovering another Pacific, in this already many times discovered inland sea.

Overland emigration from the Missouri to the Pacific began about the year 1841. It was small at first, but increased yearly, until at the close of 1844 two or three thousand men, women and children had settled on the Pacific coast. Most of these were in Oregon, but California from the first had her share. Among those who reached "the land of gold" via the Utah region in 1841, were John Bidwell and Josiah Belden. Some of Mr. Bidwell's pioneer reminiscences have recently appeared in the Century Magazine.

The usual route of travel from the Missouri at that time was up the Platte River, along the Sweetwater and through South Pass. Beyond that point, those going to Oregon would bend their course northward to Soda Springs and Fort Hall, one of the Hudson Bay Company's stations; while those for California would follow Bear River to within a few miles of the Great Salt Lake, and then turn westward, crossing the country to the Sierras. Later, a new

---

* Bonneville, promoted to the rank of Colonel, was in 1849 the commanding officer at Fort Kearney.

route to California, called the "Hastings Cut-Off," was planned. Of this, more anon.

Dr. Marcus Whitman, in 1842, made his celebrated ride from Oregon back to the States, passing through Utah by way of Uintah, and proceeding on to Santa Fe and St. Louis. He returned the following summer to Oregon, with a large body of emigrants.

Among the companies for Oregon in 1844 was one led by Cornelius Gilliam, of Clay County, Missouri, prominently connected with the Mormon troubles of 1838. Ex-Governor Boggs, the "exterminator," crossed over to California some time later.

In 1845, Colonel Fremont again visited the shores of the Great Salt Lake, passing thence into California, to be next heard from in connection with the Mexican war. That year the emigration westward was heavier than that of any previous season; five companies with two hundred and fifty wagons going to Oregon alone. In 1846 the emigration was not quite so large, though it was estimated at two thousand five hundred souls, mostly men; one thousand and seven hundred of whom went to Oregon and the remainder to California. The last company of the season was the ill-starred Donner party, whose tragic story, being virtually a portion of Utah's early history, we will briefly relate.

The Donner party consisted of George Donner, James F. Reed, and about eighty-five others, men, women and children. In company with others they left the frontier at Independence, Missouri, late in April or early in May, 1846. Separating west of South Pass, on the stream known as Little Sandy, from their friends who were going to Oregon, the Donner party, in the latter part of July set out for Fort Bridger.* There they tarried four days, prior to taking the "Hastings Cut-off" for California. This route, which was just beginning to be traveled, was by way of Bear River, Echo and Weber Canyons, around the south shore of Great Salt Lake, and across the

---

* Mr. Reed was the original leader of the party, but the day after separating from the Oregon emigrants George Donner was elected captain of the company, which was thenceforth known as the Donner party.

desert to the Humboldt and the Sierras. Its projector was Lansford W. Hastings, a mountaineer and guide, who, with the proprietors of Fort Bridger, being interested in the new route, were doing all in their power to induce emigration that way. Mr. Reed states that some friends of his, who had preceded him to California with pack animals, had left letters for him with Mr. Vasquez, Bridger's partner, advising the company to go by way of Fort Hall, and by no means to take the Hastings Cut-off; but that Vasquez, as he learned later, had kept these letters, thus preventing the party from being warned.

Near the mouth of Echo Canyon they found a letter sticking in a sage-brush. It proved to be from Hastings, who was then piloting a company through Weber Canyon. It stated that if the Donner party would send a messenger after him, he would return and guide them along a better way than the Weber, which was represented as being very difficult. Accordingly, Mr. Reed and two others—Messrs. McCutchen and Stanton—followed and overtook Hastings near Black Rock, at the south end of the Lake. He could not then return, but gave Mr. Reed some information concerning a "cut-off"—still another—from the mouth of Echo Canyon across the mountains into Salt Lake Valley. The latter then returned to camp.

The route now taken by his party was the one followed, next season, by the Mormon Pioneers,—up East Canyon, over the Big and Little Mountains and down Emigration Canyon into the Valley. The way was extremely difficult, and sixteen days were consumed by the Donner party in cutting a road through the canyons. Then came the crossing of the western desert, where many of their cattle gave out for want of grass and water, while others were lost or stolen by Indians, compelling them to abandon some of their wagons in the midst of the sandy waste. Delayed by these and other misfortunes, the ill-fated company did not strike the main trail on the Humboldt until late in September. By that time the last companies of the season had passed. Another month brought them to the foot of the Truckee Pass of the Sierras.

Early snows now came, completely blocking up the way. Some of the company killed their cattle and went into winter quarters near Truckee Lake, but others, hoping still to thread the pass, delayed building their cabins until heavier snows fell, burying cattle, cabins and all. It was now December, their provisions were well-nigh exhausted, and starvation stared the hapless emigrants in the face. An advance party on snow-shoes pushed ahead over the mountains, braving snow and ice and wintry blasts, to obtain relief for their suffering companions. Before reaching New Helvetia—now Sacramento—several of the party died from cold, hunger and exhaustion, and the others, freezing and starving, were compelled to eat their flesh.

Captain Sutter, of Sutter's Fort, near Sacramento, and others nearer the coast, on learning of the terrible fate impending over the snow-bound travelers, fitted out relief parties and sent them to the rescue. This timely action saved most of the sufferers, but out of the original eighty-seven, persuaded into taking this death-trail across the Basin, thirty-nine perished from cold and starvation. The survivors, when found, had been subsisting for weeks—horrible extremity!—upon the bodies of their dead companions. Such was the sad fate of the Donner Party. The last one rescued, a German, who had become a ferocious cannibal, was picked up in April, 1847.

CHAPTER XVII.

1847.

THE MORMON PIONEERS—THEIR JOURNEY ACROSS THE GREAT PLAINS—PAWNEES AND SIOUX—THE PIONEER BUFFALO HUNT—FORT LARAMIE—THE MISSISSIPPI MORMONS—SOUTH PASS—MAJOR HARRIS—COLONEL BRIDGER—"A THOUSAND DOLLARS FOR THE FIRST EAR OF CORN RAISED IN SALT LAKE VALLEY"—A DISCOURAGING PROSPECT—ELDER BRANNAN AGAIN—SOME OF THE BATTALION BOYS—FORT BRIDGER—MILES GOODYEAR—ECHO CANYON—THE VALLEY OF THE GREAT SALT LAKE.

LET us now bring forward into the Great Basin the vanguard of the migrating Mormons encamped upon the Missouri. "The word and will of the Lord concerning the Camp of Israel in their journeyings to the West," was issued by President Young at Winter Quarters on the 14th of January, 1847. A few paragraphs of this manifesto—the first of its kind penned by the Prophet's successor—will convey some idea of the nature of the preparations for the continued exodus:

Let all the people of the Church of Jesus Christ of Latter-day Saints, and those who journey with them, be organized into companies, with a covenant and promise to keep all the commandments and statutes of the Lord our God.

Let the companies be organized with captains of hundreds, captains of fifties, and captains of tens, with a president and his two counselors at their head, under the direction of the Twelve Apostles;

And this shall be our covenant, that we will walk in all the ordinances of the Lord.

Let each company provide themselves with all the teams, wagons, provisions, clothing, and other necessaries for the journey that they can.

When the companies are organized, let them go to with their might, to prepare for those who are to tarry.

Let each company with their captains and presidents decide how many can go next spring; and then choose out a sufficient number of able-bodied and expert men, to take teams, seeds, and farming utensils, to go as pioneers to prepare for putting in spring crops.

Let each company bear an equal proportion, according to the dividend of their property, in taking the poor, the widows, the fatherless, and the families of those who have

gone into the army, that the cries of the widow and the fatherless come not up into the ears of the Lord against this people.

Let each company prepare houses, and fields for raising grain, for those who are to remain behind this season, and this is the will of the Lord concerning his people.

Let every man use all his influence and property to remove this people to the place where the Lord shall locate a Stake of Zion;

And if ye do this with a pure heart, in all faithfulness, ye shall be blessed; you shall be blessed in your flocks, and in your herds, and in your fields, and in your houses, and in your families.

* * * * * * * * *

Seek ye and keep all your pledges one with another, and covet not that which is thy brother's.

Keep yourselves from evil to take the name of the Lord in vain, for I am the Lord your God, even the God of your fathers, the God of Abraham, and of Isaac, and of Jacob.

I am he who led the children of Israel out of the land of Egypt, and my arm is stretched out in the last days to save my people Israel.

Cease to contend one with another, cease to speak evil one of another.

Cease drunkenness, and let your words tend to edifying one another.

If thou borrowest of thy neighbor, thou shalt return that which thou hast borrowed; and if thou canst not repay, then go straightway and tell thy neighbor, lest he condemn thee.

If thou shalt find that which thy neighbor has lost, thou shalt make diligent search till thou shalt deliver it to him again.

Thou shalt be diligent in preserving what thou hast, that thou mayest be a wise steward; for it is the free gift of the Lord thy God, and thou art his steward.

If thou art merry, praise the Lord with singing, with music, with dancing, and with a prayer of praise and thanksgiving.

If thou art sorrowful, call on the Lord thy God with supplication, that your souls may be joyful.

Fear not thine enemies, for they are in mine hands, and I will do my pleasure with them.

My people must be tried in all things, that they may be prepared to receive the glory that I have for them, even the glory of Zion, and he that will not bear chastisement, is not worthy of my kingdom.

Agreeable to these instructions the Saints went to work with a will, and as spring opened all was life, bustle and stir at their camps on the Missouri, and at their other settlements on the prairies of Iowa.

The personnel of the pioneer band, selected to precede the main body, was as follows. They are here given as divided into companies of "Tens:"

HISTORY OF UTAH.

FIRST TEN.

Wilford Woodruff, Captain, Orson Pratt,   Marcus B. Thorpe,
John S. Fowler,   Joseph Egbert,   Geo. A. Smith,
Jacob D. Burnham,   John M. Freeman,   Geo. Wardle.

SECOND TEN.

Ezra T. Benson, Captain,   Amasa M. Lyman,   George Brown,
Thomas B. Grover,   Starling Driggs,   Willard Richards,
Barnabas L. Adams,   Albert Carrington,   Jesse C. Little.
Roswell Stevens,   Thomas Bullock,

THIRD TEN.

Phinehas H. Young, Captain, Addison Everett,   Bryant Stringham,
John Y. Green,   Truman O. Angell,   Joseph S. Scofield,
Thomas Tanner,   Lorenzo D. Young,   Albert P. Rockwood.
Brigham Young,

FOURTH TEN.

Luke S. Johnson, Captain,   George R. Grant,   Harry Pierce,
John Holman,   Millen Atwood,   Wm. Dykes,
Edmund Ellsworth,   Samuel B. Fox,   Jacob Weiler.
Alvarus Hanks,   Tunis Rappleyee,

FIFTH TEN.

Stephen H. Goddard, Captain, Sylvester H. Earl,   George Scholes,
Tarlton Lewis,   John Dixon,   Wm. Henrie,
Henry G. Sherwood,   Samuel H. Marble,   Wm. A. Empey.
Zebedee Coltrin,

SIXTH TEN.

Charles Shumway, Captain,   Erastus Snow,   Wm. Vance,
Andrew Shumway,   James Craig,   Simeon Howd,
Thos. Woolsey,   Wm. Wordsworth,   Seeley Owen.
Chauncey Loveland,

SEVENTH TEN.

James Case, Captain,   Wm. Carter,   Franklin B. Stewart,
Artemas Johnson,   Franklin G. Losee,   Monroe Frink,
Wm. C. A. Smoot,   Burr Frost,   Eric Glines,
Franklin B. Dewey,   Datus Ensign,   Ozro Eastman.

EIGHTH TEN.

Seth Taft, Captain,   Alma M. Williams,   Elijah Newman,
Horace Thornton,   Rufus Allen,   Levi N. Kendall,
Stephen Kelsey,   Robert T. Thomas,   Francis Boggs,
John S. Eldredge,   James W. Stewart,   David Grant.
Charles D. Barnum,

HISTORY OF UTAH. 301

NINTH TEN.

Howard Egan, Captain, Hosea Cushing, Edson Whipple,
Heber C. Kimball, Robert Byard, Philo Johnson,
Wm. A. King, George Billings, Wm. Clayton.
Thomas Cloward,

TENTH TEN.

Appleton M. Harmon, Captain, Orrin P. Rockwell, Francis Pomeroy,
Carlos Murray, Nathaniel T. Brown, Aaron Farr,
Horace K. Whitney, R. Jackson Redding. Nathaniel Fairbanks.
Orson K. Whitney, John Pack,

ELEVENTH TEN.

John S. Higbee, Captain, Joseph Rooker, James Davenport,
John Wheeler, Perry Fitzgerald, Henson Walker,
Solomon Chamberlain, John H. Tippetts, Benjamin Rolfe.
Conrad Klineman,

TWELFTH TEN.

Norton Jacobs, Captain, Stephen Markham, Andrew Gibbons,
Charles A. Harper, Lewis Barney, Joseph Hancock,
George Woodard, George Mills, John W. Norton.

THIRTEENTH TEN.

John Brown, Captain, Lyman Curtis, David Powers,
Shadrach Roundy, Hans C. Hansen, Hark Lay (colored),
Levi Jackman, Matthew Ivory, Oscar Crosby (colored).

FOURTEENTH TEN.

Joseph Matthews, Captain, Charles Burke, Norman Taylor,
Gilbroid Summe, Alexander P. Chessley, Green Flake (colored),
John Gleason, Rodney Badger, Ellis Eames.

A few of these were non-Mormons, who had cast in their lot with the Saints. As seen, twelve times twelve men had been chosen —whether designedly or otherwise we know not—but one of their number, Ellis Eames, falling sick after the company left Winter Quarters, returned, leaving the pioneer roll at one hundred and forty-three.

Besides the men, there were three women and two children in the camp. The women were Harriet Page Wheeler Young, wife of Lorenzo D. Young; Clara Decker Young, wife of Brigham Young, and Ellen Sanders Kimball, wife of Heber C. Kimball. The children were Isaac Perry Decker, stepson, and Lorenzo Sobieski, own son of Lorenzo D. Young.

According to that veteran, it was no part of the original plan to include women and children in the pioneer company. The hardships and dangers in prospect were foreseen to be such as would test the strength and endurance of the hardiest and healthiest men, who had consequently been chosen. The idea of taking delicate women and helpless children along, to hinder—as it was naturally presumed they would—the march to the mountains, if thought of, was not for a moment entertained. "Uncle Lorenzo," still living to tell the story, claims to have made the suggestion which gave to the pioneer band its triad of heroines. His wife Harriet being in feeble health, which was further imperilled by the damp, malarial atmosphere of the Missouri bottoms, pleaded so earnestly for the privilege of accompanying her husband, that the President, his brother, yielding to their entreaties, finally consented. The children of course were permitted to go with their parents. The other women were then included as well. Clara D. Young and Isaac Perry Decker were brother and sister, children of Harriet Young by a former marriage. More than once during that rugged journey to the mountains did these heroic women, in their capacity of "ministering angels"— nurses to the sick—prove that no mistake was made when they were permitted to accompany the pioneers on their long pilgrimage.

Heber C. Kimball was the first of the leaders to move toward the mountains. On the 5th of April, taking six of his teams, he left Winter Quarters and formed a camp about four miles westward, beside a spring, at or near a place called Cutler's Park. This camp was the nucleus of the pioneer company.

The general conference of the Church convened at Winter Quarters on April 6th. On the 8th, such of the Apostles as had joined the camp returned to meet their confrere, Parley P. Pratt, who had just arrived from Europe. At a council held that evening in the office of Dr. Willard Richards, Parley reported the condition of affairs

abroad. Reuben Hedlock and others, promoters of the Joint Stock Company, had been severed from the Church and their speculative operations among the British Saints brought to an end. A final settlement had been made with the stock-holders. A general reform was in progress throughout the mission, and the spiritual was once more ascendant over the temporal. Such was the substance of Elder Pratt's report.

On the 9th another start was made for the mountains. The leaders, however, had no sooner rejoined the camp, now west of the Elk Horn, than they again started back to Winter Quarters, this time to greet Apostle John Taylor, who had also returned from Europe, bringing with him over two thousand dollars in gold, contributed to the Church by its British members. Apostles Pratt and Taylor had both come by way of New Orleans. Their associate, Orson Hyde, had landed at New York, and was on his way west. These three did not join the pioneer band, but remained to help organize some of the succeeding companies. Parley P. Pratt and John Taylor followed in the wake of the pioneers that season, but Orson Hyde tarried on the frontier.

Leaving general affairs on the Missouri in the hands of these Apostles, and having appointed a special committee, consisting of Isaac Morley and Newel K. Whitney, to superintend the emigration, President Young and the other leaders again joined their camp beyond the Elk Horn. They crossed that stream, one of the north tributaries of the Platte, on a raft constructed by some of their company who had gone before. It was now the 15th of April. They were twelve miles west of the Elk Horn, and forty-seven miles from Winter Quarters.

On April 16th, at about 2 p. m., the pioneers broke camp and traveled three miles. On the 17th they proceeded seven miles farther, camping that night near a cotton-wood grove. In order to save their corn they felled hundreds of these trees, and permitted their teams to browse on the foliage.

During the next few days the camp was thoroughly organized

under the direction of President Young. In addition to the captains of tens, already named, there were captains of hundreds and fifties appointed. The captains of hundreds were Stephen Markham and Albert P. Rockwood; of fifties, Addison Everett, Tarlton Lewis and James Case. There was also a military organization, the officers of which were as follows: Brigham Young, Lieutenant-General; Jesse C. Little, Adjutant; Stephen Markham, Colonel; John Pack and Shadrach Rounty, Majors; Thomas Tanner, captain of artillery. The artillery consisted of one cannon, carried at first in a wagon, but subsequently mounted on a separate pair of wheels. It was taken along to overawe hostile Indians, or perform more serious execution if found necessary. Captain Tanner had eight men to assist him in its management.

Thomas Tanner and Burr Frost were the blacksmiths of the camp. On them devolved the duty of repairing wagons, resetting wheel tires, etc.; a portable forge and tools having been provided for that purpose. Farmers with plows, mechanics with tools, builders and colonizers in general were all included in the company. Like Cæsar's legions in Gaul and Britain the pioneers went prepared, not only to fight if necessary, but to make roads, build bridges, construct boats and do all things necessary in the settlement of a new country.

Thomas Bullock was clerk of the camp, and Willard Richards and William Clayton its historians. Besides, many others kept daily journals of events, thus preserving a very complete record for the use of the historian in after years. Among the best of these may be mentioned those of Wilford Woodruff, Orson Pratt and Horace K. Whitney. From these records we learn that the pioneers had, at starting, seventy-two wagons, ninety-three horses, fifty-two mules, sixty-six oxen and nineteen cows. The census of the camp also comprised seventeen dogs and some chickens. In addition to the animals used in the teams, there were only eight or ten horses. Mounted men consequently were few. Most of the pioneers walked nearly all the way from the Missouri River to the Great Salt Lake, a distance of over a thousand miles. The same is true of the vast majority of Utah's early settlers who subsequently crossed the plains.

General Young instructed the camp as follows: The men were to travel in a compact body, each with his loaded gun in hand, or, if a teamster, in his wagon, ready for instant use. If the gun were a cap-lock, he was to take off the cap and put on a piece of leather to exclude moisture and dirt; if a flint-lock he must take out the filling and fill the pan with tow or cotton. Each man was to keep beside his wagon, and not leave it except by permission. The vehicles were to travel two abreast wherever practicable, and in case of hostile demonstrations by savages, four or five abreast. At five o'clock in the morning the bugle would sound the call to rise, assemble for prayers, feed teams, and get breakfast, and at seven give the signal for starting. At 8:30 p. m., at the sound of the bugle, each was to retire for prayers in his own wagon, and at 9 o'clock all but the sentries to bed.

The sentries were selected from a body of fifty men, with Stephen Markham as their captain; twelve guards were on duty at a time, and the night was divided into two watches. These guards were not to leave the vicinity of the wagons. Whenever it became necessary to stake out the horses and cattle to graze at a distance from the camp, an extra guard was provided. The stock, however, were generally kept inside the enclosure formed by corralling the wagons, according to the custom of the plains. In forming the corral, the tongues of the wagons were placed outside, with a fore-wheel of each vehicle locked in a hind wheel of the one ahead. At one or both ends of the circular or oblong enclosure thus formed, an opening would be left. These gateways were carefully guarded. Sometimes, near a lake or river, the camp would form a semi-circle, resting on the bank.

The pioneers sacredly observed the Sabbath; no unnecessary toil or travel being done on that day. Divine services were held regularly. As formerly, excessive levity was frowned upon by the leaders.

Thus organized, equipped and instructed, the pioneers proceeded on their way, slowly traveling up the north bank of the Platte. The regular route at that time was along the south bank, where grass was more plentiful and the Indians less troublesome. Few if any travelers chose the north side, which was regarded as more difficult and dangerous. The pioneers preferred it for one reason: that their people who followed them would thus escape contact with the migrating Missourians, who sought every occasion to quarrel with the Mormons whenever they met them. For several hundred miles, therefore, they virtually broke a new road over the plains; a road subsequently traveled by tens of thousands of their people with ox-teams and hand-carts. It was known for many years as "the old Mormon trail." Much of it is now covered by the track of the Union Pacific Railway.

Pursuing their journey from the Elk Horn, the pioneers, in the latter part of April, found themselves in the heart of the Pawnee Indian country. These savages were still quite numerous, though their ranks had lately been decimated by the warlike Sioux, their implacable enemies. Thus far they had been very troublesome to the pioneers, stampeding and stealing their stock, and burning the prairie grass before and around them, destroying the feed upon which they mainly depended for their teams. But the Indians had offered no violence.

It was about one o'clock in the afternoon of April 21st that the pioneers halted on the bank of a long, narrow lake close by the river. They had scarcely formed their wagons in a semi-circle and placed their guards, when they were surrounded by swarms of savages, male and female, coming from all directions. Many had forded the river some distance below and followed the pioneers to their camp-ground. Among them was Shefmolm, chief of the Pawnee nation. Their manner was not hostile, and their motive, as soon appeared, purely mercenary. Presenting certificates, signed by various travelers, to the effect that the Pawnees were friendly and that it was the custom to make them small presents for the privilege of passing through their country, they intimated by a young Indian interpreter that similar gifts would be acceptable from the pioneers. The latter readily responded, imparting of their limited stores a few articles, such as powder, lead, salt, tobacco and flour, in quantities proportionate to the

amounts possessed. But the red men were not satisfied. Like Oliver Twist, they wanted "more." More the pioneers could not afford to give, and so informed them. The Pawnees professed the fear that their "white brothers" would scare away the buffalo in passing along, and hinted that from such a large company they expected bigger presents. Further parleying ensued, and finally the savages left, still unsatisfied, though not at all unfriendly. That night, which was cold and stormy, the cannon was limbered and placed outside the camp, while an extra guard stood armed and ready to repel any assault that might be made by the Indians. But the night wore away in peace, and the pioneers were not molested. Some of the guards, overpowered by the previous day's toil, fell asleep at their posts, and their guns and hats were removed by their waggish comrades. Their mortification on awaking served in lieu of a reprimand, and the sleeping act was not repeated.

Next came the difficult passage of the Loup Fork, another of the Platte's numerous tributaries, rolling like that majestic river over treacherous beds of quicksand. Some of the teams narrowly escaped drowning, and heavily laden vehicles came near capsizing. The water was only two feet deep, but the quicksands would nearly pull a wagon to pieces, making a sound like the rattling of wheels over a stony pavement. Fording with the loaded vehicles was finally discontinued, and rafts were constructed to carry the loads, leaving the empty wagons to be drawn across by teams. A boat of leather called the *Revenue Cutter*, which had been brought as a wagon-box from Winter Quarters, was also used in crossing this and other streams. This boat had formerly belonged to Ira Eldredge. The passage of the Loup Fork was finally effected without accident.

During the next few days several valuable horses were lost, two being killed by the accidental discharge of firearms and the others stolen by Indians. This loss was considered serious, as there were scarcely enough horses in camp to make traveling "at all comfortable." Several men were shot at by Indians while out hunting for the stolen animals.

Prior to crossing the Loup Fork, some of the pioneers had picked up a few plowshares and other pieces of iron lying around the site of a government station which had recently been burned to the ground during an incursion of the hostile Sioux. President Young would not permit this appropriation of property except upon the score of the government's indebtedness to James Case, one of the company, who had been employed as an Indian farmer. Those who took the iron were required to settle for it with Father Case, who was in turn directed to report to the proper authorities the amount he had thus collected on account.

The country through which they were passing, though monotonous in aspect, was nevertheless pleasing to the eye. Before and behind, on right and left, a vast level prairie, its waving grass, swept by gentle winds, limited on the right at a distance by a continuous range of majestic bluffs. On the left the muddy waters of the Platte, rolling ceaselessly over beds of quicksand; the river often hid from view by many handsome cottonwood groves fringing its sandy shores. The soil was everywhere of a sandy nature, promising little at that time to agriculture. Such was the general appearance of that region, where the iron-horse now thunders along the river's majestic course, and where flourish and wave the golden corn-fields of Nebraska.

Grand Island was reached about the 1st of May. Here the prairies swarmed with buffalo. A grand hunt was indulged in by the pioneers,—a dozen horsemen and as many footmen having previously been detailed for that purpose. After much exciting sport, ten of the animals were killed and brought to camp. Most of the company had never seen a buffalo before. Some of the hunters were verdant enough to attempt to kill one by shooting him full in the forehead, from which the bullets rebounded without making the least impression. The hide on the skull-piece of one of the dead bisons was found to be an inch thick, and covered with a coarse mat of hair —in itself a helmet of defense—which fully accounted for the pheno-

menon of rebounding balls.* The proceeds of this buffao hunt,—
one bull, three cows and six calves,—were carried to camp in five
wagons, temporarily unloaded for the purpose. The meat was
equally distributed among the tens, each company receiving about
one quarter.

After this day's sport the President instructed his men not to
kill game wantonly, as was the custom with many who crossed the
plains,—a custom which has done much to render the buffalo race
extinct. "If we slay when we have no need," said he, "we will need
when we cannot slay." Game continued more or less plentiful, the
hunters supplying the camp with buffalo, deer, antelope, geese,
ducks, etc., as often as necessary, and as they approached the mountains fine trout began to be taken from the streams. A grizzly bear
and her cubs also became trophies of their skill.

Early in May a French trader named Charles Beaumont, returning
with furs from Fort Laramie to the frontier, visited the pioneer camp,
fording the Platte for that purpose, but leaving his wagons on the
southern shore. Many embraced the opportunity thus afforded of
sending letters back to Winter Quarters. Hitherto they had been
content to improvise post-offices by the way, using the skull of a dead
buffalo, or some other conspicuous and sheltering object, in which to
deposit the missives left for their friends who were to follow. Fifty or
sixty letters were now written, all of which Mr. Beaumont courteously
undertook to deliver. The pioneers at this point were strongly
tempted to cross the river and continue their journey along the regular route. There grass and game were abundant, and travelers were
not so much molested, while on the north side the Indians kept up
their prairie-burning tactics, and horses and cattle were at times
almost famished for feed. The temptation, however, was resisted,
for reasons already given, and up the north bank they proceeded.

* A favorite method of the Indians for killing buffalo was to chase them until they
were "winded," and then, riding up alongside, strike one with an arrow in the lower part
of the spine. The beast, falling paralyzed, could then be hamstrung, and the chase continued *ad libitum*.

On May 21st they put up a guide-board, reading: "From Winter Quarters 409 miles; from the junction of the north and south forks (of the Platte) 94 miles. * * * According to Fremont, this place is 132 miles from Laramie." Similar guide-boards they had placed, and continued to place, at various points for the benefit of future emigration. Their method of measuring distances was by means of an ingenious machine invented by William Clayton and constructed by Appleton M. Harmon, a skillful mechanic. The machinery of the "roadometer" was so arranged that the revolutions of a wagon wheel, acting by screws and cogs upon smaller wheels, the whole attached to an axle-tree of one of the wagons, indicated from day to day the miles and parts of miles traveled.*

Near Chimney Rock, on the 24th of May, the pioneers encountered a band of mounted Sioux, about thirty-five in number, who forded the river and made friendly advances. These Indians were much better accoutred than the Pawnees and other tribes nearer the frontier. Many of them wore broadcloth, with fur caps, profusely decorated with beads and other ornaments, and were armed with bows, steel-pointed arrows and fire-arms. The chief sent his men to lodge some distance from the camp, but requested for himself the privilege of remaining with the pioneers over night. They granted his request, spreading a tent for his accommodation, and feeding him and his band that night and the next morning. These Sioux carried with them the American flag, and bore a recommendation

---

* The machine is thus described by its inventor:

"The whole machinery consists of a shaft about eighteen inches long, placed on gudgeons, one in the axle-tree of the wagon, near which are six arms placed at equal distances around it, and in which a cog works which is fastened on the hub of the wagon wheel, turning the shaft once around at every revolution of the wagon wheel. The upper gudgeon plays in a piece of wood nailed to the wagon box, and near this gudgeon, on the shaft, a screw is cut. The shaft lays at an angle of 45 degrees. In this screw a wheel works on an axle (fixed in the side of the wagon) of 60 cogs, and which makes one revolution for each mile traveled. In the shaft on which this wheel runs four cogs are cut on the forepart, which plays in another wheel of 40 cogs, which shows the miles and quarters of miles up to ten miles. The box incasing the whole is 18 inches long, 15 inches high and 3 inches thick."

written in French, from a Mr. Papan, agent of the American Fur Company.

About June 1st the pioneers arrived opposite Fort Laramie. According to their reckoning, they were now five hundred and forty-three miles from Winter Quarters. They had traveled this distance in about seven weeks. The first half of their westward journey was now over.

Before crossing the river — North Platte — they were visited by several men from the Fort, who announced themselves as Mormons from Mississippi, a portion of a company which, with Captain James Brown and the invalid detachments of the Mormon Battalion, had spent the winter at Pueblo. Of the Mississippians the Crow and Therlkill families and a few others—seventeen in all—had come on to Laramie to join the pioneers and accompany them over the mountains. They had been waiting at the Fort for two weeks.* They had five wagons, one cart, eleven horses, twenty-four oxen, twenty-two cows, and a few bulls and calves. Captain Brown's command, they said, expected soon to be ordered to California, by way of Fort Laramie and the South Pass.

From a party of traders who arrived from the west, the pioneers received rather discouraging reports regarding the route ahead. The snows, they were told, were so deep on the Sweetwater, and deeper still in the mountains, that no grass for feed could be found.

President Young and several of the Apostles now crossed the river in their leathern skiff and walked up to the Fort to confer with the resident authorities. Fort Laramie, at this time, was a trading post of the American Fur Company. It had been established in 1834, by William Sublette and Robert Campbell, with a view to monopolizing the trade as well as resisting the attacks of those warlike tribes, the

---

*Their names were as follows: Robert Crow, Elizabeth Crow, Benjamin R. Crow, Harriet Crow, Elizabeth Jane Crow, John McHenry Crow, Walter H. Crow, William Parker Crow, Isa Vinda Exene Crow, Ira Minda Almarene Crow, George W. Therlkill, Matilda Jane Therlkill, Milton Howard Therlkill, James William Therlkill, Archibald Little, James Chesney, Lewis B. Myers.

Arapahoes, Cheyennes and Sioux, roaming over the plains between the Missouri river and the Black Hills. It was situated upon Laramie River, a branch of the North Platte; Laramie being the name of a French trapper killed by the Arapahoes on that stream. Sold in 1835 to Milton Sublette, James Bridger and others, Fort Laramie had been rebuilt, and was now the chief trading post on the great overland route.

The principal man at the Fort was James Bordeaux, a Frenchman. He received President Young and his party very politely, and as they had decided to travel from that point on the south side of the river, owing to reports that the north side was no longer practicable, he hired to them his ferry-boat for the reasonable sum of fifteen dollars. He informed them that their old enemy, ex-Governor Boggs, of Missouri, had passed that way with a company some time before, and had warned him to look after his horses and cattle when the Mormons came along. According to Mr. Bordeaux, the ex-Governor did not succeed in prejudicing him to any great extent, for he had answered that let the Mormons be what they might, they could not be worse than Boggs and his party, who were quarreling and separating continually. "Mr. Bordeaux told us," says Wilford Woodruff, "that we were the best behaved company that had come that way." He said the Crow Indians were very troublsome in that region, having lately run off all the mules and horses belonging to the Fort.

The pioneers now crossed the Platte; the ferry averaging four wagons an hour. While thus engaged the rumor reached them that companies of emigrants, aggregating two thousand wagons, mostly from Missouri, Illinois, and Iowa, and bound for Oregon, were on the way west. Some of them expected to reach Fort Laramie next day. Many other trains were said to be forming on the frontier. Camping near the Fort, the pioneers set up their forges and repaired some of their wagons prior to resuming their journey.

Amasa M. Lyman, Thomas Woolsey, John H. Tippitts, and Roswell Stevens were now sent horse-back to Pueblo to take charge of the main body of the Mississippi Saints, and bring them over the mountains in the trail of the pioneers. It was supposed that Captain Brown's detachment would come also. Indeed the Battalion men had already started, and were now marching toward Fort Laramie.

Friday, June 4th, the pioneers resumed their journey. Deducting Apostle Lyman's party, and adding the Mississippians who had already arrived, the company was now increased to one hundred and sixty-one. They started about noon, taking the regular emigrant trail toward the mountains. On the 5th, while resting to let their cattle graze, a small company of eleven wagons, bound for Oregon, rolled ahead of them. Next day—the Sabbath—another company, numbering twenty-one wagons, passed. A third company, with thirteen wagons, went ahead during the noon halt of the 7th. On the 8th a small company from the west was encountered. These wagons were from Fort Bridger, the first trading post beyond the mountains, and were laden with furs and peltries for Fort Laramie. The day following, three men with fifteen horses, mostly pack animals, overtook and passed the pioneers. They were from Santa Fe, and bound for the Bay of San Francisco, via the Great Salt Lake.

In the Black Hills region the pioneers consumed a week, recrossing the Platte. Here the river was usually fordable, but it was now the high water season and fording was impracticable. The stream was fifteen feet deep and a hundred yards wide. To this point the President had previously sent a detachment of men with their boat, the *Revenue Cutter*, to ferry over the Oregon companies. When the main body of the pioneers reached the river this work was in progress. The little skiff carried the loads and the empty wagons were floated. Some of them were whirled over several times by the swift current. For each wagon and load the ferrymen received $1.50, and were glad to take their pay in flour, meal and bacon at Missouri prices. A little money was also realized. Other companies that soon arrived were carried over at the same rates. The proceeds of this labor, excepting a few extra dollars for the ferrymen, were equally divided among the members of the camp.

These supplies were as timely as they were totally unexpected. Their provisions were well-nigh exhausted, and to have their flour and meal bags replenished in this far-off region, and at the hands of their old enemies, the Missourians, was regarded by them as little less than a miracle. Apostle Woodruff compared it to the feeding of Israel with manna in the wilderness.

Besides their boat, two or three light rafts, constructed on the spot, were used by the pioneers at this ferry. It being demonstrated that "swimming" the wagons injured them, a heavier raft was built, strong enough to bear a loaded vehicle, and by means of this the rest of the wagons were taken over. This raft consisted of two large cottonwood canoes, placed parallel to each other, a few feet apart, firmly pinned with cross-pieces, and with nailed slabs running lengthwise. A rudder and oars were attached, with a little iron work, and the "boat" was complete. The only loss sustained during this crossing was one horse belonging to the Crow company, drowned while swimming the river.

It occurred to President Young that this was an eligible place to establish a ferry for the benefit of the companies that were to follow. Accordingly, nine men were detailed for that purpose. They were Thomas Grover, Captain; John S. Higbee, Luke S. Johnson, Appleton M. Harmon, Edmund Ellsworth, Francis M. Pomeroy, William Empey, James Davenport and Benjamin F. Stewart. They were instructed to remain at the ferry for about six weeks, or until the next company from Winter Quarters came along, by which time it was thought they would have earned enough to supply the needy with provisions. They were then to join that company and come on to the mountains. Eric Glines, against the President's wish, insisted on remaining at the ferry, but a few days later reconsidered his design and following, rejoined the main body.

On the 19th of June the camp continued its journey. The order of traveling was as follows: Each company of ten took its regular turn in the lead; the first ten one day, the second ten next day, and so on; every ten taking its turn in van and rear.

They reached Independence Rock* on the 21st of June. A mile or two beyond they forded the Sweetwater, and, contrary to report, found plenty of good grass along that river. But they had to beware of the poisonous alkaline waters of the vicinity, which proved so fatal to the cattle and horses of succeeding companies. Five days later they arrived at South Pass, the celebrated dividing ridge separating the waters here flowing east and west toward the Atlantic and the Pacific oceans. Now began the western descent of the Rockies.

At Pacific Springs, two miles west of the Pass, the pioneer vanguard met Major Moses Harris, a noted scout and trapper, who had accompanied to that point a party of travelers from Oregon, going east. He intended now to return, as guide to some of the emigrant companies bound for the north-west. From him the pioneers derived some information regarding the region of their destination,—the valley of the Great Salt Lake. His report, like Fremont's, was rather discouraging. He spoke of the country as sandy and destitute of timber and vegetation, excepting sagebrush. He gave a more favorable account of "a small region under the Bear River mountains, called Cache Valley," where trappers and traders were in the habit of "caching" their furs and other effects to hide them from the Indians. Cache Valley, Major Harris said, was "a fine place for wintering cattle." He presented for the perusal of the pioneers a file of Oregon papers beginning with the date of February 11th, 1847; also a number of the *California Star*, published by Samuel Brannan at Yerba Buena, and edited by E. P. Jones.

In this neighborhood also, according to Erastus Snow, they encountered another veteran mountaineer, Thomas L. Smith—surnamed "Pegleg"—who lived in the Bear River mountains, near Soda Springs. He advised them to direct their course toward Cache Valley, and plant their colony in that region.

In the forenoon of June 28th, the pioneers arrived at the point

---

* So named from the fact that a passing party had there celebrated the 4th of July.

where the Oregon and California roads diverged. Taking the latter or left-hand route, they crossed the Little Sandy, and that evening met Colonel James Bridger, of Bridger's Fort, accompanied by two of his men. They were on their way to Fort Laramie. In conversation with President Young and the other leaders, with whom he encamped that night, Bridger gave them in his peculiar way additional information regarding the route ahead, and the region toward which they were traveling. His report was synopsized by historian Clayton as follows:

We will find better grass as we proceed; there is no blacksmith shop at his fort at present; there was one but it was destroyed. Nearly a hundred wagons have gone over the Hastings route through Weber's Fork. They crossed the Black's Fork, and went a little south of west from his place. It is impossible for wagons to follow down Green River. Neither can it be followed in boats. * * * From Bridger's Fort to the Great Salt Lake, Hastings said, was about one hundred miles. Bridger himself had been through fifty times, but could form no correct idea of the distance. Mr. Hastings' route leaves the Oregon road at Bridger's. We could pass over the mountains further south but in some places we would meet with heavy bodies of timber and would have to cut our way through. In the Bear River Valley there is oak timber, sugar trees, cottonwood and pines. There is not an abundance of sugar maple, but plenty of beautiful pines. There is no timber on the Utah Lake, but some on the streams emptying into it. Into the outlet of the Utah Lake three well timbered streams empty. In the valleys southeast of the Salt Lake there is an abundance of blue grass and white clover. The outlet of the Utah Lake does not form a large river, neither a rapid current, but the water is muddy and the banks of the river low. Some of his men have been around the Salt Lake in canoes. But while they went out hunting, their horses were stolen by the Indians. They then spent three months going round the lake in canoes hunting beavers, the distance being five hundred and fifty (?) miles. The Utah tribe of Indians live around the lake and are a bad people, if they catch a man alone they are sure to rob and abuse him, if they don't kill him, but parties of men are in no danger. These Indians are mostly armed with guns. * * * There was a man who had opened a farm in Bear River Valley, where the soil is good and likely to produce grain, were it not for the excessive cold nights. There is a good country south of the Utah Lake or southeast of the Great Basin. Three rivers unknown to travelers enter into the Sevier Lake. There is also a splendid country north of the California mountains, calculated to produce every kind of grain and fruit, and there are several places where a man might pass from it over the mountains to the California settlements in a day. * * * The great desert extends from the Salt Lake to the Gulf of California, which is perfectly barren. Mr. Bridger supposes it to have been an arm of the sea. There is a tribe of Indians in that country who are unknown to either travelers or geographers. They make farms and raise an abundance of grain of various kinds. He can buy any quantity of the very best wheat from them. * * * This country lies south of Salt Lake, distant about twenty days' travel, but the country through which one would have to go to reach it is bad, and there would be no grass for animals to subsist on. He supposes there might be access to it from Texas. * * * He never saw any grapes on the Utah Lake, but there are plenty of cherries and berries of several kinds. He thinks the region around the Utah Lake is the best country in the vicinity of the Salt Lake, and the country is still better the farther south one goes until the desert is reached, which is upwards of two hundred miles south of the Utah Lake. There is plenty of timber on all the streams and mountains and an abundance of fish in the streams. * * * He passed through the country a year ago last summer in the month of July; there is generally one or two showers of rain every day, sometimes very heavy thunder storms but not accompanied by strong winds. * * * He said we would find plenty of water from here to Bridger's Fort, except after crossing Green River, when we have to travel about twenty miles without water, but there is plenty of grass. * * * We need not fear the Utah Indians, for we could drive the whole of them in twenty-four hours. Mr. Bridger's theory was not to kill them, but make slaves of them. The Indians south of the Utah Lake raise as good corn, wheat and pumpkins as were ever raised in old Kentucky.

In conclusion, the erratic Colonel expressed the opinion,—similar to that of Major Harris,—that it would be unwise to bring a large colony into the Great Basin until it had been proven that grain could be raised there. He said that he would give a thousand dollars for the first ear of corn that ripened in Great Salt Lake Valley.

Crossing and journeying down the right bank of the Big Sandy, the pioneers on the last day of June came to Green River. Several of them there fell sick with mountain fever, causing delirium; though none of the cases were considered dangerous, or threatened to be of long duration. The river was high and rapid,—about eighteen rods wide, with from twelve to fifteen feet of water in the channel. Fording was therefore out of the question. Two rafts were constructed from the cottonwood trees lining the banks of the river, and preparations for crossing the stream at once begun.

Just at this juncture, who should ride into camp but Elder Samuel Brannan, the same who, in February, 1846, had sailed from New York for California on the ship *Brooklyn*. He was just from the Bay of San Francisco, having left there with two companions on the 4th of April, one day before the pioneer vanguard started from Winter Quarters. Elder Brannan and his companions had crossed the Sierras over the deep snows which had buried the Donner party,—whose ghastly relics in skulls and scattered bones they had beheld in passing,—and come by way of Fort Hall to meet the pioneers. Brannan informed the President that his colony, which had reached the Bay of San Francisco on the 31st of the previous July, were settling on the San Joaquin river. He had brought with him from the coast sixteen copies of the *California Star*, the paper he had there established. Brannan's main purpose in coming to meet the President was to induce him to settle with his people on the Pacific coast. In this he was unsuccessful.

Green River was now crossed and before noon on the 3rd of July all the wagons were safe over. A camp was formed three miles below the point of crossing. The President now gave such of the pioneers as had families in the next company the privilege of returning to meet them. Five only decided to return, namely: Phinehas H. Young, George Woodward, Aaron F. Farr, Eric Glines and Rodney Badger. Taking the *Cutter* wagon they started eastward on the morning of the 4th. They were accompanied to the ferry by President Young, Heber C. Kimball and a few others. They there met thirteen of Captain Brown's Battalion men, out in pursuit of horse-thieves, who had stolen from them at Pueblo and were now supposed to be at Fort Bridger. One of the soldiers—William Walker—decided to return with the five pioneers. The others, escorted by the President and his party, joined the pioneer camp. The "glorious 4th," it being the Sabbath, was sacredly observed by the pioneers on Green River.

Resuming their journey, they continued a few miles down the right bank of the river, then leaving it and ascending some bluffs, crossed a gently undulating sandy plain, and descended upon Black's Fork. Following up that stream they forded Ham's Fork, crossed and recrossed the Black, and finally on July 7th arrived at Fort Bridger. This celebrated post—the second permanent one established on the great overland route—consisted of two adjoining log houses,

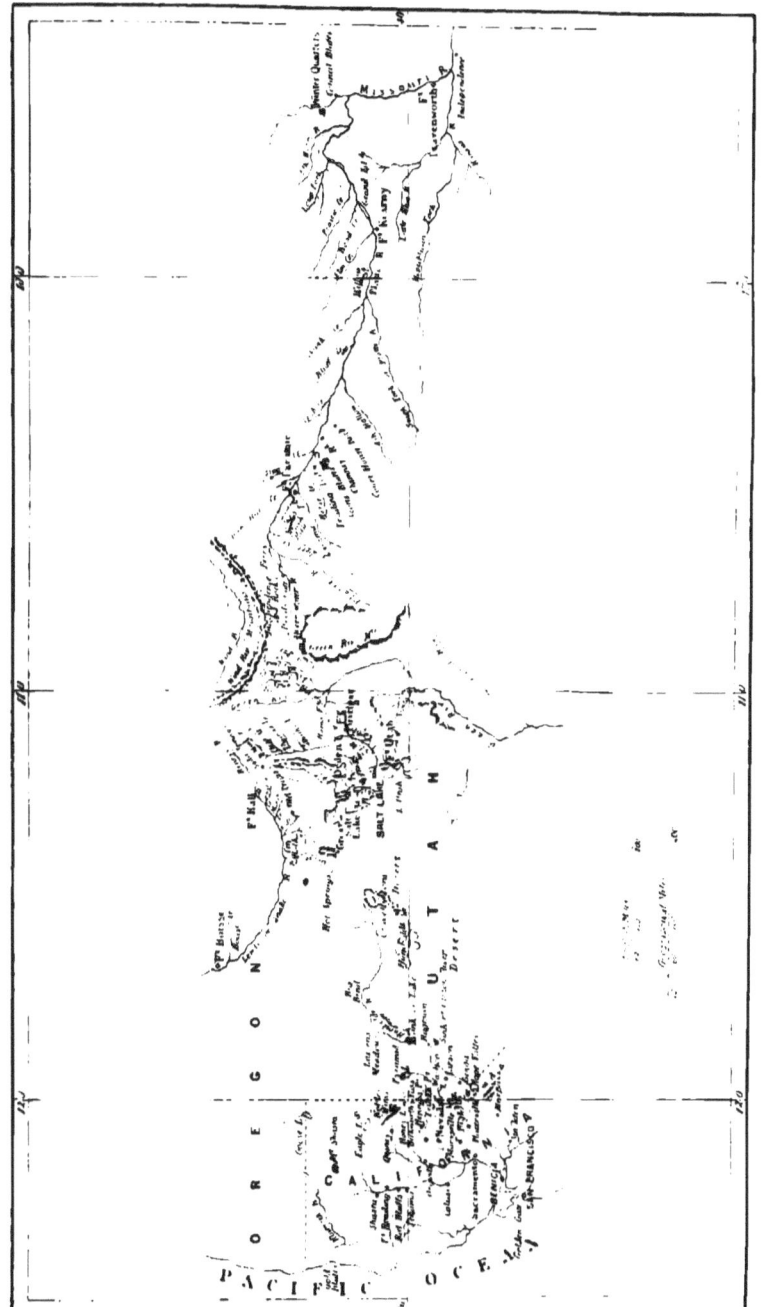

The Pioneer Route, 1847.

with dirt roofs, surrounded by a stockade of logs eight feet high. It was built upon one of several small islands formed by as many branches of Black's Fork. These islands were covered with excellent grass, and had considerable timber; mostly cottonwood and willow. The fort, still owned by Bridger and Vasquez, was the abode of a score or more of human beings, white men, Indian women, and half-breed children. In the vicinity were nine Indian lodges, where dwelt the families of other trappers and hunters who had also taken squaws for wives.

Here the pioneers again set up their forges, shoeing horses and repairing wagons, prior to undertaking the rough mountainous journey now before them. Despite all adverse reports, President Young had decided to penetrate to and colonize, if possible, the desert shores of the Great Salt Lake. The route thither lay to the southwest, along the rugged spurs of the towering Uintahs, snow-capped and glistening in the July sun.

On the 9th they set out from Fort Bridger, by way of the Hastings Cut-off. Samuel Brannan and a few others returned toward South Pass to meet Captain Brown and his detachment. Near Bear River the pioneers encountered Miles M. Goodyear, another mountaineer, who was also somewhat acquainted with Great Salt Lake Valley. He owned a place on Weber River, where he had built a stockade similar to Fort Bridger, and was engaged in trading, trapping and stock-raising. He gave them little or no encouragement, but spoke of hard frosts, cold climate and the difficulty of raising grain and vegetables in that region. Still they pressed on undaunted. Fording Bear River, which stream yielded them some fine trout, they continued following the dim wagon trail of previous emigration, as it rose over steep hills or plunged into deep and rocky ravines now in their path.

At noon on the 12th President Young, who was stricken with mountain fever, fell behind with a few wagons, but requested the main body to move on. They did so, and that night camped near a large and curious cave, which they named for one of their number

Redding's Cave,—Jackson Redding being one of the first to visit it. This was at the head of Echo Canyon.

Next morning messengers were sent back to meet the President. Returning with Heber C. Kimball, they reported that the President was better, but would not travel that day. Orson Pratt was requested to take wagons and men, and preceding the main body down the canyon, endeavor to find near its mouth the Reed and Donner trail across the mountains to the Great Salt Lake. Weber Canyon, the route generally followed from the mouth of Echo, had been reported impassable owing to high water.

At about 3 p. m. Orson Pratt's vanguard, consisting of forty-two men with twenty-three wagons, started down Echo Canyon. This company was composed as follows:

Orson Pratt, (commanding),	Benjamin B. Crow,	Lewis B. Myers,
Stephen Markham, (aide),	John S. Eldredge,	Elijah Newman,
John Brown,	Joseph Egbert,	David Power,
C. D. Barnum,	Nathaniel Fairbanks,	O. P. Rockwell,
Charles Burk,	John S. Freeman,	Jackson Redding,
Francis Boggs,	Green Flake,	Shadrach Roundy,
A. P. Chessley,	John S. Gleason,	James W. Stewart,
Oscar Crosby,	David Grant,	Gilbroid Summe.
Lyman Curtis,	Hans C. Hansen,	Horace Thornton,
James Chessney,	Levi Jackman,	Marcus B. Thorpe,
Walter Crow,	Stephen Kelsey,	George W. Therlkill,
John Crow,	Levi N. Kendall,	Norman Taylor,
Robert Crow,	Hark Lay,	Seth Taft,
Walter H. Crow.	Joseph Matthews,	Robert Thomas,

The women and children of the Crow family accompanied them, and were thus among the first to enter Salt Lake Valley.

Echo Canyon,—which was destined to become more historic still in Utah annals,—was described by Orson Pratt as a narrow valley from ten to twelve rods wide, upon each side of which the hills rose abruptly to a height of from eight to twelve hundred feet, with vertical and overhanging precipices of red pudding-stone and red sandstone, dipping to the north-west in an angle of about twenty degrees. The canyon ran south-west. The rocks were worked into many curious shapes, probably by the rains, and the country was very mountainous in every direction. The road down the canyon was quite rough, crossing and recrossing the stream—Red Fork or Echo Creek—many times. Willow and aspen grew in the valley and upon the slopes, and there were some scrub cedars clinging to the rocks and upon the hills. Echo Creek, toward the mouth, was a small stream eight feet across, putting into the Weber from its right bank. Weber River at this point was about seventy feet wide and two or three feet deep, with a rapid but clear current rolling over a bottom of boulders. Its course was west-north-west. The height above the sea at the junction of the two streams was found to be 5,301 feet.

Such was Echo Canyon in July, 1847. Ten years and a few months later that narrow valley, walled in by vertical and overhanging cliffs, blocked with ice and snow—a veritable bulwark of Nature—wore a somewhat different aspect, and became the scene of one act of an intensely interesting drama, in which the nation whence the pioneers had fled, and the mountain-girt state which they and their compatriots here framed, played principal and opposing parts. Whatever the merits of that controversy—and the full truth of it has never yet been told—Echo Canyon and its warlike episode are immortal. The bridge that Horatius kept, the storied pass of Thermopylae, are not more securely niched in History's golden temple of the past, than Echo Canyon in her pantheon of the present and the future.

The most difficult part of the pioneer journey was still before them. Level plains and rolling prairies were long since past. Their path now lay wholly among the mountains. High hills, deep ravines, rugged canyons, rock-obstructed and choked with brush and timber,—over and through these they must cut and dig their way.

Passing down the Weber about four miles, crossing that stream and striking the Donner trail—now so dim as to be hardly discernible —the Pratt vanguard proceeded toward East Canyon.* A dozen men

---

* The statement sometimes made that the Mormon Pioneers, on their way from Echo Canyon in July, 1847, entered Parley's Park, is an error.

with spades and axes went before the wagons. Six miles up a ravine, through which flowed a small, clear stream, brought them to a dividing ridge, whence they descended slowly another ravine so choked and obstructed as to be all but impassable. Four hours were consumed in going about two miles.

At length they reached East Canyon. Up that difficult gorge they toiled for eight weary miles, crossing and recrossing its crooked willow-fringed torrent thirteen times. Large grey wolves, startled out of their lairs, glared fiercely at them as they passed, and reluctantly retired up neighboring glens and ravines. The deadly rattlesnake—the policeman among reptiles—sounded his warning as if summoning assistance to arrest the further progress of these daring and dangerous human intruders. Here and there the fresh track of a buffalo, some wanderer of his race, appeared; the brush at the roadside, against which the brute had rubbed in passing, still retaining some of its hair.

Leaving East Canyon the trail turned up a ravine to the west, and finally crossed over another ridge or summit,—Big Mountain.

Hitherto naught but a seemingly endless succession of Alps on Alps, hills piled on hills, had greeted the tired vision of the struggling vanguard, pushing through these mountain fastnesses. But now, from the summit of this pass, a broader and grander view was obtained. Glimpses of the open country appeared. To the south-west, through a vista of sloping mountains,—the V of the canyon prospect changed to a W by the intervention of a massive peak towering in the distance —two small sections of Salt Lake Valley were visible. The lake was yet unseen, but beyond loomed the blue and snow-tipped Oquirrhs, and peering above them a shadowy summit of the far-off Onaqui range, dimly outlined against the western sky. It was from this summit—Big Mountain—that Orson Pratt and John Brown, riding horseback ahead of their company, on Monday, July 19th, 1847, caught the first glimpse had by any of the pioneers of the Valley of the Great Salt Lake.

Having descended Big Mountain,—a steep and dangerous slide,

First Glimpse of "The Valley."

where wheels were double-locked lest teams and wagons should rush on to destruction,—the hopeful vanguard pushed on cheerily, their spirits and strength materially renewed by what they had seen. A few miles farther the trail, avoiding a canyon on the left, rose abruptly over another high hill—Little Mountain—whence it descended into the gorge since known as Emigration Canyon.

A mile below Little Mountain, on July 21st, Pratt's company halted for noon beside a swift-running stream which they named Last Creek. Here they were overtaken by Erastus Snow, a messenger from the rear. The pioneer company was now traveling in three detachments. Elder Snow said that it was President Young's impression that on emerging from the mountains they should bear to the northward and stop at the first convenient place for putting in seed.

That afternoon, Orson Pratt and Erastus Snow, taking a single saddle-horse, preceded the rest of the company down the canyon. Near the mouth of the gorge,—which they found to be impassable, owing to a dense thicket, where rocks, brush and timber completely choked the way,—they crossed to the south side of the creek and followed the trail up over a steep and dangerous hill,—"so very steep," says the record, "that it was almost impossible for heavy wagons to ascend, and so narrow that the least accident might precipitate a wagon down a bank of three or four hundred feet." From the summit of this hill the two pioneers saw for the first time the broad, open valley, belted with snow-capped peaks, and the blue waters of the lake flashing and shimmering in the summer sunbeams. A shout of rapture broke from their lips, and having drunk their fill of the inspiring scene, they descended from the hills to the plateau or bench below.

Meantime the middle or main company, after repairing some of their wagons,—broken in passing over the rocky and stumpy route,— had almost overtaken the vanguard in Emigration Canyon. The rear wagons, with the sick President, were at the same time approaching East Canyon. On the 22nd they encamped there, and on the

23rd crossed Big Mountain. The President, reclining in Apostle Woodruff's carriage, requested to have it turned upon the summit so that he might see those portions of the Valley that were now visible. Gazing long and earnestly at the prospect, he exclaimed: "Enough. This is the right place. Drive on."

That night the President's party encamped in a small birch grove, whence issued a beautiful spring. It was about midway between the Big and Little mountains, near the cozy canyon nook now called Mountain Dell. Here, at Birch Spring, on the evening of July 23rd, the party was joined by John Pack and Joseph Matthews, who had returned to report that the companies ahead had cut their way through the mouth of the canyon, entered and partly explored the Valley, and made choice of a spot for putting in crops. It was late in the forenoon of the day following—the memorable 24th—that the rear wagons rolled through the mouth of Emigration Canyon, and Brigham Young, the founder of Utah, looked his first upon the full glory of the Valley by the Lake.

Great Salt Lake Valley, July, 1847.

HISTORY OF UTAH.   325

CHAPTER XVIII.
1847.

PEN PICTURE OF SALT LAKE VALLEY—HOW IT LOOKED TO THE PIONEERS—CONTRASTED IMPRESSIONS—ORSON PRATT AND ERASTUS SNOW THE FIRST EXPLORERS—THE CAMP ON CITY CREEK—PLOWING AND PLANTING—ARRIVAL OF THE PRESIDENT—THE FIRST SABBATH SERVICE IN THE VALLEY—ORSON PRATT'S SERMON TO THE PIONEERS—BRIGHAM YOUNG LAYS DOWN THE LAW—APOSTLE LYMAN AND ELDER BRANNAN ARRIVE—EXPLORING AND COLONIZING—ENSIGN PEAK NAMED—THE GREAT SALT LAKE VISITED—BLACK ROCK CHRISTENED—TOOELE VALLEY—UTAH LAKE SEEN—SALT LAKE CITY PLANNED AND LOCATED.

IT WAS no Garden of the Hesperides upon which the Pioneers gazed that memorable July morning. Aside from its scenic splendor, which was indeed glorious, magnificent, there was little to invite and much to repel in the prospect presented to their view. A broad and barren plain hemmed in by mountains, blistering in the burning rays of the midsummer sun. No waving fields, no swaying forests, no verdant meadows to rest and refresh the weary eye, but on all sides a seemingly interminable waste of sagebrush bespangled with sunflowers,—the paradise of the lizard, the cricket and the rattlesnake. Less than half way across the baked and burning valley, dividing it in twain—as if the vast bowl, in the intense heat of the Master Potter's fires, in process of formation had cracked asunder—a narrow river, turbid and shallow, from south to north in many a serpentine curve, sweeps on its sinuous way. Beyond, a broad lake, the river's goal, dotted with mountain islands; its briny waters shimmering in the sunlight like a silver shield.

From mountains snow-capped, seamed and craggy, lifting their kingly heads to be crowned by the golden sun, flow limpid, laughing streams, cold and crystal clear, leaping, dashing, foaming, flashing, from rock to glen, from peak to plain. But the fresh canyon streams are far and few, and the arid waste they water, glistening with beds of salt and soda and pools of deadly alkali, scarcely allows them to reach the river, but midway well nigh swallows and absorbs them in its thirsty sands. Above the line of gray and gold, of sage and sunflower, the sloping hillsides and precipitous steeps clothed with purple and dark-green patches. These, the oak-bush, the squaw-berry, and other scant growths, with here and there a tree casting its lone shadow on hill or in valley; a wire-grass swamp, a few acres of withered bunch-grass, and the lazily waving willows and wild-rose bushes fringing the distant streams, the only green things visible.

Silence and desolation reign. A silence unbroken, save by the cricket's ceaseless chirp, the roar of the mountain torrent, or the whir and twitter of the passing bird. A desolation of centuries, where earth seems heaven-forsaken, where hermit Nature, watching, wailing, weeps, and worships God amid eternal solitudes.

A voice breaks the stillness. It is the voice of Brigham Young. Pale and wasted from his recent illness, and still reclining wearily in the light vehicle which has borne him through the mountains, the pioneer chieftain sweeps with a prescient glance the gorgeous panorama spread out before him,—the contrasted splendors of mountain, valley, lake and stream, glorious and glittering in the summer sunlight. Far over and beyond all these extends that inspired gaze. It sees not merely the present, but the future; not only that which is, but that which is to be, when from these barren sands shall rise, as rose proud Venice from the sea, a city fair as Adriatic's island queen, and no less wealthy, famed and powerful. It sees the burning plains to blooming gardens turn; the desert change to an oasis; the sterile valley, the reproach of Nature, which naught before had borne, teeming with varied life and yielding rich fruits and rare flowers for the sustenance and delight of man. An inanimate Sarah, a barren Rachel, transformed by the touch of God to a joyful mother of children. The curse of centuries is lifted, the fetters of ages are stricken off, and the redeemed earth, like a freed captive, looks up to heaven and smiles. Cities, towns and hamlets multiply; farms, fields, orchards and vineyards fill all the land. Egypt, the wilderness, are past; another Canaan appears; and here a Moses who shall smite the rock, a Joshua to sit in judgment and divide to Israel his inheritance.

Still he gazed on. Still rolled before that enraptured sight, in waves of prophetic imagery, the sunlit panorama of the future. Saw he no cloud? Yes, one. He thought upon the oppressor and he frowned, for he was human, and he remembered the past: upon the Master and His mission of mercy, and a softened look played upon the wan and wasted features. Yes, he too could forgive, as he hoped with all men to be forgiven. If the Gentile came he should be welcome, blessing should be given for cursing, and the olive branch, and not the sword, would Ephraim extend to Japheth. But he must come peaceably, give friendship for friendship, and honor the laws of the commonwealth. No stirrers-up of strife, no mobocracy would be tolerated. Japheth, if he desired it, should indeed "dwell in the tents of Shem," but he must dwell there in peace and in propriety, or his room would be preferable to his company.

Is it all fancy? Did no such thoughts sweep through the mind of the Mormon leader that day—one who believed himself, as tens of thousands believed him, a divinely appointed law-giver, a Moses indeed to another and a veritable Israel? Did no such sentiments swell his breast, as he surveyed for the first time the land, the desert land, which his directing genius and his people's united industry were destined to redeem and render immortal? Perhaps we shall see as we proceed.

"The very place." Such were his simple words, but they were words that spoke volumes. Says Wilford Woodruff, who, with Heber C. Kimball, Lorenzo D. Young and others had remained behind with the President, and now stood with him upon the narrow plateau near the mouth of Emigration Canyon: "We gazed in wonder and admiration upon the vast valley before us, with the waters of the Great Salt Lake glistening in the sun, mountains towering to the skies, and streams of pure water running through the beautiful valley. It was the grandest view we had ever seen till this moment.

Pleasant thoughts ran through our minds at the prospect that not many years hence the house of God would be established in the mountains and exalted above the hills, while the valleys would be converted into orchards, vineyards and fruitful fields, cities erected to the name of the Lord, and the standard of Zion unfurled for the gathering of the nations. President Young expressed his entire satisfaction at the appearance of the valley as a resting place for the Saints, and felt amply repaid for his journey. While lying upon his bed in my carriage, gazing upon the scene before us, many things of the future, concerning the Valley, were shown to him in vision."

Some of the pioneers, however, weary and worn by their long pilgrimage, were far from enchanted at the prospect of remaining in such a desolate place. Their hearts sank within them at the announcement of their leader, that this was the very spot,—a spot which he claimed to have previously seen in vision, as held in reserve by the Almighty for His people.* Said Harriet Young: "Weak and weary as I am, I would rather go a thousand miles farther than remain in such a forsaken place as this." Ellen Kimball, her sister pioneer, felt likewise. Clara D. Young was the only one of the three who felt at all satisfied with the situation. Said she in later years: "It did not look so dreary to me as it did to the other ladies. They were terribly disappointed because there were no trees. My poor mother was almost heart-broken. I don't remember a tree that could be called a tree." Lorenzo D. Young says there was a scrub-oak or a cottonwood here and there, but that the general outlook was dreary and disheartening. And thus were opinions and impressions divided. All in all it is evident, from the concensus of these views, which might be multiplied *ad libitum*, that beyond the scenic glory of Salt Lake Valley, which still remains unrivalled, its inviting features at that time were more visible to the eye of faith than to the natural vision.

* Says Erastus Snow: "It was here he had seen the tent settling down from heaven and resting, and a voice said unto him, 'Here is the place where my people Israel shall pitch their tents.'"

Continuing, Apostle Woodruff says: "After gazing awhile upon this scenery, we moved four miles across the table-land into the valley, to the encampment of our brethren, who had arrived two days before us. They had pitched upon the banks of two small streams of pure water, and had commenced plowing. On our arrival they had already broken five acres of land, and had begun planting potatoes in the Valley of the Great Salt Lake."

Orson Pratt had been the first of the pioneers to tread the site of Salt Lake City. We left him and Erastus Snow on the afternoon of the 21st of July, descending the hills near Emigration Canyon, after drinking in with rapture the inspiring scene which had burst some moments before upon their view. As said, they had but one horse between them, and Erastus was now riding. The day being warm,—the temperature about 96° Fahr.,—he had taken off his coat and flung it loosely over the saddle. When about three miles from the canyon he missed his coat, and returned to look for it. Orson Pratt meanwhile walked on alone, descending from plateau to plain. After traversing a circuit of about twelve miles, the two returned to their camp in the canyon.

Erastus Snow states that after entering the valley they first directed their course toward the stream now called Mill Creek, where the tall canes along its banks "looked like inviting grain." Disappointed by the delusion, and remembering the President's injunction to "bear to the northward," they turned in that direction and came to the banks of City Creek. This creek then divided in twain a little above Temple Block; one branch running westward and the other southward. It was 9 or 10 o'clock p. m. when they rejoined their companions. Pratt's company, after their leader left them, had only advanced three miles down the canyon and were now encamped one-and-a-half miles above the mouth.

Next morning, the main company having arrived, Orson Pratt, George A. Smith and seven others rode into the valley to explore, leaving the others to follow them and make practicable the "narrows" at the mouth of the canyon. Descending into the valley about five miles, the explorers turned northward toward the Lake. "For three or four miles," says Orson Pratt, "we found the soil of a most excellent quality. Streams from the mountains and springs were very abundant, the water excellent, and generally with gravel bottoms. A great variety of green grass, and very luxuriant, covered the bottoms for miles where the soil was sufficiently damp, but in other places, although the soil was good, the grass had nearly dried up for want of moisture. We found the drier places swarming with very large crickets, about the size of a man's thumb. This valley is surrounded by mountains, except on the north; the tops of some of the highest being covered with snow. Every one or two miles streams were emptying into it from the mountains on the east, many of which were sufficiently large to carry mills and other machinery. As we proceeded towards the Salt Lake, the soil began to assume a more sterile appearance. *   *   *   We found, as we proceeded on, great numbers of hot springs issuing from near the base of the mountains. These springs were highly impregnated with salt and sulphur. The temperature of some was nearly raised to the boiling point. We traveled for about fifteen miles after coming down into the valley; the latter parts of the distance the soil being unfit for agricultural purposes."

Returning from this jaunt, which evidently took in the neighborhood of the Warm and Hot Springs, they found their wagons encamped in the valley, four or five miles below Emigration Canyon.

On the morning of the 23rd, after despatching messengers to meet the President and inform him of what had been seen and done, the camp removed to the south branch of City Creek, near the Eighth Ward or Washington Square, not far from where the Methodist Church and its palatial neighbor the Hotel Knutsford now stand. A meeting was there called. Orson Pratt prayed and dedicated the land and camp to the Lord, and he and Willard Richards addressed those assembled. Various committees were then appointed, and preparations at once made for putting in crops. The planting season being virtually past, no time was to be lost if they hoped to

reap any results from their labors. Within two hours from the time they arrived on City Creek, ground was broken a short distance from camp—in the very business heart of Salt Lake City—and three plows were kept going during the rest of the day. George W. Brown, William Carter and Shadrach Roundy ran the first furrows plowed by white men in Salt Lake Valley.* Owing to the extreme dryness of the soil, plowing was at first very difficult, and more than one plowshare was broken in the hard sun-baked earth. But a dam having been placed in the creek, and the surrounding soil well flooded, the work was rendered comparatively easy. At 3 o'clock p. m. the pioneer thermometer indicated 96° F. A thunder shower swept over from the west that afternoon, but scarcely enough rain fell to lay the dust. A heavier shower fell next evening.

These rains were particularly welcome and gratifying, not only on account of the prevailing heat and dryness, but from the fact that the pioneers had received the impression, in spite of Colonel Bridger's report, that such phenomena as mid-summer showers were unknown in the Great Basin. They saw many days during that and ensuing seasons, when, but for the memory of these refreshing rains, that early impression would certainly have been confirmed.

On the morning of the 24th the pioneers began planting, first putting in their potatoes. Having planted a few acres they turned the waters of the creek upon their little field and gave the soil "a

---

* George W. Brown, now residing at Charleston, Wasatch County, Utah, writes: "We moved camp from Emigration Creek to City Creek near where the Deseret Bank now stands. A meeting was called soon after we halted. Orders were given to begin plowing. (I had turned my oxen out with their yoke on). A rush was made to begin. All eager to get started first. I succeeded in being the first one to hitch up. John S. Eldredge furnished the plow (having it all ready). I picked up my whip and both drove and held the plow and turned the first sod in Utah Territory. This occurred about 11 o'clock a. m. July 23rd, 1847."

William Carter, of St. George, Washington County, says: "July 23rd, 1847, I put in my plow on the south side of the Thirteenth Ward, opposite Tuft's Hotel, on the west side of the block. Levi Kendall and Bishop Taft put in their plow and broke the beam. This was close to camp and they could not plow. I plowed about half an acre before any other teams came. This took place about noon."

good soaking." This was the beginning of their vast and successful system of irrigation—since famous throughout the civilized world—which has done so much toward redeeming the desert Basin, and making Utah a veritable Eden in the midst of a barren waste.

About midday, or early in the afternoon, President Young and his party arrived at the camp on City Creek. It was in his honor that July 24th—the day of his arrival—was set apart by the pioneers to commemorate their advent into the valleys of the mountains.

The day following was the Sabbath. The grateful pioneers did not forget it. Assembling at 10 a. m. in the circle of their encampment, they paid their devotions to the Most High. George A. Smith was the first speaker, and he was followed by Heber C. Kimball and Ezra T. Benson. All expressed themselves as satisfied with the country to which they had come, with their present situation and future prospects. Apostle Kimball drew attention to the fact that not one human life had been lost during their long journey from the Missouri, and that they had been favored by divine providence in various ways. In the afternoon the Sacrament was administered, after which the assembly was addressed by Wilford Woodruff, Orson Pratt and Willard Richards; Lorenzo D. Young, John Pack and others also making a few remarks. But the sermon of the day was delivered by Apostle Orson Pratt, who took for his text Isaiah 52: 7, 8:

> How beautiful upon the mountains are the feet of him that bringeth good tidings, that publisheth peace; that bringeth good tidings of good, that publisheth salvation; that saith unto Zion, Thy God reigneth!
>
> Thy watchmen shall lift up the voice; with the voice together shall they sing: for they shall see eye to eye, when the Lord shall bring again Zion.

The Apostle proceeded to show that these inspired words, and not only these but many other predictions of the ancient seers, bore directly upon the situation of the pioneers and their people, who were now beginning to plant their feet in the midst of the Rocky Mountains. The prophets of old, he declared, had foreseen this very establishment of the Lord's house in the "tops of the mountains," where it was "exalted above the hills," and "all nations" would yet "flow unto it."

Whether or not the Apostle's literal view be taken, there is no denying that in the light of those prophecies the situation of the pioneers was particularly striking, and that these descendants of the Pilgrims and Puritans, as ready as their New England ancestors to recognize God's hand in their westward flight, had ample reason, from their standpoint, to accept, as they undoubtedly did, their Apostle's interpretation as true and genuine. Would not their feet be indeed "beautiful upon the mountains" to those who were even now awaiting the "glad tidings," soon to be sent back to them, of a home of peace and safety unto which the Lord was about to "bring Zion?"

The President, though his feeble condition would not permit him to preach a sermon that day, added a few practical words from his arm chair, where he sat while he addressed them. "He told the brethren," says Apostle Woodruff, "that they must not work on Sunday; that they would lose five times as much as they would gain by it. None were to hunt or fish on that day, and there should not any man dwell among us who would not observe these rules. They might go and dwell where they pleased, but should not dwell with us. He also said that no man who came here should buy any land; that he had none to sell;* but every man should have his land measured out to him for city and farming purposes. He might till it as he pleased, but he must be industrious and take care of it."

While there exists no proof that it was the purpose of the Mormon leader to set up anew at that time the system of the United Order, the character of his instructions on this occasion were strikingly reminiscent of the past history and operations of the Saints under the great social plan introduced and partly established by their Prophet. The proposed measuring out to each member of the community of that portion of land which he was required to industri-

---

* None of them had any title to the land at that time. It was still Mexican soil.

ously cultivate, was in perfect keeping with the plan of the United Order, and strongly suggestive of the mission once given to Bishop Edward Partridge in Jackson County, Missouri. "He might till it as he pleased," but he must not sell it, nor work it on the Sabbath. Though each man was to have an "inheritance" as an individual possession, he was expected to hold and use it in a way not inconsistent with the public weal; "every man seeking the interest of his neighbor and doing all things with an eye single to the glory of God."

The Israelitish, or at all events ancient genius of the United Order is apparent. Nothing is plainer than that Joseph Smith's concept of a community, while subsequent in enunciation and practice to the theories of the French socialists and Robert Owen, was not inspired by modern socialism and its methods. If he had ideals, they were ancient and biblical, not modern and secular. They were Moses and Joshua, rather than Owen and Saint-Simon. Joseph and Brigham in their time were each compared to Moses, and that, too, by Gentile writers; Brigham, no doubt, because he was not only, like Joseph, a law-giver, but actually led a people, as Moses led Israel, through a wilderness to their "land of promise." But he was not one whit less a Joshua in dividing to an Israel their "inheritance." And yet, be it remembered, it was the order of Enoch, "the seventh from Adam," and not an order of Moses and Joshua, that Joseph Smith had sought to establish. The patriarchal or plural marriage system of the Saints,—now known to the Church in general, and about to be openly avowed to the world,—was also Israelitish in theory and in practice, as were their patriarchal family organizations, formed at Nauvoo and Winter Quarters, according to "the law of adoption."

Before proceeding with our narrative, let us here touch upon another point.

Brigham Young, soon after his arrival in Salt Lake Valley, is said to have remarked: "Now if they"—the Gentiles—"will let us alone for ten years, I'll ask no odds of them." Some have construed this as a covert threat against the Federal Government, signifying a

settled purpose on the part of the Mormon leader to set up an independent government, hostile to and even militant against the United States. Such a conclusion is wholly unwarrantable. Aside from all considerations of Mormon loyalty, so many times proven, the idea of a handful of people numbering only a few thousand souls, whose religion forbade strife and bloodshed, hurling themselves against a nation of thirty or forty millions, and that nation the United States, is so ridiculous as to carry with it its own refutation. Brigham Young has been deemed a fanatic, but no one ever accused him of being a fool. Defensive measures he might, and did employ, as we shall see, against United States troops, sent, as he believed and as they themselves boasted, to re-enact in Salt Lake Valley the bloody scenes of Jackson County and Far West, but never did he lift finger or lisp word in aggressive warfare against the Union. On the contrary when its life seemed hanging by a thread, which the shears of Secession were put forth to sunder, he not only repelled all overtures from the South to join Utah to the Confederacy, but offered to President Lincoln material aid in the nation's defense. No; all that Brigham Young could have meant, when he said that if let alone for ten years he would "ask no odds of them" was that by that time, Mormonism in all probability would have demonstrated to the world its true spirit and motives, so much misunderstood,—demonstrated them by practical results; and if that would not avail to win it friends, then its numerical strength, combined with its admirable strategic position behind the rocky ramparts of Nature's own rearing, would enable it to successfully withstand the assaults of mobs, such as had formerly sought its destruction.

Brigham Young, having "laid down the law" to the pioneer congregation that Sunday afternoon—July 25th, 1847—next directed the organization of three exploring parties, to start out next morning and explore the country to the north, south and west. Said he: "It is necessary that we should learn the facilities of the country and be able to report to our brethren whose eyes are turned towards us. But I can tell you before you start," he added, "that you will find many good places and many facilities for settlements all around us, and you will all return feeling satisfied that this is the most suitable place, and *the* place for us to make our commencement. Here is the place to build our city." Experience has certainly proven, since that hour, the truth of the great colonizer's forecast.

Monday morning, July 26th, the pioneers resumed their secular labors. Plowing and planting began early, so anxious were they to get in their crops while there yet remained hope of a harvest. Carpenters and blacksmiths were at work rigging up plows and other implements, with a view to increasing at once the force of husbandmen. The explorers also started out according to instructions, the President heading one party in person, and leaving the camp about 10 o'clock a. m. This party consisted of Brigham Young, Heber C. Kimball, Willard Richards, Wilford Woodruff, George A. Smith, Ezra T. Benson, Albert Carrington and William Clayton. Messrs. Kimball, Woodruff, Benson and Smith had ascended City Creek Canyon several miles the Saturday evening before. The party now climbed the hills west of the canyon and proceeded northward, the President still riding. "A good place to raise an ensign," he remarked—a fragment of Apostle Pratt's sermon probably lingering in his mind—as the party planted their feet upon a prominent peak near the western edge of a mountainous spur partly enclosing the valley on the north. "Ensign Peak," the mountain was accordingly named, which title it still bears. Wilford Woodruff was the first to ascend it. The President, still feeble, could hardly climb, even with assistance, to the summit. From the top of Ensign, the view on all sides was more than ever sublime. Descending to the valley, the party visited the Warm Springs, in which some of them bathed, finding the waters "very pleasant and refreshing." They were especially beneficial to those who had been afflicted with mountain fever. They returned to camp about 5 p. m.

Joseph Matthews and John Brown, returning from the western mountains, reported the distance across the valley as being about fifteen miles. The soil west of the river they found to be of inferior quality to that upon the east side. No fresh water was discovered after leaving the "Utah Outlet,"* which was about two miles from camp. They had brought back a stray horse, found near the mountains, and supposed to have been lost by the Donner party, or some other company that had passed that way.

Other explorers returning reported that the canyons in the vicinity contained plenty of timber, such as sugar-maple, ash, oak, fir and pine.

While the explorers had been absent, the farmers had planted three more acres with potatoes, and several acres with corn, peas and beans. These crops, planted so late, were not destined to mature; though a few small potatoes "from the size of a pea upward to that of half an inch in diameter" were obtained as excellent seed for another year's planting.

Early on the morning of the 26th, before the President's exploring party had set out, Lorenzo D. Young obtained permission to remove his wagons from the south branch of City Creek to a more elevated, and as he believed, healthier site on the branch running westward, near what was afterwards known as the Whitney Corner, opposite the north-east corner of Temple Block. There stood a solitary scrub-oak, one of the few trees at first visible in the valley. Beneath the scant shade of this exile of the forest,—for it was neither monarch nor resident of the wood,—he placed his covered wagon-box, lifting it from the wheels for that purpose, and did all in his power to make a comfortable and cozy little nook for his dejected wife, so sadly dispirited over the treeless and desolate aspect of their new home. The President and his party, passing by on their way to the mountains, decided that this was a better campground than the one then occupied. Other wagons were therefore directed to remove to that vicinity, which, being done, it was thence-

---

* The name given to the river Jordan, the outlet of Lake Utah, by the trappers and guides of the Great Basin.

forth known as the Upper Camp. In the neighborhood a spot for a garden was selected, and its cultivation immediately begun.

Early on the morning of the 27th, a couple of Indians—Utes—visited the camps and traded with the pioneers, exchanging two ponies for a rifle and a musket. The red men were quite friendly, and seemed very anxious to trade.

About half past eight Amasa M. Lyman, Rodney Badger and Roswell Stevens, who had parted from the pioneers at Fort Laramie to go to Pueblo, arrived at head-quarters on City Creek. They were accompanied by Samuel Brannan. They reported Captain Brown's command as being within two days' march of the Valley.

Half an hour later, the President's exploring party, including the Apostles, Elder Brannan and several others, started for the Great Salt Lake, taking with them a carriage, several riding and pack animals, with bedding and provisions for a two days' journey. The Utah Outlet, which they forded, was described as being about six rods wide and three feet deep, with a gravel bottom; the water, unlike that of the mountain streams, being unclear, and the current not very rapid. Thirteen miles over a level plain covered with sage-brush and greasewood, with here and there a stagnant alkaline pool, or dry bed of a lake, baked and cracked by the sun, brought them to the "point of the mountain," near the southern shore of the lake. Nooning at a large spring in that vicinity, the waters of which were slightly brackish, they rode on a few miles farther to where a large, black rock stood upon the shore. The somber color of this lone basaltic cliff readily suggested the name it should bear, and they called it Black Rock, bestowing upon it the same title as that given it by the Donner party, according to Mr. Reed, the season before. It was not then, as now, separated from the shore by water. The pioneers walked to it dry-shod. Brigham Young was the first to lave his hand in the lake. After a bath in its briny and buoyant waters, the wonderful properties of which much impressed them, they partly explored Tooele Valley, west of the Oquirrh mountains. At dusk they set out to return to the place of their noon halt, and there encamped for the night.

Next morning Apostle Woodruff, while out hunting for his carriage whip, lost the evening before, descried in the distance a band of about twenty Indians, whom he at first mistook for bears. Being unarmed, he turned his horse's head and trotted slowly toward camp. One of the Indians called to him, and then, mounting a pony, rode at full speed to overtake him. The savage, on coming up, informed the pioneer, who had waited for him, that he and his company were Utes, and that they wanted to trade. He accompanied Elder Woodruff to camp. Having no time to spare, the President's party at once set out for the south, along the eastern base of the Oquirrhs, leaving the Indian to await the coming of his companions.

The land now passed over for about ten miles was barren and devoid of water. A few miles south of a place where they halted for noon, Orson Pratt, ascending a high ridge, saw for the first time Utah Lake. Goats, sheep and antelope were seen at various points frisking about and among the hills. Re-crossing the valley the party returned to the banks of City Creek, fully convinced, from all they had yet seen, that the most eligible site for their city lay in that locality.

Accordingly, that evening the President, accompanied by the Apostles, proceeded to a spot between and a little below the forks of City Creek, and striking his cane in the earth, said: "Here will be the Temple of our God. Here are the forty acres for the Temple. The city can be laid out perfectly square, north and south, east and west." It was then and there decided that the building of the city should begin at that point; the Temple block to contain forty acres, and the city blocks surrounding, ten acres each, exclusive of the streets. The smaller blocks were to be sub-divided into lots of ten rods by twenty, giving one-and-a-quarter acres to each lot. The streets were to be eight rods wide, intersecting at right angles, with sidewalks twenty feet in width on either hand. The houses should stand in the centres of the lots, twenty feet back from the front. Four city blocks were reserved for public squares.

Such was the plan adopted by these city-building Apostles in council. Afterwards, the entire body of pioneer settlers convened at the Temple grounds, and ratified by unanimous vote this action of their leaders. The Apostles were appointed a committee to superintend the laying out of the city.

Thus was Salt Lake City, the Mormon metropolis, planned and located; the date of the event being Wednesday, July 28th, 1847. Subsequently some modifications were made in the original plan, such as reducing the size of Temple Block from forty to ten acres, as being "more convenient," and as the city grew up over the foot-hills or benches, the formation of blocks of two-and-a-half acres in lieu of ten. Some of them were irregular, also, instead of being perfectly square, owing to the peculiar lay of the land. But in general the original plan remained unchanged. Beyond the city limits, in the farming and pasturing districts, fields of five, ten and twenty acres were laid out; the smallest ones being nearest the city, and the others graded according to size beyond them.

City Creek, Salt Lake's main water supply, was in due time changed from its original channel, or channels, and made to run in one straight aqueduct down North Temple Street, from the mouth of the canyon westward to the Jordan. Near the canyon's mouth, and at various points along the principal channel, the waters were diverted for irrigating and domestic purposes, pleasant little rills flowing down most of the streets, along the outer edges of the sidewalks. Tree-planting was encouraged, not only in the lots, where rich orchards in time brought forth luscious fruits—apples, pears, peaches, plums, apricots, cherries, currants, etc.,—but also along the side-walks, where cottonwood, box-elder and locust soon cast a grateful shade, and clear and sparkling streams cooled the air, delighted the eye, and made music as they murmured by. Not many seasons elapsed, after the pioneer year 1847, before the main city of the Saints, which served as a model for scores of others, with its wide and regular streets flanked with shade-trees, neat and substantial dwellings embowered in groves and gardens, crystal streams fresh from the towering snow-crowned hills, flowing down both sides of its charming and healthful thoroughfares, presented the appearance, especially in summer when orchards were all abloom, of one vast, variegated bouquet, radiant with beauty and redolent of mingled perfumes. The transformation from sage-brush and sun-flower was truly wonderful, and the fair and peaceful city,—as peaceful as it was fair,—was a perpetual delight, not only to its builders and inhabitants, but likewise to the stranger guest, the weary traveler and passing pilgrim from abroad.

CHAPTER XIX.
1847.

THE PIONEER SETTLERS RE-INFORCED—CAPTAIN JAMES BROWN AND HIS COMPANY—THE MISSISSIPPI MORMONS—AN INDIAN AFFRAY UTES AND SHOSHONES—THE "OLD FORT" PROJECTED—THE FIRST CITY SURVEY—UTAH VALLEY EXPLORED—"RENEWING COVENANTS" AND "SELECTING INHERITANCES"—CACHE VALLEY VISITED—ASCENT OF TWIN PEAKS—THE FIRST HOUSE FINISHED IN SALT LAKE CITY—THE FIRST WHITE CHILD BORN IN UTAH—FIRST DEATH IN THE PIONEER COLONY—THE OX-TEAM COMPANIES RETURN TO WINTER QUARTERS—GREAT SALT LAKE CITY NAMED—THE PIONEER LEADERS RECROSS THE PLAINS —IMMIGRATION OF 1847—CAPTAINS OF HUNDREDS AND FIFTIES—THE FIRST STAKE OF ZION IN THE ROCKY MOUNTAINS—ARRIVALS FROM THE WEST—WINTER AT THE FORT—HARRIET YOUNG'S ADVENTURE—INDIAN CAPTIVES AND CAPTORS—CEDAR AND RUSH VALLEYS EXPLORED—CLOSE OF THE YEAR 1847.

THE pioneer settlers of Salt Lake Valley now began to receive re-inforcements. The first to arrive was Captain James Brown's detachment of the Mormon Battalion, accompanied by the main portion of the Mississippi Saints who had joined the soldiers at Pueblo. Being aware of their approach, President Young and others on the 29th of July mounted their horses and went out to meet them.

The advance columns were encountered about three miles from camp; the main body, with Captains Brown and Higgins and Lieutenant Willis, some distance behind them in Emigration Canyon. A thunder-storm accompanied by a cloud-burst occurred while they were yet in the canyon, swelling the mountain streams, causing them to rush and roar tumultuously down their rocky channels, over-flow their banks in places and flood the surrounding soil. Simultaneously a shower spread over a large portion of the valley. Having emerged from the gorge, Captain Brown's company, escorted by the President and his party, marched to the inspiring strains of martial music to the camps on City Creek, arriving at the lower one about 4 p. m. They received a joyful welcome. The soldiers, some of whom were mounted, numbered over one hundred; the Mississippians about the same. They brought with them sixty wagons, one carriage, one hundred horses and mules, and three hundred head of cattle; adding materially to the strength of the pioneer colony.

It had been the design of Captain Brown, on leaving Pueblo, to push on without delay to the Bay of San Francisco. But the Battalion's term of enlistment having expired, and his teams being jaded and many of his wagons broken, he now decided to tarry in Salt Lake Valley and await further orders from his military superiors. The soldiers formed a separate camp on City Creek, about midway between the two camps of the pioneers.

At a general meeting held next evening, the President, in behalf of the whole people, publicly thanked the Battalion for the important service they had rendered their country and their co-religionists. He expressed the belief that the Church had been saved from destruction by the enlistment of these troops on the frontier. Similar sentiments were voiced by him to the main body of the Battalion after their arrival from California.

Captain Brown's men, at the request of the President, constructed, two days after their arrival, a bowery in which to hold public meetings on Temple Block. This primitive structure—the first building of any kind erected by the Mormons in the Rocky Mountains—was similar to the boweries constructed by them at their various settlements between the Mississippi and the Missouri. Posts were set in the ground, and upon these rude pillars long poles were laid and securely fastened with wooden pegs or strips of rawhide. This framework, overlaid with timbers and brush, formed an umbrageous if not a very substantial roof; a good shelter from the sun and a fair though insufficient one from wind and rain. Its dimensions were forty by twenty-eight feet,—large enough to accommodate the assembly of the entire camp.

At one end of these boweries it was customary to erect a platform and stand, well boarded in at the back, for the use of presiding officers and speakers; a space in front being reserved for the choir. At first seats would be improvised from whatever articles came handy, but in due time rude benches would follow, resting upon a floor or on the ground; the character and extent of the improvements would largely depend upon the permanency of the settlement of which the bowery was the center of worship, social amusement and gatherings in general. Though top and sides were well covered and closed in, the meetings held in such buildings would be virtually in the open air, and during bad weather would have to be suspended and in winter time discontinued. Until the "Old Tabernacle" was built—the forerunner of the present Tabernacle—these boweries were the only regular places of public worship in Salt Lake Valley.

The original bowery, erected by the Battalion boys, must not be confounded with the "Old Bowery," subsequently built on Temple Block, which, after several years' use as a house of worship, was transformed into a theater,—the original Thespian temple of Utah. Concerning this particular structure, in connection with the local history of music and the drama, we shall have more to say hereafter.

July 31st—the day the first bowery was erected—witnessed an exciting and bloody affray between two small bands of Indians, Utes and Shoshones, who were trading at the camps on City Creek. Two young men, one of either tribe, began disputing over a theft alleged to have been committed by the Ute. He was accused of stealing a horse belonging to the Shoshones and trading it to one of the settlers for a rifle. Being detected, he refused to relinquish either horse or rifle. Hence the quarrel, followed by a combat, between the two young warriors. During the fight one broke his gun-stock over the other's head. The affair was waxing warm, and matters began getting serious, when an old man, father of one of the combatants, strove to separate them. For this purpose he lashed with a heavy thong of rawhide their heads and faces. The son's antagonist struck

the old man, whereupon the latter seized a stick of timber and shattered it over the warrior's head. The two were finally separated, and the Ute retired to one of the lower camps. While there a horse belonging to the Shoshones wandered by. Mounting his own pony, the Ute started to drive the other animal toward the mountains. The Shoshones, being apprised of this new theft, sent four of their number in hot pursuit. Overtaking the thief they shot him dead, likewise killing his horse. Returning, they brandished a bloody rifle, and informing the other Utes of what they had done, intimated by fierce looks that the trouble might not yet be over.

It seems that there was bad blood between the two tribes, owing to the Utes coming over the line from the valleys southward to trade with the settlers, a privilege which the Shoshones, who claimed the land where the camps were situated, desired to monopolize. They showed marked displeasure toward all who traded with the Utes, regarding it as an infringement of their rights. They expressed their willingness to sell the land for fire-arms, powder and lead.

The excitement attending this tragic incident having somewhat abated, the slayers of the Ute sat down and proceeded to devour with great apparent relish some large crickets they had caught, of the kind infesting the valleys. They harvested these insects for bread, as a farmer would wheat or corn. We have heard more than one pioneer speak of these "cricket cakes" of the savages, but never knew one to admit having tasted them.*

It was now Saturday evening. A little over a week had the Pioneers been in Salt Lake Valley. A summary of their labors during that time was reported by Colonel Markham as follows: Three lots of land, aggregating fifty-three acres, had been plowed, and

---

* The California Indians offered to Fremont's explorers in 1845 a very superior quality of meal, which the white men purchased, and made into bread. One day some wings and legs of grasshoppers were found in the meal, which led to the discovery, much to the disgust of the buyers and users of the commodity, that it was pounded up grasshoppers they had been eating and relishing.

planted with potatoes, peas, beans, corn, oats, buckwheat, garden seeds, etc., and about three acres of corn and some beans and potatoes were already beginning to sprout. Thirteen plows and three harrows had been worked during the week, and various repairs made to broken implements. The valley had been explored, the several canyons visited, and a road made to the timber. A saw-pit had also been constructed, and a large pine log, brought down from the mountains for the purpose, converted into lumber for a skiff.

Sunday morning, August 1st, the camp assembled for worship in the Bowery. The President, who was again ill, did not attend, but the other Apostles were present. Heber C. Kimball presided, and was the first speaker. His remarks were very practical. He enquired if there was a guard out around the cattle. If not, he advised that one be placed immediately, as the Indians, after remaining in camp over night, had left very suddenly that morning without assigning any reason for their abrupt departure. He was followed by Orson Pratt, in a characteristic sermon on the ancient prophecies; continuing his theme of the Sunday before. Apostle Kimball then spoke again, still in a very practical vein, and still upon the subject of the Indians. He warned the settlers against selling guns and ammunition to the savages, or allowing them, through carelessness, to steal from them. Several guns, he said, had been stolen by their dusky visitors the day before. As to the land upon which they had settled, it did not belong to the red men, and to pay them for it, as they desired, would impoverish the community. No man must sell his inheritance. The speaker predicted that five years would not elapse before they and their people who followed them would be better off than ever they were at Nauvoo.

Willard Richards, Amasa M. Lyman and others addressed the afternoon meeting, when it was decided to concentrate the three camps in one, and work more unitedly than heretofore. The project of building a stockade, for further protection against thieving and hostile savages, was also mooted. Colonel Rockwood, Captains Brown and Lewis and Lieutenant Willis spoke to this question, which involved that of building and inhabiting houses during the coming winter, instead of dwelling in tents and wagons. It was thought that a log house, sixteen by eighteen feet, would cost about forty dollars, and one of adobes—sun-burnt bricks—about half that sum. Samuel Brannan favored adobe houses, one of which, he said, might be built in a week. His printing office in California had been put up and a copy of his paper issued in fourteen days. Samuel Gould and James Dunn reported themselves as lime-burners, and Sylvester H. Earl, Joel J. Terrill, Ralph Douglas and Joseph Hancock as brickmakers. It was decided by vote that a stockade of logs and adobes be at once erected. Thus the famous "Old Fort" had its origin.

Next morning the three camps moved all their wagons to a spot a little east of the upper camp-ground, and formed them into an oblong corral between the two branches of City Creek. A dam was put in the stream some distance above, and the waters so diverted that pleasant little rivulets were soon running down outside as well as inside the corral of wagons. The Indians, on account of their stealing proclivities, were not now permitted inside the enclosure.

On the morning of August 2nd Orson Pratt and Henry G. Sherwood began the survey of Salt Lake City. Heber C. Kimball's teams went into the canyon and brought the first loads of logs for the fort, and other laborers began making adobes and preparing mounds for the same purpose. The day was very warm and the camp exceedingly busy.

Ezra T. Benson and Porter Rockwell were now sent back to meet the next companies from Winter Quarters, supposed to be somewhere on the plains between the Missouri River and the mountains. They started about noon of the 2nd, going horseback, and taking with them the following letter:

PIONEER CAMP, VALLEY OF THE GREAT SALT LAKE, Aug. 2, 1847.
To General Charles C. Rich and the Presidents and Officers of the Emigrating Company.

DEAR BRETHREN.—We have delegated our beloved brother, Ezra T. Benson, and escort to communicate to you by express the cheering intelligence that we have arrived in the most beautiful valley of the Great Salt Lake; that every soul who left Winter Quarters with us is alive, and almost every one enjoying good health. That portion of the Battalion that was at Pueblo are here with us, together with the Mississippi company that accompanied them, and they are generally well. We number about four hundred souls, and we know of no one but what is pleased with our situation. We have commenced the survey of a city this morning. We feel that the time is fast approaching when those teams that are going to Winter Quarters this fall should be on the way. Every individual here would be glad to tarry if their friends were here, but as many of the Battalion as well as the Pioneers have not their families here, and do not expect that they are in your camp, we wish to learn by express from you the situation of your camp as speedily as possible, that we may be prepared to counsel and act in the whole matter. We want you to send us the name of every individual in your camp, or, in other words, a copy of your whole camp roll, including the names, number of wagons, horses, mules, oxen, cows, etc., and the health of your camp; your location, prospects, etc. If your teams are worn out, if your camp is sick and not able to take care of themselves, if you are short of teamsters, or if any other circumstance impedes your progress, we want to know it immediately, for we have help for you, and if your teams are in good plight, and will be able to return to Winter Quarters this season, or any portion of them, we want to know it. We also want the mail, which will include all letters and papers and packages belonging to our camp, general and particular. Would circumstances permit, we would gladly meet you some distance from this, but our time is very much occupied, notwithstanding we think you will see us before you see our valley. Let all the brethren and sisters cheer up their hearts and know assuredly that God has heard and answered their prayers and ours, and led us to a goodly land, and our souls are satisfied therewith. Brother Benson can give you many particulars that will be gratifying and cheering to you which I have not time to write, and we feel to bless all the Saints.

In behalf of the council,   Brigham Young, President,
                                                    Willard Richards, Clerk.

Utah Valley was next explored. Jesse C. Little and a party, returning on the 5th of August from a tour in that vicinity, reported that there was a fine country east of Utah Lake, the soil being well adapted for cultivation. They virtually confirmed the report of Escalante, the Spaniard, who had discovered that lake and valley seventy-one years before.

On the 6th of August the President and the Apostles who were with him, namely: Heber C. Kimball, Orson Pratt, Willard Richards, Wilford Woodruff, George A. Smith and Amasa M. Lyman, "renewed their covenants" by baptism. President Young, entering the water —City Creek—immersed each of the others according to the usual mode, after which he laid hands upon and confirmed them, resealing upon each his Apostleship. Heber C. Kimball—next to Brigham

Young the senior of the Twelve—then baptized and confirmed the President in like manner. This example of "renewing covenants" was subsequently followed by the entire camp, and by all their brethren and sisters who came after them. Even to this day it is the custom with those who "gather to Zion," to receive rebaptism on reaching the settlements of the Saints in the Rocky Mountains.

A weather note of August 7th tells of "a terrible whirl-wind" that struck the camp about noon, doing considerable damage. It whirled a fowl high in air, tore tents and wagon-covers and shook things in general violently.

In the afternoon of that day the Apostles repaired to Temple Block and selected their "inheritances." Brigham Young took a block east of the Temple site and running south-east, upon which to settle his family and friends. Heber C. Kimball took a block north of the Temple, Orson Pratt a block south, and Wilford Woodruff a block cornering on the Temple grounds. George A. Smith chose one on the west, and Amasa M. Lyman one near Wilford Woodruff's. Willard Richards was not in camp at the time, but it was supposed that he would prefer settling on the east near the President, to whom he was related. Subsequently other selections of lands were made by the Apostles for their friends who were yet to come.

On the 9th of August Captain James Brown, Samuel Brannan and others set out for San Francisco by way of Fort Hall. The object of Captain Brown's trip to the coast was to draw the pay due from Government to the men of his detachment; the Battalion to which they belonged having been honorably discharged at Los Angeles on the 16th of July. The Captain took with him the muster roll of his detachment, with power of attorney from each man to sign for and receive his pay. Those besides Samuel Brannan who accompanied him were Abner Blackburn, Gilbert Hunt, John Fowler, William Gribble, Henry Frank, Lysander Woodworth and Jesse S. Brown, the Captain's eldest son. Elder Brannan acted as their guide.

It is believed that he returned to California somewhat crestfallen, having failed to convince the Mormon leaders that the Pacific coast, where he had located his colony, was a more desirable place for the Saints to settle and build up a State, than the desert shores of the Great Salt Lake. Elder Brannan, always more a man of the world than a devout religionist, probably surveyed the subject from a business standpoint. Considering that alone he was undoubtedly correct. But Brigham Young and his associates, as shown, had other than material ends in view. Hence their determination to remain separate—at least for a season—from the Gentiles, whose worldly aims and pursuits, if in the majority, would have tended to thwart the spiritual plans and purposes of the Mormon colonists; rendering the "building up of Zion" difficult if not impossible.

Captain Brown's party were accompanied as far as Bear River by Jesse C. Little, Lieutenant Willis, Joseph Matthews, John Brown and John Buchanan. Passing up the eastern shore of the Great Salt Lake they came to Weber River, where, as stated, Miles M. Goodyear, whom the Pioneers met on their way to the Valley in July, had built a log fort and was engaged in trapping and trading. Captain Brown called at the fort and conversed with its proprietor. This, perhaps, was the beginning of negotiations between them, ending, as we shall see, in the purchase of the Goodyear fort, lands and improvements by the Captain, on his return from California.

Colonel Little and his party, after separating from Brown and Brannan, explored Cache Valley, of which Major Harris had spoken so favorably to the Pioneers at South Pass. Lewis B. Myers and a companion also visited that valley about the same time. Returning, they confirmed the reports relating to that section. Cache Valley, it was found, was not only "a fine place for wintering cattle," but, when watered, an excellent farming region as well. It is known today as "Utah's Granary."

The explorers of the north returned to Salt Lake Valley on the 14th of August. A few days later, Albert Carrington, John Brown and others started on an exploring trip to Twin Peaks, being the first of the Pioneers and probably the first white men to plant their feet upon those well-nigh inaccessible summits, tipped with perpetual snow. The ascent was made on the 21st of August.

Meantime work on the stockade had begun and was progressing rapidly. The site selected for the fort was about three-quarters of a mile south-west of the City Creek encampment. A portion of the Sixth Ward of Salt Lake City still bears the familiar name of the "Old Fort Block," though the fort itself, which once enclosed it, has long since disappeared. There, on the 10th of August, 1847, were laid the foundations of the first houses erected in Salt Lake Valley,—the first built by the Mormons west of Winter Quarters. Brigham Young started four of these houses, Heber C. Kimball four, Stephen Markham one, Willard Richards one, and Lorenzo D. Young one. This was the beginning of the Old Fort. The first house finished and occupied was Lorenzo D. Young's. These houses extended continuously along the east line of the stockade, beginning at the nort-heast corner. Their order was as follows: Brigham Young, four rooms; Lorenzo D. Young, two; Heber C. Kimball, five; Willard Richards, two; Wilford Woodruff, two; George A. Smith, two; Amasa M. Lyman, two; and Erastus Snow, one. These first dwellings were of logs. They had poles for rafters, willows for roofs and in lieu of shingles earth; an insufficient shelter, as was found later, from autumn rains and winter's melting snows. Floors and ceilings were rare, and of the rudest and most primitive kind, while window glass was almost an unknown quantity.

Plowing and planting by this time had been suspended, thirty additional acres having been put under cultivation, making eighty-three in all. Most of the settlers were now busily occupied, chopping and hauling logs, making adobes and preparing to build.

The first white child born in Utah opened its eyes to the light on Monday, August 9th, 1847—two weeks and two days after the arrival of the Pioneers. This infantile re-inforcement was a girl, the daughter of John and Catharine Campbell Steele, both of the Mormon Battalion, who came into the Valley in Captain Brown's company on the 29th of July. Their child was born at 4 o'clock

a. m., in her father's tent on Temple Block. She was named Young Elizabeth Steele, after President Young and Queen Elizabeth. The father, John Steele, was a mason, and according to his account built nearly one-third of the "Old Fort" with his own hands, using a trowel made by Burr Frost out of a saw-blade. Mr. Steele also claims to be the pioneer shoe-maker of Utah. He resides at Toquerville, in the southern part of the Territory. His daughter lives at Kanarra, in Kane County, and is now Mrs. James Stapley.

The first death in the pioneer colony followed hard upon the heels of the original birth. It occurred just two days later. The victim was a little three-year-old child of George and Jane Therlkill, —a grand-child of Robert Crow. Wandering away from camp a little to the south, it had fallen into the creek, where it was discovered, drowned, about five o'clock in the afternoon. Every possible effort was made to restore it, but without avail. The parents mourned bitterly their loss, and a shadow of sympathetic gloom rested for a season upon the whole encampment.

On August 12th an observation was taken by Orson Pratt and William Clayton to ascertain the height of Temple Block. It was discovered to be 4,300 feet above the sea level, and sixty-five feet above the Utah outlet. Ascending City Creek canyon one mile the altitude above the Temple grounds was found to be 214 feet.

Surveyor Sherwood and his aids were still busy laying out the city. Messrs. Tanner, Frost and their fellow sons of Vulcan were engaged in shoeing oxen and re-setting wheel tires for the companies that were about to return to Winter Quarters. Some of these were Battalion men who had not seen their families since bidding them adieu on the frontier thirteen months before. A party of men who had been to the lake to boil down salt, returned, reporting that they had found, lying between two sand-bars on the lake-shore, a beautiful bed of salt all ready to load into wagons. Several loads were brought to camp, and two of them taken east by the company that set out a few days later for the Missouri River.

HISTORY OF UTAH. 353

August 16th was the day of their departure. Most of the ox-teams started and traveled to the mouth of Emigration Canyon, where they were joined next day by the residue of the company. There were seventy-one men, with thirty-three wagons and ninety-two yoke of oxen; also some horses and mules. Their organization was similar to that of the Pioneers. There were two divisions, made up of companies of tens. Tunis Rappleyee and Shadrach Roundy were the two captains of divisions, and William Clayton was historian. The personnel of the company was as follows:

FIRST DIVISION:

Tunis Rappleyee, Captain.

FIRST TEN (SIX WAGONS):

Joseph Skein, Captain,	George Cummings,	Joseph Shipley,
Artemas Johnson,	Thomas Richardson,	Samuel Badlam,
James Cazier, captain of guard	William Burt,	Roswell Stevens.
of first division,	James Dunn,	

SECOND TEN (FIVE WAGONS):

Zebedee Coltrin, Captain,	Samuel H. Marble,	Joshua Curtis,
Chauncey Loveland,	George Scholes,	John S. Eldredge,
Lorenzo Babcock,	William Bird,	Horace Thornton.

THIRD TEN (FIVE WAGONS):

| Francis Boggs, Captain, | Seeley Owen, | Clark Stillman, |
| Sylvester H. Earl, | George Wardle, | Almon M. Williams. |

SECOND DIVISION:

Shadrach Roundy, Captain.

FIRST TEN (FIVE WAGONS):

R. Jackson Redding,	John Pack,	Thomas Colward,
William Carpenter,	Robert Byard,	Lisbon Lamb,
Henry W. Sanderson,	Benjamin W. Rolfe,	William Clayton.
Bailey Jacobs,		

SECOND TEN (FIVE WAGONS):

John H. Tippitts, Captain,	William C. McLelland,	John S. Gleason, captain of
Francis T. Whitney,	Norman Taylor,	guard of second division,
James Stewart,	Lyman Stevens,	Myron Tanner,
Charles A. Burke,	Lyman Curtis,	Rufus Allen.

THIRD TEN (FOUR WAGONS):

Allen Compton, Captain,	Philip Garner,	Harmon D. Persons,
John Bybee,	Barnebas Lake,	Solomon Tindell,
Jeduthan Averett,	Franklin Allen,	Charles Hopkins.
John G. Smith,	David Garner,	

FOURTH TEN (THREE WAGONS):

Andrew J. Shupe, Captain,	Benjamin Roberts,	John Calvert,
Francillo Durfee,	Jarvis Johnson,	Daniel Miller,
Erastus Bingham,	Albert Clark,	Luther W. Glazier,
Loren Kinney,	James Hendrickson,	Thomas Bingham.

The third and fourth tens of the second division were members of the Mormon Battalion, returning to meet their families on the plains or the frontier. For each man there had been provided eight pounds of flour, nine pounds of meal, and a few pounds of beans. For the rest of their subsistence they were to depend upon game killed by the way. A new roadometer was constructed for this company by William A. King; William Clayton having received special instructions from President Young to carefully re-measure the distance back to Winter Quarters, and collect such other information as might be serviceable to future emigration.

Their journey back to the Missouri consumed a little over nine weeks. It was prosperous and comparatively uneventful. Beyond Green River, on Big Sandy, they met Ezra T. Benson and Porter Rockwell, returning west with the mail, after delivering the President's letter to General Rich and the on-coming trains. The leading one—Captain Daniel Spencer's first fifty—was encountered by the east-bound wagons on the 31st of August, at the "first crossing" of the Sweetwater. Here Shadrach Roundy joined his family and returned west, and John G. Smith took his place as captain of the second division. The other companies were met at various points within the next three days.|

Heavy rains, with snow, set in early in September. The provisions—breadstuffs—of the returning company gave out, and for several weeks dried buffalo meat was their sole subsistence. During the latter part of the journey the Indians annoyed them considerably,

HISTORY OF UTAH.   355

burning the prairies before them and stealing their stock. At the North Platte ferry they met Luke Johnson, William A. Empey and Appleton M. Harmon, of the nine men left there by the pioneers in June, and at Loup Fork Captain Hosea Stout and a party of mounted police from Winter Quarters, going out to meet President Young, who was now supposed to be on his way back to the Missouri

Captain Rappleyee's wagons rolled into Winter Quarters on the 21st of October. The distance from Salt Lake Valley, as re-measured by William Clayton, was found to be 1032 miles—twenty-two miles less than the former reckoning of the Pioneers.

In the Valley, after the departure of the "ox-teams," the work of exploring, building and surveying went steadily on. The laying out of the city was completed on August 20th; 135 blocks of ten acres each being included in this original survey. The building of the fort was pushed forward as rapidly as possible and by the last of the month twenty-nine houses had been erected at the stockade.

In the latter part of August President Young and the Apostles prepared to return to Winter Quarters. Though much remained to be done before the feet of the infant colony would be firmly planted, anxiety was felt by the leaders for the welfare of the Church on the frontier, and the success of the next year's emigration. None could so well organize and lead the main body of their people across the plains to their mountain retreat, as these experienced guides and colonizers of the Great Basin. That was doubtless the main reason why they resolved to return to the Missouri that season, instead of spending the winter with their friends in Salt Lake Valley.

Prior to their departure a special conference was convened on Sunday the 22nd of August, when the pioneer settlers assembled in the Bowery to receive the parting instructions of their leaders. It was emphatically a business conference, called to consider the temporal affairs of the colony. It was decided by vote to fence in and cultivate the city plat during the coming year, in preference to lands lying outside, also to organize in Salt Lake Valley a Stake of Zion, with Father John Smith, the Prophet's uncle, as President. Father Smith had not yet arrived, but was expected in the coming emigration. Other nominations were deferred until it should be known who were in the next trains.

The pioneer city then received its name. "I move," said Brigham Young, "that we call this place the Great Salt Lake City of the Great Basin of North America." The motion was seconded and carried. On the President's motion the post office was called "The Great Basin Post Office." Heber C. Kimball, by motion, named the river running through the valley "The Western Jordan," and Brigham Young christened City Creek, Mill Creek, Red Butte Creek, Emigration Creek, and Canyon (now Parley's) Creek, in like manner. It was many years before the city's title was abbreviated by legislative enactment to "Salt Lake City," but the "Western Jordan" became plain "Jordan" almost immediately.

Colonel A. P. Rockwood, overseer of the stockade, was released from that position to return with the President, and Tarlton Lewis was appointed overseer in his stead. William McIntyre was chosen clerk to keep an account of public labor, and Edson Whipple was given charge of the distribution of water over the plowed lands. The President's parting injunction was as follows:

> It is necessary that the adobe yard (the stockade) should be secured so that Indians cannot get in. To accommodate those few who shall remain here after we return; it would only be necessary to build one side of the fort, but common sense teaches us to build it all round. By and by men of means will be coming on, and they will want rooms, and the men who build them will then be entitled to their pay. Make your walls 4½ feet high, so that they can keep the cattle out. Build your houses so that you will have plenty of fresh air in them, or some of you will get sick, after being used to sleeping in your wagons so long. We propose to fence in a tract of land thirty rods square, so that in case of necessity the cattle can be brought inside and the hay also be stacked there. In the spring this fence can be removed and a trench be plowed about twenty feet from the houses to enable the women to raise garden vegetables. I want to engage 50,000 bushels of wheat and the same amount of corn and other grain in proportion. I will pay you $1.25 per bushel for wheat and 50 cents for corn. Why cannot I bring glass for you and you raise corn for me? Raise all the grain you can, and with this you can purchase sheep, cows, teams, etc., of those who come here later on. We desire you to live in that stockade until we come back again, and raise grain next year.

On the 26th of August the pioneer leaders bade farewell to their friends who were to remain, and set out upon their return journey to the Missouri. Such of the Pioneers and Battalion men present as had families at Winter Quarters or on the way west, were selected to accompany the President and his party.

The weather was now beautiful. The oppressive heat of summer was pretty well past, and the cool, bright days of our delightful mountain autumn were just about beginning. The roads, however, were very dusty, and the way through the canyons, though more passable than before, was still rough and difficult. Their noon halt on the 29th was at the head of Echo Canyon. There Ezra T. Benson joined them, bringing news of the approaching trains. Porter Rockwell came up later. After crossing Bear River the company was called together and organized. The full list of names was as here given:

Brigham Young,	William Wardsworth,	Alex. P. Chessley,
John P. Greene,	Datus Ensign,	Thomas C. Chessley,
Truman O. Angell,	John Dixon,	John C. Gould,
Joseph S. Schofield,	Simeon Howd,	Samuel Gould,
Albert P. Rockwood,	Seth Taft,	Amasa M. Lyman,
Stephen H. Goddard,	John P. Wriston,	Albert Carrington,
Millen Atwood,	Stephen Kelsey,	John Brown,
Thomas Tanner,	Charles D. Barnum,	George A. Smith,
Addison Everett,	Wilford Woodruff,	Joel J. Terrill,
Sidney A. Hanks,	Dexter Stillman,	Solomon Chamberlain,
George Clark,	William C. A. Smoot,	William Terrill,
J. G. Luce,	James W. Steward,	Nathaniel Fairbanks,
John G. Holman,	Robert T. Thomas,	Charles A. Harper,
George R. Grant,	Jabez Nowlin,	Perry Fitzgerald,
Davis S. Laughlin,	James Case,	Isaac N. Wriston,
William Dykes,	James C. Earl,	Ozro Eastman,
Jacob Weiler,	Judson Persons,	Horace Monroe Frink,
David Grant,	Orson Pratt,	Levi N. Kendall,
Thomas Woolsey,	Joseph Egbert,	Stephen Markham,
Haywood Thomas,	Marcus B. Thorpe,	George Mills,
Samuel W. Fox,	George Wilson,	Conrad Klineman,
Willard Richards,	Jesse Johnson,	Horace K. Whitney,
Thomas Bullock,	John Brimhall,	Orson K. Whitney,
Benjamin Richmond,	A. L. Huntley,	George P. Billings,
Harvey Pierce,	Rodney Badger,	Ralph Douglas,

Ezra T. Benson,	William W. Rust,	Elijah E. Holden,
Matthew Ivory,	Joseph Matthews,	William Gifford,
David Powell,	Joseph G. Camp,	Albert Sharp,
Erastus Snow,	William Park.	Abel M. Sargent,
William McIntyre,	Green Flake.	Andrew S. Gibbons,
George Brown,	Benjamin F. Stewart,	Thurston Larson,
Orrin P. Rockwell,	John Crow,	Heber C. Kimball,
Charles Shumway,	Peter J. Meeseck,	Howard Egan,
Andrew P. Shumway,	C. Rowe,	Hosea Cushing,
Burr Frost,	William Rowe,	William A. King,
William Carter,	Barnabas L. Adams,	Carlos Murray,

The camp comprised one hundred and eight men, with thirty-six wagons and about three times that number of horses and mules. Stephen Markham was chosen captain of hundred; Barnabas L. Adams and Joseph Matthews, captains of fifties; Brigham Young, John Brown, Howard Egan, George Clark, George Wilson, Erastus Snow, Thomas Tanner and Charles A. Harper, captains of tens. Thomas Bullock was again appointed Clerk. The President's ten included six of his fellow Apostles, with Albert P. Rockwood, Stephen H. Goddard and Joseph Schofield.

Fording Green River, which was now quite low, the company, having crossed Big Sandy, came upon Daniel Spencer's first fifty there encamped. It was now the 3rd of September.

At this point let us briefly sketch the experience of these westbound companies, the first to follow in the wake of the pioneers. They had been organized on the Elk Horn in June, under the direction of Father Morley and Bishop Whitney, the committee previously appointed for that purpose. Due deference had been paid by this committee, however, to the Apostles, Parley P. Pratt and John Taylor, who were present and took part in the organization. They were invited by the committee, inasmuch as it was their purpose to accompany the emigration, to exercise a general superintendency over all the trains. These aggregated five hundred and sixty wagons, with about fifteen hundred men, women and children, and five thousand head of stock. Most of the wagons were drawn by oxen.

The companies were organized as follows: John Young, brother

of Brigham Young, had immediate general command, and John Van Cott was marshal. There were four captains of hundreds, namely: (1) Daniel Spencer, under whom Ira Eldredge and Peregrine Sessions were captains of fifties; (2) Edward Hunter, with Jacob Foutz and Joseph Horne as captains of fifties; (3) Jedediah M. Grant, with Joseph B. Noble and Willard Snow as sub-captains, and (4) Abraham O. Smoot, under whom were Captains George B. Wallace and Samuel Russell. There was also another company called "the artillery company," having with it several pieces of cannon. It was more or less distinct and independent in organization, and was commanded by General Charles C. Rich. As usual, the divisions of fifties were sub-divided into tens.

Parley P. Pratt generally traveled with Daniel Spencer's hundred and John Taylor with Edward Hunter's. George Q. Cannon, then a youth of twenty, was with his uncle, Apostle Taylor, in this emigration. In Captain Grant's hundred was the poetess, Eliza R. Snow. Other notable names connected with this emigration were Father John Smith, Lorin Farr, Hezekiah, Moses and George W. Thatcher, Samuel and John Bennion, William Hyde, Jacob Gates, Archibald and Robert Gardner, John Neff, Jacob Houtz, Abraham Hoagland, William Bringhurst, Thomas Callister, John, George, Peter and Henry Nebeker, L. E. Harrington, Millen and Miner Atwood, Isaac Chase, Charles Crismon, Levi E. and William W. Riter, Silas S. and Jesse N. Smith, Joseph C. Kingsbury, Elijah F. Sheets, William C. Staines, Bryant Stringham, Harrison Sperry, Chauncey W. West and many others.

The first company left the Elk Horn on the 18th of June; the last one on or about the 4th of July. During the first few days considerable ill-feeling was manifested, owing to misunderstandings as to the order of traveling, but a general halt having been called, and a meeting of officers held, these differences were adjusted and the journey resumed. Then came stampedes and loss of cattle, almost crippling some of the companies, and sadly hindering their progress.

A good idea of a stampede,—though not in this, as in most instances, caused by Indians,—is conveyed in the following bit of description penned by one of the pilgrims to the Valley that season. Says the writer: "Some one was carelessly shaking a big buffalo robe at the back of a wagon, from which some of the cattle in the corral took fright and started on the run; these frightened others; they commenced bellowing; and all in a huddle ran for the gateway of the enclosure, which being altogether too narrow for the egress of the rushing multitude that thronged into the passage, they piled one on top of another until the top ones were above the tops of the adjacent wagons, moving them from their stations, while the inmates, at this early hour, being so suddenly and unceremoniously aroused from their morning sleep, and not knowing the cause of this terrible uproar and confusion, were some of them almost paralyzed with fear. At length those that could, broke from the enclosure, the bellowing subsided and quiet was restored; but the sad effect of the fright caused much suffering to some whose nerves were not sufficient for the trying scene. In the encounter two wagon wheels were crushed, Captain K.'s only cow was killed, and several oxen had horns knocked off."

This stampede resulted from an accident. But the Indians resorted to just such tricks as shaking buffalo robes or blankets in order to frighten and scatter the horses and cattle of passing trains. It was their habit to follow them for hundreds of miles,—as sharks at sea some vessel with a dead body aboard,—warily concealing themselves and awaiting an opportunity to effect their purpose. Dark and rainy nights were their delight. Creeping like snakes through the long, dank prairie grass, so stealthily as to completely elude the eyes and ears of the watchful guard, they would cut the lariats of the horses, if staked outside the wagons, and then scare and scatter them pell-mell in every direction. After the trains had passed on, if pass they could after losing much of their stock, these cunning prowlers of the plains would hunt and capture the missing animals at leisure.

Late in July and early in August, the companies from Winter Quarters met a squad of fourteen soldiers, members of the Mormon Battalion, the escort of General S. F. Kearney, then on his way from San Francisco to Fort Leavenworth. There they expected to be discharged. These soldiers were husbands and sons of women traveling in the companies. Their meetings therefore were more than ordinarily joyful. Nathaniel V. Jones was one of Kearney's escort. Colonel John C. Fremont was traveling with the party, being in custody, on his way to Washington, there to answer to the charge of insubordination in refusing to recognize Kearney's authority in California.

Six or seven deaths—mostly of children—occurred among the emigrants. The first death was that of Jacob Weatherbee, who was shot by Omaha Indians between Winter Quarters and the Elk Horn, on the 19th of June. Captain Jedediah M. Grant had just lost a child, and his wife was lying at the point of death, when he met Captain Rappleyee's wagons on the 3rd of September. Mrs. Grant died before reaching the Valley, but her remains were taken there for burial. Captain Grant's companies were particularly unfortunate. The alkali lands—or waters—along the Sweewater, killed many of their cattle, and a score of their horses were stolen by Indians. But death and disaster did not have it all their own way. Several children were born on the plains and after the emigrants passed the Rocky Mountains.

President Young, on meeting Captain Spencer's companies at Big Sandy, advised them to go on to Green River, and from there send back teams to assist the other trains which had lost so heavily in cattle. Several pioneers, having met their families, now returned.

At Little Sandy, on September 4th, the Apostles met their confrere, Parley P. Pratt, and went into council. Two of the Twelve were sharply reproved by the President for undoing what the majority of the Apostles had done in organizing the camps for traveling. Good feeling being restored the President's company pushed on.

Three days later they met Edward Hunter's wagons on the Sweetwater. It was now snowing, but the weather continued mild. A feast had been prepared for the President at the instance of Apostle Taylor and Bishop Hunter; the tables, richly laden with nature's bounties, tastefully prepared, being set in a grove under a bowery on the banks of the river. "It was a rare sight indeed," says Wilford Woodruff, "to see a table so well spread with the 'good things of this life,' in the heart of the wilderness so remote from civilization. The bill of fare consisted of roast and broiled beef, pies, cakes, biscuit, butter, peach-sauce, coffee, tea, sugar, and a great variety of good things. Fully one hundred people sat down to the table. The remains of the feast were distributed among the soldiers and pioneers, and the ceremonies of the afternoon were concluded with a dance." Another council of the Apostles was held at this point, and other differences adjusted.

Next day Jedediah M. Grant's hundred was encountered. Captain Grant, who was recently from Philadelphia, informed the President that Senator Benton, of Missouri, like Saul of Tarsus, was still "breathing out threatenings and slaughter against the Saints." While on the Sweetwater, the pioneer party, allowing their usual vigilance to relax in the cheering society of their friends, had about thirty of their horses stolen by Indians. The emigrants at the same time lost about twenty head.

On the morning of September 21st, an exciting though bloodless affray occurred between the pioneers and a band of Sioux, who were trying to stampede their stock. It was just after breakfast, and the camp was getting ready to start. Being detected in their manœuvres, the Indians shot at several of the guards, and seizing one, attempted to carry him off. He freed himself with his fists, knocking one of the red-skins down. The rest sounded an alarm, and in a moment the scene was alive with savages, coming from the bluffs and timber near by. There were fully two hundred mounted warriors. Firing a volley, they charged upon the camp. Wilford Woodruff had already given warning, and he, with Heber C. Kimball, Colonel

Rockwood, Joseph Matthews and others sprang into their saddles, returned the Indian fire, and made a counter-charge, putting the savages to flight. Making signs of peace, the Sioux now returned and apologized to the pioneers for attacking them, claiming that they had mistaken them for Crows or Snakes, with whom they were at war. They wanted to smoke the pipe of peace with the leaders, and invited the President to visit their village, five miles away, where about eight hundred Sioux were encamped. It was not deemed prudent for the President to go, but Heber C. Kimball and a few others went instead, and smoked the calumet with the savages. They proved to be the same Indians who had stolen the horses on the Sweetwater. Through the courage and diplomacy of Apostle Kimball, many of the stolen horses were recovered.

At Fort Laramie the pioneer leaders dined, by invitation, with Commodore Stockton, who, with forty men, had just arrived from the Bay of San Francisco. The Commodore was described as a polite and affable gentleman. He purposed traveling from that point with President Young, but changed his plan and took the south side of the river. A few days later the pioneers heard that he had been attacked by Indians and one of his men killed.

Journeying down the Platte, over the road they had formerly traveled, the President's company, on the 18th of October, met Captain Hosea Stout and his mounted squad, coming to meet them. These were the old "Nauvoo Police," now the peace-officers of Winter Quarters. They were Hosea Stout, George D. Grant, G. J. Potter, William H. Kimball, Jacob Frazier, George W. Langley, W. J. Earl, W. Meeks, W. Martindale, William Huntington, Luman H. Calkins, James W. Cummings, S. S. Thornton, Levi Nickerson, James H. Glines and Chauncey Whiting. Messrs. Grant and Kimball had brought with them two wagons loaded with grain and provisions, of which the jaded company, which had been scantily provisioned from the start, now stood much in need. On the 30th they crossed the Elk Horn and were joined by Bishop Whitney and many others, with twenty wagons laden with supplies. Twenty-four hours later they marched in order into Winter Quarters, the streets of the town being lined with people waiting to welcome them.

Upon the mutual joy of husbands, wives, parents and children, meeting after such a separation, we need not dwell. Suffice it that during the absence of the pioneers, peace and prosperity had generally prevailed among their friends on the frontier. During the first few months, there had been much sickness and some deaths, but the atmosphere and climate, once so damp and sickly, were now much healthier, and the soil, being well tilled, had responded generously to the touch of the husbandman.

Returning now to the emigrants en route for Salt Lake Valley. It was in the latter part of September that the companies began arriving there. Early in October the last of the trains had reached the valley in safety.

A conference was held at the Fort on the 3rd of October. On that day the Stake organization previously provided for went into effect. Father John Smith was sustained as President of the Stake and Charles C. Rich and John Young as his counselors. A High Council was also organized, with the following named members: Henry G. Sherwood, Thomas Grover, Levi Jackman, John Murdock, Daniel Spencer, Lewis Abbott, Ira Eldredge, Edson Whipple, Shadrach Roundy, John Vance, Willard Snow and Abraham O. Smoot. Tarlton Lewis was chosen Bishop. Thus was organized the first Stake of Zion in the Rocky Mountains. A reorganization was effected after the return of the President from Winter Quarters.

The next arrivals in the Valley were from the west. They were members of the Mormon Battalion, recently mustered out of service in California. Soon after their discharge at Los Angeles, eighty-one of these volunteers, at the earnest solicitation of Governor Mason, previously mentioned, had re-enlisted for six months, and been ordered back to garrison San Diego. The main body started east, and hearing that the Pioneers had entered Salt Lake Valley directed their course thither. West of the Sierras they met Samuel Brannan and Captain James Brown, and learned from them that it was Pres-

ident Young's advice for such of the discharged soldiers as were without means to remain in California, work through the winter, and come on to the Valley with their earnings in the spring. Accordingly, about half the soldiers returned, some to secure employment at Sutter's Mills,* and to be heard from a little later in a way not dreamed of that September day, when they turned their faces westward and started back for the land of gold. The others continued on their way, arriving in Salt Lake Valley on the 16th of October. Two days later thirty-two of them, including Serjeant Daniel Tyler,† set out for the Missouri river, braving the dangerous prospect of wintry storms and blockading snows in their anxiety to join their families on the frontier. After much hardship and suffering they reached their destination on the 18th of December.

The Battalion men, returning from California, brought to the Valley wheat, corn, potatoes and garden seeds. Subsequently some of the settlers visited the coast and returned bringing more seeds and live stock. Soon afterward trade was opened up with Fort Hall,‡ and a little later with the frontier states.

As winter drew near, the colonists, having finished their late sowing, moved into the stockade to await the coming spring. The fort was now enclosed, the east side with log houses, and on the north, south and west with adobe walls. Two additional blocks, or parts of blocks, on the south were being enclosed in like manner by the newly arrived immigrants, whom the original fort could not accommodate. Meanwhile, many were living in tents and wagons. The additions were merely extensions of the first stockade, with which they communicated by gates. There was a large gate on the east, which was kept carefully closed by night. The roofs of the

---

* Now Coloma, El Dorado County, California.

† Author of the valuable and interesting "History of the Mormon Battalion."

‡ Captain Grant of Fort Hall, was the first person outside the Mormon community who brought goods to the Utah market for sale. He sold sugar and coffee at one dollar a pint, calicoes at 50 and 75 cents per yard, and other articles in proportion. *Deseret News* Sept. 28, 1854.

houses, or huts, all slanted inward. The doors and windows faced the interior, but each house had a small loop-hole looking out. The houses last erected were in some respects superior to the first, though even the best of them were poor. The mistake of making the roofs almost flat, instead of sharply slanting, eventually caused much discomfort. The fore part of the winter was exceptionally mild, but as the season advanced, heavy snows fell, then melted, and soaking through the dirt and willow roofs, descended in drizzling streams upon the heads, beds and larders of the miserable inmates; spoiling at once their tempers and their provisions. Apostle Taylor, whose house was one of the best,—having among other superior points a rough, whip-sawed plank floor,—had plastered the ceiling and walls with white clay, a fine quality of which was found in the neighborhood. But alas! the merciless water trickled through all the same, carrying with it in solution or in lumps the treacherous plastering. Umbrellas were in great demand, even while in bed, and it was no uncommon sight to see a good housewife bending over her stove, upon which the drops from above unceasingly dripped and sizzled, holding an umbrella in her left hand, while turning a beef-steak or stirring a mush-kettle with her right. The situation of the fort-dwellers, that season, though often ludicrous, was far from pleasant, and at times almost pitiable; quite so, indeed, where there was sickness, and a lack of needed shelter.

Other causes of discomfort were swarms of vermin,—mice, bed-bugs, etc.—infesting the fort. The bugs were indigenous, being brought in the green timber from the mountains. The mice were also "native and to the manor born" though some may have been carried to the Valley in the grain wagons of the immigrants. Great white wolves also prowled around the fort, making night hideous with their howling, and attacking cattle on the range. So intolerable became this nuisance that hunting parties were finally organized, to make war upon the wolves and other wild-beasts. Their depredations then gradually grew less. As for the vermin, they were dealt with according to the best approved exterminating methods

then in vogue. Cats, if good mousers, were in high favor,—quite as much so as umbrellas.

It was probably owing to these discomforts that Lorenzo D. Young—ever on the lookout to better his own or his friends' condition—as early as October sold his house in the fort, and having built a new log cabin on City Creek, north-east of the stockade, in December moved into it with his family.* Their leaving the fort was much against the wishes of their friends, who feared that they might be killed by Indians. "I'll risk that, and no one but myself shall be responsible," said "Uncle Lorenzo," and off to his new home went.

An incident occurred that winter which probably convinced him that the anxiety for his safety felt by his friends at the fort was not entirely groundless. It also illustrates the coolness and courage possessed by those early heroines, the pioneer women of Utah. It happened thus: Harriet Young was sitting with her infant child† in their solitary home one day,—her husband and the rest of the family being absent,—when an Indian came to the door and asked for "biscuit." He was a fierce, ill-looking fellow, known throughout the region as "a bad Indian." Mrs. Young, going to her humble larder, gave the savage two of three small biscuits—all the bread that she had in the house. He took them and asked for more. She gave him the remaining one, but still he demanded more. More she did not have, and so informed him. Furious he advanced, and fitting an arrow to his bow, aimed it at her heart, fiercely repeating the request. Cool and collected the brave woman faced her swarthy foe, and for a moment thought that her last hour and that of her helpless babe had come. Not yet. An idea strikes her. In the

---

* This humble abode, which was on the site now occupied by the Bee-Hive House, was the first building erected outside the fort in Salt Lake Valley. The first tree planted by the Pioneers still stands in the yard of the Bee Hive House. It is a locust, and was planted by Harriet P. Young.

† Lorenzo Dow Young, junior, born September 20th, 1847,—the first white male child born in Utah.

next room, securely fastened, is a large dog, a powerful mastiff, purchased by her husband on leaving the fort, and kept upon the premises for just such emergencies as the danger now threatening. Making a sign to the savage, as of compliance with his request, she passed into the next room, and hastily untying the dog, exclaimed "seize him." Like lightning the mastiff darted through the doorway, and a shriek of terror, quickly followed by a howl of pain, as the sharp canine teeth met in the red-skin's thigh, told how well the faithful brute comprehended his mistress' peril, and the duty required of him in her defense. In all probability, the Indian, prostrate and pleading vociferously for his life, would never again have risen, had not our heroine, in whose generous heart pity for the vanquished wretch at once took the place of the just anger she had momentarily felt, after prudently relieving him of his bow and arrow, called off the dog and set the wounded savage at liberty. He was badly hurt, and cried bitterly. Mrs. Young magnanimously washed the wound, applied a large sticking plaster to the injured part, and sent him away a wiser if not a better Indian.

But the settlers of Salt Lake Valley were not much molested by the red men. Other settlements, formed later, fared worse. Fierce, at times, were the fights of the savages among themselves. One of the customs in vogue with them was to torture and kill, if they could not sell, their prisoners of war. Several Indian children were ransomed, the first winter, by settlers at the fort, to save them from being shot or tortured to death by their merciless captors. One of these, a girl, was purchased by Charles Decker, who gave her to his sister, Clara D. Young, by whom she was civilized and reared to womanhood.

Owing to the mildness of the first winter in the valley, logging, building and exploring were continued at intervals until spring. The heaviest snows fell in March, after the spring plowing had begun. During December, Parley P. Pratt and others went on horseback to Utah Lake, taking with them a boat and fish-net in a wagon drawn by oxen. At the foot of the lake they launched their boat and began

fishing. It was believed by Parley that these were "probably the first boat and net ever used on this sheet of water in modern times." They took a few trout and other fish, but on the whole met with poor success piscatorially. Having explored a day or two in that vicinity, most of the party returned, but Parley and a man named Summers remained. Striking westward from the foot of Utah Lake they partly explored Cedar Valley, afterwards the site of Camp Floyd, then passed over the mountains and through Rush and Tooele valleys. Continuing on to the Salt Lake, they turned eastward, crossed the Jordan and came home. So passed away the first winter of the pioneer settlers in Salt Lake Valley.

CHAPTER XX.
1847-1849.

FOUNDING NEW SETTLEMENTS—BRIGHAM YOUNG AS A COLONIZER—DAVIS COUNTY OCCUPIED—THE GOODYEAR PURCHASE—THE CRICKET PLAGUE—SAVED BY THE GULLS—DAYS OF FAMINE—THE FIRST HARVEST FEAST—HOW GOLD WAS DISCOVERED IN CALIFORNIA—IMMIGRATION OF 1848—MATTERS SPIRITUAL AND TEMPORAL.—LANDS DISTRIBUTED TO THE SETTLERS—THE FIRST UTAH CURRENCY—MORE APOSTLES ORDAINED—THE STAKE ORGANIZED—SALT LAKE CITY DIVIDED INTO BISHOPS' WARDS.

ALMOST the first steps taken by the pioneer colony in 1848 were toward the founding of additional settlements. Indeed, before the new year dawned movements had been made in that direction.

As Brigham Young had predicted, the day after entering the Valley, when organizing his exploring parties to traverse the surrounding region in quest of eligible sites for other settlements, no place so suitable for their chief city had been found or was destined to be discovered by those explorers in all their subsequent wanderings and searchings. And yet the pioneer leader had made that prediction intuitively, not from any previous acquaintance with this region; had made it, too, in the very face of reports received from experienced mountaineers, men thoroughly familiar with the country,—reports uniformly adverse to Salt Lake Valley as a place in which to plant a colony, and all favoring other localities. But Brigham Young knew better. The reports of the Fremonts, the Harrises and the Bridgers were nothing to him, when once his eye had rested upon the scene and surveyed the situation. Here was a place for a great city, and he knew it, and his "oracular soul" told him that in all this inter-mountain region no other place so suitable was to be found.

It is said that the great Napoleon, at the very beginning of a battle, as with the instinct of Mars himself, was able almost invariably to foretell the outcome; and that on one occasion, at least, before the battle had fairly joined, he scribbled upon his saddle-bow a dispatch reading: "Victory is ours," and sent it off post-haste to Paris and Josephine. Brigham Young's victories were of peace, not of war, yet there was something Napoleonic in his genius,—in his marvelous intuition and foresight.

The fact is, Brigham Young was a born colonizer,—as much so, perhaps, as Napoleon was a born warrior; one of the greatest colonizers that the world has seen; a builder of cities, a founder of empire, second to none in the annals of the ages. This is not flattery. The world, sometimes slow, but always sure at last to open its eyes to the truth, will one day acknowledge it. The broad-minded and intelligent, whose attention has been drawn to the subject, recognize it already. Even bigotry will follow suit some day. Men may not credit, as Brigham Young did, as his people still do, divine inspiration with his success; for he always maintained that Mormonism made him, that it made Joseph Smith, and not they Mormonism. But men will yet acknowledge, far more widely than they now do, and impartial history, whose page is the past and present, but whose pen is the future, will yet record that Brigham Young was a great man, one of Time's greatest, and that genius, if not divinity, was manifest in his methods and achievements.

A man may have faults, and yet be great, as water may be clear though holding soil in solution; as the sun may have spots, and yet supremely shine. Brigham Young had his faults, as Washington, as Lincoln and Grant had theirs. But if greatness were denied to men because of their defects,—those shadows that form the back-ground of the most brilliant picture,—who of all men, save One, would be great? The incident referred to, though a mere straw in the wind, serving to show its direction, will illustrate in part the intuition and foresight of which Brigham Young was undoubtedly the possessor.

Salt Lake Valley was indeed, as he declared, the best place for a city—a metropolis—in all this inter-mountain region. The whole world knows it now. But there were other places in the vicinity, as he also declared, possessing every facility of situation, soil, climate and surroundings, for the formation of thriving settlements, and of future flourishing towns and cities. True, most of them were then barren and desolate, cheerless and forbidding in the extreme; but the sagacious eye saw past all this, and the future became present to its gaze. A few spots there were that were even then promising; where water was not so scarce, where verdure sprang spontaneously and the soil was naturally fertile. Among these were some of the lands now included in Davis County, and the Goodyear lands on the Weber, where the next settlements of our Territory were formed. Both these sections are comprised in a narrow alluvial strip lying between the western base of the Wasatch Mountains and the eastern shore of the Great Salt Lake. In fact those lands are a portion, a mere extension northward of Salt Lake Valley.

Peregrine Sessions, the original pioneer of Davis County—next to Salt Lake County the first part of Utah occupied and settled,—was, as we have seen, a captain of fifty in Daniel Spencer's hundred; the very vanguard of the migrating trains that began arriving in Salt Lake Valley in the latter part of September, 1847. On the 28th of that month, a few days after reaching the valley, Mr. Sessions moved northward about ten miles and camped that night about half a mile from the spot where he now resides, and where sprang up Sessions' Settlement, since called Bountiful. Hector C. Haight, following Captain Sessions' example, camped six or seven miles north of him, on what was afterwards known as Haight's Creek, a little south-west of the present site of Kaysville. This was also in the latter part of 1847. There may have been others who moved into that section about the same time. Such was the beginning of the settlement of Davis County.

The object of these men in separating themselves so early from the society of their friends at the pioneer fort—the immediate object at least—was to find pasturage for their stock, the range of the

Jordan Valley being inadequate for all the cattle of the immigrants. These cattle, some of which had to be killed at once for beef, were almost worn to skeletons by their long pilgrimage over the plains. So literally was this the case that one of the new-comers,—who was no other than Apostle John Taylor,—while sawing up one of these bony, juiceless beeves for the winter, remarked with grim humor to his assistant, Captain Joseph Horne, that he guessed they would "have to grease the saw to make it work." But though pasturing stock was the original purpose of the pioneers of Davis County, it was not the only one. At all events, though they did little else than herd cattle and horses through the winter, they began to till the ground the following spring, and thus formed the nuclei of some of the present flourishing settlements in that vicinity.

It was in March, 1848, that Peregrine Sessions, assisted by Jezreel Shoemaker, broke the first ground in Davis County for agricultural purposes. Later, came into the county at various times such men as Thomas Grover, Daniel Wood, A. B. Cherry, Anson Call, Daniel C. Davis, John Stoker, Joseph Holbrook, Nathan T. Porter, the Smiths, the Parrishes, the Duels, the Millers, William Kay, Christopher Layton and many others to be mentioned hereafter. Davis County was named for Captain Daniel C. Davis, of the Mormon Battalion, commander of the re-enlisted volunteers, a portion of whom, being disbanded at San Diego in March, 1848, rejoined their people in Salt Lake Valley in June. Captain Davis settled on a creek a little south of the present town of Farmington.

And now as to the inception of Weber County, the nucleus of which—speaking of its settlement by white men—antedates by several years either Davis or Salt Lake County. The greater part of the lands now comprised in Weber County were owned, or claimed, in 1847 by Miles M. Goodyear, whose name has more than once been mentioned in these pages. He was a protege, it is said, of Captain Grant, a well known, eccentric character of those days, representing the Hudson's Bay Company at Fort Hall. Goodyear claimed the Weber lands by virtue of a grant from the Mexican government made to him in 1841. His claim was particularly described as follows: Beginning at the mouth of Weber Canyon, and following the base of the mountains north to the Hot Springs, thence westward to the Great Salt Lake, southward along the shore of the lake to a point opposite Weber Canyon, and thence to the point of beginning. Its extent is said to have been twenty miles square. This tract, at that time, was one of the most desirable spots in all this region. On these lands Goodyear had built a picket fort, enclosing a few log cabins, situated on the right bank of the Weber, about two miles above the junction of that stream with the Ogden river. Having established himself as a trapper and trader he was there living with his Indian family, and a few mountaineers and half-breeds, when the pioneers entered Salt Lake Valley.*

It has been related how Captain James Brown, on his way to San Francisco in August, 1847, called at the Goodyear Fort and became acquainted with its proprietor. Goodyear's principal reason for offering his place for sale,—as he is said to have done soon afterwards,—was his lack of success in farming. It was also due, no doubt, to the advent of local immigration, which would necessarily interfere with his success in trapping. As soon as Captain Brown returned from the coast, the purchase of the Goodyear lands, improvements and live stock was by him negotiated and effected.

The Captain returned to the Valley some time in December, 1847. He brought with him from San Francisco $10,000 in Spanish doubloons, most if not all of it the amount received from the U. S. Paymaster for the men of his detachment. This was the first money put in circulation among the Mormon colonists, save perhaps a few coins remaining to them after purchasing the outfits with which they had crossed the plains. Captain Brown was accompanied

---

* The Goodyear Fort was situated near a large sand mound, still visible, about half a mile south-west of the Union Railway Depot in Ogden.

Most of the mountaineers living in the west had squaws. Barney Ward, well remembered by the early settlers of Salt Lake Valley, was dwelling with his Indian family in this region when the pioneers arrived.

on his return by his son Jesse, Abner Blackburn and Lysander Woodworth, of the party who had gone with him from the Valley, and by Samuel Lewis, a member of the Battalion, who joined them at Sutter's Fort. The rest of his party remained in California. Threading the Truckee Pass, at the foot of which so many of the Donner party had miserably perished, and taking the Hastings Cut-Off, the Captain and his party accomplished the hazardous winter journey in safety. Immediately on his return he entered into or concluded negotiations with the proprietor of the Goodyear lands, and late in December, or early in January, 1848, purchased them for the sum of $3,000.

It has more than once been published that this purchase was made on the 6th of June of that year, and that a part of the amount brought by Captain Brown from California was in gold dust. We have it on the authority of the Captain's sons, Jesse, Alexander, William and Moroni, that January and not June was the time. Jesse and Alexander, who accompanied their father when he first took up his abode on the Weber, state positively that the snow was on the ground,—which would hardly be the case in June,—and that they "kept bachelor's hall at the fort all winter." This being so, and Captain Brown's returning from the coast in December, 1847, renders highly improbable the statement that he brought any gold dust with him; as gold was not discovered in California until January, 1848. Whether or not the Goodyear purchase was made at the suggestion of President Young—who was then at Winter Quarters—it was manifestly in perfect keeping, as was the occupation of the Davis County lands, with the grand colonizing scheme of the pioneer President, as foreshadowed in his instructions to the explorers in July, 1847.

In about a month after the purchase of the Goodyear tract the treaty of Guadalupe Hidalgo was signed—February 2nd, 1848—and the vast region now known as California, Nevada, Utah, New Mexico and Arizona, previously Mexican territory, was ceded to the United States. The terms of the treaty, it was expected, would confirm

Captain Brown's title to the Goodyear lands, but for some reason it was not recognized, and the Federal Government, many years later, ignored the claim, assumed ownership of the lands,* gave to the Union Pacific Railway on its subsidy each alternate section of the tract, and required the old settlers, including Captain Brown's immediate descendants, to re-purchase the homes and farms that they had held for two decades. The inference is that Government, not purposely oppressive and unjust, did not regard the grant to Goodyear from Mexico as valid. Similar cases occurred in California.

In the spring of 1848, Captain Brown, his sons and hired help, went to work with a will on the Weber, plowing and sowing a few acres with wheat, the seed of which he had brought with him from California. He also planted corn, potatoes, cabbage, turnips, and water-melons. A man named Wells, who had formerly dwelt at the fort, told the Browns, as Goodyear had previously told them, that their crops would not mature. The frost, he said, would kill the corn about the time it began silking,—at least such had been his experience as a farmer in that region. Nothing daunted, they went on putting in their crops, and in due time reaped a goodly harvest. Jesse S. Brown, the Captain's eldest son, today wears a medal for plowing the first furrow in Weber County. Mary Black, the Captain's wife, was the pioneer cheese-maker of Utah. While awaiting their first harvest they procured supplies of flour from Fort Hall. And thus was laid the foundation of Weber County.

Other Mormon settlers soon followed the Browns to that locality. Retaining but two or three hundred acres of his immense purchase for himself, the Captain generously allowed his brethren to settle on the tract, and would take no pay from them for the lands they built upon and cultivated. The Farrs, Canfields, Moores, Brownings, Wests, Shurtliffs, Herricks, Peerys, Richardses and other representative Weber County families,—too numerous to mention here, but all

---

*Fort Bridger, purchased of its proprietors by Brigham Young in 1853, shared a similar fate. Bridger had claimed the property by virtue of a Mexican grant, which claim, in Brigham Young, the United States government ignored.

of whom shall receive due notice at the proper time,—eventually took up their abode in the county, and helped to make it what it is today. Lorin Farr, who has before been mentioned, though not the pioneer of Weber County, was the virtual founder of Ogden, Utah's second city, of which he was the first Mayor, many times re-elected.

The opening of the spring of 1848 in Great Salt Lake City saw nearly seventeen hundred souls dwelling in upwards of four hundred log and adobe huts inside the "Old Fort." Over five thousand acres of land had been brought under cultivation, nearly nine hundred of which had been sown with winter wheat, the tender blades of which were now beginning to sprout.* A few months more and the settlers, whose breadstuffs and provisions of all kinds were getting quite low, and would just about last, with due economy, until harvest-time, would be rejoicing with their friends in the north in reaping and partaking of their first harvest in the Rocky Mountains.

But now came a visitation as terrible as it was totally unexpected. It was the cricket plague. In May and June of that year myriads of these destructive pests, an army of famine and despair, rolled in black legions down the mountain sides and attacked the fields of growing grain.† The tender crops fell an easy prey to their fierce voracity. They literally swept everything before them. Starvation with all its terrors seemed staring the poor settlers in the face. In the northern sections the situation was much the same, though at Brownville, on the Weber, the ravages of the crickets were not so great.

With the energy of desperation, the community, men, women and children, thoroughly alarmed, marshaled themselves to fight and if possible repel the rapacious foe. While some went through the

---
* To be exact, there were 1671 souls, 423 houses, 5133 acres of cultivated land, and 875 acres sown with winter wheat.

† Says Anson Call: "The Rocky Mountain cricket, as now remembered, when full grown, is about one-and-a-half inches in length, heavy and clumsy in its movements, with no better power of locomotion than hopping a foot or two at a time. It has an eagle-eyed, staring appearance, and suggests the idea that it may be the habitation of a vindictive little demon."

fields killing the crickets, and at the same time, alas! crushing much of the tender grain, others dug ditches around the farms, turned water into the trenches, and drove and drowned therein myriads of the black devourers. Others beat them back with clubs and brooms, or burned them in fires set in the fields. Still they could not prevail. Too much headway had been gained by the crickets before the gravity of the situation was discovered, and in spite of all that the settlers could do, their hopes of a harvest were fast vanishing, and with those hopes the very hope of life.

They were saved, they believed, by a miracle,—just such a miracle as, according to classic tradition, saved ancient Rome, when the cackling of geese roused the slumbering city in time to beat back the invading Gauls.* In the midst of the work of destruction, when it seemed as if nothing could stay the devastation, great flocks of gulls appeared, filling the air with their white wings and plaintive cries, and settled down upon the half-ruined fields. At first it seemed as if they came but to destroy what the crickets had left. But their real purpose was soon apparent. They came to prey upon the destroyers. All day long they gorged themselves, and when full, disgorged and feasted again, the white gulls upon the black crickets, like hosts of heaven and hell contending, until the pests were vanquished, and the people were saved. The heaven-sent birds then returned to the lake islands whence they came, leaving the grateful people to shed tears of joy at the wonderful and timely deliverance wrought out for them.

Is it strange that among the early acts of Utah's legislators there should be a law making the wanton killing of these birds a

---

* This event is said to have occurred in the year 390, B. C. The Gauls were invading Roman territory, and had inflicted a disastrous defeat upon the Romans just outside the city. Marius Manlius, at the head of a handful of his countrymen, held the citadel against the barbarians, but according to the legend had neglected to place sentinels to warn him against a night attack. A few of the geese, considered holy by the Romans, had been spared by the famishing soldiers, and during the siege the Gauls determined upon a night attack. They were advancing toward the citadel, when the geese, alarmed at their approach, set up a cackling and aroused the defenders, who drove off the besiegers.

punishable offense? Rome once had her sacred geese. Utah would henceforth have her sacred gulls. Ye statesmen and state-makers of the future! When Utah's sovereign star, dawning above the dark horizon of factional strife, shall take its place in the blue, unclouded zenith of freedom's empyrean, and it is asked by those who would frame her escutcheon, What shall her emblem be? Name not at all the carpet-bag. Place not first the beehive, nor the eagle; nor yet the miner's pick, the farmer's plow, nor the smoke-stack of the wealth-producing smelter. Give these their places, all, in dexter or in middle, but whatever else the glittering shield contains, reserve for the honor point, as worthy of all praise, the sacred bird that saved the pioneers.

And barely saved them, too, for even as it was, there was famine in Utah before another year. This was largely owing to the crickets, but was due also to drought and frost. These mishaps, with the coming of the fall immigration, depending upon the settlers for much of their support, rendered the harvest wholly inadequate, and caused much inconvenience and some suffering before another crop could be raised. During the days, or rather months of scarcity, such as had food put themselves and their families upon rations, while those who were without or had but little, dug sego and thistle roots, and cooked and ate raw-hides to eke out their scanty store. Wild vegetation of various kinds was used for "greens" by the half-famished people, many of whom went for weeks without tasting bread. The raw-hides were boiled and converted into a gelatinous soup, which was drank with eager relish. The straitness began to be felt even before the crickets came, and after that event, owing to the prevailing scarcity, the arrival of the fall immigration was looked forward to with positive apprehension.*

---

* "During this spring and summer," says Parley P. Pratt, "my family and myself, in common with many of the camp, suffered much for want of food. * * * We had lost nearly all our cows, and the few which were spared to us were dry. * * * I had ploughed and subdued land to the amount of near forty acres. * * * I nthis labor every woman and child in my family, so far as they were of sufficient age and

Before the worst of those days arrived, however, on August 10th, 1848, the glad settlers celebrated with a feast their first harvest home. It was quite a grand affair with them. In the center of the fort a bowery had been erected, and underneath its shade, tables were spread richly and bounteously laden. Bread and beef, butter and cheese, cakes and pastry, green corn, water-melons and vegetables of nearly every variety composed the feast. For once at least, that season, the hungry people had enough to eat. Says Parley P. Pratt: "Large sheaves of wheat, rye, barley, oats and other productions were hoisted on poles for public exhibition, and there was prayer and thanksgiving, congratulations, songs, speeches, music, dancing, smiling faces and merry hearts. In short it was a great day with the people of these valleys, and long to be remembered by those who had suffered and waited anxiously for the results of a first effort to redeem the interior deserts of America."

The fort now contained eighteen hundred inhabitants; the increase since March being due to the arrival from the west of several parties of the disbanded Mormon volunteers. They returned laden with gold-dust from the California mines.* The discovery of the precious metal west of the Sierras being due to the labor of Utah men, it is but proper to give here a brief account of that very important event.

It has already been related that in September, 1847, a party of the discharged Battalion men, on their way to Salt Lake Valley, met, east of the Sierras, Captain James Brown and Samuel Brannan, and that a portion of the soldiers, pursuant to advice sent them by President Young, turned back to obtain work for the winter in California. These men, about forty in number, secured employment

---

strength, had joined to help me, and had toiled incessantly in the field, suffering every hardship which human nature could well endure. Myself and some of them were compelled to go with bare feet for several months, reserving our Indian moccasins for extra occasions. We toiled hard and lived on a few greens, and on the thistle and other roots."

with them two brass cannon purchased for $512 and used as a means of protection against hostile Indians.

at Sutter's Fort, the proprietor of which, Captain John A. Sutter, was just then in need of help for the erection of a flour-mill and a saw-mill. A site for the flour-mill was selected near the fort, and most of the men were put to work thereon. But the saw-mill had to be built among the mountains, in the little valley of Coloma, forty-five miles away. To that place Sutter sent ten men, one of whom was his partner, James W. Marshall, who superintended the erection of the mill. The other nine worked under him. Of these, six were Mormons and late members of the Battalion. Their names were Alexander Stephens, James S. Brown, James Barger, William Johnston, Azariah Smith and Henry W. Bigler. The other three were non-Mormons, who had been more or less associated with the Saints since the days of Nauvoo. They were Peter Wimmer, William Scott and Charles Bennett. Sutter also employed about a dozen Indians. For four months these men labored at Coloma, and the saw-mill was approaching completion. Late in January, 1848, the water was turned into the race to carry away some loose dirt and gravel. It was then turned off, and the superintendent, Mr. Marshall, walked along the tail-race to ascertain the extent of some slight damage that had been done by the water near the base of the building. While pursuing his investigation, his eye caught sight of some yellow metallic particles on the rotten granite bed-rock of the race. He picked up several of them, the largest of which were about the size of wheat grains. He believed—but did not know—that they were gold. Subsequently they were assayed, and the fact of the great discovery was verified.

The first record of the finding of the gold was made by Henry W. Bigler, a Mormon,—now a citizen of St. George, Utah. To him, among the first, Marshall announced his discovery. A diary note in Bigler's journal, made on the same day, runs as follows:

"Monday, 24th. This day some kind of metal was found in the tail-race that looks like gold."

Another note of January 30th, which was Sunday, reads: "Clear, and has been all the last week. Our metal has been tried and proves to be gold. It is thought to be rich. We have picked up more than a hundred dollars' worth last week."

Thus was originally chronicled the world-renowned discovery at Coloma. Henry W. Bigler, of St George, Azariah Smith, of Manti, in Utah; and Peter L. Wimmer, of San Diego, California, are today the three survivors of the party of workmen whose picks and shovels first brought to light the auriferous wealth of California.

Meantime on the far-off frontier, President Young and his associates, early in 1848, had set about organizing the main body of their people prior to leading them to the Rocky Mountains. On the 27th of the previous December, at a conference of the Saints held in a new log tabernacle on the east side of the Missouri, the First Presidency—vacant since the death of Joseph Smith—had been reorganized. Brigham Young was now President of the Church of Jesus Christ of Latter-day Saints in all the world, and Heber C. Kimball and Willard Richards were his Counselors.* This event was supplemented by preparations for a general emigration in the spring. Still it was desirable to maintain, for the benefit of future emigration, an out-fitting post on the frontier. Winter Quarters was soon to be vacated, but the Legislature of Iowa granted a petition for the organization of Pottowatomie County—east of the river—and there, on the site where stood their historic Log Tabernacle, the Mormons built the town of Kanesville, a few miles above the present city of Council Bluffs. Kanesville became for several years a point of outfit and departure for Mormon emigration. Their companies from Europe by way of New Orleans would now steam up the Mississippi and the Missouri to Kanesville. The first company to follow this river route was one led by Franklin D. Richards. It sailed from Liverpool in February, 1848, and reached Winter Quarters some time before the early summer emigration started across the plains.

It was about the beginning of June that the First Presidency

---

*This action was pursuant to a decision of the Council of the Apostles made on the 5th of December.

broke up their camp on the Elk Horn, and again set out for the Valley of the Great Salt Lake. First went Brigham Young, with a company of 1229 souls and 397 wagons; next, Heber C. Kimball, whose trains numbered 662 souls and 226 wagons. Willard Richards brought up the rear, with 526 souls and 169 wagons. The last wagon left Winter Quarters on the 3rd of July. That place was now nearly deserted.

Along with this large emigration went such notables as Daniel H. Wells, who, having joined the Church at Nauvoo in August, 1846, had left the city with the expelled remnant of his people and joined the main body in their prairie homes; Lorenzo Snow, who had figured in the British Mission before the Prophet's death, and was now fast rising to prominence; Franklin D. Richards, of whom that mission had also heard and was destined to hear much more; Joseph F. Smith, who, however, was only a lad of nine years, in the care of his heroic mother, Mary Fielding Smith, who, with other Mormon women of that period, drove her own ox-team wagon across the plains. Bishop Newel K. Whitney also accompanied this emigration, which carried with it such notable women as his wife, Elizabeth Ann Whitney, Vilate Kimball and Mary Ann Angell Young. Robert T. Burton, George D. Grant, William Kay, Phineas Richards, Horace S. Eldredge, Hosea Stout and others who became prominent or well known in Utah history were also included.

Brigham Young had general command of all the companies, and Daniel H. Wells was his aide-de-camp. Horace S. Eldredge was marshal, and Hosea Stout captain of the night-guard. Amasa M. Lyman, Erastus Snow and other prominent men who had returned with the President from the Valley, now went back with him, having charge of various sub-divisions of the emigration. Several of the Apostles remained at Kanesville; some to go upon missions, and some to superintend Mormon affairs on the frontier. One of these was Orson Hyde, who had not yet been to the Valley, and still tarried behind to transact important business for the Church. A few months after the President's departure, Apostle Hyde began the publication, at Kanesville, of a semi-monthly paper called the *Frontier Guardian*.*

On went the emigration, crossing the plains and the Rocky Mountains along the same route formerly traveled by the Pioneers. President Young, with a portion of his division, reached Salt Lake Valley on the 20th of September. Heber C. Kimball came a few days later, and within another month the trains had all arrived.

President Richards' companies lost many of their cattle through the alkali on the Sweetwater. This so hindered his progress that teams from the Valley had to be sent out to help in the rear trains.

Immediately after the President's arrival a conference was called to convene on the 8th of October. This conference, which was held in the Fort Bowery, ratified the action of the Apostles and the main body of the Saints on the frontier, relative to the reorganization of the First Presidency. Newel K. Whitney was sustained as Presiding Bishop of the Church, and John Smith was appointed its Patriarch. This caused a vacancy in the Stake Presidency, which Charles C. Rich was chosen to fill; John Young and Erastus Snow were his counselors.

These spiritual matters attended to, the temporal needs of the colony came in for their share of thought and labor. The recent immigration, which aggregated nearly 2500 souls, had swelled the population in the valley to between four and five thousand. These people must be housed and fed through the winter. How, was the problem facing the Mormon leaders that fall, as the signs of a long and unusually severe winter began to show themselves. More houses might be built, for the materials were at hand, and before the heavy snows fell the number of huts might be materially increased. Some of the families could make shift with their wagons until spring. But where was the food to come from,—the loaves and fishes to feed these five thousand? The immigrants had not all brought sufficient,

---

* The first number of this paper was issued February 7th, 1849.

and the valley harvest, upon which they had largely depended, had measurably failed. Thus the food question was the principal problem, and before it was fully solved, there had been much suffering and privation in the Valley by the Lake.

It was during these days of scarcity, when the half-starved, half-clad settlers hardly knew where to look for the next crust of bread, or for rags to hide their nakedness,—for clothing had become almost as scarce with them as breadstuffs,*—that Heber C. Kimball, in a public meeting, declared to the astonished congregation that it would not be three years before "States goods" would be sold in Salt Lake Valley cheaper than in the eastern cities. The astonishment of his hearers was not based upon any expectation that this prediction would or could be realized. Rather were they astounded at the seemingly preposterous statement. "I don't believe a word of it," said Charles C. Rich, and he but expressed the sentiments of nineteen-twentieths of the congregation. President Kimball, after a moment's reflection, rather doubted the prediction himself. And yet, as we shall see, it was literally fulfilled, and in a manner totally unanticipated.

During 1848 various improvements for the public benefit were planned and effected in Salt Lake Valley and the vicinity. Roads were constructed in divers directions, and bridges thrown across the Jordan River and several of the mountain streams. A bath house was also erected at the Warm Springs. To defray the expense of some of these improvements the roadmaster—Daniel Spencer—was authorized to levy a poll and property tax; the rate of the latter being one per cent. Most of the assessments were paid in labor on the roads. In October a Council House was projected, to be built by donation, or labor-tithing. Daniel H. Wells was appointed to superintend its construction. Grist-mills and saw-mills had been and were being erected on City Creek, Mill Creek and other streams, water being the motive power used. Some of this machinery had

---

* "Nearly every man was dressed in skins."—Heber C. Kimball.

come with the first immigration and was in operation during the following spring and summer. More machinery for milling, and some for carding; also printing presses, type, and other materials of "the art preservative," were brought in the immigration of 1848. Among the pioneer mill-builders may be mentioned Charles Crismon, Isaac Chase, John Neff, Samuel Thompson, Archibald and Robert Gardner.

During the autumn the city lots were given out to the settlers, and when all had been distributed, others were laid out in extensions to the original plat, and allotted in like manner. A vast field of eight thousand acres was surveyed south of and bordering upon the city, plotted in five and ten-acre fields and distributed by lot to the people. Each man was to help build a fence around the "Big Field," and construct a canal along the east side for irrigating purposes. These lands were not sold, but given, as in the first instance when the Apostles selected their "inheritances." But a small fee was required from each holder to pay the surveyor.

Before winter set in, some of the people began leaving the fort and moving out upon their city lots. Most of them, however, remained in the stockade until spring. They then took their houses with them—such of the domiciles as were portable—and set them down, according to rule, in or near the centers of their lots. Thus as the city grew the fort began to disappear, and soon there was little left of it but a few adobe walls to show where once it stood.

The lack of a circulating medium among the settlers had long been felt. The inconvenience of buying wheat with corn, and paying for pigs in chickens, is apparent. The advent of gold-dust, much of which was brought by the Battalion men and others from California, had put an end to much of this embarrassment, and yet bags of gold-dust were not the most convenient money in the world. To obviate the trouble, pending the procuring of a stamp wherewith to coin some of the precious metal now becoming so abundant, a paper currency was issued in January, 1849. The first bill—one dollar—bore the signatures of Brigham Young, Heber C. Kimball and

HISTORY OF UTAH. 387

Thomas Bullock. The first type-setting in Salt Lake Valley—by Brigham Young and Thomas Bullock—was for this primitive Utah currency. Some months later $2.50, $5, $10 and $20 gold pieces were coined in a mint temporarily established by the Mormons. These coins, which were improvised purely for local use, bore no resemblance to the Government coins. They were of unalloyed, virgin gold, and as fast as they were superseded by legal money were disposed of as bullion to the Federal mints.*

The winter of 1848-9, unlike its predecessor, was uncommonly severe. Heavy snows and violent winds prevailed, and the weather, from the 1st of December until late in February, was extremely cold. The coldest day was the 5th of February, when the mercury fell to 33° F. below zero. An inventory of breadstuffs taken early that month showed about three-fourths of a pound per day for each soul in the Valley, until the beginning of July. The pressure of the famine was severely felt, but the community generally shared alike, and extreme suffering was thus prevented. The earth that season yielded abundantly, and the famine again was staid.

Early in February the Church authorities resumed the task of perfecting the ecclesiastical organization. In December fellowship had been withdrawn from Apostle Lyman Wight and Bishop George Miller, who had previously separated from the Church, refusing to longer follow its destinies.† Four vacancies now existed in the council of the Twelve. They were filled on February 12th, 1849, by

* The veteran jeweler, J. M. Barlow, senior, of Salt Lake City, contributes this: "The first dies, consisting of a $2.50, a $5 and a $20 piece, were made by John Kay and an old blacksmith, but were very crude. At the request of Governor Young I had made in my office by Dougal Brown, a set of dies for $5 pieces, and for a number of years (until Governor Cumming ordered its discontinuance) I refined the gold and coined it into money. If I do say so myself, it was as perfect a piece of money as ever came from any mint. I also made the first and only solid silver spoons ever made in Utah, and the silver cups now in use in the administration of the sacrament at the Tabernacle."

† During November, 1848, at far-off Kanesville, Oliver Cowdery came back into the Church, to die in the Mormon faith a few months later, but never to reach the Rocky Mountains.

the calling and ordination of Charles C. Rich, Lorenzo Snow, Erastus Snow and Franklin D. Richards to the Apostleship. On the 13th of that month a more permanent Stake organization was effected, as follows: Daniel Spencer, President; David Fullmer and Willard Snow, first and second Counselors. The members of the High Council were Isaac Morley, Phinehas Richards, Shadrach Roundy, Henry G. Sherwood, Titus Billings, Eleazer Miller, John Vance, Levi Jackman, Ira Eldredge, Elisha H. Groves, William W. Major and Edwin D. Woolley.

Next day—the 14th—Great Salt Lake City was divided into nineteen ecclesiastical wards. The following named were the Bishops: First Ward, Peter McCue; Second, John Lowry; Third, Christopher Williams, Fourth, Benjamin Brown; Fifth, Thomas Winters; Sixth, William Hickenlooper; Seventh, William G. Perkins; Eight, Addison Everett; Ninth, Seth Taft; Tenth, David Pettigrew; Eleventh, John Lytle; Twelfth, Benjamin Covey; Thirteenth, Edward Hunter; Fourteenth, John Murdock, senior; Fifteenth, Abraham O. Smoot; Sixteenth, Shadrach Roundy; Seventeenth, Joseph L. Heywood; Eighteenth, Presiding Bishop Whitney; Nineteenth, James Hendricks. Each of these wards comprised, as far as practicable, three blocks square; the enumeration beginning at the southeast corner of the city, where the First Ward lies, and running west to the city limit, where the Fifth Ward ends. The enumeration then continued on the next tier of blocks from west to east, then back again, and so on until all the wards were formed.

www.ingramcontent.com/pod-product-compliance
Lightning Source LLC
Chambersburg PA
CBHW022134300426
44115CB00006B/181